German aesthetic and literar
Winckelmann, Lessing, H
Herder, Schiller, Goethe

German aesthetic and literary criticism: Winckelmann, Lessing, Hamann, Herder, Schiller, Goethe

Edited and introduced by H. B. Nisbet

Professor of Modern Languages (German)
University of Cambridge, and Fellow
of Sidney Sussex College

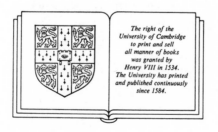

The right of the
University of Cambridge
to print and sell
all manner of books
was granted by
Henry VIII in 1534.
The University has printed
and published continuously
since 1584.

Cambridge University Press

Cambridge
London   New York   New Rochelle
Melbourne   Sydney

Published by the Press Syndicate of the University of Cambridge
The Pitt Building, Trumpington Street, Cambridge CB2 1RP
32 East 57th Street, New York, NY 10022, USA
10 Stamford Road, Oakleigh, Melbourne 3166, Australia

First published 1985

Printed in Great Britain by
the University Press, Cambridge

British Library cataloguing in publication data
German aesthetic and literary criticism.
1. German literature – 18th century – History and criticism
2. German literature – 19th century – History and criticism
I. Nisbet, H. B.
830.9'006   PT311

Library of Congress cataloguing in publication data
Main entry under title:
German aesthetic and literary criticism. Winckelmann,
Lessing, Hamann, Herder, Schiller, Goethe.
Bibliography: p.
Includes index.
1. Aesthetics, Germany – 18th century – Addresses, essays, lec-
tures.   2. Aesthetics, Germany – 19th century – Addresses, essays,
lectures.   3. Criticism – Germany – History – 18th century – Ad-
dresses, essays, lectures.   4. Criticism – Germany – History – 19th
century – Addresses, essays, lectures. I. Nisbet, Hugh Barr.
BH221.G3G47   1986   700'.1   85-11348

ISBN 0 521 23509 X hard covers
ISBN 0 521 28009 5 paperback

Contents

Acknowledgement

I am grateful to T. J. Reed for his constructive criticisms of the Introduction to this volume, and to Caroline Murray for correcting a number of errors in the text.

A note on the translations

All of the translations included in this volume, apart from those of Lessing's *Laocoon* and Schiller's *On Naive and Sentimental Poetry*, are published here for the first time. Those of Winckelmann's *Thoughts on the Imitation of the Painting and Sculpture of the Greeks* and of Goethe's *Winckelmann* are by the editor of the volume. The translation of Lessing's letter to Nicolai of 26 May 1769, of Hamann's *Aesthetica in nuce*, and of Herder's essays on Ossian and on Shakespeare, are by Joyce P. Crick, with modifications by the editor.

The translation of Lessing's *Laocoon* is taken from *Laocoon. Nathan the Wise. Minna von Barnhelm*, edited by William A. Steel, Everyman's Library (London and New York, 1930) with modifications by the editor of the present volume, and is reprinted by permission of the publisher.

The translation of Schiller's *On Naive and Sentimental Poetry* is taken from Schiller, *'Naive and Sentimental Poetry' and 'On the Sublime'*, translated by Julius A. Elias, Frederick Ungar Publishing Co. (New York, 1966), and is reprinted, with some modifications, by permission of the publisher.

The texts of the works by Winckelmann, Hamann, Schiller, and Goethe are unabridged, as is that of Herder's essay *Shakespeare*. The last four chapters (Chapters 26 to 29) of Lessing's *Laocoon*, along with most of Lessing's footnotes, have been omitted, since they are of purely antiquarian interest and extraneous to his arguments. All points of substance and essential references in them are incorporated in the notes to the translation. Only that portion of Lessing's letter to Nicolai which deals with aesthetic and critical matters has been included; the remainder deals with personal matters unconnected with Lessing's work as a critic. The translation of Herder's essay on Ossian is also abridged. The numerous examples of folksong which he quotes are omitted, as are some of the more repetitive passages in the essay. Details of these omissions, and of any matters of substance in the omitted passages, are supplied in the notes to the translation.

Introduction

This volume is one of a series of three anthologies of aesthetic theory and criticism by German thinkers from Winckelmann to Hegel. The period in question (approximately 1750 to 1830) was an exceptionally fruitful time in the cultural and intellectual history of Germany. It includes that momentous literary revival which, from the work of Lessing to the classicism of Goethe and Schiller and the rise of Romanticism, transformed German literature from a pale imitation of foreign models (chiefly French) into an original creative achievement of European significance. In aesthetics and critical theory, it is no less productive; it encompasses the first attempts, by Alexander Gottlieb Baumgarten, to establish a new science of aesthetics (*Aesthetica*, 1750), Lessing's celebrated treatise on the differences between the poetic and visual arts (*Laocoon*, 1766), the programmes of Winckelmann, Goethe, and Schiller for a rejuvenated, Hellenising classicism, the aesthetic systems of Kant and Hegel, and that ferment of theorising on art and aesthetics which is associated with the German Romantic movement. The repercussions on both art and aesthetic theory in other countries – especially Britain and France – were profound.

Many of the theoretical and critical writings of the time have never been translated into English, and the translations of many others are either inadequate or out of print. The aim of this series is to bring together as many as possible of the major contributions to the debate – for it was indeed an ongoing debate for much of the time – and to illustrate all of its principal phases. Since literary criticism, poetics, aesthetic theory, and philosophy in general were not nearly so rigidly separated as they often are today, but constantly interacted and fructified one another, examples of all these modes of discourse are included in the three volumes of the series.

Each of the volumes has a unity of its own, however. The unifying theme of the present volume, which covers the earliest phase of the development, is classicism: four of the six writers represented here – Winckelmann, Lessing, Schiller, and Goethe – are in various ways concerned to define and defend classical values in art, taking the art and thinking of ancient Greece as their ultimate standard. Before Winckelmann and Lessing made their appearance, aesthetics and poetics in Germany were, in fact, already dominated by neo-classical values (as they had been, in varying degrees, since the Renaissance). But the ruling orthodoxy, as represented by the *Kritische Dichtkunst*

(*Critical Poetics*, 1732) of Johann Christoph Gottsched, the literary lawgiver of
Leipzig, was a neo-classicism of French inspiration, which looked to such
authorities as Boileau in matters of theory, and to the courtly literature of
seventeenth-century France for practical models, in the absence of any
German works of canonic status at that time. Winckelmann and Lessing,
however, by-passed the French, and reverted directly to the theory and art
of antiquity, especially Greek antiquity, as the basis of their own neo-classical
programmes. Their thinking is typical of their age in as much as their theories
are prescriptive ones; they are in no doubt that rules can be laid down for each
of the arts, and for each genre within them. This normative approach is also
shared by Schiller and Goethe during their years of collaboration.

   Herder, especially in those critical works of his early period which are
represented in this volume, was also preoccupied with neo-classical values. But
his attitude towards them is less positive than that of the four writers referred
to above. The historical approach to art, pioneered by Winckelmann in his
History of the Art of Antiquity (1764), becomes for Herder a means of justifying
art-forms outside the classical canon. He certainly shares Winckelmann's and
Lessing's respect for the art and culture of Greece. But his well-developed
historical sense leads him, particularly in his early years, to a historical and
cultural relativism which in turn impels him to reject French neo-classical
poetics as inauthentic (that is, not truly Greek), alien to Germanic traditions,
and unduly restrictive upon the poetic imagination. He accordingly defends
non-classical art forms, above all the drama of Shakespeare and the folk-poetry
of northern Europe, as fully justified in their own right. Unlike his older friend
and mentor Johann Georg Hamann – who is the great exception in this
volume, and in some ways the most eccentric figure of the entire German
Enlightenment – Herder at no time rejects rational and normative poetics
completely. His aim was not to overthrow, but merely to limit, the authority
of the classical tradition. In particular, he was anxious to legitimate those
modern and northern European forms of poetry which Francophiles such as
Gottsched had condemned. Herder's initiative was subsequently taken further
by Friedrich Schiller, who, in his *On Naive and Sentimental Poetry* of 1795, seeks
a rationale by which to explicate and justify two separate modes of art – ancient
and modern, 'naive' and 'sentimental', objective and subjective, classical and
post-classical, or (as Friedrich Schlegel was soon to redefine them) Classical
and Romantic. One of Hamann's strange and sibylline texts is included in this
volume, mainly because his revolt against rational poetics – which is only a
part of his assault on rationalism in general – is the first clear symptom of a
tendency which leads on, via the pre-Romanticism of the young Herder and
the so-called *Sturm und Drang* movement of the 1770s, to the rise of Romanticism
proper in Germany. The aesthetic and critical theory of the Romantics and
other later thinkers is documented in the other two volumes in this series.
Finally, Goethe's essay on Winckelmann (1805) is included here as an eminent
example of that classical ethos which Goethe defended during the two decades

following his journey to Italy (1786–8) and during the period of his friendship with Schiller (1794–1805). Written immediately before Schiller's death, it constitutes a defiant and late attempt on Goethe's part to reassert his own classical values in face of the rising tide of Romanticism. It also marks the end of that phase of neo-classicism in Germany inaugurated exactly fifty years before by the essay with which this volume begins – Winckelmann's *Thoughts on the Imitation of the Painting and Sculpture of the Greeks* (1755)

Thus the tension between ancient and modern runs, explicitly or implicitly, through most of the writings included here. In this respect, the preoccupations of the writers concerned may be seen as a prolonged epilogue to the *Querelle des anciens et des modernes* of the preceding century. Winckelmann, Lessing, and the classical Goethe are, on the whole, on the side of the ancients, although their attitude is by no means one of nostalgic resignation: their aim is to promote a new art and literature in Germany, based on principles sanctioned by the classical tradition. Herder and Schiller share the respect of the others for antiquity, but they also seek to justify and consolidate the achievements of the modern age – and, in Schiller's case, even to transcend the dichotomy of ancient and modern by postulating a third and higher phase of art, which would combine the merits of both its predecessors. Hamann is once again the exception in this group. He is on the side of antiquity rather than of the modern age; but the antiquity he looks to is primarily that of the Bible, the Judaeo-Christian legacy which, in his opinion, has been betrayed by modern secular rationalism with its vain and presumptuous glorification of man.

Winckelmann's writings relate almost exclusively to visual art, but their significance and impact are altogether wider. He became for his age the leading exponent of the Hellenic ideal, and of classical perfection in art. Focussing the diffuse insights of earlier antiquarian scholarship on the basis of that first-hand, encyclopaedic knowledge of ancient art which he acquired during his years in Rome, he made of Greece a coherent, luminous, indeed brilliant image, which became a guiding light for the neo-classical movement in its final phase – above all in Germany, but beyond its frontiers as well. The Greek ideal as he taught it is, of course, predominantly an aesthetic one. But it is a good deal more. It incorporates moral, cultural, and political elements which extended its influence beyond the visual arts to literature, historiography, ethics, anthropology, and other areas. What Winckelmann proclaimed was in fact a myth, and an extremely potent one in its time. Its appeal was enhanced by the fact that he wrote in a popular and emotionally charged style and – especially after his move to Rome – with the empirical directness of a field-worker in immediate contact with the latest discoveries from Herculaneum, Pompeii, and other Italian sites. What, precisely, were the qualities which Winckelmann detected (or read into) classical art? And why did they appeal so profoundly to his century?

The answer to the first of these questions lies in his conception of Greek beauty. Or more exactly, in his conception of the supreme variety of Greek beauty. Nowhere does he offer a rigorous conceptual definition of beauty, such as Hogarth, Kant, and other eighteenth-century theoreticians attempted. It is rather, for him, something which can be pointed to in certain Greek sculptures, but which cannot be adequately expressed in words. The nearest he comes to defining it is perhaps in that celebrated formula he uses in his essay of 1755 to characterise what he considers the finest Greek statues, especially the Laocoon group in the Vatican:

> the universal and predominant characteristic of the Greek masterpieces is a noble simplicity and tranquil grandeur, both in posture and expression. Just as the depths of the sea remain forever calm, however much the surface may rage, so does the expression of the Greek figures, however strong their passions, reveal a great and dignified soul.[1]

Clearly, Winckelmann's formula – 'a noble simplicity and tranquil grandeur' (*eine edle Einfalt und eine stille Größe*) – is not a narrowly aesthetic one. It encompasses moral and spiritual qualities on the one hand, and aesthetic attributes on the other. The first epithet, *edel* (noble), refers to the stoical fortitude with which the Greek heroes, such as Laocoon, retain their spiritual composure even in the face of calamity. And the first noun, *Größe* (grandeur or greatness), emphasises the superiority of the Greek heroes to ordinary mortals; they exist on a higher moral and spiritual plane. *Größe* is only one of the many terms denoting height, elevation, or sublimity which Winckelmann uses of the classical figures.[2] They represent for him an ideal of humanity, of human completeness and self-sufficiency, which has much in common with the later ideal of *Humanität* as propounded by the older Herder, and by Goethe in his classical phase.

The word *Einfalt* (simplicity), however, denotes an aesthetic as well as a moral quality, and the quality Winckelmann has in mind is fundamental to the neo-classical art of his century. Greek art, in his eyes, is an art of essentials. In its greatest masterpieces, all ornament and accretion are absent. The figures, indeed, are usually naked or near-naked; and they are stripped not only of clothes, but of all adventitious characteristics, all accidents of life, all transitory passions and emotions. This is why beauty, for Winckelmann, is the opposite of *Ausdruck* (expression). Such expression of emotion as is present in the Greek statues is reduced to an absolute minimum; for passion is a fleeting thing, and it is with the constant and ideal aspects of humanity that the Greeks were concerned. The Greek figure is timeless and universal, and devoid of individual character (in so far as individual character entails subjection to the casual influences of experience). The statues which Winckelmann, like Goethe after him, admired most were those which seemed serenely impassive, lacking in any distinct expression. It is this economy and restraint in the rendering of human forms which he describes as *Einfalt*. And it is this same quality which accounts for his austerely linear conception of art, shared by the painters, sculptors, and architects of eighteenth-century neo-classicism. He places much emphasis on line (or 'contour', as he calls it), and has virtually nothing to say on colour, texture, or mass.

As for the adjective *still* (tranquil), it too has both aesthetic and spiritual connotations. Rest or tranquillity, not movement, is the condition with which beauty, for Winckelmann, is essentially linked; for motion, in the human body, tends to be accompanied by passion and expression, by transitory and fortuitous conditions. But in the notion of tranquillity, as so often in Winckelmann's aesthetic theory, secularised religious values are also present.[3] The German mystics of the sixteenth and seventeenth centuries had envisaged God as residing in *Stille* (tranquillity, calm), above and beyond the turmoil of time and experienced reality. This spiritual as well as aesthetic preference for the immobile and serene is one of the reasons why Winckelmann so strenuously objects to the art of the Baroque and the Rococo, particularly the sculptures of Bernini, with their ecstatic expression and impassioned movement.

But Winckelmann's conception of beauty embodies not only the absolute and timeless ideals just mentioned. It is simultaneously a relative category, for he often points out that Greek beauty was the unique product of a particular climate, age, and culture. He never properly resolves this paradox: on the one hand, Greek beauty is relative to a specific historical and geographical context; yet on the other hand, he enjoins his contemporaries, in a different age and culture, to emulate it. Obviously, we cannot recreate the Greek climate in the north. The most we can do is to travel south, as Winckelmann and so many of his German admirers did. And if we allow the Greek ideal to influence and permeate our lives as well as our art – which Winckelmann certainly intends his public to do – we can perhaps reproduce the necessary conditions for a truly classical neo-classicism.

Winckelmann's ideal of Greek beauty had a compelling attraction for his contemporaries. Its pronounced moral element – as in the stoic self-restraint of Laocoon – appealed to the moralistically inclined German Enlightenment; its humanism appealed to an ever more secular age; and the linear proportion and economy with which it was associated appealed to the century of rationalism. But the eighteenth century was also the century of sensibility, of *Empfindsamkeit*; and there can be little doubt that the highly emotional quality of Winckelmann's style and personality added to his charisma. His poetic descriptions of the Belvedere Torso of Hercules, of the Belvedere Apollo, and – in the essay included in this volume – of Laocoon's torments, are hymns of praise to divine human forms; they are prose counterparts to the odes of Klopstock, which the generation of the 1760s and 1770s in Germany greeted with boundless enthusiasm. This visionary and subjective style of criticism, entering into the spirit of its object, prefigures that of Herder and the Romantics. Yet there is also a clarity and simplicity about Winckelmann's prose; he attempts to create a linguistic analogue of the style he discerned in the best of Greek art. At the time of his death in 1768, his only rival as a master of German prose was Lessing.

But Winckelmann's Greece, as already remarked, is a mythical construct. Indeed, it is one of the most potent myths of the eighteenth century. It is a world of serene, whole, and happy individuals, living in the eternal springtime of mankind; it is a world of beauty, lightness, form, and order, which reflects the brightest aspects of the Olympian pantheon. The irrational side of Greek religion and culture is ignored or suppressed. (Not until the time of Nietzsche was the realm of tragic suffering, of cruel and arbitrary fate, of priapism, of the orgiastic festivals of the wine-god – in short, everything that Nietzsche called the 'Dionysian' – proclaimed as the dark but essential obverse of the radiant Olympian image.) The morality of Winckelmann's Greeks, despite the powerful eros which animates his descriptions of their art and society, has a quality of Stoicism, even of Puritanism, about it. Greek art, for Winckelmann, is the antithesis of Baroque exuberance, and of the hedonism and licentiousness of the Rococo, which he and the German middle classes associated with aristocratic decadence and with the courtly French culture whose grip on the ruling classes in Germany they resented. The Greek ethos, as he depicts it, owes something to the moralism of the contemporary middle-class public. And this was shortly reinforced and modified by another far-reaching influence: the primitivism of Rousseau and the myth of the noble savage. For Winckelmann, Lessing, Herder, Schiller, and many others, the Greeks are a 'naive' people, living a frugal but healthy existence close to nature; they are primitives in the most positive sense of the word. Lessing, in his *Laocoon*, enlarges on this supposed naturalness of the Greeks, and he does so at the expense of Winckelmann's Stoicism. The Greeks, he contends, expressed their emotions freely and naturally, and even their most warlike heroes did not hesitate to release their suffering in tears. And for the age of *sensibilité*, such open displays of emotion were the surest index of uncorrupted, natural virtue. In short, the German Hellenists discovered in Greece a moral ideal which they presented as the antithesis of modern sophistication and aristocratic immorality. On the less acceptable face of antiquity, they simply turned their backs; and such works as Wilhelm Heinse's novel *Ardinghello* (1787) and Goethe's *Roman Elegies* (published 1795) which dared to glorify antique sensualism, were widely deplored as immoral and indecent.[4]

Enthusiasm for Greece was particularly strong in Germany, whose foremost writers in the eighteenth century were acutely troubled by the lack of a national culture. Their readiness to associate themselves with the myth of Greece was part of that search for a German national identity which continues, in various forms, into the twentieth century. The Greek myth, in the latter half of the eighteenth century, provided an antidote to French culture. But it also seemed to offer an alternative to the current evils of social inequality and political absolutism, with all the curbs which these imposed on individual development.

For one of the most attractive features of Winckelmann's myth was its emphasis on individual freedom. (The institution of slavery was conveniently ignored.) Winckelmann's vision of Athens as a happy polis of free individuals gave political inspiration to several of his successors: Hölderlin was captivated by it, and its echoes are to be found in Shelley, and of course in Byron, who died in the cause of Greek independence. But there were few political activists in eighteenth-century Germany. More influential than the dream of political emancipation was Winckelmann's stress on Greek individualism, on the wholeness and completeness of the individual personality in ancient Greece. This individualism, indeed, becomes a hallmark of German classicism, although it never lost its peculiar association with Greek antiquity. It became the goal of that process of *Bildung* or self-cultivation which Goethe, Schiller, and Wilhelm von Humboldt recommended as the basis of all education; it received literary expression in the *Bildungsroman*, the novel of individual development, from Wieland's *Agathon* and Goethe's *Wilhelm Meister* onwards; and it became in turn a fundamental principle of nineteenth-century German liberalism. (It is also one of the main themes of Goethe's essay on Winckelmann in the present volume.) The laments of the German Hellenists on the one-sidedness of the modern individual and his remoteness from the classical ideal of the integral personality are echoed once again in the individualism of the young Karl Marx and in his theory of alienation.

Thus, Winckelmann's vision of Greece, though based largely on his studies of Greek art, is compounded of more than just aesthetic elements. His impact on art and aesthetics was nevertheless considerable. He is the founder of modern art-history; his artistic ideals were realised in the painting and sculpture of European neo-classicism in its later phases; and his aesthetic theories were an inspiration to Lessing, Herder, Goethe, and many others. Yet ultimately, his view of art is an intolerant and restrictive one. Whole schools, genres, and centuries of art – including the Middle Ages, the Dutch school, landscape, still-life, and genre-painting – were dismissed as misguided or vulgar. His all-too-exclusive classicism demanded correction and supplementation; Herder and Schiller were among those who attempted this task. But his most profound influence was as a cultural critic and educator, as Goethe surely recognised when he said to Eckermann: 'One *learns* nothing on reading him, but one *becomes* something.'[5]

Winckelmann's observations on the statue of Laocoon, however, also had momentous repercussions. As a result of his preoccupation with it, it became a cult-object for the German Hellenists. It was discussed at length not only by Winckelmann and Lessing, but also by Herder, Goethe, Schiller, Heinse, Hegel, and numerous others, including the Romantics A. W. Schlegel and Novalis.[6] It is hard for us today to understand why this extraordinary, and even grotesque Hellenistic sculpture was so esteemed by so many. One of the reasons why Winckelmann lavished so much attention on it was that it was generally regarded in his day – that is, before the Elgin marbles and other works of the best period in Greek art became known in Europe – as the greatest sculpture of antiquity, and indeed of all time. In ancient Rome, the Elder Pliny had accorded it the highest praise, and this was echoed by Michelangelo when the group was rediscovered in 1506. Another reason why Winckelmann chose this example may well have been the shrewd calculation that, if he could convince his public that even this most violent, indeed baroque, of all Greek sculptures was an instance of calm, restraint, and nobility, they would surely accept that his thesis applied even more aptly to all other works of the Greeks.

Lessing's treatise *Laocoon* is a brilliant, if tendentious, analysis of the limits of poetry and visual art. Characteristically, he takes a disagreement with Winckelmann over the interpretation of the Laocoon group as his point of departure. (Lessing is always at his most original when he has someone to disagree with, and his best ideas were often developed through controversy and polemics.) His disagreement with Winckelmann is, on the face of it, a minor one. For he accepts Winckelmann's fundamental premise that the supreme law which governed the visual arts in antiquity was the law of beauty. What he objects to is the *moral* component in Winckelmann's theory of beauty. He does not deny that the Greeks were morally admirable: he denies merely that their visual art, as distinct from their literature and way of life, was determined by moral considerations. Thus, Laocoon's half-closed mouth is not a sign of his stoical fortitude, that is, of his moral excellence. For as Lessing points out, Laocoon *does* scream aloud in Virgil's version of the story in the *Aeneid*, and other Greek heroes did not consider it unmanly to do likewise in similar predicaments. The statue shows him at the moment just before he screams; because to show him actually screaming, with his mouth gaping open, would offend the rule of beauty. It was therefore solely in the interests of beauty that the sculptors avoided showing him screaming, whereas in literature (for example, the *Aeneid*), the law of beauty does not apply as it does in the visual arts, so that the poet is perfectly free to describe Laocoon's screams. In other words, Lessing insists on a narrowly aesthetic definition of classical beauty. Winckelmann's supporting, ethical arguments, though not incompatible with the aesthetic thesis, have the effect of blurring a distinction which Lessing wishes above all to establish.

Lessing uses his apparently minor disagreement with Winckelmann to demonstrate something fundamental to aesthetics: that poetry and visual art are subject to quite different laws. His aesthetic principles, like those of his age as a whole, are normative: each art-form has rules of its own, and the arts must not be assimilated to one another, as the Horatian dictum *ut pictura poesis* had suggested. The central arguments in Lessing's *Laocoon* are not new, of course.[7] But they had never before been stated so fully and so lucidly. The treatise *Laocoon* shows Lessing at his analytical best: he is a master of logical distinctions. And although he attempted, in the final version of his work, to give it as informal and relaxed an appearance as possible (before Winckelmann and

Lessing, German aesthetics, having grown out of academic philosophy, had been all too addicted to abstract systems, like that of Baumgarten), it had in fact begun as a rigorous piece of deduction from the concepts of space and time, along the lines of Chapter 16 in the final version. Like the aesthetic theories of most of his immediate predecessors, Lessing's is a mimetic, representational one: it is the business of art to render imaginary objects present, to create an illusion of reality. It follows from this that there must be a natural relationship between sign and signified. Poetry uses words, which follow each other in time, hence it must deal with objects which follow each other in time, that is, actions. The visual arts use shapes and surfaces, which coexist in space, hence they must depict objects which coexist in space, that is, bodies. It is one of the strengths of Lessing's treatise that it supplements, and indeed builds up to, these *a priori* arguments with empirical ones derived from the practice of the Greeks: Homer, as a poet, depicted primarily actions, and the Greek sculptors depicted primarily bodies. Lessing thus arrives at identical conclusions by two distinct routes: by the deductive methods of Baumgarten, Moses Mendelssohn, and other thinkers of the Leibniz-Wolffian school, and by the empirical methods favoured by the art-historian Winckelmann.

Lessing's treatise extends to literature the service which Winckelmann had performed for the visual arts. Just as Winckelmann had drawn his conclusions directly from the art of antiquity, so does Lessing formulate the laws of poetry by direct reference to Homer, Sophocles, and (in his essays on drama, the *Hamburg Dramaturgy* of 1767–9) the *Poetics* of Aristotle. French neo-classicism is either ignored, or (again in the *Hamburg Dramaturgy*) attacked as weakly derivative and inauthentic. It is a great misfortune that the *Laocoon* is unfinished. Its continuation was to have dealt, among other things, with music, dance, and mime, and with drama as an art form which combines visual art and poetry. As a dramatist himself, Lessing would have been well qualified to tackle this issue. The *Hamburg Dramaturgy* is no real substitute, for it consists of unsystematic reflections, chiefly designed to undermine the authority of French tragedy as practised by Corneille and Voltaire, and to supply a theoretical justification for psychological and domestic drama in a more realistic idiom such as Lessing himself, Diderot, and a few other contemporaries were then developing. The continuation of the *Laocoon* would have approached drama more systematically, working from first principles. We have, however, an indication in Lessing's letter of 26 May 1769 to Friedrich Nicolai (a translation of which is included in this volume) of how he would have proceeded.

The deductive framework of the *Laocoon* is provided by Lessing's semiotic theory – his theory of 'natural' and 'arbitrary' signs. A 'natural' sign resembles the object it signifies, as do the shapes and colours of figurative sculpture and painting. An 'arbitrary' sign (and all language, with a few rare exceptions such as onomatopoetic words, consists of 'arbitrary' signs) has no necessary connection with its object: the connection is a purely conventional one. Since the aim of all art, according to Lessing's mimetic theory, is to present the imitated object to the intuitive cognition of the recipient in as direct a manner as possible, it follows that poetry must endeavour by all possible means to transform its 'arbitrary' (that is, conventional) linguistic signs into 'natural' ones. In depicting only actions and eschewing description of bodies – for the visual arts are more suited to the latter task – poetry takes a major step in this direction. Its use of images and metaphors (rather than abstractions) also enhances its concreteness and immediacy. But the genre of poetry best equipped to convert symbolic or linguistic cognition into intuitive or perceptual cognition – that is, to convert 'arbitrary' signs into 'natural' signs – is drama, as Lessing explains in the letter to Nicolai. For drama is not an *imitation* of speech, as the third-person narrative often is: the sign (the dramatic dialogue) coincides completely with the signified (the speech of the characters); and the linguistic signs are reinforced by the purely 'natural' signs of the actors' gestures and expression.[8]

It cannot be denied, however, that Lessing's interest is above all in poetry, and that the visual arts come off poorly by comparison. E. H. Gombrich exaggerates only slightly when he says that the *Laocoon* 'is not so much a book about as against the visual arts'.[9] As was pointed out earlier, Winckelmann's conception of classical beauty was itself narrow and restrictive. Lessing has the same limitations, in that he is just as indifferent as his predecessor towards landscape, genre painting, still-life, and other non-classical art-forms. But he adds further restrictions on top of these. While endorsing Winckelmann's contention that the visual arts should depict beautiful and idealised human figures, he goes on to maintain that this is their exclusive task. Not only does he outlaw the ethical content of Winckelmann's conception of beauty; he also condemns allegorical and historical painting – forms held in high esteem by Winckelmann – as unwarranted intrusions by the visual arts upon the province of poetry. His censures of descriptive poetry (descriptive in the sense of indulging in enumeration of physical detail) diminish the province of poetry far less drastically than his corresponding strictures on whole areas of sculpture and painting diminish that of the visual arts. And whereas he deals separately with the different genres of poetry – and he would have distinguished between them further if he had completed his treatise – he simply lumps together painting and sculpture as if they were a single art-form. (It was left to Herder, in his essay *Plastic Art* (*Plastik*) of 1778, to supplement Lessing's work with a separate aesthetics of sculpture as a three-dimensional form, relating less to vision than to the sense of touch.) The effect of all this was to confine the visual arts to depicting only a restrained and, in the last resort, empty variety of human beauty. Poetry, meanwhile, remains undisputed sovereign of the realm which interested the dramatist Lessing most: the boundless sphere of human activity, which affects us far more immediately than the lofty, but ultimately frigid beauty of Greek art. It is probable, as Gombrich suggests, that Lessing's attack on Winckelmann's interpretation of Laocoon as a paragon of fortitude is part of his campaign against French classicism, against the idealised stoical heroes of Cornelian tragedy. By banishing heroic images to the visual arts, and at the same time emptying them of all but aesthetic content, Lessing hopes to clear the way for literature to get on with more important things, and to enjoy a monopoly of realism.

The limitations of the *Laocoon* are thus conspicuous, particularly in its treatment of the visual arts. As regards poetry, its limitations are not so much those of Lessing himself, as of the representational aesthetics and neo-classical principles of his time. The mimetic theory is less than adequate to the more subjective varieties of poetry, especially the lyric. The role of unconscious factors in expression, the role of mood and atmosphere, and of the associative qualities of language, are almost completely neglected. And although Lessing tries valiantly, in his *Hamburg Dramaturgy*, to harmonise Aristotle's *Poetics* with modern forms of drama, his attempts are strained. Despite his frequent praise of Shakespeare, he nowhere seriously attempts to reconcile Shakespeare's plays with his own neo-classical principles. Based as the latter were on the art-forms of antiquity, their inadequacy in relation to newer, post-Renaissance forms was becoming ever more obvious. Herder's historical relativism and his expressive theory of poetry, further developed by Schiller and the Romantics, were among the first attempts to fill this gap.

Johann Georg Hamann was neither artist, critic, aesthetician, nor theorist of art. His published works all date from after the decisive experience of his life, his religious conversion of 1758. All of them, even those few which touch on art and poetry, are religious tracts of one description or another. Nevertheless, his strange personality and style fascinated the young artists and writers of the *Sturm und Drang* in the 1770s, including Goethe and Herder. They took from him, however, only what they could use – notably his taste for popular literature, his belief in the senses and feelings as the basis of cognition, and his hostility towards rationalism and abstraction. But even his closest disciple, Herder, at no time fully accepted his paradoxical and mystical teachings.

Reality, for Hamann, is ultimately mysterious and unfathomable, except with the help of Christian faith. The philosophers of the German *Aufklärung*, from Leibniz and Wolff to Moses Mendelssohn and Hamann's friend Immanuel Kant (still in his 'pre-critical' phase in the 1760s and 1770s), are guilty of a gross misrepresentation in trying to explain the universe as a rational system. Reality is infinitely more complex and elusive than their philosophies would allow. The Bible, as the revelation of God, is the primary means of interpreting it. But there are two other revelations of God besides the Bible: these are the undeciphered books of nature and of human history respectively. They speak to us not just through our reason (Hamann never rejected reason as such, and is not a complete irrationalist, as often used to be claimed); they speak to us more vividly and powerfully through our senses and emotions. For Hamann as for Pascal, the God of the philosophers is a lifeless abstraction. The concrete world is more alive to us than are the reasonings of the schoolmen, and he who would move us most must address us through images, through signs and pictures – although even these are never entirely adequate to express the rich and complex reality through which the creator manifests himself. With their belief in the omnipotence of human reason, the philosophers are also guilty of the sin of pride, of vastly overrating the powers and significance of man.

In his crusade against the rationalists, Hamann chose his tactics with mischievous irony. He drew support from two of the traditions which the Enlightenment most respected – British empiricism, and the thought of classical antiquity. For instance, he often cites approvingly the doctrines of Francis Bacon that all true knowledge comes to us through experience, through the senses, and that we should distrust abstractions and hypotheses. Bacon, of course, had used these principles as a constructive basis for empirical science; but Hamann uses them as a destructive weapon against rationalism. He found further support in the writings of David Hume, whose *Dialogues concerning Natural Religion* he subsequently translated into German. For Hume himself, sceptical philosophy served to undermine rational theology and to promote agnosticism – hence his popularity with the most radical of the *philosophes* in France. But as the history of philosophy has so often demonstrated, scepticism can just as easily serve to support fideism instead. Hamann accordingly employed Hume's arguments not only to attack rationalism, but also to defend his own belief in feeling and intuition, and in the need for Christian faith. In a similar spirit, he chose the figure of Socrates – another hero of the Enlightenment – as his spokesman in his first published work, the *Socratic Memorabilia (Sokratische Denkwürdigkeiten)* of 1759. In this case, it was the irony of Socrates which served Hamann's purpose. Socratic irony, of course, consisted in the claims of Socrates, in Plato's dialogues, that he knew nothing. This feigned ignorance emboldened his interlocutors to propound philosophical theories themselves, theories which Socrates would proceed to demolish, thereby revealing that he knew a great deal more than he professed. With double irony, Hamann took Socrates at his word, and made him, like Hume, another ally in his campaign to demonstrate the inadequacy of human reason. But he went further still. Socrates's contention that he had a personal *daimon* or guiding spirit which, when he was faced with difficult decisions, would advise him how to act, again enabled Hamann to reinterpret him in his own interests. For firstly, the *daimon* made Socrates into a prototype of Christ, who was similarly guided by the Holy Spirit. Secondly, Socrates's reliance on his *daimon* seemed to confirm Hamann's belief that the feelings and intimations of the heart are surer guides than reason. And thirdly, the *daimon* of Socrates could be likened to the inspiration of the poetic genius, who finds rational rules – as in the poetics of neo-classicism – of little help, and follows his own creative urges instead. In this remarkable little work, Hamann transforms Socrates from an apostle of reason and cult-figure of the Enlightenment into a spokesman of ignorance and humility, of genius and feeling. It was Hamann's image, not that of the rationalists, which the young Goethe had in mind when he planned to write a drama on the figure of Socrates.

The greatest obstacle to understanding Hamann's thought is the style and presentation of his works, which are difficult and obscure in the extreme. He once confessed that he often could not himself understand what he had earlier written.[10] But all this was part of a deliberate policy. The stylistic and philosophical ideal of the rationalists, from Descartes to the eighteenth century, was maximum clarity and freedom from contradiction. Hamann is the first thinker of the *Aufklärung* to challenge this ideal, and he writes in open defiance of the stylistic norms of rationalism. In keeping with his own doctrines, he avoids abstract concepts and sustained logical argument, and relies heavily on images. For images, he believes, can point beyond themselves to truths which rational concepts cannot communicate. Thus his style constantly points beyond itself. It is full of (often cryptic) allusions to other works and individuals, and many of these references are of a satirical and even personal nature. There are innumerable quotations in many languages – most often from the Bible, but also frequently from the classics, and from Shakespeare, whom Hamann greatly revered. His manner of writing is invariably indirect, and he is especially fond of periphrasis and other figures of substitution. He cultivates a sibylline, oracular mode of utterance, a 'cabbalistic prose' (as the subtitle of his *Aesthetica in nuce* puts it). Words are used paradoxically, with exalted expressions for trivial or ridiculous things, and traditionally negative terms endowed with positive values (the one-eyed Cyclops, for instance, is a figure for the poetic genius). Similarly, he often includes an elaborate apparatus of learned footnotes – not so much to elucidate what he says, but chiefly in order to parody and satirise the scholarship of the *Aufklärung*. This, of course, is ironic; and irony is Hamann's favourite rhetorical device. But the sense underlying the paradoxes and multiple ironies of his 'cabbalistic prose' is always ultimately the mystery of Christian revelation.

The *Aesthetica in nuce* is the only work of Hamann which is concerned substantially with aesthetic and poetic questions. Even so, what he has to say on these matters has to be sifted out of a great deal of other material. Much of the work consists of veiled satire on Johann David Michaelis (a rationalist commentator on the Scriptures) and various other scholars, including Lessing and Moses Mendelssohn. A full translation of the work is included here, however, since it is impossible to separate its aesthetic and critical content from the rest of the text: Hamann is frequently talking on more than one plane of reference at once, and what he says about the creator, for example, may simultaneously apply to the poet, and vice versa. As with most of Hamann's writings, any adequate commentary on this work (more than one is available in German)[11] must be considerably longer than the work itself. Space forbids such a commentary here; I shall confine myself in this introduction to elucidating what seem to be Hamann's main observations on aesthetics and poetry, and, in the notes to the text, to elucidating his literary references.

Shaftesbury and Edward Young, followed by the German writers of the *Sturm und Drang* with their cult of the artistic genius, liked to refer to the poet as a second creator, a Prometheus, or a god in miniature. Hamann, in the *Aesthetica*, uses the same analogy; but characteristically, he uses it in reverse, thereby removing its overtones of human presumption. God is like a poet, 'the poet at the beginning of days'. Creation is the poetry of God, which speaks to us by means of images. And poetry, if it imitates nature, will itself be an image of creation – and, like the Bible (which is also poetry), an image of God, embodying something of the creator's divinity. The kind of poetry which Hamann values most is that which is richest in concrete images, symbols, and myths; he finds these qualities at their most developed in Homer and Shakespeare – and, of course, in the Bible itself. Besides, God is revealed often in the lowliest, even the ugliest phenomena, as in the crucified Christ, who suffered the death of the basest criminal. (His prototype, Socrates, was reputedly an ugly man, as Hamann points out in the *Socratic Memorabilia*.) The parables of Christ treat of the humblest aspects of daily life; the Bible speaks not in polished cadences, in the language of wit and elegance (Hamann is no friend of neo-classicism), but in simple and earthy tones. All primitive and natural language is poetic; poetry is older than prose, just as images are older than abstractions. 'Poetry is the mother-tongue of the human race...The entire store of human knowledge and happiness consists in images.' 'O for a muse like a refiner's fire, and like a fuller's soap!', he exclaims. 'She will dare to purify the natural use of the senses from the unnatural use of abstractions.'

Sentiments such as these helped to arouse the young Herder's enthusiasm for 'natural poetry' (*Naturpoesie*) and popular literature, and for the poetic qualities of ancient myth – themes which were further developed by the German Romantics thirty years later. Hamann's ideas prepared the ground for that reassessment of the traditional genres of poetry which took place in Germany during the 1770s and again at the end of the century. His teachings had a liberating effect – and especially in their negative aspects. Most of what Hamann rejected – rationalistic poetics, neo-classicism on the French model, abstract didacticism in literature – was also rejected, in varying degrees, by the *Sturm und Drang* movement. His positive doctrines as a Christian prophet and mystic had only a limited resonance: the secularism of the Enlightenment had by then taken too strong a hold. But his emphasis on the senses and on concrete experience, on the feelings and passions, on genius and inspiration as the basis of poetic creativity, was echoed by the younger generation, to whom Herder acted as a mediator of Hamann's ideas. Hamann himself disapproved of the cult of the artistic genius which arose in the 1770s. For him, it was but another form of human self-glorification, no better than the complacency of the rationalists for whom no mystery existed which could not be dispelled by reason.

What Hamann had to say on aesthetics and poetry was fragmentary and obscure. But it contained the germ of developments which were soon to end the authority of neo-classical poetics. But even in comparison with Herder and the Romantics, for whom he prepared the way, he remains remarkable for the extreme subjectivity of his hermeneutic principles. He has no use whatsoever for objective historical methods in the interpretation of earlier texts, whether of poetry or of Scripture.[12] To an extent quite exceptional for his time, he looks to the creative response of the reader as the key to the sense – a sense which, moreover, need not have been foreseen or intended by the original writer. His method is typological, and it is modelled on Biblical criticism; but, unlike earlier typologists, he claims no objective basis for his typology. For Hamann, it is legitimate not only to consider Socrates as the prototype of Christ, but also to interpret the literature of the past in the light of the reader's personal experience and situation in the present.

The writings by Johann Gottfried Herder which appear in this volume deal with Shakespeare and with the folk poetry of northern Europe – that is, with post-classical forms of literature. This subject-matter, together with the exclamatory and breathless style which Herder cultivated in his early years, can easily give the impression that he has broken completely with neo-classical values, including those of Winckelmann and Lessing. In fact, Herder had the greatest respect for these two writers, and much of his early work is indebted or even devoted to them.

Unlike Herder, Winckelmann was no historical relativist: the example of Greek art remained unconditionally valid for all ages. Nevertheless, as the first critic to treat Greek art historically and to define the principal phases in its evolution (in his *History of the Art of Antiquity*), he helped Herder to develop a historical approach to art and culture which he then extended to the post-classical centuries as well. Winckelmann had maintained that Greek art was the product of the physical and cultural environment of Greece; Herder applied the same argument to later phases of art, and concluded that each is the product of its own age and context, and as such, equally justified. Herder's essay on Shakespeare illustrates this development clearly. He applies to ancient tragedy the same kind of deterministic theory which Winckelmann had applied to ancient sculpture, and then extends it to Shakespearean tragedy, arriving quite consistently at a position of historical relativism.

Similarly, the figure of Lessing bulks large in Herder's early productions. A major section of one early work is devoted entirely to Lessing's *Laocoon*, which Herder attempts to enlarge and supplement rather than to refute (the first of his *Critical Miscellanies*, 1769). And his other major work of the 1760s, the *Fragments on Recent German Literature* (1767–8), was intended as a supplement to the *Letters concerning Recent Literature* (1759–65), a collaborative work to which Lessing had been the chief contributor. Herder, then, was scarcely an enemy of neo-classicism. He simply objected to the narrowness of its base and the exclusivity of its normative pretensions, and tried to do justice to non-classical and modern art-forms as well.

Herder endorsed Hamann's primitivism to the extent that he considered all early or primitive languages, including the language of Homer and of the Bible, as inherently more poetic than language in its more advanced stages. The later stages of language, in his view, are increasingly abstract and rational – that is, increasingly lacking in poetic qualities such as concreteness, spontaneity, wealth of synonyms and idioms, and local reference. For Herder, the expressive qualities of language and poetry – indeed of all art – are paramount. His aesthetic is no longer primarily representational or mimetic like that of Winckelmann and Lessing, but expressive. On an individual level, the work of art expresses the personality and feelings of the artist; on a more general level, the art of a given time and place expresses the values, aspirations, and cultural milieu of the society which produces it. Thus, the art of every historical era is equally legitimate – at any rate, more or less equally so, for the products of more advanced cultures may lack the spontaneity of their earlier, more organic counterparts, and derivative or imitative forms (such as French classicism) will inevitably be inferior to their original models.

For Lessing, the supreme form of poetry is drama. For Herder, it is the lyric. Like Hamann, he believes that primitive language is essentially lyrical, and that the lyric is the earliest and most authentic form of poetry, from which other, later forms are derived. Greek tragedy arose out of the 'impromptus' or dithyrambic song of the chorus; and the epics of Homer, and of Ossian (Herder refused to believe that the Ossianic poems were the forgery of James Macpherson) were originally collections of separate, but thematically related lyrical songs. Herder is one of the first, before F. A. Wolf, to hint at a multiple authorship of the Homeric poems.

Like Lessing, the young Herder was profoundly discontented with the present state of German literature, particularly with its dependence on France. The chief remedy he offers is not, however, a classical revival, but rather a return to native Germanic and northern traditions. The collection of five essays in which he included his own contributions on Shakespeare and Ossian – as well as a piece by the young Goethe on Gothic architecture – was entitled *Von deutscher Art und Kunst* (*On German Character and Art*, 1773). The term 'German' is obviously used here in a wider than usual sense, and is roughly equivalent to 'Germanic' (Herder treats the Celtic tradition of Ossian as cognate to English), but suggestive of northern culture in general as an organic and natural alternative to the mannered, artificial tradition of the French. The seed of nationalism is certainly present in Herder's early works; but it is a cultural, not a political nationalism (although the German nationalists of a later age were to claim Herder as one of their own). *On German Character and Art* is the nearest thing we have to a programme or manifesto of the *Sturm und Drang* movement of the 1770s. The central and most creative figure in this group, the young Goethe (who is apostrophised by Herder at the conclusion of his essay on Shakespeare), put Herder's doctrines into practice in a new lyric poetry of personal expression, modelled on the folksong, and in his first major dramatic success, the 'Shakespearean' drama of German chivalry, *Götz von Berlichingen*. These works satisfied Herder's criterion of *Volkspoesie* (popular poetry), a term which encompasses much more than just folksong and the anonymous literature of folk tradition: *Volkspoesie*, for Herder, includes all poetry which reflects and expresses the national culture from which it grew. It accordingly applies to most of the world's great literature, from Homer to Dante and Shakespeare, as well as to the poetry of his young disciple Goethe.

Herder's essay on Ossian and folk poetry takes the form of letters to an imaginary correspondent who upholds all the neo-classical and rationalistic prejudices against popular poetry, seeing it as crude and formless literature, unworthy of the educated critic's attention. To such prejudices, Herder opposes his (and Hamann's) contention that primitive poetry is more concrete, spontaneous, and expressive, and hence more genuinely poetic, than its refined literary equivalents. The scorn of the imaginary correspondent for Herder's arguments is likened to Voltaire's ridicule of Rousseau's primitivism. (Herder thereby implicitly acknowledges Rousseau as one of his main ideological allies.) Natural man is superior to civilised man – and natural poetry is superior to the poetry of modern sophistication. Herder's essay is disjointed and repetitive; his choice of the epistolary form allows him that degree of informality and stylistic latitude he is happiest with. Much of the work consists of examples of folksong from various countries, which are quoted at considerable length. These extended quotations and the most repetitive parts of the essay are omitted in the translation included here; all the main points of Herder's argument are retained.

Herder's remarks on the poetic imagination were new and stimulating to his contemporaries, for the psychological principles he employed were not the familiar ones of rationalism. The logic of the imagination, he points out, is not that of discursive thinking. And the poetic illusion which it creates cannot be assessed by any objective criterion of verisimilitude (as in the representational aesthetic theory of the rationalists). The test of a successful poetic illusion is a subjective one: the internal coherence of the poem is not that of rationality, nor can the imaginative reality it expresses be formulated in rational terms. Its coherence is associative (the young Herder was familiar with the associationalist psychology of David Hartley),[13] and the associations in question arise naturally out of the poet's feelings and the world as he experiences it. The laws of the imagination are more closely analogous to those of organic growth than to the laws of mechanics. Herder's fondness of organic analogies reflects this conviction: 'There is the same connection between the sections of these songs as there is between the trees and bushes of the forest' (p. 160). It marks the beginning of a reaction in Germany, which culminated in the *Naturphilosophie* of the Romantics, against the mechanistic principles of the Enlightenment and in favour of new, organic models of nature and human experience.

It follows from Herder's principles that the reader or listener can appreciate folk poetry only by an effort of the imagination, by transposing himself empathetically into the world of the poet. And since much of this poetry is the product of other societies and ages than our own, a well-developed historical and geographical sense is necessary if we are to understand it properly. The *a priori* rules of rational poetics are totally inadequate for this purpose. Besides, the task of the reader or critic is not in any case to evaluate the poetry he studies, according to Herder, but rather to interpret it and appreciate it in the light of the author's own aims and cultural context. The only evaluation that is required is the initial one of distinguishing *Volkspoesie* from inauthentic or artificial modes, which are themselves unworthy of consideration – other than as a warning to poets on what they should avoid.

One of the greatest services which the essay on Ossian performed was to call for a collection of German folk poetry, on the model of Thomas Percy's *Reliques of Ancient Poetry* (1765) from which Herder drew several of his illustrations. Herder himself published a substantial collection of such poetry, foreign as well as German, in 1778–9, and this became in turn the precursor of the more famous anthologies of folk literature compiled by the German Romantics.

The essay on Shakespeare, a full translation of which is included here, is a fine example of Herder's genetic and historical approach to criticism. Greek tragedy and Shakespearean tragedy, he argues, are equally natural, and hence equally legitimate products of their respective historical contexts. French tragedy, however, is derivative and unnatural. (Here and elsewhere in this essay, Herder echoes views already expressed by Lessing in his *Hamburg Dramaturgy*.) The effect of this argument – and the main purpose of the essay – is to defend Shakespeare's dramatic practice against the strictures of neo-classical poetics, with their insistence on the unities, the *bienséances*, the purity of genre, etc. Yet Herder has surprisingly little to say on the form of Shakespeare's plays, not to mention their theatrical qualities and stageworthiness. He alludes briefly to these questions almost at the end of the essay, saying 'At this point the heart of my enquiry might begin' (p. 174), but breaks off shortly afterwards. For in fact, his main aim – the justification of Shakespeare on historical grounds – has already been accomplished. This lack of attention on Herder's part to dramatic form, and indeed his praise of Shakespeare precisely for his non-adherence to classicistic rules of form, had far-reaching consequences for the burst of dramatic writing which followed in Germany. The pseudo-Shakespearean dramas of the *Sturm und Drang* – by Lenz, Maler Müller, Klinger, and others – vied with each other in ostentatious disregard for every variety of structural and formal unity, with multiple actions, constant changes of time, scene, and stylistic level, and free intermingling of tragic and comic, lyrical and narrative elements. Such licence seemed to be sanctioned, more-over, by Herder's exaltation of the poetic genius as a quasi-divine being, invulnerable to the petty cavillings of critics. The effect of his historical rela-tivism was equally liberating; but since it placed all literature on one level, so long as it fitted the (generously conceived) definition of *Volkspoesie*, it could also serve as an excuse for much inferior writing. Most of the dramas of the 1770s are now understandably forgotten (the most notable exceptions being Goethe's *Götz von Berlichingen* and his as yet incomplete *Faust*). They have a certain historical importance, however, as the first experiments in Germany in freer dramatic forms which in some ways anticipate the work of Büchner, Wedekind, Brecht, and other more recent playwrights. As to Herder himself, he was alarmed at the poetic excesses of his followers, and soon dissociated himself from the cult of genius. He even alleged – somewhat unfairly and perhaps not altogether ingenuously – that Goethe's *Götz* had been ruined by Shakespeare's influence.

Herder is a difficult thinker to pin down, because his is an eclectic rather than a systematic mind. He was active in many intellectual areas, as philosopher, critic, theologian, historian, poet, and more besides, and he made little attempt to keep these roles separate. He was by inclination a syncretist, and much of his thought consists in attempts to harmonise traditionally distinct or even irreconcilable positions.[14] This led him at times into inconsistency and contradiction, but it also meant that his influence was a particularly diverse one. As a critic, his principal achievements were to undermine the normative poetics of neo-classicism, to rehabilitate non-classical forms of literature, and to illuminate the functions of imagination and expression in poetry, thereby preparing the ground for Romanticism. But it was all a question of emphasis: he perceived an imbalance which needed correction, but he did not cease to admire and defend the classical tradition and the more rational and didactic varieties of poetry while pressing the case for their opposites. There is a good example of this even in his most impassioned defence of 'natural' and spontaneous poetry, the essay on Ossian, where he acknowledges that another kind of poetry is permissible, and indeed desirable – a poetry of rational reflection:

...What I said recently about the first spontaneous draft of a poem in no way justifies the careless and bungling efforts of our young would-be poets. For what deficiency is more obvious in their work than the very indefiniteness and uncertainty of their thoughts and words? They themselves never know what they want to say or should say. But if someone lacks even that knowledge, how can any corrections ever teach him it? Can anyone fashion a marble statue of Apollo out of a kitchen skewer?

It seems to me, given the state of our poetry at present, that two main possibilities are open to us. If a poet recognises that the mental faculties which are required partly by his subject and by the poetic genre he has chosen, and which also happen to be predominant within him, are the representational and cognitive faculties – he must reflect thoroughly on the content of his poem, comprehend it, turn it over, and order it clearly and distinctly until every letter is, as it were, engraved upon his soul, and his poem need only reproduce this in a complete and honest manner. But if his poem requires an outpouring of passion and feeling, or if this class of faculties supplies the most active and habitual kind of motivation he needs for his work – then he will abandon himself to the inspiration of the happy hour, and will write and enchant us.

(pp. 159f.)

A similar psychological distinction between two fundamentally different poetic modes or attitudes, supplemented by the historical distinction between ancient and modern eras, enables Friedrich Schiller, in his essay *On Naive and Sentimental Poetry*, to associate classical and post-classical forms of poetry with different varieties of consciousness.

Schiller's essay *On Naive and Sentimental Poetry* of 1795–6 is the most important work of poetics to appear in Germany since Lessing's *Laocoon* thirty years earlier. Unlike the *Laocoon*, it deals only with poetry. And although Schiller shares Lessing's neo-classical principles to a large extent, he does not adopt his formal and semiotic methods of classification. Instead, he classifies poetry in terms of the attitudes of poets to the world they live in. This was a momentous step. For, since Schiller's two main categories – 'naive' and 'sentimental' – coincided broadly with the traditional distinction between ancient and modern, he was able to formulate this time-honoured antithesis in a new and challenging way, and to focus attention on those characteristic attitudes of mind which distinguish most poetry of the modern era from that of antiquity. His concept of 'sentimental' or modern poetry became, shortly afterwards, the basis of Friedrich Schlegel's definition of 'Romantic' poetry.

Schiller's entire thinking, especially in his later years, tends to operate in antitheses. The antithesis of 'naive' and 'sentimental' is only one of them, and it is by no means exhausted by the cognate distinctions of ancient and modern or Classical and Romantic. Since his early studies of medicine and psychology in the 1770s, he had habitually worked with dualistic models of the human psyche – animal and spiritual natures, sense and intellect, and so on.[15] This tendency was greatly reinforced, and its conceptual basis considerably refined, by his studies of Kant's critical philosophy in the early 1790s. For Kant's idealism furnished the dualistic model of human nature which is central to Schiller's major aesthetic treatise, the *Letters on the Aesthetic Education of Man*, completed a year before the essay *On Naive and Sentimental Poetry*: the educative function of art, of aesthetic experience, is to reconcile and reintegrate the warring impulses within man – sense and intellect, nature and reason – and so to foster the development of full and balanced individuals, and ultimately of a harmonious culture and society. Art is uniquely placed to perform this task successfully, since it is itself an indissoluble compound of sensuous and rational elements.[16]

But the relative balance of these two elements will vary in each work of art, in relation to the genre it belongs to, the age in which it was created, and even the personality of the artist who produced it. Thus in poetry, for example (with which Schiller, as a poet himself, was chiefly concerned), the relative predominance of sense and reason, of nature and intellect, of spontaneity and reflection, can provide a means of classifying different genres and periods, as well as different kinds of poet.

Schiller regarded himself, quite rightly, as a primarily reflective poet, inclined to philosophical analysis. As such, he was acutely aware of the gulf between ideal and reality, thought and experience, and between himself as a self-conscious, rational being and the spontaneous life of nature and natural impulse of which he did not feel part. What made this awareness a decisive experience for him, particularly in relation to his work as a poet, was his friendship with Goethe, which began in 1794. Goethe, whose eminence and success Schiller had watched and envied from a distance for years, seemed to him to possess the very kind of poetic gifts which he himself lacked, and to represent the antithesis of himself as a poetic type: intuitive, spontaneous, at one with nature and at home in the world of the senses, objective in the way he depicted reality, a classicist by inclination, and as such more akin to the poets of antiquity than to those of the modern age. In short, he was a 'naive' poet. Schiller attempted to define the essential differences between his own and Goethe's poetic disposition in his famous letter to Goethe of 23 August 1794, which marks the beginning of that decade of collaboration between the poets which ended with Schiller's death in 1805. Schiller's characterological distinction had much truth in it – although, in the interests of a neat antithesis, there is undoubtedly exaggeration on both sides. Schiller's own mode of production, especially as a lyric poet, had a greater element of intuition and spontaneity about it than his simplified schema suggests.[17] And Goethe's complex nature includes elements of introspection and self-analysis to which Schiller's characterisation does less than justice. (Schiller implicitly acknowledges as much in his attempts to reconcile Goethe's *Werther*, *Tasso*, and *Faust* and the extreme self-consciousness of their heroes with his image of the 'naive' poet in the essay, pp. 206 f.) Nevertheless, this initial attempt by Schiller to characterise Goethe and himself as antithetical types contains the nucleus of his later distinction between 'naive' and 'sentimental' poets. And one of Schiller's reasons for making the distinction was clearly to justify his own, more reflective attitude towards poetic production as different from, yet no less valid than, Goethe's more 'natural' and apparently effortless mode of creativity.[18]

Thus, Kant's philosophy supplied the conceptual foundation, and the friendship with Goethe the characterological basis, of Schiller's classification of poetry. Its third main component – its historical application – rests on that chronological distinction between nature and artifice which, from Rousseau onwards, runs through most eighteenth-century accounts of cultural history.

'Nature', for Schiller (as for most of his contemporaries) represents a moral value as well as an empirical reality. It is associated with primitive ages and cultures, and with innate human virtue, uncorrupted by excessive civilisation. Already for Winckelmann and Lessing, it had associations with classical antiquity, and with Greece in particular. Homer is the archetypal natural

genius, whose art is based on eternal principles of nature and follows laws akin
to those of nature itself. Schiller's 'naive' poetry is poetry of this kind. The
nature on which it is based is itself an ideal: it is 'true' nature (*wahre Natur*)
as distinct from 'actual' nature (*wirkliche Natur*), and represents the eternal
principles on which all healthy life and harmonious art are based. It has none
of the associations of unvarnished naturalism in art or of licence in personal
behaviour which it had possessed for the *Sturm und Drang* two decades
before. Its affinities with neo-classicism are obvious; Schiller actually applies
Winckelmann's famous phrase 'noble simplicity' (*edle Einfalt*) to the 'naive'
character (p. 184).

'Sentimental' poetry, by way of contrast, is the poetry of a later, more
modern age. (Schiller does not say exactly when this age began; but it certainly
comes after the rise of Christianity, which taught men to look on nature and
spirit as inherently hostile principles.) It is an age of divided consciousness, in
which feeling and intellect have become divorced, and nature – both in life and
in art – figures only as a lost ideal of harmony. All 'sentimental' poetry is in
some way concerned with the discrepancy between this ideal and present
reality. Like Rousseau's era of civilisation, Schiller's 'sentimental', modern era
has a post-lapsarian quality about it. But Schiller rejects the yearning for a
lost Arcadia, which he associates with Rousseau, as regressive, and seeks instead
to restore the unity of nature and intellect in a new, higher 'Elysium'; this
is represented in poetry by what he calls the 'idyll', and in human culture in
general by what, in his earlier treatise on aesthetic education, he had called
the 'aesthetic state'. He is one of the first to treat the relation between the
modern artist and society as an inherently problematic one. (Goethe had
already done so several years before, in a poetic context, in his artist-drama
Torquato Tasso.) The 'sentimental' poet is painfully aware that he is himself
inwardly divided, and that modern culture, fragmented by the progressive
division of labour, no longer presents him with a unified object or audience.
Hence in the modern age, as Schiller puts it, 'our feeling for nature is like the
feeling of an invalid for health' (p. 190). But art itself can offer a way out of
this unhappy predicament. A special kind of 'idyll' in particular, through
presenting the lost ideal as a present reality, might enable the 'sentimental'
poet to achieve, by his own distinctive method, a result comparable to what
the 'naive' poet, in more favourable circumstances, accomplished with relative
ease. (Schiller's efforts to justify his own position in relation to that of Goethe
are once again apparent.)

The structure of Schiller's essay, like that of the earlier treatise on aesthetic
education, is tripartite. His scheme of cultural and artistic development, unlike
Rousseau's two-stage model of cultural history, entails a third and higher
phase, a future synthesis, in which qualities of the earlier two phases will be
combined.[19] Yet there is an ambiguity about Schiller's third phase of poetry,
just as there had been about the third phase of cultural development in the
Aesthetic Letters. In the latter work, the original 'state of nature' is succeeded

by a 'rational state', in which man's moral reason is more fully (if one-sidedly) developed. But it is not always clear whether the third phase is merely an enhancement of the second phase, brought about through the mediation of art, or whether it is synonymous with that 'aesthetic state' in which nature and reason are held in balance. Similarly, in the later essay, Schiller seems uncertain whether the future goal of poetry represents a culmination of 'sentimental' poetry (i.e. of the second phase), or a synthesis of the two original poetic modes, the 'naive' and the 'sentimental'. His remarks on the 'idyll' suggest the former. But he seems to envisage the latter possibility when he declares (p. 224) 'neither the naive nor the sentimental character, each considered alone, quite exhausts that ideal of beautiful humanity that can only arise out of the intimate union of both'. It may be that he is referring, on the latter occasion, to the complementarity of two types of poet (as exemplified in his own friendship with Goethe), and on the former, to the future development of poetry itself.

Nevertheless, there are many obscurities in Schiller's essay. Most of them are caused by his using established terms in unfamiliar senses, identical terms in varying senses, and mixing together aesthetic and non-aesthetic categories. For example, 'naive' is not primarily an aesthetic term, but it is invested with more and more aesthetic connotations as the essay proceeds. 'Sentimental' is not an aesthetic term either, and Schiller introduces it in a new and unusual sense, virtually as a synonym for 'reflective'. By the end of the essay, the two terms have acquired so strong an aesthetic colouring that Schiller feels obliged to introduce two new terms to denote the non-aesthetic counterparts of 'naive' and 'sentimental' types of poet – namely the 'realist' and the 'idealist'. The fact that Schiller's terms have both historical and characterological (or psychological) meanings causes further problems: poets of a 'naive' disposition can be encountered in modern times (Shakespeare and Goethe), just as 'sentimentally' inclined poets are to be found even in antiquity (Euripides and Horace). And when Schiller says that 'every true genius must be naive, or it is not genius' (p. 186), it is plain that the historical dimension is completely lacking. At times it appears that 'naive' and 'sentimental' characters and attitudes are perennial, supra-historical phenomena; at other times, they seem rather the products of whatever age they occur in. The issue is further complicated by the fact that Schiller gives to the subdivisions within 'sentimental' poetry names borrowed from traditional sub-genres of poetry – satire, elegy, and idyll – but endows them with new senses. And at the same time, he attempts to accommodate other actual sub-genres, particularly tragedy and comedy, within his scheme; but the attempt is somewhat strained, since comedy appears, under slightly different guises, as a variety of both 'satire' and 'idyll'. To complicate matters further, two other categories of traditional aesthetics – the sublime and the beautiful – are brought in as cognates of 'punitive' and 'playful' satire respectively. Schiller's definition of the 'idyll' as a future mode of poetry is particularly indeterminate. It is not at all easy to imagine what

such a work would look like, since none as yet exists; and Schiller's own plan
for an idyll on the marriage of Hercules and Hebe, which is all too suggestive
of pallid neo-classical allegory, never came to fruition.[20]

We have, then, a curious amalgam of old and new poetic terminology, used
in shifting and multiple senses. This is a symptom not so much of confusion
on Schiller's part as of the incipient breakdown of neo-classical poetics. The
old formal definitions of pure and unchanging genres took inadequate account
of the changing function of these genres in history, and Schiller accordingly
supplements them by a new classification in terms of the 'modes of perception'
(*Empfindungsweisen*) of the poets themselves. But he is too much of a neo-classicist
himself to abandon the traditional definitions entirely, and his ultimate
standard remains the art of classical antiquity, to whose achievement modern
art should approximate, albeit by a process of competition rather than of mere
imitation. And although he is moving away from a normative poetics of genre
in the direction of a historical and descriptive classification, he does retain
certain general norms associated with classicism: all art should have a universal
representativeness, which excludes the purely local and contingent; and the
extremes of naturalism, of narrowly personal and local reference on the one
hand, and of excessive abstraction and loss of reality on the other, are to be
avoided. But this is nevertheless a long way from the rigorously prescriptive
poetics of Boileau, Gottsched, and the early Enlightenment. Schiller's category
of the 'sentimental' in particular is an open and dynamic one. As such, it threw
into relief important characteristics of modern poetry which the older poetics
did not adequately account for, and furnished the Schlegel brothers' new
concept of Romantic poetry with much of its substance.

Schiller's essay thus points ahead to Romanticism. But when the new movement first emerged in the late 1790s, both he and Goethe viewed it with
suspicion and disapproval. Despite their own early *Sturm und Drang* productions, their endeavour was now to sustain and enrich the neo-classical
tradition of the century they had grown up in. They did not merely theorise
about it, but produced major works of poetry on the classical model or
embodying classical values. Weimar classicism was a brief and remarkable
interlude, essentially the achievement of two men over less than two decades.
But although Goethe continued for many years thereafter to defend the values
associated with it, it was to all intents and purposes over by 1805 with the death
of Schiller. Hölderlin's classicism was over by then too – but it had been
predominantly elegiac from the start. For Hölderlin, the Hellenic ideal was
very much a thing of the past, and his dreams of a future rebirth have a
desperate and unreal quality about them. It is fitting that, in 1805, Goethe
was able, despite a severe illness, to conclude the chapter of German classicism
on a triumphant note with his splendid tribute to Winckelmann. In it, he
reaffirms the classical tradition, pays homage to its first authentic spokesman
in Germany, and bids defiance to its enemies, the Romantics.

The occasion for Goethe's essay was the publication of a collection of Winckelmann's letters which had recently come to light in Weimar. Goethe resolved to edit a volume on Winckelmann, including contributions by the art-historians Heinrich Meyer and Carl Ludwig Fernow and by the classical philologist F. A. Wolf, as well as the letters themselves. The title of the volume, *Winckelmann and his Century* (an obvious echo of Voltaire's *Siècle de Louis XIV*), indicates the importance which Goethe accorded to Winckelmann as the representative figure of his age. By far the most substantial contribution is the essay by Goethe himself, which is simultaneously a biographical tribute to Winckelmann and a statement of Goethe's own Hellenic and classical ideals. The latter embody not only a programme for art, but also an ethos for living.

The essay is an *éloge* or panegyric rather than a historical analysis or detached biography. It is a monument to Winckelmann, and the figure of Winckelmann himself is monumentalised. Goethe is not concerned with the incidents of Winckelmann's life, except in so far as they can be made to illustrate representative values. (The sordid circumstances surrounding his murder in Trieste, for example, are nowhere mentioned.) Many of the headings to the sections within the essay underline the values which Winckelmann epitomises: *Antiquity, Friendship, Beauty, Paganism*, etc. The figure of Winckelmann is, as it were, chiselled in marble: he is a living myth, a Greek reborn, an incarnation of classical culture in modern times.

The essay as a whole and various passages within it are characterised by that upward, idealising movement which Goethe sometimes described as *Steigerung* (enhancement, intensification), and which is evident in many of his poetic works – particularly those which culminate on an ideal or transcendental plane – from *Egmont* to *Faust*, Part II. It is coupled here on one occasion with a triadic formula similar to that which Schiller was fond of using. In the present case, Goethe distinguishes three ascending degrees of human achievement (in the section *Antiquity*, which is the key to the whole essay):

Man may achieve much through the purposeful application of isolated faculties, and he may achieve the extraordinary by combining several of his capacities; but he can accomplish the unique, the totally unexpected, only when all his resources are uniformly united within him. The latter was the happy lot of the ancients, especially of the Greeks in their best period; fate has assigned the two former possibilities to us moderns.

(p. 237)

In the last sentence, the tripartite progression is simplified so as to yield a straight antithesis, which provides the other main structural principle of the essay: the distinction between ancients and moderns, between whole men and fragmented individuals. But in order to raise the third and highest order of human achievement – the attainment of a balanced, harmonious, and fulfilled personality – to an even higher level, Goethe goes on to present it, in a daring hyperbole, as the goal of the entire creative process, as the *telos* of the universe:[21]

When the healthy nature of man functions as a totality, when he feels himself in the world as in a vast, beautiful, worthy, and valued whole, when a harmonious sense of well-being affords him pure and free delight – then the universe, if it were capable of sensation, would exult at having reached its goal, and marvel at the culmination of its own development and being. For what is the use of all the expenditure of suns and planets and moons, of stars and galaxies, of comets and nebulae, of completed and developing worlds, if at the end a happy man does not unconsciously rejoice in existence?

For all its hyperbole, this passage is a fine expression (albeit a late one) of the humanism and optimism of the eighteenth century, and of its belief that man, if not the earth itself, is the goal and centre of the universe. And no sooner have we been told that the consummate human achievement, the whole man, belongs only to the past, to antiquity, than Winckelmann is reintroduced, with an effect like that of a miracle. For in him, the antique personality was once more made flesh: 'From the very moment when he won the freedom he required, he appeared whole and complete, entirely in the spirit of antiquity.'

But the very fact that Winckelmann is presented as a remarkable exception confirms that Goethe was highly sceptical about the possibility of realising the ancient ideal in the modern world, of crossing the barrier which separates fragmented moderns from integrated ancients. He suggests, just as Schiller had done, that a fundamental division within human nature has become apparent since antiquity, and says of the ancients: 'Feeling and reflection were not yet fragmented, that perhaps irreparable rift had not yet opened up within the healthy powers of man' (p. 238).[22] It was this gulf which Goethe himself strove to bridge, and the one figure in his own times who, according to him, successfully overcame it was Winckelmann. For Winckelmann fulfils the same function in Goethe's essay as Goethe himself had fulfilled in Schiller's essay of ten years before.[23] Goethe, of course, is perfectly aware of this – his essay contains numerous echoes of Schiller. He is consciously identifying himself with Winckelmann, on to whose personality and destiny he projects many of his own qualities, including those which Schiller had attributed to him. For example, in the section *Character* – although he avoids using Schiller's term – he endows Winckelmann with the essential attributes of the 'naive' personality: lack of self-consciousness ('He thinks only *of* himself, not *about* himself'), and a spontaneous, intuitive approach to his work. He repeatedly applies to Winckelmann the words *Glück* (fortune, happiness) and *glücklich* (fortunate, happy), words which he often applied to himself as a favourite of fortune. The Winckelmann of this essay also lives out the Goethean doctrine of seizing the moment, of expanding the fleeting instant to temporal saturation by means of ceaseless activity. And what Goethe says about Winckelmann's experiences and self-fulfilment in Rome resonates with memories of his own Italian years and the educative value they had held for him, even down to the detail of Winckelmann being mistaken for an artist (Goethe had himself travelled incognito as an artist in Italy). The section *Rome*, with an appropriate quotation from his friend Wilhelm von Humboldt, is a celebration of Goethe's own experience of the classical south.

But finally, it is perhaps in his comments on religion and morality that Goethe's self-identification with Winckelmann is most striking – all the more so since no distortion of Winckelmann is involved. He praises Winckelmann's free and unconventional style of living in Rome, and contrasts it with the stiffness and ceremony of his German homeland. He has no word of reproach for Winckelmann's flouting of convention, as in his devotion to male friendships on the antique model which Goethe mentions with approval. We have here an attitude akin to that expressed in the greatest lyrics of Goethe's classical period, the *Roman Elegies* and *Venetian Epigrams*, in which the bohemianism, sensualism, and contempt for prudery of his own Italian phase and its aftermath are at their most conspicuous. And in the section *Paganism*, Goethe positively revels in Winckelmann's 'remoteness from all Christian sentiments' (p. 239), and he subsequently refers to his 'thoroughly pagan nature' (p. 242); these again are turns of phrase he liked to apply to himself. Like Goethe, Winckelmann was free from the Christian revulsion against the senses; and despite his religious conversion – which Goethe describes as essentially a matter of convenience – his concern was above all with things of this world.

It is obvious from all this that Goethe's essay conveys a stylised and in some ways tendentious impression of its subject. Its aim is to present the respected Winckelmann as a forerunner of Weimar classicism – and to enlist him as an ally against the German Romantics, with whom Goethe had by now lost patience and whom he saw as the main threat to his classical values. In the very year of this essay, Goethe had denounced the Romantic fraternity for portraying the art of antiquity as spiritually empty and elevating Christian art as far superior. He said of such judgements, in a famous outburst:

Who can fail to notice the neo-Catholic sentimentality in these phrases? That monasticising, Sternbaldising mischief which poses a greater threat to the visual arts than all the Calibans who clamour for greater realism.[24]

The essay is not only a manifesto of Goethe's classicism, but also a polemic against Romanticism, which is associated, by implication, with a one-sided and stunted humanity. The religious revival of the nineteenth century was sweeping away the humanism of the eighteenth; the Goethe's essay is one of his chief attempts to stem the tide. It is no wonder that it was bitterly resented by Friedrich Schlegel and his circle.

Goethe describes Winckelmann's last published work as 'a legacy to all future ages' (p. 253). The same words could be used of his own essay. It is a testament of those values in art and life which Goethe considers permanently binding. And they are not the values of a closed and immobile classicism: Goethe repeatedly stresses the provisional and fluid quality of even the greatest achievements, which remain open to the future as a challenge and inspiration.[25] In his sonorous conclusion, he not only pays Winckelmann the highest compliment a classicist could bestow: 'He lived as a man, and as a complete man he went from hence.' He even represents his premature death as an advantage to posterity, in that it encourages later generations to continue where he left off.

German classicism begins, then, with Winckelmann, and culminates in Goethe, whose achievement retrospectively illuminates that of his predecessor. Walter Pater, whose own essay on Winckelmann is largely inspired by that of Goethe, rightly emphasises their connection (even if he is a little unfair to Winckelmann in the process):

The aim of a right criticism is to place Winckelmann in an intellectual perspective, of which Goethe is the foreground. For, after all, he is infinitely less than Goethe; and it is chiefly because at certain points he comes in contact with Goethe, that criticism entertains consideration of him.[26]

Part 1
Winckelmann

Johann Joachim Winckelmann

(1717–68)

Winckelmann was born in 1717 at Stendal in Prussia. He grew up in poverty, and received a basic education in Latin, followed by some tuition in Greek at a Berlin grammar school. He enrolled as a student of theology at the University of Halle, where he also studied philosophy. After earning enough, as a house tutor, to continue his studies he matriculated at the University of Jena, but soon abandoned his studies of medicine and mathematics. After several miserable years as a schoolteacher, he became a research assistant to Count Bünau at his castle near Dresden (1748), and made full use of the Count's excellent library. Winckelmann's years in Dresden, during which he began systematic studies of the literature and art of antiquity, ended with his conversion to Catholicism (1754), as a preliminary to his planned move to Italy, and with the publication of his first and most seminal work, the *Thoughts on the Imitation of the Painting and Sculpture of the Greeks* (1755). This work marks the beginning of that passion for the Hellenic ideal in art and literature which runs through German intellectual life from Goethe, Schiller, and Hölderlin to Nietzsche. (Before Winckelmann, classical education in Germany had been based almost exclusively on Latin, and Greek was taught only as an aid to New Testament studies.)

Winckelmann's career in Rome from 1755 onwards and his increasing eminence as a scholar and connoisseur of Greek art are memorably described by Goethe in his biographical tribute, the essay *Winckelmann*, a translation of which is included in this volume (pp. 236–58). His professional career culminated in his appointment to the office of Prefect of Antiquities and to a post at the Vatican Library in Rome (1763), and his career as a scholar in the publication of his epoch-making *History of the Art of Antiquity* (1764), which for the first time identified the main phases in the development of Greek art and laid the foundations of modern art history. He became a legend in his own time, and his tragic murder in Trieste in 1768 added to the fascination with which he was regarded by his German contemporaries. Winckelmann's achievement gave a decisive impetus to classical studies in Germany, which were to lead the world within a century of his death. His vision of Greece and the aesthetic ideals he based upon it helped to shape the later phases of neo-classicism in Europe. The debts of Lessing, Schiller, and Goethe to him are plainly visible in the works by these writers which are included in this volume.

Further reading

The standard edition of Winckelmann's works is that by Joseph Eiselein (see Bibliography for this and subsequent titles), and the letters are collected in *Winckelmanns Briefe* (1952–7). A useful collection of his writings in English translation is David Irwin's *Winckelmann: Writings on Art* (1972). The standard biography is that of Justi (1923, reprinted 1956). Walter Pater's essay on him in his *The Renaissance* (1873) is still worth reading. Hatfield (1943 and 1964) relates his achievement to the context of German Hellenism, and Honour (1968) to that of European neo-classicism.

Thoughts on the Imitation of the Painting and Sculpture of the Greeks[1]

1755

Translated by H. B. Nisbet.
German text in *Sämtliche Werke*, edited by Eiselein (1825–9), I, 7–56.

I Nature

Good taste, which is gaining ever wider currency throughout the world, first began to develop under the skies of Greece. All the inventions of foreign nations came, so to speak, only as a germinating seed to Greece, and took on another nature and form in the country which Minerva, it is said,[2] selected before all others because of the temperate seasons she encountered there, and assigned to the Greeks to inhabit as a country which would produce wise intellects.

The kind of taste which this nation bestowed on its works has remained peculiar to it; it has seldom travelled far from Greece without losing something, and in remote regions it has become known only in later times. In northern climes, it was certainly completely alien in that period when the two arts of which the Greeks are the great instructors found few devotees; in that period, that is, when the most admirable of Correggio's productions were hung in front of the windows of the royal stables in Stockholm to serve as blinds.

And we must confess that the reign of the great Augustus[3] marks precisely that happy moment at which the arts, as a foreign colony, have been introduced to Saxony. Under his successor, the German Titus,[4] they have become naturalised in this country, and through their influence, good taste is becoming universal.

It is a permanent monument to the greatness of this monarch that, in order that good taste may develop, the greatest treasures of Italy, and whatever perfect works the painters of other countries have produced, are exhibited to the public gaze. And his zeal to perpetuate the arts has not finally rested until truly authentic works of Greek masters – works, moreover, of the first importance – have been made available for artists to imitate.

The purest springs of art now flow freely: happy is he who finds them and tastes their waters! To seek these springs is to journey to Athens; and henceforth, Dresden will be the Athens of the artists.

The only way for us to become great, and indeed – if this is possible – inimitable, is by imitating the ancients. And what someone said of Homer, that he who has learned to understand him well has learned to admire him, is also true of the art of the ancients, and of the Greeks in particular. One must become familiar with their works as with a friend in order to find the Laocoon group as inimitable as Homer. With such close familiarity, our judgement will be like that of Nicomachus, who said of the Helen of Zeuxis to an ignorant critic who presumed to censure the work: 'Take my eyes, and you will see in her a goddess.'

It was with such eyes that Michelangelo, Raphael, and Poussin looked at the works of the ancients. They drew good taste from its original source, and in Raphael's case, from the very land where it first developed; for it is known that he sent young artists to Greece to sketch the relics of antiquity for him.

An ancient Roman statue will always stand in the same relation to a Greek original as Virgil's Dido, whom he likens with her retinue to Diana amidst her Oreads, does to Homer's Nausicaa, whom Virgil was trying to imitate.

The Laocoon group was to the artists of ancient Rome precisely what it is to us today: the rule of Polycleitus,[5] a perfect model for art.

I need not point out that there are certain instances of negligence in the most famous productions of the Greeks: the dolphin which accompanies the Medici Venus along with the playing children, and the workmanship of Dioscorides – apart from the central figure – in his rendering of Diomedes with the Palladium, are cases in point. We also know that the work on the obverse of the finest coins of the Egyptian and Syrian kings is rarely of the same quality as the heads. But great artists are wise even in their negligence, and even their errors are instructive. We should look at their works as Lucian tells us to look at the Jupiter of Phidias: at Jupiter himself, and not at his footstool.

The connoisseurs and imitators of the works of the Greeks find in their masterpieces not only the highest beauty of nature, but something more than nature: namely certain ideal beauties which, as an ancient commentator of Plato puts it, 'are based on images constructed solely by the mind'.[6]

The most beautiful human body to be found among us might perhaps resemble the most beautiful Greek body no more closely than Iphicles resembled his brother Hercules. A mild and clear sky influenced the childhood development of the Greeks, but it was their early physical exercises which determined their noble form. Take, for instance, a Spartan youth, the offspring of heroes, who was never constricted in infancy by swaddling-clothes, who slept on the bare earth from his seventh year onwards, and who was trained since childhood in wrestling and swimming; compare him with a young Sybarite of our time, and then decide which of them an artist would choose as the model for a young Theseus, an Achilles, or even a Bacchus. The latter would produce a Theseus reared, as it were, on roses, the former a Theseus reared on meat (to use the terms which a Greek painter[7] applied to two different versions of this hero).

The Olympic Games were for all young Greeks a powerful incentive to physical exercise, and the laws required them to train for ten months at Elis, the actual site where the Games were held. And the highest awards were not always won by men, but often by youths, as Pindar's odes indicate. The supreme ambition of the young was to rival the god-like Diagoras.[8]

Consider the fleet-footed Indian who hunts the deer on foot: how swift his circulation becomes, how quickly and flexibly his nerves and muscles react, and how lightly his whole frame is constructed! Thus Homer draws his heroes, and his Achilles is distinguished above all by his lightness of foot.

These exercises gave the bodies of the Greeks that great and manly contour which the Greek masters imparted to their statues, with no vague outlines or superfluous accretions. The young Spartans had to appear naked every ten days before the ephors,[9] who imposed a stricter diet on those who began to show signs of fat. Indeed, the rules of Pythagoras included one which warned against excess weight. Perhaps it was for this same reason that, in the earliest times in Greece, youths presenting themselves for wrestling contests were allowed only a diet of milk during their training period.

All physical evils were carefully avoided, and after Alcibiades as a boy refused to learn the flute because it distorted his face, the young Athenians followed his example.

Accordingly, the entire dress of the Greeks was designed not to impose the slightest constraint on the formative power of nature. Growth and beauty of form were in no way impaired by the various accoutrements of modern clothing, which cramps and restricts the body, particularly around the neck, hips, and thighs. Even the fair sex among the Greeks knew no anxious constraint in its attire: the young Spartan girls were dressed so lightly and scantily that they were known as 'the girls who reveal their hips'.

It is also well known what pains the Greeks took to produce beautiful children. Quillet, in his *Callipaedia*,[10] suggests fewer ways of attaining this end than were already familiar to the Greeks. They even went to the length of trying to turn blue eyes into black ones. With a similar end in view, beauty contests were organised. They were held at Elis, and the prize consisted of weapons which were displayed in the temple of Minerva. There was no lack of exacting and well-qualified judges; for the Greeks, as Aristotle tells us,[11] taught their children to draw chiefly because they believed it would make them better equipped to observe and assess physical beauty.

The fine complexion of the inhabitants of most Greek islands, though mixed with so many varieties of foreign blood, and the exquisite charms of the fair sex in those regions, particularly on the island of Chios, allow us to form a sound estimate of how beautiful both sexes must have been at the time of their forefathers, who boasted of being the original inhabitants, a race older than the moon.

Even today, there are whole nations among whom beauty is not considered a merit, because everyone is beautiful. The writers of travelogues say this unanimously of the Georgians, and the same is reported of the Kabardines, a Crimean Tartar race.

Those diseases which are so destructive of beauty and which ravage the noblest features were as yet unknown among the Greeks. There is no mention of smallpox in the writings of the Greek physicians; and no physical description of any Greek (although Homer often refers to the minutest characteristics) includes so distinctive a feature as a pock-marked face.

Venereal diseases, and their progeny, the English malady,[12] had not yet marred the natural beauty of the Greeks.

All the precepts and injunctions on the cultivation of the body from birth to adulthood, and on its preservation, nurture, and embellishment by natural and artificial means, were designed to enhance the natural beauty of the ancient Greeks; they justify us in asserting, with the highest degree of probability, that the outstanding physical beauty of the Greeks far surpassed our own.

But in a country where nature was impeded in its operations by stricter laws – as was the case in Egypt, the alleged homeland of the arts and sciences – the most perfect creations of nature would have been only partially and imperfectly known to the artists. In Greece, however, whose inhabitants were dedicated from childhood to joy and delight, and where our present-day criteria of respectability never interfered with the freedom of manners, natural beauty revealed itself naked for the instruction of the artist.

The schools of art were the gymnasiums, where the young people – though modesty required them to wear clothes in public – performed their exercises completely naked. Philosophers and artists accompanied them – Socrates in order to teach Charmides, Autolycus, and Lysis, and Phidias in order to enrich his art through studying their beauty. Here, one could learn the movements of the muscles and the attitudes of the body; one could study physical outlines or the contour of the body in the impressions left by the young wrestlers in the sand.

The nude at its most beautiful was displayed here in varied, authentic, and noble attitudes and postures, of a sort which could never be reproduced by a hired model required to pose in our academies.

Authentic expression springs from inner sentiment; and the draughtsman who wishes to convey this quality of truth to his academy will not achieve a shadow of it unless he himself supplies what the heart of an unmoved and indifferent model does not feel, and cannot express through an action appropriate to a given emotion or passion.

The opening passages of many of the Platonic dialogues which begin in the gymnasiums of Athens give us an impression of the inward nobility of the youths, and permit us to infer that their actions and postures in their training were of a corresponding character.

The most beautiful young people danced naked in the theatre; and the great Sophocles, in his youth, was the first to entertain his fellow citizens in this manner. Phryne bathed before the eyes of all Greece at the Eleusinian Games, and gave the artists their model for Venus Anadyomene as she emerged from the water; and we know that the young girls of Sparta danced naked before the assembled youth at one of their festivals. Strange as this may seem, it becomes more credible when we consider that the early Christians, men and women alike, were likewise baptised or immersed in water together, completely naked, in one and the same font.

Thus every Greek festival gave the artists an opportunity to become thoroughly conversant with natural beauty.

The humanity of the Greeks, at the time when their freedom was at its height, precluded the introduction of bloody spectacles. Or if, as some believe, such spectacles were at one time customary in Ionic Asia, they had not been held for a considerable time before. Antiochus Epiphanes, King of Syria, imported gladiators from Rome, and put these unfortunate people on show before the Greeks, who at first regarded such spectacles with loathing; but with time, humane sentiments became blunted, and these displays too became schools for the artist. Here, Ctesilaus studied his dying gladiator, and one could tell from the statue how much life still remained in him.

These frequent opportunities for observing nature led the Greek artists to take a further step: they began to formulate certain general concepts of beauty, with reference both to individual parts of the body and to its overall proportions – concepts which sought to transcend nature itself. Their model in this case was an archetype of nature constructed solely in the mind.

Raphael created his Galatea in this way, as we learn from his letter to Count Balthasar Castiglione, where he writes: 'Since there are so few beauties among the female sex, I have worked from a certain imaginary idea.'

The Greeks created their gods and men from such concepts, exalted far above the ordinary realm of material form. In their gods and goddesses, the brow and nose form an almost straight line. The heads of famous women on Greek coins have the same profile, although there was nothing arbitrary about the choice of ideal models. Alternatively, we might conjecture that this profile was as peculiar to the ancient Greeks as flat noses are to the Calmucks, or small eyes to the Chinese. The large eyes of the Greek heads on gems and coins might lend support to such conjectures.

The Roman empresses were depicted in the same manner by the Greeks on their coins: the head of Livia or Agrippina has the same profile as that of Artemisia or Cleopatra.

In all these instances we can see that the law which the Thebans imposed on their artists – namely that they should imitate nature to the best of their ability, or suffer a penalty for failure to do so – was recognised as binding by other Greek artists too. Where the smooth Greek profile could not be introduced without prejudicing the likeness, they remained true to nature, as can be seen in the beautiful head of Julia, daughter of the Emperor Titus, engraved by Euodus.[13]

But the supreme law recognised by the Greek artists was that people should be faithfully depicted, yet at the same time beautified; this presupposes an intention on the master's part to work towards a more beautiful and perfect nature. Polygnotus always adhered to this rule.

And when we are told that some artists followed the example of Praxiteles, who modelled his Cnidian Venus on his concubine Cratina, or of other painters who took Lais as their model for the Graces, I believe that they did so without deviating from those general laws of art described above. Sensuous beauty was the model for the beauty of nature; ideal beauty for its sublime features – the former for the human, the latter for the divine.

Let anyone who is perspicacious enough to fathom the secrets of art compare all the other aspects of the Greek figures with most of their modern equivalents – particularly those based rather on nature than on antique taste – and he will often discover hitherto undetected beauties.

In most figures executed by modern masters, those parts of the body which are subjected to pressure will display small but all-too-conspicuous folds of skin; but where the same folds occur on the same constricted parts in Greek statues, each rises from the other in gentle undulations, so that they all form a single unit and seem to be the combined product of a single noble pressure. These masterpieces show us a skin which is not tightly stretched, but gently drawn over a healthy flesh, which fills it out without distended protuberances and follows all the movements of the fleshy parts of the body in a single unified direction. The skin never forms separate folds distinct from the flesh, as on the bodies of modern figures.

Similarly, modern works are distinguished from those of the Greeks by numerous little hollows, by too many and too conspicuous dimples. Where these do occur in the works of the ancients, they are employed with wise economy, in keeping with the more perfect and complete nature of the Greeks; they are merely hinted at, and are often apparent only to a trained sensibility.

In every such instance, there is a clear probability that, in the physical beauty of the Greeks and in the works of their masters, there was a greater unity of construction, a nobler integration of parts, and a higher degree of completeness, without the lean, drawn contours and sunken outlines of the present-day physique.

This can be no more than a probability, of course. But as such, it merits the attention of our artists and connoisseurs – all the more so since it is necessary, in paying due respect to the Greek monuments, to free ourselves from the common prejudice that the only credit to be gained through imitating them derives from their aura of antiquity.

But this point, on which the opinions of artists are divided, would require a more thorough investigation than is possible within the scope of this work.

It is well known that the great Bernini was one of those who sought to deny the Greeks the distinction of possessing a greater natural beauty and of attaining an ideal beauty in their compositions. He was also of the opinion that nature, in all its parts, yields every kind of beauty we require, and that art consists merely in discovering it. He boasted of having overcome a prejudice under which he had initially laboured with regard to the Medici Venus, whose charms he had considered unique until, after painstaking research, he encountered them here and there in nature.[14]

Thus it was the statue of Venus which taught him to discover beauties in nature which he had previously considered peculiar to the statue, and which, without the statue, he would never have looked for in nature. Does it not follow from this that the beauty of the Greek statues can be discovered more readily than the beauty of nature, and that the former is more affecting, less scattered, and more completely united than the latter? The study of nature must therefore be at the very least a slower and more laborious way of discovering perfect beauty than the study of ancient art; and in directing young artists primarily to the chief beauties of nature, Bernini was not showing them the shortest route to their destination.

The imitation of natural beauty is either based on a single object, or it collects observations from various distinct objects and unites them into a whole. The former we call copying or portraying a likeness; it is the method by which the Dutch artists create their forms and figures. The latter, however, is the way to universal beauty and its ideal images; it is the way of the Greeks. But there is this difference between them and us: the Greeks were able to create such images even without basing them upon particularly beautiful bodies, because they had daily opportunities for observing natural beauty such as we do not see every day, and which we rarely see in the manner an artist would wish for.

Nature, in our times, will not readily produce a body as perfect as the Antinous Admirandus;[15] and no idea can surpass the more than human proportions of divine beauty as exemplified in the Vatican Apollo:[16] all that nature, mind, and art have been able to accomplish stands here before us.

I believe that imitating the Greeks can teach us artistic insight more quickly than any other method. For on the one hand, their art embodies the essence of what is scattered throughout nature; and on the other, it shows us how far nature, at its most beautiful, can surpass itself in bold yet judicious compositions. It can teach us to think and to design with confidence, for it enables us to fix precisely the upper limits of human and divine beauty.

If the artist builds on this foundation, and lets the Greek rule of beauty guide his hand and his senses, he is on the surest route to successful imitation of nature. The concepts of totality and perfection which he discovers in the nature of antiquity will refine and give concrete shape to the diffuse concepts he abstracts from the nature of today: he will learn to combine the beauties he finds in it with ideal beauty, and, with the help of the sublime forms which are constantly present to him, he will then be able to legislate for himself.

Then, and then only, can the painter in particular embark on the imitation of nature, as in those instances where his art allows him to deviate from his marble models (in representing drapery, for example) and to take the kind of liberties which Poussin took; for, as Michelangelo puts it, he who constantly follows others will never lead the way himself; and whoever can produce nothing of value from his own resources will not make profitable use of the work of others either.

Those individuals whom nature has favoured

> quibus arte benigna
> Et meliore luto finxit praecordia Titan[17]

have nothing to stop them from becoming original artists.

It is in this spirit that we should interpret what De Piles[18] tells us of Raphael – namely that, shortly before his death, he intended to abandon the ancient marbles and follow nature alone. The true taste of antiquity would have continued to be his guide in the realm of ordinary nature, and everything he observed therein would, by a kind of chemical transformation, have become of one substance with his own nature and being.

Perhaps he would then have given his paintings more variety, fuller draperies, more colour, and more light and shade: but they would certainly have benefited less from all this than from that noble contour and sublime spirit which the Greeks taught him to impart to his works.

Nothing would more clearly demonstrate the superior advantage to be gained from imitating the ancients, as distinct from nature, than if one were to take two equally talented young people, and direct one to the study of antiquity and the other solely to nature. The latter would represent nature as he found it: as an Italian, he would perhaps paint figures like Caravaggio; as a Dutchman, like Jacob Jordaens (if he were lucky);[19] as a Frenchman, like Stella.[20] But the former would represent nature as it should be represented, and paint figures like those of Raphael.

II Contour

But however much the artist may gain from the imitation of nature, it can never teach him that precision of contour which can be learned from the Greeks alone.

The noblest contour unites or circumscribes every component of natural and ideal beauty in the figures of the Greeks; or rather, it is the supreme expression of both. Euphranor, whose fame dates from after the time of Zeuxis, is considered to be the first to have treated it in the more sublime manner.

Many modern artists have tried to imitate the Greek contour, but very few have succeeded. The great Rubens is far from having captured the Greek outline, particularly in those of his works which he executed before he went to Italy and studied the antiques.

The dividing line between completeness and superfluity in nature is a fine one, and the greatest of modern masters have deviated too far in both directions from this intangible mean. Those who have tried to avoid an emaciated contour have erred on the side of corpulence, while others have made their figures excessively lean.

Michelangelo is perhaps the only artist who may be said to have equalled the ancients; but he does so only in strong, muscular figures, in characters from the heroic age. He is less successful with delicate youthful figures, and with those of women, who, in his hands, become Amazons.

The Greek artist, on the other hand, judged the contour of all his figures to within a hair's breadth, even in the most delicate and laborious compositions such as those on engraved gems. One need only consider the Diomedes and Perseus of Dioscorides,[21] or the Hercules and Iole of Teucer[22] to see how inimitable the Greeks are in such work.

Parrhasius is generally regarded as the supreme master of contour.

Even beneath the garments of the Greek figures, the masterly contour prevails as the chief aim of the artists, who makes the beautiful physique of his figures stand out even through the marble, as if through the kind of transparent fabric manufactured in Cos.

The statue of Agrippina, executed in the lofty style, and the three Vestals in the royal collection in Dresden call for mention in this connection. Agrippina is probably not the mother of Nero, but the elder Agrippina, the wife of Germanicus. She closely resembles another standing figure, allegedly of this same Agrippina, in the entrance hall of the library of St Mark's in Venice.[23] Our Agrippina, however, is a seated figure of more than life size, with her head supported by her right hand. Her beautiful features suggest a soul immersed in profound meditation, rendered insensible to all external impressions by grief and sorrow. We might conjecture that the artist sought to depict the heroine at that sad moment when she received the news of her banishment to the island of Pandataria.[24]

The three Vestals merit our esteem for two reasons. They are the first major discoveries from Herculaneum; and they are even more valuable because of the grand manner in which their draperies are executed. In this respect all three of them, but particularly the one which is more than life size, can be put in the same class as the Farnese Flora and other Greek works of the first importance. The other two figures, of life size, are so alike that they appear to be the work of the same artist; the only difference is in their heads, which are not of equal merit. In the better of the two, the curled hair is parted in the middle, drawn back from the forehead, and tied together at the back. On the other head, the hair runs smoothly over the scalp, except at the front, where it is curled and tied with a ribbon. It is conceivable that this head is the work of a later, albeit able hand, and has been substituted for the original.

The fact that the heads of these two figures wear no veil does not mean that they cannot be Vestals, for there is evidence that priestesses of Vesta are depicted elsewhere without veils. Or rather, it seems from the heavy folds of drapery behind their necks that the veil, which is of one piece with the garment (as can be seen from the largest of the figures), is thrown back over their shoulders.

It is worth mentioning that these three divine figures supplied the first clue which led to the discovery of the subterranean treasures of Herculaneum.

They came to light when its memory had virtually been obliterated, just as the city itself lay buried under the rubble of its own buildings – at a time, that is, when almost the only knowledge that remained of the sad fate which befell it was the younger Pliny's report of his uncle's death during the destruction of Herculaneum.

These great masterpieces of Greek art were removed to Germany and admired there before Naples, so far as one can tell, could boast of a single monument from Herculaneum.

They were found in a buried vault at Portici near Naples in the year 1706, when the foundations were being dug for the Prince d'Elbeuf's country house. Immediately afterwards, along with other statues of marble and bronze discovered in the same locality, they came into the possession of Prince Eugene, and were taken to Vienna.

This great connoisseur, seeking a suitable place to display them, had a *sala terrena*[25] built specially for these three figures, and they were duly placed there along with a few other statues. When the first rumour arose that they were to be sold, the whole academy and all the artists in Vienna were incensed, and everyone looked on with sadness when they were removed to Dresden.

Before they were removed, the famous Mattielli,[26] 'to whom Polycleitus gave his rule, and Phidias his chisel', as Algarotti[27] puts it, copied all three Vestals in clay, with immense effort, to compensate himself for their loss. He followed them himself a few years later, however, and filled Dresden with enduring monuments of his art. Yet even here, the priestesses remained his model for drapery (in which his chief skill consisted) until his last years, which is a sure testimony to their excellence.

III Drapery

The word 'drapery' denotes everything taught by art concerning the clothing of nakedness and the folds of garments. After natural beauty and a noble contour, this particular expertise is the third outstanding characteristic of the works of antiquity.

The drapery of the Vestals is executed in the most exalted manner: the lesser folds emerge in gentle undulations from the broadest surfaces, and disappear again into these with a noble freedom and gentle harmony overall, but without concealing the beautiful contour of the underlying physique. How few modern masters are free from fault in this area!

But we must not be unjust to a few great artists of modern times (especially painters) who have in certain cases successfully deviated from the usual practice of the Greek masters in relation to drapery, without prejudice to nature or truth. Greek drapery is usually modelled on thin and wet garments, which, as artists know, cling tightly to the skin and body, and thereby reveal the underlying contours. The entire outer garment of Greek ladies was of extremely thin material known as perlon, a kind of veil.

The ancients did not always stick to delicately folded garments, however, as can be seen from their reliefs and paintings, and particularly from the ancient busts. This is confirmed by the fine bust of Caracalla in the royal collection of antiquities in Dresden.

In modern times, the artist has had to pile one garment on top of the other, some of them of heavy material, so that they cannot fall into the gentle flowing folds of their ancient counterparts. This accordingly gave rise to the modern practice of employing broad surfaces in drapery, which allows the artist to display his skill no less effectively than in the usual manner of the ancients.

Carlo Maratta[28] and Francesco Solimena[29] may be considered the greatest exponents of this technique. But artists of the new Venetian school, in attempting to go even further, have exaggerated this manner; and, by confining themselves to large surfaces, they have rendered their draperies stiff and metallic.

IV Expression

Finally, the universal and predominant characteristic of the Greek masterpieces is a noble simplicity and tranquil grandeur, both in posture and expression.[30] Just as the depths of the sea remain forever calm, however much the surface may rage, so does the expression of the Greek figures, however strong their passions, reveal a great and dignified soul. Such a soul is depicted in the face of Laocoon, and not only in his face, despite his most violent torments. The pain which is evident in his every muscle and sinew, and which, disregarding his face and other parts of his body, we can almost feel ourselves simply by looking at his painfully contracted abdomen – this pain, I maintain, nevertheless causes no violent distortion either to his face or to his general posture. He raises no terrible clamour, as in Virgil's poetic account of his fate. His mouth is not wide enough open to allow it, and he emits instead an anxious and oppressed sigh, such as Sadoleto describes.[31] The physical pain and spiritual greatness are diffused with equal intensity throughout his entire frame, and held, as it were, in balance. Laocoon suffers, but he suffers like the Philoctetes of Sophocles: his misery touches us to the heart, but we envy the fortitude with which this great man endures it.

The expression of so great a soul far surpasses the forms of natural beauty; the artist had to feel within himself the strength of spirit which he imprinted on his marble. Greece possessed artists and philosophers in one and the same person, and had more than one Metrodorus.[32] Wisdom reached out its hand to art, and inspired its figures with more than ordinary souls.

Had Laocoon worn a garment such as the artist ought to have given him as a priest, his pain would have been only half as graphic. Bernini even claimed to detect the first effect of the snake's venom in the paralysis of one of Laocoon's thighs.

All actions or postures in Greek art which were not distinguished by this character of wisdom, but were too passionate and uncontrolled, fell into an error which the ancient artists called *parenthyrsus*.[33]

The calmer the state of a body, the fitter it is to express the true character of the soul: in all physical postures too far removed from the state of rest, the soul is not in the condition most proper to it, but subject to violence and constraint. The soul becomes more expressive and recognisable in powerful passions: but it is great and noble only in the state of unity, the state of rest. In the case of Laocoon, his pain, if depicted in isolation, would have been *parenthyrsus*; hence, in order to combine the expressive and the noble aspects of his soul into a single unity, the artist put him in a position as close to the state of rest as was compatible with his agony. But in this state of rest, the soul must be characterised by features peculiar to the individual concerned; it must be at rest yet at the same time active, tranquil yet neither indifferent nor lethargic.

The true antithesis of this, the diametrically opposite extreme, is the taste most common among today's artists, particularly the beginners. The only works they applaud are those characterised by strange contortions and brazenly impassioned actions, and which they say are executed with spirit, with *franchezza*.[34] Their favourite concept is contrast, which for them is the quintessence of all the original qualities of the perfect work of art. They demand in their figures a soul of comet-like eccentricity; they look for an Ajax or a Capaneus in every one of them.

The arts have their infancy just as men do, and their beginnings are like those of artists, who at first are satisfied only with the bombastic and extraordinary. The tragic muse of Aeschylus was of this kind, and his hyperboles in the *Agamemnon* make parts of it more obscure than anything Heracleitus[35] ever wrote. Perhaps the earliest Greek painters drew in the same way as their first good tragedian wrote.

In all human activities, violence and haste come first, and dignity and thoroughness come last. But the latter qualities need time to be appreciated, and are the prerogative of great masters; violent passions, however, are a recommendation in the eyes of their pupils.

Those with artistic wisdom know how difficult it is to produce works which are apparently so easy to imitate:

> ut sibi quivis
> Speret idem; sudet multum, frustraque laboret
> Ausus idem.[36]

Lafage,[37] though a great draughtsman, could not reach the level of ancient taste. Everything in his works is in movement, and our attention is divided and scattered in contemplating them, as in a company where everyone tries to speak at once.

The noble simplicity and tranquil grandeur of the Greek statues are also the hallmark of Greek writing in its best period, as in the works of the school of Socrates. And it is these qualities which constitute the pre-eminent greatness of Raphael, who acquired them through imitating the ancients.

A beautiful soul such as his, housed in a beautiful body, first made it possible for the true character of the ancients to be rediscovered and appreciated in modern times. And he had the great good fortune to succeed in this when he was still of an age at which vulgar and half-formed souls remain insensible to true greatness.

One must approach his works with an eye trained to appreciate these beauties, and schooled in the true taste of antiquity. Only then will the calm and tranquillity of the main figures in his Attila, which many regard as lifeless, appear to us as highly significant and sublime. The Roman bishop, opposing the plan of the King of the Huns to attack Rome, does not appear with the gestures and movements of an orator, but as a venerable man whose presence alone is enough to quell a disturbance; he recalls the lines of Virgil

> Tum pietate gravem ac meritis si forte virum quem
> Conspexere, silent arrectisque auribus adstant;[38]

as he stands before the tyrant, his face full of divine confidence. The two apostles look down from the sky not like destroying angels, but (if the sacred may be compared with the profane) like Homer's Jupiter, who shakes Olympus with the wink of his eye.

Algardi,[39] in his famous representation of this same story in low relief on an altar in St Peter's in Rome, either omitted to endow the figures of his two apostles with the active tranquillity his great predecessor had achieved, or was unable to do so. Raphael's apostles appear like messengers of the Lord of Hosts; Algardi's like mortal warriors with the weapons of man.

How few connoisseurs have been able to appreciate Guido Reni's fine St Michael in the Church of the Capuchins in Rome, and to understand the grandeur of expression with which the artist has endowed his archangel! They usually prefer the archangel of Conca,[40] because its face has an angry and vengeful expression; whereas Guido's St Michael, having vanquished the enemy of God and man, hovers above him with a serene and untroubled countenance.

A similar calm and tranquillity characterise the avenging angel which the English poet describes as hovering over Britannia, and which he likens to the hero of his poem, the victor of Blenheim.[41]

The royal picture-gallery in Dresden now contains among its treasures a worthy example of Raphael's work, a painting executed in his best period (as Vasari and others testify). It is a Madonna and Child, with St Sixtus and St Barbara kneeling on either side, and two angels in the foreground.[42]

This picture was the central panel of the altarpiece in the monastery of St Sixtus in Piacenza. Art-lovers and connoisseurs flocked there to see this

Raphael, just as they did in earlier times to Thespiae to see the beautiful Cupid of Praxiteles.

Just look at the Madonna, a figure of more than female stature and with her face full of innocence, in a posture of blessed calm, and with that tranquillity which the ancients imparted to the statues of their deities! How grand and noble is her whole contour!

The child in her arms is exalted above ordinary children by a face from which a ray of divinity seems to shine forth through the innocence of childhood.

St Barbara kneels below her at her side in adoring tranquillity of spirit, but remains far beneath the majesty of the main figure. The great artist has compensated for her lower station by giving her features a gentle grace.

The saint opposite her is a venerable old man, whose face seems to bear witness to his dedication to God since his youth.

That reverence which St Barbara shows towards the Madonna, and which is given more tangible and affecting expression through the beautiful hands she clasps to her breast, is partly conveyed in the case of St Sixtus by the movement of one of his hands. This action expresses the ecstasy of the saint, which the artist, for greater variety, wisely tried to associate rather with male vigour than with female modesty.

Time has admittedly removed much of the visual splendour of this painting, and the intensity of the colours has faded to some extent; but the soul which its creator breathed into his handiwork animates it to this day.

Some may approach this and other works of Raphael in the hope of finding in them those minor beauties which are so highly esteemed in the works of the Dutch painters: the laborious assiduity of Netscher[43] or Dou,[44] the ivory flesh of Van der Werff,[45] or the scrubbed manner of some of Raphael's compatriots in our own time: such people, I say, will look in vain for the great Raphael in Raphael's own works.

V Working techniques

After studying the natural beauty, contour, drapery, and noble simplicity and tranquil grandeur of the works of the Greek masters, the artist who seeks to imitate them ever more successfully must carefully examine their working techniques.

It is well known that they often fashioned their original models in wax. Modern masters, however, have chosen clay or other easily moulded substances instead, finding them more suited to rendering flesh in particular than is possible with wax, which they regard as too sticky and unyielding for this purpose.

This is not to say, however, that the method of modelling in wet clay was unknown or unusual among the Greeks. We even know the identity of the man who first attempted this technique, namely Dibutades of Sicyon;[46] and Arcesilaus,[47] the friend of the great Lucullus, owed his fame rather to his models in clay than to his finished works. He made for his friend a clay figure representing happiness, which Lucullus bought for 60,000 sesterces; and the Roman knight Octavius paid the same artist the sum of one talent just for the plaster model of a large cup which he wished to have executed in gold.

Clay would indeed be the most suitable medium for modelling figures if it retained its moisture. But since this evaporates when it is dried and fired, its more solid parts will contract in consequence, so that the mass of the figure is diminished and occupies a smaller space. If the figure contracted equally at every point and in all its parts, it would retain its original proportions despite its reduction in size. But the smaller parts will dry out more quickly than the larger ones, and the body of the figure, being the most substantial part, will dry out last, so that the former will lose more mass than the latter over the same interval of time.

Wax does not have this disadvantage: none of its substance is lost, and there is also a way of giving it the smoothness of flesh which other methods of modelling can achieve only with the greatest of difficulty.

The technique in question is to form one's model in clay, make a plaster mould of it, and then cast it in wax.

But the actual method which the Greeks employed to translate their model into marble appears not to have been the same as that employed by most modern artists. All the marbles of the ancients betray the confidence and sureness of purpose of the master, and even among their inferior works it is hard to find anywhere too much has been cut away. This sure and accurate craftsmanship of the Greeks must have been guided by rules more specific and reliable than those we adhere to today.

The usual method employed by our sculptors, after they have first studied their model exhaustively and moulded it to the best of their ability, is to cover it with a network of horizontal and perpendicular lines. They then proceed much as one would do in copying or enlarging a painting, namely by transferring the same number of intersecting lines to the marble.

Thus, every little square on the model has its counterpart in a larger square on the marble. But since these outlines give no indication of relative volume, they cannot supply an accurate guide to the correct degrees of elevation and depth on the surface of the model. Consequently, the artist may well be able to give his projected figure something of the model's proportions; but since he must rely only on the evidence of his eye, he will constantly be uncertain as to whether he has cut too shallow or too deep in relation to his model, and has removed too much or too little material.

Nor can he determine, by means of such a network, either the overall outlines, or those which – often by the merest hint – indicate the inner parts of the model, or those which run towards its centre; he has no infallible method of transferring these lines to the marble with precise accuracy.

Besides, if his work is too extensive for a single sculptor to execute, he is compelled to rely on the help of assistants, who are not always skilful enough to realise their master's intentions. And once a false cut has been made – for it is impossible by this method to fix precise limits on depth – the error is irreparable.

In this connection, it may be said in general of every sculptor who chisels out the deeper parts of his figure in full at the first stage of his work, and does not approach them gradually so as to give them their ultimate depth only at the final stage, that such an artist will never be able to eliminate faults from his work.

Another major disadvantage of this method is that the lines drawn on the marble are constantly being cut away and have to be remeasured and redrawn repeatedly, not without risk of inaccuracy.

The uncertainty of this procedure compelled artists to look for a more reliable method; the one devised by the French Academy in Rome and first used for copying antique statues was accordingly adopted by many of them, even when working from models.

The first step is to fix above the statue which one wishes to copy a square of corresponding size, and to suspend plumb-lines from it at equal intervals. These will mark the extremities of the figure more accurately than was possible with the former method of surface lines, every point on which represented an outer limit. They also give the artist a more tangible measure of some of the most pronounced elevations and depressions by the relative distance between these and the points covered by the plumb-lines, thereby allowing him to proceed with greater confidence.

But since the course of a curved line cannot be plotted exactly by means of a single straight line, this method too gives the artist only a very approximate indication of the outlines of a figure, and as soon as they deviate in the slightest from their mean course, he again finds himself without help or guidance.

It is also very plain that the true proportions of figures are difficult to determine by this method, and horizontal lines intersecting the plumb-lines are employed for this purpose. But the rays of light reflected from the figure through the squares formed above its surface by these lines will strike the eye at wider angles, and consequently appear larger, according to the relative height from which they are viewed.

The method of plumb-lines still retains its value as an aid to copying antique statues, which have to be handled with care, and no surer or easier method has yet been devised for this purpose. But for the reasons already specified, this method is not sufficiently accurate when it comes to working from models.

Michelangelo adopted a technique unknown before his time, and it is remarkable that no subsequent sculptors appear to have followed his example, given that they venerate him as the supreme master of his art.

As one might have expected, this latter-day Phidias, the greatest sculptor since the Greeks, seems to have hit upon the very method employed by his great teachers – or at any rate, no other method is known by which all conceivable physical properties and beauties of the model can be transferred to the figure itself and given expression in it.

Vasari gives a rather imperfect description of this discovery. The essence of his report is as follows.

Michelangelo took a vessel of water, in which he immersed his model of wax or other harder material; he then gradually raised it to the surface. In this way, the elevated portions emerged first, and the lower remained submerged, until finally the whole model was exposed and clear of the water. Vasari adds that Michelangelo worked his marble in precisely the same way. He first cut the outlines of the elevated parts, and gradually proceeded towards the lower.

It seems either that Vasari failed to understand his friend's procedure properly, or that the vagueness of his account leads us to imagine something different from what he actually describes.

The form of the water-vessel is not indicated sufficiently clearly. The gradual raising of the model out of the water from below would be extremely laborious, and presupposes more problems than the biographer of the artists saw fit to inform us of.

We can be sure that Michelangelo made exhaustive studies of the method he invented, and applied it in as convenient a manner as possible. In all probability he proceeded as follows.

He took a vessel of the same proportions as his figure – for example, an elongated rectangle. He divided the surface of its sides into marked sections, which he reproduced on a larger scale on his block of marble, and inscribed a graduated scale on the inside of his container, from top to bottom. He next laid his model in the container (if it was of heavier material), or fastened it to the base (if it was made of wax). Then, perhaps, he placed on top of the container a lattice with the same divisions as before, and drew corresponding lines on his marble; he probably added the outlines of his figure immediately afterwards. He poured water over the model until it reached the top of the uppermost parts, and after noting which part would have to be most prominent on the figure he had drawn, he drained off enough water to uncover more of the top of his model. He then began work on this part as it emerged by degrees from the water. If another part of the model emerged at the same time, it was copied too (in so far as it was visible). He fashioned all the upper parts in the same manner.

More water was released until the lower parts appeared in turn. The gradations on the container always registered the water-level as it subsided, and the surface of the water indicated the precise positions of the lowest parts. The equivalent gradations on the marble gave him an exact measure.

The water enabled him to trace not only the highest and lowest points, but also the contour of his model; and the distance between the inner sides of the container and the outline traced by the surface of the water, a distance recorded by the gradations on the other two sides, gave him at every point an indication of how much marble he could remove.

His work now had its initial, but already correct form. The surface of the water had drawn for him a line of which the highest points of the model were a part. As the water subsided in the vessel, this line likewise descended horizontally, and the artist had followed its movement with his chisel until the water exposed the lowest declivities of the elevated parts, at the point where they merge with the broader surfaces. He had thus matched each smaller gradation in the container with a corresponding, larger gradation on his figure, and had thereby followed the line of the water beyond the lowest contour of his work, so that the model now stood fully exposed.

His figure still lacked formal *beauty*. He again immersed his model in water to the required depth, and then counted the gradations on the container up to the water-level, which gave him the height of the topmost point. He then laid his rule horizontally across the top of his figure, and measured the distance from its lower edge to the base. If he then found that the number of smaller gradations in the container matched the number of larger gradations on the figure, he had a kind of geometric measure of their content which proved that he had followed the correct procedure.

When he repeated the operation, he attempted to reproduce in his figure the pressure and movement of muscles and sinews, the outlines of the other lesser parts, and all the artistic subtleties of his model. The water, encompassing even the most imperceptible parts, traced their outline with the utmost clarity, and drew their contours with maximum precision.

This method does not prevent the artist from placing the model in every possible position. Laid on its side, it will reveal to the artist everything he may have overlooked. It will also show him the external contours of the elevated and inner parts, and the whole model in section.

All this, and the hope of a successful outcome, presupposes a model fashioned by skilful hands in accordance with the true taste of antiquity.

This is the path which led Michelangelo to immortality. His reputation and the rewards he received afforded him the leisure to work in so painstaking a manner.

An artist of our times, whom nature and industry have given the capacity to rise to greater heights, and who has seen that this method promises true and accurate results, is nevertheless compelled to work for a living rather than for renown. He therefore sticks to the course he know best, thinking that he can display more skill in so doing, and continues to rely on the judgement of his eye, trained by long practice, as his guideline.

This ocular judgement on which he must chiefly depend has attained its all-important position as a result of practical techniques which are sometimes of a highly questionable nature. How fine and unerring this judgement might have become if the artist had trained it from youth on the basis of infallible rules!

If aspiring artists, on first learning to work in clay or other materials, were instructed in the sure method which Michelangelo devised after long researches, they could indeed hope to come as near to the Greeks as he did.

VI Painting

Everything that can be said in praise of Greek sculpture applies in all probability to their painting too. But time and the barbarity of men have deprived us of the evidence we need to make any conclusive pronouncement on this subject.

The Greek painters are credited with draughtsmanship and expression – and nothing more. Perspective, composition, and colouring are denied them. This judgement is based partly on bas-reliefs, and partly on ancient (one cannot say Greek) paintings discovered in recent times in and around Rome, in subterranean vaults of the palaces of Maecenas, Titus, Trajan, and the Antonines. Not much more than thirty such works survive intact, and some of them are only mosaics.

Turnbull has included in his work on ancient painting[48] a collection of the most famous items, drawn by Camillo Paderni and engraved by Mynde; these alone give some worth to the excellent and otherwise wasted paper of his book. Two of them are based on originals in the collection of the celebrated London physician Richard Mead.

Others have already noted that Poussin made studies of the so-called Aldobrandini Wedding, that drawings still exist which Annibale Carracci made of the presumed portrait of Marcus Coriolanus, and that some have detected a close resemblance between the heads in Guido Reni's works and those on the well-known mosaic of the Rape of Europa.

If it were possible to base sound judgements of ancient painting on frescoes of this kind, it would no doubt be denied, on the evidence of such fragments as survive, that the ancients had any proficiency even in draughtsmanship and expression.

For we are assured that the life-size paintings on the walls of the theatre at Herculaneum, which were removed along with the walls themselves, give only a poor idea of the latter qualities. The Theseus, with Athenian youths kissing his hands and embracing his knees after his victory over the Minotaur, the Flora with Hercules and a faun, and the so-called Judgement of the Decemvir Appius Claudius are all, on the testimony of an artist who saw them, either mediocre or badly drawn. Most of the heads, we are told, are not only devoid of expression, but those in the painting of Appius Claudius are not even properly characterised.

But this very fact proves that these paintings are the work of very mediocre artists. For the science of beautiful proportions, contour, and expression, with which the Greek sculptors were familiar, must also have been known to their best painters.

This acknowledged proficiency of the ancient painters in certain areas still leaves the moderns superior in many others.

For example, they undoubtedly have the advantage in perspective, and no apologist of the ancients, however scholarly his credentials, can deny that the moderns are superior in this department. The laws of composition and the arrangement of figures were known to the ancients only imperfectly and in part, as witnessed by the reliefs of the period when the Greek arts were flourishing in Rome.

In colour likewise, the accounts of ancient writers and the remains of ancient painting seem to give the advantage to the moderns.

Several types of representation in painting have also reached a higher degree of perfection in modern times. All the evidence suggests that our artists have surpassed the ancients in animal painting and in landscapes. The ancients do not seem to have been familiar with the more beautiful species of animals found in other countries – if we may generalise from individual cases such as the horse of Marcus Aurelius, the two horses on Monte Cavallo, the so-called Lysippean horses above the portal of St Mark's in Venice, the Farnese Bull, and the other animals in that group.

It may be remarked in passing that, in their representations of horses, the ancients failed to observe the diametric motion of their legs, as is evident from the horses in Venice and on ancient coins. Some modern artists have followed their example out of ignorance, and have even been defended for so doing.

Our landscapes, particularly those of the Dutch painters, owe their beauty chiefly to the use of oils: these have given their colours more strength, vivacity, and prominence; and even nature, in the aspects it assumes under our heavier and rainier skies, has helped not a little to extend this branch of art.

These, and some other advantages of modern painters over the ancients, deserve to be given greater emphasis and substantiated by more detailed arguments than has hitherto been the case.

VII Allegory

Another major step remains to be taken to enlarge the frontiers of art. The artist who begins to diverge from the common path, or has actually done so, may venture on this course; but his foot hesitates before what amounts to the steepest precipice in art, and he remains helpless where he is.

The lives of saints, mythological themes, and metamorphoses have been the constant and almost exclusive subjects of modern painters for several centuries. They have been varied and elaborated in a thousand different ways, so that aversion and boredom must eventually overcome the discerning critic or connoisseur of art.

Any sensitive and thoughtful artist must find his mind idle and unoccupied when he embarks on a Daphne and Apollo, an Abduction of Proserpine or Europa, or other similar subjects. He would prefer to show himself as a poet, and to present figures by means of images – that is, to paint *allegorically*.

Painting extends to supra-sensory things, which are its supreme object. The Greeks also shared this aim, as the writings of the ancients testify. It is said that Parrhasius,[49] a painter who, like Aristides,[50] could express the soul itself, was even able to render the character of an entire nation. He painted the Athenians as both generous and cruel, frivolous and determined, courageous and cowardly. If such a representation is at all possible, it can be so only by means of allegory – that is, by images which convey general concepts.

But here, the artist is lost as if in a desert. The languages of the savage Indians, which are almost devoid of such concepts and contain no words for such things as gratitude, space, duration, etc., are no worse off in this respect than is painting today. Every painter who thinks beyond his palette longs for some learned compendium he could consult, and from which he could extract significant and concrete signs to denote supra-sensory objects. No complete work of this kind is yet available: the attempts so far made are too circumscribed to measure up to this grand design. The artist will already know how inadequately he is served by Ripa's *Iconology*,[51] or by van Hooge's *Emblems of the Ancient Nations*.[52]

This is the reason why the greatest artists have chosen only familiar themes. Annibale Carracci, instead of using general symbols and concrete images – that is, the methods of allegorical painting – to record for the Farnese gallery the most illustrious deeds and events in the history of the Farnese family, devoted all his efforts merely to familiar mythological subjects.

The royal picture-gallery in Dresden is undoubtedly a treasure-house of works by the greatest masters, and perhaps surpasses all other galleries in the world; and His Majesty, as the wisest of artistic connoisseurs, has selected on strict principles only the most perfect examples of each genre. But how few historical works there are in this royal collection! And there are even fewer paintings of an allegorical or poetic variety.

The great Rubens is the most eminent of the major painters who, as a sublime poet, has ventured on to this untrodden path of painting and produced appropriate compositions on a large scale. His greatest work, the gallery of the Luxembourg Palace, has been introduced to the world at large through the work of the best engravers.

After Rubens, no more sublime work has been conceived and executed in this manner than the cupola of the Imperial Library in Vienna, painted by Daniel Gran, and engraved by Sedelmayer. The Apotheosis of Hercules at Versailles, painted by Lemoyne[53] in allusion to Cardinal Hercules de Fleury, and vaunted in France as the greatest composition in the world, is a very ordinary and myopic allegory in comparison with the learned and ingenious painting of the German artist: it is like a panegyric whose strongest sentiments are lavished merely on names in the calendar. Here was an opportunity to achieve something really great, and one can only wonder at its failure. But one can also see what the painter lacked, even supposing that the apotheosis of a minister was a suitable subject for the main ceiling of a royal palace.

What the artist needs is a work which brings together from the whole of mythology, from the best poets of ancient and modern times, from the esoteric wisdom of many nations, and from the monuments of antiquity on gems, coins, and implements, all those concrete images and figures by which general concepts have been represented poetically. This rich material should be conveniently classified, and so arranged as to instruct the artist in how to apply and interpret it in relation to possible individual cases.

This would at the same time offer much new scope for imitating the ancients, and would impart to our works something of the sublime taste of antiquity.

Since Vitruvius's bitter complaints about the decline of good taste in decoration,[54] the position has deteriorated even further in recent times. This is due partly to the grotesques brought into fashion by Morto da Feltro,[55] and partly to the insipid interior decoration of our own day. A more thorough study of allegory might also purify our taste in this respect, and lend it sense and veracity.

Our convoluted patterns and modish shell-designs, which are now regarded as essential in all decoration, are at times as unnatural as the candelabra of Vitruvius, which were surmounted by little castles and palaces. But allegory could supply us with the knowledge we need to make even the smallest ornaments harmonise with their chosen location:

> Reddere personae scit convenientia cuique.[56]

Paintings on ceilings and above doors serve mainly to fill the space they occupy, and to cover those areas which cannot be gilded over. They not only lack all connection with the station and circumstances of their owner, but often actually cast a prejudicial light on these.

It is thus the horror of a vacuum which fills up empty walls; and pictures devoid of thought must make good the deficiency.

This is the reason why the artist, left to his own devices, will often, for lack of allegorical images, select subjects which tend to satirise rather than to glorify his patron; and perhaps as a safeguard against this, the latter will shrewdly calculate that it is better to ask for pictures with no meaning whatsoever.

It is often difficult to find even these, until at last

> velut aegri somnia, vanae
> Fingentur species.[57]

Thus painting is deprived of its supreme function, the depiction of invisible things and things past and future.

But those paintings which could gain special significance in a particular setting lose their effect when placed in arbitrary or unsuitable surroundings.

The owner of some new building

> Dives agris, dives positis in foenore nummis[58]

will perhaps place above the high doors of his rooms and salons small pictures incompatible with the angle of vision and the laws of perspective. (I am referring here to those items which form part of the fixed and permanent decor, not to those which are arranged symmetrically as part of a collection.)

The choice of architectural ornaments is sometimes just as ill-founded. Arms and trophies will always be as incongruous on a hunting-lodge as Ganymede and the eagle or Jupiter and Leda are among the reliefs on the bronze doors at the entrance to St Peter's in Rome.[59]

All the arts have a double aim: they should delight and at the same time instruct.[60] Hence many of the greatest landscape-painters believe they have only half-fulfilled the aim of their art if they do not include some figures in their landscapes.

The artist's brush should be dipped in reason, as someone once said of the pen of Aristotle. It should afford more food for thought than material for the eye; and the artist will achieve this aim if he has learned to clothe – but not hide – his ideas in allegory. And if he has chosen or been given a poetic subject, or one capable of poetic treatment, his art will inspire him and awaken in him the fire which Prometheus stole from the gods. The connoisseur will find plenty to reflect upon, and the amateur will learn to do likewise.

Part 2

Lessing

Gotthold Ephraim Lessing

(1729–81)

Lessing was born in 1729 at Kamenz in Saxony, the son of a Lutheran pastor. He seemed destined for a distinguished career in theology, for which he enrolled at Leipzig University, but his interests quickly moved to literature and the theatre, and he devoted himself increasingly to dramatic composition and to literary journalism. On his move to Berlin in 1748, Lessing became one of the first Germans to support himself by writing (mainly journalistic criticism for the growing educated public of largely middle-class readers). His greatest journalistic success was the periodical *Letters concerning Recent Literature* (*Briefe, die neueste Literatur betreffend*, 1759–65), to which he and his friends Friedrich Nicolai and Moses Mendelssohn were the chief contributors. Their literary criticism set new standards in Germany, and did much to end the French domination of German literary culture. Lessing's championship of Shakespeare prepared the way for the Shakespeare cult of Herder and the *Sturm und Drang* movement of the 1770s.

Lessing's appetite for analytical criticism and polemics found new outlets in antiquarian studies during his sojourn in Breslau (1760–5) as secretary to a Prussian general. The chief fruit of these was the *Laocoon*. His years in Hamburg (1767–70) were chiefly devoted to dramatic criticism (*Hamburg Dramaturgy*, 1767–9), in which he attempted to reconcile Aristotelian and neo-classical models with the realism he was himself cultivating, under the influence of Diderot's dramatic theory, in his own dramas (*Minna von Barnhelm*, 1767; *Emilia Galotti*, 1772).

During the last phase of his life (1770–81) as librarian to the Duke of Brunswick in Wolfenbüttel, Lessing was able to develop his already formidable learning in numerous disciplines, including philosophy, history, philology, and theology. After 1777, he became embroiled in acrimonious polemics with various theologians as a result of his publishing the *Fragments* of the freethinker H. S. Reimarus, which criticised the Bible from a position of deistic rationalism. One positive result of the controversy was Lessing's last drama, *Nathan the Wise*, with its message of enlightened cosmopolitanism and religious tolerance.

Lessing's forceful personality and rigorous analytical intellect made him the dominant figure in German literary life before Goethe's rise to fame. His three major plays helped to end the provincialism of German literature, his work as a critic ended the hegemony of French literary models in Germany, and his *Laocoon* gave neo-classical poetics a new philosophical basis and a more secure foundation in the literature of ancient Greece – a foundation on which the Weimar classicism of Goethe and Schiller was to build in the closing decade of the century.

Further reading

The standard edition of Lessing's works is that of Lachmann and Muncker (1886–1924), which also contains Lessing's correspondence. There are less complete, but useful modern editions by Rilla (second edition, 1968) and Göpfert (1970–9). English translations include those by Steel (1930) of the *Laocoon, Nathan the Wise,* and *Minna von Barnhelm,* by Zimmern (1962) of the *Hamburg Dramaturgy,* and by Chadwick (1956) of selected theological writings. The standard biography is that of Schmidt (fourth edition, 1923). The best general accounts in English are Garland (second edition, 1962) and Brown (1971). Robertson (second edition, 1965) deals with the dramatic theory, Allison (1966) with philosophical aspects, and Wellbery (1984) with Lessing's aesthetics.

Laocoon

or

On the Limits of Painting and Poetry[1]

1766

Translated by W. A. Steel (slightly modified).
German text in *Sämtliche Schriften,* edited by Lachmann and Muncker (1886–1924), IX, 1–177.

Preface

The first who likened painting and poetry to each other must have been a man of delicate perception, who found that both arts affected him in a similar manner. Both, he realised, present to us appearance as reality, absent things as present; both deceive, and the deceit of either is pleasing.

A second sought to penetrate to the essence of the pleasure and discovered that in both it flows from one source. Beauty, the conception of which we at first derive from bodily objects, has general rules which can be applied to various things: to actions, to thoughts, as well as to forms.

A third, who reflected on the value and the application of these general rules, observed that some of them were predominant rather in painting, others rather in poetry; that, therefore, in the latter poetry could help out painting, in the former painting help out poetry, with illustrations and examples.

The first was the amateur; the second the philosopher; the third the critic.

The two former could not easily make a false use either of their feeling or of their conclusions. But in the remarks of the critic, on the other hand, almost everything depends on the justice of their application to the individual case; and, where there have been fifty witty to one clear-eyed critic, it would have been a miracle if this application had at all times been made with the circumspection needful to hold the balance true between the two arts.

Supposing that Apelles and Protogenes[2] in their lost treatises upon painting confirmed and illustrated the rules of the same by the already settled rules of poetry, then one can certainly believe it must have been done with the moderation and exactitude with which we still find Aristotle, Cicero, Horace, Quintilian, in their writings, applying the principles and practice of painting to eloquence and poetry. It is the prerogative of the ancients, in everything to do neither too much nor too little.

But we moderns in several things have considered ourselves their betters, when we transformed their pleasant little byeways to highroads, even if the shorter and safer highroads shrink again to footpaths as they lead us through the wilds.

The startling antithesis of the Greek Voltaire,[3] that painting is a dumb poetry, and poetry a vocal painting, certainly was not to be found in any manual. It was a sudden inspiration, such as Simonides had more than once; the true element in it is so illuminating that we are inclined to ignore what in it is false or doubtful.

Nevertheless, the ancients did not ignore it. Rather, whilst they confined the claim of Simonides solely to the effect of the two arts, they did not omit to point out that, notwithstanding the complete similarity of this effect, they were yet distinct, both in their subjects and in the manner of their imitation (ὕλη καὶ τρόποις μιμήσεως).[4]

But entirely as if no such difference existed, many of our most recent critics have drawn from that correspondence between painting and poetry the crudest conclusions in the world. Now they force poetry into the narrower bounds of painting; and again, they propose to painting to fill the whole wide sphere of poetry. Everything that is right for the one is to be granted to the other also; everything which in the one pleases or displeases is necessarily to please or displease in the other; and, obsessed by this notion, they utter in the most confident tone the shallowest judgments; and we see them, in dealing with the works of poets and painters beyond reproach, making it a fault if they deviate from one another, and casting blame now on this side and now on that, according as they themselves have a taste for poetry or for painting.

Indeed, this newer criticism has in part seduced the virtuosos themselves. It has engendered in poetry the rage for description, and in painting the rage for allegorising, in the effort to turn the former into a speaking picture without really knowing what she can and should paint, and to turn the latter into a silent poem without considering in what measure she can express general concepts and not at the same time depart from her vocation and become a freakish kind of writing.

To counteract this false taste and these ill-founded judgements is the primary

object of the pages that follow. They have come together incidentally,
according to the order of my reading, instead of being built up by a methodical
development of general principles.[5] They are, therefore, rather unordered
collectanea for a book than themselves a book.

Yet I flatter myself that even as such they are not wholly to be despised. Of
systematic books there is no lack amongst us Germans. Out of a few assumed
definitions to deduce most logically whatever we will – this we can manage as
well as any nation in the world.

Baumgarten[6] confessed that for a great part of the examples in his *Æsthetics*
he was indebted to Gesner's Dictionary.[7] If my argument is not as conclusive
as Baumgarten's, at all events my examples will taste more of the original
sources.

As I started, as it were, from Laocoon and return to him several times, I
have desired to give him a share in the superscription. Some other little
digressions concerning various points in the history of ancient art contribute
less to my purpose, and they only stand here because I cannot hope ever to
find for them a more suitable place.

I would further remind the reader that under the name of Painting I
include the plastic arts in general, and am not prepared to maintain that
under the name of Poetry I may not have had some regard also to the other
arts whose method of imitation is progressive.

I

The general distinguishing excellence of the Greek masterpieces in painting and
sculpture Herr Winckelmann places in a noble simplicity and quiet greatness,
both in arrangement and in expression. 'Just as the depths of the sea', he says,

always remain quiet, however the surface may rage, in like manner the expression in
the figures of the Greek artists shows under all passions a great and steadfast soul.

This soul is depicted in the countenance of the Laocoon, and not in the countenance
alone, under the most violent sufferings. The pain which discovers itself in every muscle
and sinew of the body, and which, without regarding the face and other parts, one seems
almost oneself to feel from the painfully contracted abdomen alone – this pain, I say,
yet expresses itself in the countenance and in the entire attitude without passion. He
raises no agonising cry, as Virgil sings of his Laocoon; the opening of the mouth does
not permit it: much rather is it an oppressed and weary sigh, as Sadoleto[8] describes it.
The pain of the body and the greatness of the soul are by the whole build of the figure
distributed and, as it were, weighed out in equal parts. Laocoon suffers, but he suffers
like the Philoctetes of Sophocles: his misery touches us to the soul; but we should like
to be able to endure misery as this great man endures it.

The expression of so great a soul goes far beyond the fashioning which beautiful
Nature gives. The artist must have felt in himself the strength of spirit which he
impressed upon the marble. Greece had artist and philosopher in one person, and more
than one Metrodorus.[9] Wisdom stretched out her hand to Art and breathed more than
common souls into the figures that she wrought, etc., etc.

The remark which is fundamental here – that the pain does not show itself in the countenance of Laocoon with the passion which one would expect from its violence – is perfectly just. This, too, is incontestable, that even in this very point in which a sciolist might judge the artist to have come short of Nature and not to have reached the true pathos of the pain: that just here, I say, his wisdom has shone out with especial brightness.

Only in the reason which Winckelmann gives for this wisdom, and in the universality of the rule which he deduces from this reason, I venture to be of a different opinion.

I confess that the disapproving side-glance which he casts on Virgil at first took me rather aback; and, next to that, the comparison with Philoctetes. I will make this my starting-point, and write down my thoughts just in the order in which they come.

'Laocoon suffers like the Philoctetes of Sophocles.' How, then, does the latter suffer? It is singular that his suffering has left with us such different impressions – the complaints, the outcry, the wild curses, with which his pain filled the camp and disturbed the sacrifices and all the sacred functions, resounded no less terribly through the desert island, as it was in part they that banished him thither. What sounds of anger, of lamentation, of despair, by which even the poet in his imitation made the theatre resound! People have found the third act of this drama disproportionately short compared with the rest. From this one gathers, say the critics, that the ancient dramatists considered an equal length of acts as of small consequence. That, indeed, I believe; but in this question I should prefer to base myself upon another example than this. The piteous outcries, the whimpering, the broken ἆ, ἆ, φεῦ, ἀτταταῖ, ὦ μοι, μοι![10] the whole long lines full of παπα, παπα,[11] of which this act consists and which must have been declaimed with quite other hesitations and drawings-out of utterance than are needful in a connected speech, doubtless made this act last pretty well as long in the presentation as the others. On paper it appears to the reader far shorter than it would to the listeners.

To cry out is the natural expression of bodily pain. Homer's wounded warriors not seldom fall to the ground with cries. Venus scratched screams loudly; not in order that she may be shown as the soft goddess of pleasure, but rather that suffering Nature may have her rights. For even the iron Mars, when he feels the spear of Diomedes, screams so horribly, like ten thousand raging warriors at once, that both hosts are terrified.

However high in other respects Homer raises his heroes above Nature, they yet ever remain faithful to her when it comes to the point of feeling pain and injury, and to the utterance of this feeling by cries, or tears, or abusive language. By their deeds they are creatures of a superior order, by their sensibilities mere men.

I am well aware that we Europeans of a wiser posterity know better how to control our mouth and our eyes. Politeness and dignity forbid cries and tears. The active fortitude of the first rude ages has with us been transformed into the fortitude of endurance. Yet even our own ancestors were greater in the latter than in the former. Our ancestors, however, were barbarians. To conceal all pains, to face the stroke of death with unaltered eye, to die smiling under the teeth of vipers, to bewail neither his sin nor the loss of his dearest friend, are the marks of the ancient Northern hero. Palnatoko[12] gave his Jomsburgers the command to fear nothing nor once to utter the word fear.

Not so the Greek! He both felt and feared; he uttered his pain and his trouble; he was ashamed of no human weaknesses; but none must hold him back on the way to honour or from the fulfilment of duty. What with the barbarian sprang from savagery and hardness, was wrought in him by principle. With him heroism was like the hidden sparks in the flint, which sleep quietly so long as no outward force awakes them, and take from the stone neither its clearness nor its coldness. With the barbarian, heroism was a bright devouring flame, which raged continually and consumed, or at least darkened, every other good quality in him. When Homer leads out the Trojans to battle with wild outcries, and the Greeks, on the other hand, in resolute silence, the commentators remark with justice that the poet in this wishes to depict those as barbarians and these as civilised people. I am surprised that they have not remarked in another passage a similar characteristic contrast. The opposing hosts have concluded a truce; they are busy with the burning of their dead, which on neither side takes place without hot tears: δάκρυα θερμὰ χέοντες.[13] But Priam forbids his Trojans to weep; οὐδ᾽ εἴα κλαίειν Πρίαμος μέγας.[14] He forbids them to weep, says Dacier,[15] because he dreads that they will weaken themselves too much and return to battle on the morrow with less courage. Good! But I ask, Why must Priam dread this? Why does not Agamemnon, too, give his Greeks the same command? The sense of the poet goes deeper. He would teach us that only the civilised Greek can at the same time weep and be brave, whilst the uncivilised Trojan in order to be so must first stifle all human feeling. Νεμεσσῶμαί γε μὲν οὐδὲν κλαίειν,[16] in another place, he puts in the mouth of the understanding son of wise Nestor.

It is worthy of remark that amongst the few tragedies that have come down to us from antiquity two pieces are to be found in which bodily pain is not the smallest part of the calamity that befalls the suffering hero: there is, besides the Philoctetes, the dying Hercules.[17] And even the latter Sophocles represents complaining, whining, weeping and crying aloud. Thanks to our polite neighbours, those masters of the becoming,[18] today a whimpering Philoctetes, a screaming Hercules, would be the most laughable, the most unendurable persons on the stage. It is true one of their latest dramatists has ventured on Philoctetes.[19] But would he venture to show them the true Philoctetes?

Amongst the lost dramas of Sophocles is numbered even a 'Laocoon'. Would that Fate had only granted us this Laocoon also! From the slight references made to it by some ancient grammarians it is not easy to gather how the theme was handled. Of one thing I feel sure: that the poet will not have depicted

Laocoon as more of a stoic than Philoctetes and Hercules. All stoicism is untheatrical, and our pity is always proportionate to the suffering which the interesting subject expresses. If we see him bear his misery with greatness of soul, then indeed this greatness of soul will excite our admiration, but admiration is a cold emotion, whose passive wonder excludes every other warmer passion as well as every other more significant representation.

And now I come to the inference I wish to draw. If it is true that outcries on the feeling of bodily pain, especially according to the ancient Greek way of thinking, can quite well consist with a great soul; then the expression of such a soul cannot be the reason why, nevertheless, the artist in his marble refuses to imitate this crying: there must be other grounds why he deviates here from his rival, the poet, who expresses this crying with obvious intention.

II

Whether it be fable or history that Love prompted the first attempt in the plastic arts,[20] it is at least certain that she was never weary of lending her guiding hand to the ancient masters. For if painting, as the art which imitates bodies on plane surfaces, is now generally practised with an unlimited range of subject, certainly the wise Greek set her much straiter bounds, and confined her solely to the imitation of beautiful bodies. His artist portrayed nothing but the beautiful; even the ordinary beautiful, beauty of inferior kinds, was for him only an occasional theme, an exercise, a recreation. In his work the perfection of the subject itself must give delight; he was too great to demand of those who beheld it that they should content themselves with the bare, cold pleasure arising from a well-caught likeness or from the daring of a clever effort; in his art nothing was dearer to him, and to his thinking nothing nobler, than the ultimate purpose of art.

'Who will wish to paint you, when no one wishes to see you?' says an old epigrammatist concerning an extremely misshapen man. Many a more modern artist would say, 'Be you as misshapen as is possible, I will paint you nevertheless. Though, indeed, no one may wish to see you, people will still wish to see my picture; not in so far as it represents you, but in so far as it is a demonstration of my art, which knows how to make so good a likeness of such a monster.'

To be sure, with pitiful dexterities that are not ennobled by the worth of their subjects, the propensity to such rank boasting is too natural for the Greeks to have escaped without their Pauson, their Pyreicus.[21] They had them; but they did strict justice upon them. Pauson, who confined himself entirely to the beauty of vulgar things and whose lower taste delighted most in the faulty and ugly in human shape, lived in the most sordid poverty. And Pyreicus, who painted, with all the diligence of a Dutch artist, nothing but barbers' shops, filthy factories, donkeys and cabbages, as if that kind of thing had so much charm in Nature and were so rarely to be seen, got the nickname of the rhyparograph, the dirt-painter, although the luxurious rich weighed his works against gold, to help out their merit by this imaginary value.

The magistrates themselves considered it not unworthy of their attention to keep the artist by force in his proper sphere. The law of the Thebans, which commanded him in his imitation to add to beauty, and forbade under penalties the exaggeration of the ugly, is well known. It was no law against the bungler, as it is usually, and even by Junius,[22] considered. It condemned the Greek Ghezzis;[23] the unworthy artifice of achieving likeness by exaggeration of the uglier parts of the original: in a word, caricature.

Indeed, it was direct from the spirit of the Beautiful that the law of the Hellanodiken[24] proceeded. Every Olympian victor received a statue; but only to the three-times victor was an Iconian statue[25] awarded. Of mediocre portraits there ought not to be too many amongst works of art. For although even a portrait admits of an ideal, still the likeness must be the first consideration; it is the ideal of a certain man, not the ideal of a man.

We laugh when we hear that with the ancients even the arts were subject to municipal laws. But we are not always right when we laugh. Unquestionably the laws must not usurp power over the sciences, for the ultimate purpose of the sciences is truth. Truth is a necessity of the soul; and it is nothing but tyranny to offer her the slightest violence in satisfying this essential need. The ultimate purpose of the arts, on the other hand, is pleasure, and pleasure can be dispensed with. So, of course, it may depend on the law-giver what kind of pleasure, and in what measure any kind of it, he will permit. The plastic arts in particular, beyond the unfailing influence they exert on the character of a nation, are capable of an effect that demands the close supervision of the law. When beautiful men fashioned beautiful statues, these in their turn affected them, and the State had beautiful statues in part to thank for beautiful citizens. With us the tender, imaginative power of mothers appears to express itself only in monsters.[26]

From this point of view I believe that in certain ancient legends, which men cast aside without hesitation as lies, something of truth may be recognised. The mothers of Aristomenes, of Aristodamas,[27] of Alexander the Great, of Scipio, of Augustus, of Galerius, all dreamed in their pregnancy that they had to do with a serpent. The serpent was a symbol of deity, and the beautiful statues and pictures of a Bacchus, an Apollo, a Mercury and a Hercules were seldom without a serpent. The honest women had by day feasted their eyes on the god, and the bewildering dream called up the image of the reptile. Thus I save the dream, and surrender the interpretation which the pride of their sons and the shamelessness of flatterers gave it. For there must certainly be a reason why the adulterous phantasy was never anything but a serpent.

Here, however, I am going off the line. I merely wished to establish the fact that with the ancients beauty was the supreme law of the plastic arts. And this being established, it necessarily follows that all else after which also the plastic arts might strive, if it were inconsistent with beauty must wholly yield to her, and if it were consistent with beauty must at least be subordinate.

I will dwell a little longer on *expression*. There are passions and degrees of passion which express themselves in the countenance by the most hideous grimaces, and put the whole frame into such violent postures that all the beautiful lines are lost which define it in a quieter condition. From these, therefore, the ancient artists either abstained wholly or reduced them to lower degrees in which they were capable of a measure of beauty. Rage and despair disfigured none of their works. I dare maintain that they never depicted a Fury.[28]

Wrath they reduced to sternness: with the poet it was an angry Jupiter who sent forth his lightnings; with the artist the god was calmly grave.

Lamentation was toned down to sadness. And where this softening could not take place, where lamentation would have been just as deforming as belittling – what then did Timanthes?[29] His picture of Iphigenia's sacrifice, in which he imparted to all the company the peculiar degree of sadness befitting them individually, but veiled the father's face, which should have shown the supreme degree, is well known, and many nice things have been said about it. He had, says one, so exhausted himself in sorrowful countenances that he despaired of being able to give the father one yet more grief-stricken. He confessed thereby, says another, that the pain of a father in such events is beyond all expression. I, for my part, see here neither the impotence of the artist nor the impotence of art. With the degree of emotion the traces of it are correspondingly heightened in the countenance; the highest degree is accompanied by the most decided traces of all, and nothing is easier for the artist than to exhibit them. But Timanthes knew the limits which the Graces set to his art. He knew that such misery as fell to Agamemnon's lot as a father expresses itself by distortions which are at all times ugly. So far as beauty and dignity could be united with the expression of sorrow, so far he carried it. He might have been willing to omit the ugliness had he been willing to mitigate the sorrow; but as his composition did not admit of both, what else remained to him but to veil it? What he dared not paint he left to be guessed. In a word, this veiling was a sacrifice which the artist offered to Beauty. It is an example, not how one should force expression beyond the bounds of art, but rather how one must subject it to the first law of art, the law of Beauty.

And if we refer this to the Laocoon, the motive for which I am looking becomes evident. The master was striving after the highest beauty, under the given circumstances of bodily pain. This, in its full deforming violence, it was not possible to unite with that. He was obliged, therefore, to abate, to lower it, to tone down cries to sighing; not because cries betrayed an ignoble soul, but because they disfigure the face in an unpleasing manner. Let one only, in imagination, open wide the mouth in Laocoon, and judge! Let him shriek, and see! It was a form that inspired pity because it showed beauty and pain together; now it has become an ugly, a loathsome form, from which one gladly turns away one's face, because the aspect of pain excites discomfort without the beauty of the suffering subject changing this discomfort into the sweet feeling of compassion.

The mere wide opening of the mouth – apart from the fact that the other parts of the face are thereby violently and unpleasantly distorted – is a blot in painting and a fault in sculpture which has the most untoward effect possible. Montfaucon[30] showed little taste when he passed off an old, bearded head with widespread mouth for an oracle-pronouncing Jupiter. Must a god shriek when he unveils the future? Would a pleasing contour of the mouth make his speech suspicious? I do not even believe Valerius,[31] that Ajax in the imaginary picture of Timanthes should have cried aloud. Far inferior artists, in times when art was already degraded, never once allow the wildest barbarians, when, under the victor's sword, terror and mortal anguish seize them, to open the mouth to shrieking-point.

Certain it is that this reduction of extremest physical pain to a lower degree of feeling is apparent in several works of ancient art. The suffering Hercules in the poisoned garment, from the hand of an unknown ancient master, was not the Sophoclean who shrieked so horribly that the Locrian cliffs and the Euboean headlands resounded. It was more sad than wild. The Philoctetes of Pythagoras Leontinus[32] appeared to impart this pain to the beholder, an effect which the slightest trace of the horrible would have prevented. Some may ask where I have learnt that this master made a statue of Philoctetes? From a passage of Pliny which ought not to have awaited my emendation, so manifestly forged or garbled is it.

III

But, as we have already seen, Art in these later days has been assigned far wider boundaries. Let her imitative hand, folks say, stretch out to the whole of visible Nature, of which the Beautiful is only a small part. Let fidelity and truth of expression be her first law, and as Nature herself at all times sacrifices beauty to higher purposes, so also must the artist subordinate it to his general aim and yield to it no further than fidelity of expression permits. Enough, if by truth and faithful expression an ugliness of Nature be transformed into a beauty of Art.

Granted that one would willingly, to begin with, leave these conceptions uncontested in their worth or worthlessness, ought not other considerations quite independent of them to be examined – namely, why the artist is obliged to set bounds to expression and never to choose for it the supreme moment of an action?

The fact that the material limits of Art confine her imitative effort to one single moment will, I believe, lead us to similar conclusions.

If the artist can never, in presence of ever-changing Nature, choose and use more than one single moment, and the painter in particular can use this single moment only from one point of vision; if, again, their works are made not merely to be seen, but to be considered, to be long and repeatedly contemplated, then it is certain that that single moment, and the single viewpoint of that moment, can never be chosen too significantly. Now that alone is significant and fruitful which gives free play to the imagination. The more we see, the more must we be able to add by thinking. The more we add thereto by thinking, so much the more can we believe ourselves to see. In the whole gamut of an emotion, however, there is no moment less advantageous than its topmost note. Beyond it there is nothing further, and to show us the uttermost is to tie the wings of fancy and oblige her, as she cannot rise above the sensuous impression, to busy herself with weaker pictures below it, the visible fullness of expression acting as a frontier which she dare not transgress. When, therefore, Laocoon sighs, the imagination can hear him shriek; but if he shrieks, then she cannot mount a step higher from this representation, nor, again, descend a step lower without seeing him in a more tolerable and consequently more uninteresting condition. She hears him only groan, or she sees him already dead.

Further. As this single moment receives from Art an unchangeable continuance, it must not express anything which thought is obliged to consider transitory. All phenomena of whose very essence, according to our conceptions, it is that they break out suddenly and as suddenly vanish, that what they are they can be only for a moment – all such phenomena, whether agreeable or terrible, do, by the permanence which Art bestows, put on an aspect so abhorrent to Nature that at every repeated view of them the impression becomes weaker, until at last the whole thing inspires us with horror or loathing. La Mettrie, who had himself painted and engraved as a second Democritus, laughs only the first time that one sees him.[33] View him often, and from a philosopher he becomes a fool, and the laugh becomes a grin. So, too, with cries. The violent pain which presses out the cry either speedily relaxes or it destroys the sufferer. If, again, the most patient and resolute man cries aloud, still he does not cry out without intermission. And just this unintermitting aspect in the material imitations of Art it is which would make his cries an effeminate or a childish weakness. This at least the artist of the Laocoon had to avoid, if cries had not been themselves damaging to beauty, and if even it had been permitted to his art to depict suffering without beauty.

Among the ancient painters Timomachus[34] seems to have chosen by preference themes of the extremest emotion. His Frenzied Ajax, his Medea the child-murderess, were famous pictures. But from the descriptions we have of them it clearly appears that he understood excellently well, and knew how to combine, that point where the beholder does not so much see the uttermost as reach it by added thought, and that appearance with which we do not join the idea of the transitory so necessarily that the prolongation of the same in Art must displease us. Medea he had not taken at the moment in which she actually murders the children, but some moments earlier, when motherly love still battles with jealousy. We foresee the end of the fight. We tremble beforehand, about to see Medea at her cruel deed, and our imagination goes out far beyond everything that the painter could show us in this terrible moment. But for this very reason we are so little troubled by the continued indecision of Medea, as Art presents it, that rather we devoutly wish it had so continued in Nature itself, that the struggle of passions had never been decided, or had at least endured long enough for time and reflection to weaken rage and assure the victory to motherly feeling. To Timomachus, moreover, this wisdom of his brought great and manifold tributes, and raised him far above another unknown painter who had been misguided enough to represent Medea in the height of her rage, and thus to give to this transient extreme of frenzy a permanence that revolts all Nature. The poet who blames him on this account remarks, very sensibly, addressing the picture itself: 'Dost thou, then, thirst perpetually for the blood of thy children? Is there constantly a new Jason, always a new Creusa here, to embitter thee for evermore? To the devil with thee, even in picture!' he adds, with angry disgust.

Of the Frenzied Ajax of Timomachus we can judge by Philostratus' account.[35] Ajax appeared not as he rages amongst the herds and binds and slays oxen and goats for his enemies. Rather, the master showed him when, after these mad-heroic deeds, he sits exhausted and is meditating self-destruction. And that is actually the Frenzied Ajax; not because just then he rages, but because one sees that he has raged, because one perceives the greatness of his frenzy most vividly by the despair and shame which he himself now feels over it. One sees the storm in the wreckage and corpses it has cast upon the shore.

IV

Glancing at the reasons adduced why the artist of the Laocoon was obliged to observe restraint in the expression of physical pain, I find that they are entirely drawn from the peculiar nature of Art and its necessary limits and requirements. Hardly, therefore, could any one of them be made applicable to poetry.

Without inquiring here how far the poet can succeed in depicting physical beauty, so much at least is undeniable, that, as the whole immeasurable realm of perfection lies open to his imitative skill, this visible veil, under which perfection becomes beauty, can be only one of the smallest means by which he undertakes to interest us in his subject. Often he neglects this means entirely, being assured that if his hero has won our goodwill, then his nobler qualities either so engage us that we do not think at all of the bodily form, or, if we think of it, so prepossess us that we do, on their very account, attribute to him, if not a beautiful one, yet at any rate one that is not uncomely. At least, with every single line which is not expressly intended for the eye he will still take this sense into consideration. When Virgil's Laocoon cries aloud, to whom does it occur then that a wide mouth is needful for a cry, and that this must be ugly?

Enough, that *clamores horrendos ad sidera tollit*[36] is an excellent feature for the hearing, whatever it might be for the vision. Whosoever demands here a beautiful picture, for him the poet has entirely failed of his intention.

In the next place, nothing requires the poet to concentrate his picture on one single moment. He takes up each of his actions, as he likes, from its very origin and conducts it through all possible modifications to its final close. Every one of these modifications, which would cost the artist an entire separate canvas or marble-block, costs the poet a single line; and if this line, taken in itself, would have misled the hearer's imagination, it was either so prepared for by what preceded, or so modified and supplemented by what followed, that it loses its separate impression, and in its proper connection produces the most admirable effect in the world. Were it therefore actually unbecoming to a man to cry out in the extremity of pain, what damage can this trifling and transient impropriety do in our eyes to one whose other virtues have already taken us captive? Virgil's Laocoon shrieks aloud, but this shrieking Laocoon we already know and love as the wisest of patriots and the most affectionate of fathers. We refer his cries not to his character but purely to his unendurable suffering. It is this alone we hear in his cries, and the poet could make it sensible to us only through them. Who shall blame him then, and not much rather confess that, if the artist does well not to permit Laocoon to cry aloud, the poet does equally well in permitting him?

But Virgil here is merely a narrative poet. Can the dramatic poet be included with him in this justification? It is a different impression which is made by the narration of any man's cries from that which is made by the cries themselves. The drama, which is intended for the living artistry of the actor, might on this very ground be held more strictly to the laws of material painting. In him we do not merely suppose that we see and hear a shrieking Philoctetes; we hear and see him actually shriek. The closer the actor comes to Nature in this, the more sensibly must our eyes and ears be offended; for it is undeniable that they are so in Nature when we hear such loud and violent utterances of pain. Besides, physical pain does not generally excite that degree of sympathy which other evils awaken. Our imagination is not able to distinguish enough in it for the mere sight of it to call out something like an equivalent feeling in ourselves. Sophocles could, therefore, easily have overstepped a propriety not merely capricious, but founded in the very essence of our feelings, if he allowed Philoctetes and Hercules thus to whine and weep, thus to shriek and bellow. The bystanders could not possibly take so much share in their suffering as these unmeasured outbursts seem to demand. They will appear to us spectators comparatively cold, and yet we cannot well regard their sympathy otherwise than as the measure of our own. Let us add that the actor can only with difficulty, if at all, carry the representation of physical pain to the point of illusion; and who knows whether the later dramatic poets are not rather to be commended than to be blamed, in that they have either avoided this rock entirely or only sailed round it with the lightest of skiffs?

How many a thing would appear irrefragable in theory if genius had not succeeded in proving the contrary by actual achievement! None of these considerations is unfounded, and yet Philoctetes remains one of the masterpieces of the stage. For some of them do not really touch Sophocles, and by treating the rest with contempt he has attained beauties of which the timid critic without this example would never dream. The following notes deal with this point in fuller detail.

1. How wonderfully has the poet known how to strengthen and enlarge the idea of the physical pain! He chose a wound – for even the circumstances of the story one can contemplate as if they had depended on choice, in so far, that is to say, as he chose the whole story just because of the advantages the circumstances of it afforded him – he chose, I say, a wound and not an inward malady, because a more vivid representation can be made of the former than of the latter, however painful this may be. The mysterious inward burning which consumed Meleager[37] when his mother sacrificed him in mortal fire to her sisterly rage would therefore be less theatrical than a wound. And this wound was a divine judgement. A supernatural venom raged within without ceasing, and only an unusually severe attack of pain had its set time, after which the unhappy man fell ever into a narcotic sleep in which his exhausted nature must recover itself to be able to enter anew on the selfsame way of suffering. Chateaubrun[38] represents him merely as wounded by the poisoned arrow of a Trojan. What of extraordinary can so commonplace an accident promise? To such every warrior in the ancient battles was exposed; how did it come about that only with Philoctetes had it such terrible consequences? A natural poison that works nine whole years without killing is, besides, more improbable by far than all the mythical miraculous with which the Greek has furnished it.

2. But however great and terrible he made the bodily pains of his hero, he yet was in no doubt that they were insufficient in themselves to excite any notable degree of sympathy. He combined them, therefore, with other evils, which likewise, regarded in themselves, could not particularly move us, but which by this combination received just as melancholy a tinge as in their turn they imparted to the bodily pains. These evils were – a total deprivation of human society, hunger, and all the inconveniences of life to which in such deprivations one is exposed under an inclement sky. Let us conceive of a man in these circumstances, but give him health, and capacities, and industry, and we have a Robinson Crusoe who makes little demand upon our compassion, although otherwise his fate is not exactly a matter of indifference. For we are rarely so satisfied with human society that the repose which we enjoy when wanting it might not appear very charming, particularly under the representation which flatters every individual, that he can learn gradually to dispense with outside assistance. On the other hand, give a man the most painful, incurable malady, but at the same time conceive him surrounded by agreeable friends who let him want for nothing, who soften his affliction as far as lies in

their power, and to whom he may unreservedly wail and lament; unquestionably we shall have pity for him, but this pity does not last, in the end we shrug our shoulders and recommend him patience. Only when both cases come together, when the lonely man has an enfeebled body, when others help the sick man just as little as he can help himself, and his complainings fly away in the desert air; then, indeed, we behold all the misery that can afflict human nature close over the unfortunate one, and every fleeting thought in which we conceive ourselves in his place awakens shuddering and horror. We perceive nothing before us but despair in its most dreadful form, and no pity is stronger, none more melts the whole soul than that which is mingled with representations of despair. Of this kind is the pity which we feel for Philoctetes, and feel most strongly at that moment when we see him deprived of his bow, the one thing that might preserve him his wretched life. Oh, the Frenchman, who had neither the understanding to reflect on this nor the heart to feel it! Or, if he had, was small enough to sacrifice all this to the pitiful taste of his countrymen. Chateaubrun gives Philoctetes society. He lets a young Princess come to him in the desert island. Nor is she alone, for she has her governess with her; a thing of which I know not whether the Princess or the poet had the greater need. The whole excellent play with the bow he set quite aside. Instead of it he gives us the play of beautiful eyes. Certainly to young French heroes bow and arrow would have appeared a great joke. On the other hand, nothing is more serious than the anger of beautiful eyes. The Greek torments us with the dreadful apprehension that poor Philoctetes must remain on the desert island without his bow, and perish miserably. The Frenchman knows a surer way to our hearts: he makes us fear the son of Achilles must retire without his Princess. At the time the Parisan critics proclaimed this a triumphing over the ancients, and one of them proposed to call Chateaubrun's piece '*La Difficulté vaincue*'.[39]

3. After the general effect let us consider the individual scenes, in which Philoctetes is no longer the forsaken invalid; in which he has hope of speedily leaving the comfortless wilderness behind and of once more reaching his own kingdom; in which, therefore, the painful wound is his sole calamity. He whimpers, he cries aloud, he goes through the most frightful convulsions. To this behaviour it is that the reproach of offended propriety is particularly addressed. It is an Englishman who utters this reproach;[40] a man, therefore, whom we should not easily suspect of a false delicacy. As we have already hinted, he gives a very good reason for the reproach. All feelings and passions, he says, with which others can only slightly sympathise, are offensive when they are expressed too violently.

For this reason there is nothing more unbecoming and more unworthy of a man than when he cannot bear pain, even the most violent, with patience, but weeps and cries aloud. Of course we may feel sympathy with bodily pain. When we see that any one is about to get a blow on the arm or the shin-bone, and when the blow actually falls, in a certain measure we feel it as truly as he whom it strikes. At the same time, however,

it is certain that the trouble we thus experience amounts to very little; if the person
struck, therefore, sets up a violent outcry, we do not fail to despise him, because we
are not at all in the mind to cry out with so much violence.

(Adam Smith, *Theory of the Moral Sentiments*, Part I, sect. 2, chap. i, p. 41,
London, 1761)

Nothing is more fallacious than general laws for human feelings. The web of
them is so fine-spun and so intricate that it is hardly possible for the most careful
speculation to take up a single thread by itself and follow it through all the
threads that cross it. And supposing it possible, what is the use of it? There
does not exist in Nature a single unmixed feeling; along with every one of them
there arise a thousand others simultaneously, the very smallest of which
completely alters the first, so that exceptions on exceptions spring up which
reduce at last the supposed general law itself to the mere experience of a few
individual cases. We despise him, says the Englishman, whom we hear shriek
aloud under bodily pain. No; not always, nor at first; not when we see that
the sufferer makes every effort to suppress it; not when we know him otherwise
as a man of fortitude; still less when we see him even in his suffering give proof
of his fortitude, when we see that the pain can indeed force cries from him,
but can compel him to nothing further – that he will rather submit to the longer
endurance of this pain than change his opinions or his resolves in the slightest,
even if he might hope by such a change to end his agony. And all this we find
in Philoctetes. With the ancient Greeks moral greatness consisted in just as
unchanging a love to friends as an unalterable hatred to enemies. This
greatness Philoctetes maintains in all his torments. His pain has not so dried his
eyes that they can spare no tears for the fate of his old friends. His pain has
not made him so pliable that, to be rid of it, he will forgive his enemies and
allow himself willingly to be used for their selfish purposes. And this rock of
a man ought the Athenians to have despised because the surges that could not
shake him made him give forth a cry? I confess that in the philosophy of Cicero,
generally speaking, I find little taste; and least of all in that second book of
his *Tusculan Disputations*, where he pours out his notions about the endurance
of bodily pain. One might almost think he wanted to train a gladiator, he
declaims so passionately against the outward expression of pain. In this alone
does he seem to find a want of fortitude, without considering that it is frequently
anything but voluntary, whilst true bravery can only be shown in voluntary
actions. In Sophocles he hears Philoctetes merely complain and cry aloud, and
overlooks utterly his otherwise steadfast bearing. Where save here could he
have found the opportunity for his rhetorical outburst against the poets? 'They
would make us weaklings, showing us as they do the bravest of men lamenting
and bewailing themselves.' They must bewail themselves, for a theatre is not
an arena. The condemned or venal gladiator it behoved to do and suffer
everything with decorum. No complaining word must be heard from him, nor
painful grimace be seen. For as his wounds and his death were to delight the
spectators, Art must learn to conceal all feeling. The least utterance of it would

have aroused compassion, and compassion often excited would have speedily brought an end to these icily gruesome spectacles. But what here it was not desired to excite is the one object of the tragic stage, and demands therefore an exactly opposite demeanour. Its heroes must show feeling, must utter their pain, and let Nature work in them undisguisedly. If they betray restraint and training, they leave our hearts cold, and pugilists in the cothurnus could at best only excite admiration. This designation would befit all the persons of the so-called Seneca tragedies,[41] and I firmly believe that the gladiatorial plays were the principal reason why the Romans in tragedy remained so far below the mediocre. To disown human nature was the lesson the spectators learned in the bloody amphitheatre, where certainly a Ctesias[42] might study his art, but never a Sophocles. The tragic genius, accustomed to these artistic death scenes, necessarily sank into bombast and rodomontade. But just as little as such rodomontade could inspire true heroism, could the laments of Philoctetes make men weak. The complaints are those of a man, but the actions those of a hero. Both together make the human hero, who is neither soft nor hardened, but appears now the one and now the other, according as Nature at one time, and duty and principle at another, demand. He is the highest that Wisdom can produce and Art imitate.

4. It is not enough that Sophocles has secured his sensitive Philoctetes against contempt; he has also wisely taken precautions against all else that might, according to the Englishman's remark, be urged against him. For if we certainly do not always despise him who cries aloud in bodily pain, still it is indisputable that we do not feel so much sympathy for him as these outcries seem to demand. How, then, shall all those comport themselves who have to do with the shrieking Philoctetes? Shall they affect to be deeply moved? That is against nature. Shall they show themselves as cold and as disconcerted as we are really accustomed to be in such cases? That would produce for the spectator the most unpleasant dissonance. But, as we have said, against this Sophocles has taken precautions. In this way, namely, that the secondary persons have an interest of their own; that the impression which the cries of Philoctetes make on them is not the one thing that occupies them, and the spectator's attention is not so much drawn to the disproportion of their sympathy with these cries, but rather to the change which arises or should arise in their disposition and attitude from sympathy, be it as weak or as strong as it may. Neoptolemus and his company have deceived the unhappy Philoctetes; they recognise into what despair their betrayal will plunge him; and now, before their eyes, a terrible accident befalls him. If this accident is not enough to arouse any particular feeling of sympathy within them, it still will move them to repent, to have regard to a misery so great, and indispose them to add to it by treachery. This is what the spectator expects, and his expectations are not disappointed by the noble-minded Neoptolemus. Philoctetes mastering his pain would have maintained Neoptolemus in his dissimulation. Philoctetes, whom his pain renders incapable of dissimulation, however imperatively

necessary it may seem to him, so that his future fellow-travellers may not too soon regret their promise to take him with them; Philoctetes, who is nature itself, brings Neoptolemus, too, back to his own nature. This conversion is admirable, and so much the more touching as it is entirely wrought by humane feeling. With the Frenchman,[43] on the contrary, beautiful eyes have their share in it. But I will say no more of this burlesque. Of the same artifice – namely, to join to the pity which bodily pain should arouse another emotion in the onlookers – Sophocles availed himself on another occasion: in the *Trachiniae.* The agony of Hercules is no enfeebling agony, it drives him to frenzy in which he pants for nothing but revenge. He had already, in his rage, seized Lichas and dashed him to pieces upon the rocks. The chorus is of women; so much the more naturally must fear and horror overwhelm them. This, and the expectant doubt whether yet a god will hasten to the help of Hercules, or Hercules succumb to the calamity, form here the real general interest, mingled merely with a slight tinge of sympathy. As soon as the issue is determined by the oracle, Hercules becomes quiet, and admiration of his final steadfast resolution takes the place of all other feelings. But in comparing the suffering Hercules with the suffering Philoctetes, one must never forget that the former is a demigod and the latter only a man. The man is not for a moment ashamed of his lamentations; but the demigod is ashamed that his mortal part has prevailed so far over the immortal that he must weep and whimper like a girl. We moderns do not believe in demigods, but our smallest hero we expect to feel and act as a demigod.

Whether an actor can bring the cries and grimaces of pain to the point of illusion I will not venture either to assert or to deny. If I found that our actors could not, then I should first like to know whether it would be impossible also to a Garrick;[44] and if even he did not succeed, I should still be able to suppose a perfection in the stage-business and declamation of the ancients of which we today have no conception.

V

There are some learned students of antiquity who regard the Laocoon group as indeed a work of Greek masters, but of the time of the Emperors, because they believe that the Laocoon of Virgil served as its model.[45] Of the older scholars who are of this opinion I will name only Bartholomew Marliani,[46] and of the modern, Montfaucon.[47] They doubtless found so close an agreement between the work of art and the poet's description that they thought it impossible that the two should have lighted by chance upon identical details such as are far from offering themselves unsought. At the same time their presumption is that if it be a question of the honour of the invention and first conception, the probability is incomparably greater that it belongs rather to the poet than to the artist.

Only they appear to have forgotten that a third case is possible. For it may be that the poet has as little imitated the artist as the artist has the poet, and that both have drawn from an identical source older than either. According to Macrobius,[48] this more ancient source might have been Pisander.[49] For when the works of this Greek poet were still extant, it was a matter of common knowledge, *pueris decantatum*,[50] that the Roman had not so much imitated as faithfully translated from him the whole of the Capture and Destruction of Ilium, his entire Second Book. Now, therefore, if Pisander had been Virgil's predecessor also in the story of Laocoon, then the Greek artists needed not to learn their lesson from a Latin poet, and the surmise as to their era is based upon nothing.

All the same, were I obliged to maintain the opinion of Marliani and Montfaucon, I should suggest to them the following way out. Pisander's poems are lost; how the story of Laocoon was told by him no one can say with certainty; but it is probable that it was with the same details of which we still find traces in the Greek writers. Now, these do not agree in the least with Virgil's narrative, and the Roman poet must have recast the Greek legend as he thought best. His manner of telling the tale of Laocoon is his own invention; consequently, if the artists in their representation are in harmony with him, it is almost a certainty that they followed him and wrought according to his pattern.

In Quintus Calaber,[51] indeed, Laocoon displays a similar suspicion of the Wooden Horse as in Virgil; but the wrath of Minerva which he thereby draws upon himself expresses itself quite differently. The earth trembles under the warning Trojan; horror and dread seize him; a burning pain rages in his eyes; his brain reels; he raves; he goes blind. Only when, though blind, he ceases not to urge the burning of the Wooden Horse, does Minerva send two terrible dragons, and these attack only the children of Laocoon. In vain they stretch out their hands to their father; the poor blind man cannot help them; they are torn in pieces, and the serpents glide away into the earth. To Laocoon himself they do nothing; and that this account was not peculiar to Quintus, but must rather have been universally accepted, is proved by a passage in Lycophron,[52] where these serpents bear the epithet 'child-eaters'.

If, however, this account had been universally received amongst the Greeks, the Greek artists in that case would hardly have been bold enough to deviate from it, and it would hardly have happened that they should deviate from it in precisely the same way as a Roman poet did if they had not known this poet, if perhaps they had not actually had the express commission to follow his lead. On this point, I think, we must insist if we would defend Marliani and Montfaucon. Virgil is the first and only one who describes the father as well as the children destroyed by the serpents;[53] the sculptors do this likewise, while yet as Greeks they ought not: therefore it is probable that they did it at the prompting of Virgil.

I quite understand how far this probability falls short of historical certainty. But as I do not intend to draw any historical conclusions from it, I yet believe at least that it can stand as a hypothesis which the critic in forming his views may take into account. Proven or not proven, that the sculptors followed Virgil in their works, I will assume it merely to see how in that case they did follow him. Concerning the outcries, I have already explained my opinion. Perhaps a further comparison may lead us to observations not less instructive.

The idea of binding the father with his two sons into one group by the deadly serpents is unquestionably a very happy one, evincing an uncommonly graphic fancy. To whom is it to be assigned? The poet, or the artist? Montfaucon refuses to find it in the poet. But Montfaucon, as I think, has not read him with sufficient attention.

> ... Illi agmine certo
> Laocoönta petunt, et primum parva duorum
> Corpora natorum serpens amplexus uterque
> Implicat et miseros morsu depascitur artus.
> Post ipsum, auxilio subeuntem ac tela ferentem,
> Corripiunt, spirisque ligant ingentibus....[54]

The poet has depicted the serpents as of a marvellous length. They have enfolded the boys, and when the father comes to their aid, seize him also (*corripiunt*). From their size they could not at once uncoil themselves from the boys; there must therefore be a moment in which they had attacked the father with their heads and foreparts, while they still with their other parts enveloped the children. This moment is required in the development of the poetic picture; the poet makes it sufficiently felt; only the time had not yet been reached for finishing the picture. That the ancient commentators actually realised this appears to be shown by a passage in Donatus.[55] How much less would it escape the artists in whose understanding eyes everything that can advantage them stands out so quickly and so plainly.

In the coils themselves with which the poet's fancy sees the serpents entwine Laocoon, he very carefully avoids the arms, in order to leave the hands their freedom.

> Ille simul manibus tendit divellere nodos.[56]

In this the artists must necessarily follow him. Nothing gives more life and expression than the movement of the hands; in emotion especially the most speaking countenance without it is insignificant. Arms fast bound to the body by the coils of the serpents would have spread frost and death over the whole group. For this reason we see them, in the chief figure as well as in the secondary figures, in full activity, and busiest there where for the moment there is the most violent anguish.

Further, too, the artists, in view of the convolutions of the serpents, found nothing that could be more advantageously borrowed from the poet than this movement of the arms. Virgil makes the serpents wind themselves doubly about the body and doubly about the neck of Laocoon, with their heads elevated above him.

> Bis medium amplexi, bis collo squamea circum
> Terga dati, superant capite et cervicibus altis.[57]

This picture satisfies the imagination completely; the noblest parts are compressed to suffocation,and the poison goes straight to the face. Nevertheless, it was not a picture for artists, who want to exhibit the effects of the pain and the poison in the bodily frame. For in order to make these visible the chief parts must be as free as possible, and no external pressure whatever must be exercised upon them which could alter and weaken the play of the suffering nerves and straining muscles. The double coil of the serpents would have concealed the whole body, so that the painful contraction of the abdomen, which is so expressive, would have remained invisible. What one would still have perceived of the body, over, or under, or between the coils would have appeared under pressures and swellings caused not by the inward pain, but by the external burden. The neck so many times encircled would have spoiled completely the pyramidal tapering of the group which is so agreeable to the eye; and the pointed serpent heads standing out into the air from this swollen bulk would have made so abrupt a break in proportion that the form of the whole would have been repulsive in the extreme. There are doubtless draughtsmen who would nevertheless have been unintelligent enough to follow the poet slavishly. But what would have come of that, we can, to name no other instances, understand from a drawing of Franz Cleyn,[58] which can be looked on only with disgust. (This occurs in the splendid edition of Dryden's English Virgil.)[59] The ancient sculptors perceived at a glance that their art demanded an entire modification. They removed all the serpent coils from neck and body to thighs and feet. Here these coils, without injuring the expression, could cover and press as much as was needful. Here they aroused at once the idea of retarded flight and of a kind of immobility which is exceedingly advantageous to the artistic permanence of a single posture.

I know not how it has come about that the critics have passed over in perfect silence this distinction, which is exhibited so plainly in the coilings of the serpents, between the work of art and the poet's description. It exalts the artistic wisdom of the work just as much as the other which they mention, which, however, they do not venture to praise, but rather seek to excuse. I mean the difference in the draping of the subject. Virgil's Laocoon is in his priestly vestments, but in the group appears, with both his sons, completely naked. I am told there are people who find something preposterous in representing a prince, a priest, unclothed, at the altar of sacrifice. And to these people connoisseurs of art reply, in all seriousness, that certainly it is an offence against custom, but that the artists were compelled to it, because they could not give their figures any suitable attire. Sculpture, say they, cannot imitate any kind of cloth; thick folds would make a bad effect. Of two embarrassments, therefore, they had chosen the smaller, and were willing rather to offend against truth than to incur the risk of blame for their draperies. If the ancient artists would laugh at the objection, I really cannot tell what they would have said about the answer. One cannot degrade Art further than by such a defence. For, granted that sculpture could imitate the different materials just as well as painting, should then Laocoon necessarily have been clothed? Should we lose nothing by this draping? Has a costume, the work of slavish hands, just as much beauty as the work of the Eternal Wisdom, an organised body? Does it demand the same faculties, is it equally meritorious, does it bring the same honour, to imitate the former as to imitate the latter? Do our eyes only wish to be deceived, and is it all the same to them with what they are deceived?

With the poet a dress is no dress; it conceals nothing; our imagination sees through it at all times. Let Laocoon in Virgil have it or lack it, his suffering in every part of his body is, to the imagination, an evil equally visible. The brow is bound about for her with the priestly fillet, but it is not veiled. Indeed, it does not only not hinder, this fillet, it even strengthens yet more the conception that we form of the sufferer's misfortunes.

Perfusus sanie vittas atroque veneno.[60]

His priestly dignity helps him not a whit; the very symbol which secures him everywhere respect and veneration is soaked and defiled by the deadly venom.

But this accessory idea the artist had to sacrifice if the main work were not to suffer damage. Besides, had he left to Laocoon only this fillet, the expression would in consequence have been much weakened. The brow would have been partly covered, and the brow is the seat of expression. So, just as in that other particular, the shriek, he sacrificed expression to beauty, in the same way here he sacrificed custom to expression. Generally speaking, custom, in the view of the ancients, was a matter of little consequence. They felt that the highest aim of Art pointed to dispensing with the customary altogether. Beauty is this highest aim; necessity invented clothing, and what has Art to do with necessity? I grant you there is also a beauty of drapery; but what is it compared with the beauty of the human form? And will he who is able to reach the higher content himself with the lower? I am much afraid that the most finished master in draperies shows by that very dexterity in what it is he is lacking.

VI

My hypothesis – that the artists imitated the poet – does not redound to their disparagement. On the contrary, this imitation sets their wisdom in the fairest light. They followed the poet without allowing themselves to be misled by him in the slightest. They had a pattern, but as they had to transpose this pattern from one art into another, they found opportunity enough to think for themselves. And these thoughts of theirs, which are manifest in their deviation from their model, prove that they were just as great in their art as he in his own.

And now I will reverse the hypothesis and suppose the poet to have imitated the artists. There are scholars who maintain this supposition to be the truth. Whether they had historical grounds for that, I do not know. But when they found the work of art so superlatively beautiful, they could not persuade themselves that it might belong to a late period. It must be of the age when Art was in its perfect flower, because it deserved to be of that age.

It has been shown that, admirable as Virgil's picture is, there are yet various features of it which the artists could not use. The statement thus admits of being reduced to this, that a good poetic description must also yield a good actual painting, and that the poet has only so far described well when the artist can follow him in every feature. One is inclined to presume this restricted sense, even before seeing it confirmed by examples; merely from consideration of the wider sphere of poetry, from the boundless field of our imagination, and from the spiritual nature of the pictures, which can stand side by side in the greatest multitude and variety without one obscuring or damaging another, just as the things themselves would do or the natural signs of the same within the narrow bounds of space and time.

But if the less cannot include the greater, the greater can contain the less. This is my point – if not, every feature which the descriptive poet uses can be used with like effect on the canvas or in the marble. Might perhaps every feature of which the artist avails himself prove equally effective in the work of the poet? Unquestionably; for what we find beautiful in a work of art is not found beautiful by the eye, but by our imagination through the eye. The picture in question may therefore be called up again in our imagination by arbitrary or natural signs,[61] and thus also may arise at any time the corresponding pleasure, although not in corresponding degree.

This, however, being admitted, I must confess that to my mind the hypothesis that Virgil imitated the artists is far less conceivable than the contrary supposition. If the artists followed the poet, I can account for their deviations. They were obliged to deviate, because the selfsame features as the poet delineated would have occasioned them difficulties such as do not embarrass the poet. But what should make the poet deviate? If he had followed the group in every detail would he not, all the same, have presented to us an admirable picture? I can conceive quite well how his fancy, working on its own account, might suggest one feature and another; but the reasons why his imagination should think that beautiful features, already before his eyes, ought to be transformed into those other features – such reasons, I confess, never dawn upon me.

It even seems to me that if Virgil had had the group as his pattern he could scarcely have refrained from permitting the union together, as it were in a knot, of the three bodies to be at least conjectured. It was too vivid not to catch his eye, and he would have appreciated its excellent effect too keenly not to give it yet more prominence in his description. As I have said, the time was not yet arrived to finish this picture of the entwined group. No; but a single word more would perhaps have given to it, in the shadow where the poet had to leave it, a very obvious impression. What the artist was able to discover without this word, the poet, if he had seen it in the artist's work, would not have left unspoken.

The artist had the most compelling reasons not to let the suffering of Laocoon break out into a cry. But if the poet had had before him the so touching union of pain and beauty in the work of art, what could have so imperatively obliged him to leave completely unsuggested the idea of manly dignity and great-hearted endurance which arises from this union of pain and beauty, and all at once to shock us with the terrible outcries of Laocoon? Richardson says, 'Virgil's Laocoon must shriek, because the poet desires to arouse not so much pity for him as terror and horror in the ranks of the Trojans.'[62] I grant, although Richardson seems not to have considered it, that the poet does not make the description in his own person, but lets Aeneas make it, and this, too, in the presence of Dido, to whose compassion Aeneas could never enough appeal. It is not, however, the shriek that surprises me, but the absence of any gradation leading up to the cry, a gradation that the work of art would naturally have shown the poet to be needful, if, as we have supposed, he had had it for a pattern. Richardson adds, 'The story of Laocoon should lead up merely to the pathetic description of the final ruin; the poet, therefore, has not thought fit to make it more interesting, in order not to waste upon the misfortune of a single citizen the attention which should be wholly fixed on Troy's last dreadful night.' Only, this sets out the affair as one to be regarded from a painter's point of view, from which it cannot be contemplated at all. The calamity of Laocoon and the Destruction of the City are not with the poet pictures set side by side; the two together do not make a great whole which the eye either should or could take in at a glance; and only in such a case would it be needful to arrange that our eyes should fall rather upon Laocoon than upon the burning city. The two descriptions follow each other successively, and I do not see what disadvantage it could bring to the second, how greatly soever the preceding one had moved us. That could only be, if the second in itself were not sufficiently touching.

Still less reason would the poet have had to alter the coiling of the serpents. In the work of art they leave the hands busy and bind the feet. This disposition pleases the eye, and it is a living picture that is left by it in the imagination. It is so clear and pure that it can be presented almost as effectively by words as by actual material means.

> ...Micat alter, et ipsum
> Laocoönta petit, totumque infraque supraque
> Implicat et rabido tandem ferit ilia morsu
>
> .   .   .   .   .   .
>
> At serpens lapsu crebro redeunte subintrat
> Lubricus, intortoque ligat genua infima nodo.[63]

These are the lines of Sadoleto,[64] which would, no doubt, have come from Virgil with a more picturesque power if a visible pattern had fired his fancy, and which would in that case certainly have been better than what he now gives us in their place:

> Bis medium amplexi, bis collo squamea circum
> Terga dati, superant capite et cervicibus altis.[65]

These details, certainly, fill the imagination; but it must not rest in them, it must not endeavour to make an end here; it must see now only the serpents and now only Laocoon, it must try to represent to itself what kind of figure is made by the two together. As soon as it sinks to this the Virgilian picture begins to dissatisfy, and it finds it in the highest degree unpictorial.

If, however, the changes which Virgil had made in the pattern set before him had not been unsuccessful, they would yet be merely arbitrary. One imitates in order to resemble. Can resemblance be preserved when alterations are made needlessly? Rather, when this is done, the design obviously is – not to be like, and therefore not to imitate.

Not the whole, some may object, but perhaps this part and that. Good! But what, then, are these single parts that agree in the description and in the work of art so exactly that the poet might seem to have borrowed them from the latter? The father, the children, the serpents – all these the story furnished to the poet as well as to the artists. Excepting the story itself, they agree in nothing beyond the one point that they bind father and children in a single serpent-knot. But the suggestion of this arose from the altered detail, that the selfsame calamity overtook the father and the children. This alteration, as has already been pointed out, Virgil appears to have introduced; for the Greek legend says something quite different. Consequently, when, in view of that common binding by the serpent coils, there certainly was imitation on one side or the other, it is easier to suppose it on the artist's side than on that of the poet. In all else the one deviates from the other; only with the distinction that, if it is the artist who has made these deviations, the design of imitating the poet can still persist, the aim and the limitations of his art obliging him thereto; if, on the other hand, it is the poet who is supposed to have imitated the artist, then all the deviations referred to are an evidence against the supposed imitation, and those who, notwithstanding, maintain it, can mean nothing further by it than that the work of art is older than the poetic description.

VII

When one says that the artist imitates the poet, or that the poet imitates the artist, this is capable of two interpretations. Either the one makes the work of the other the actual subject of his imitation, or they have both the same subject and the one borrows from the other the style and fashion of the imitation. When Virgil describes the shield of Aeneas, it is in the first of these senses that he imitates the artist who made it. The work of art itself, not that which is represented upon it, is the subject of his imitation, and although certainly he describes at the same time what one sees represented thereon, yet he describes it only as a part of the shield, and not the thing itself. If Virgil, on the other hand, had imitated the Laocoon group, this would be an imitation of the second kind. For he would not have imitated the group, but what the group represents, and only the characteristics of his imitation would have been borrowed from it. In the first imitation the poet is original, in the second he is a copyist. The former is a part of the general imitation which constitutes the essence of his art, and he works as genius, whether his subject be a work of other arts or of Nature. The latter, on the contrary, degrades him wholly from his dignity; instead of the things themselves, he imitates the imitations of them, and gives us cold recollections of features from another's genius in place of original features of his own.

When, however, poet and artist, as not seldom happens, view the subjects that they have in common from an identical standpoint, it can hardly fail that there should be agreement in many particulars without implying the slightest degree of imitation or common aim between them. These agreements in contemporaneous artists and poets, concerning things that are no longer extant, may contribute to reciprocal illustration; but to attempt to establish such illustration by finding design in what was mere accident, and especially to attribute to the poet in every trifle a reference to this statue or that painting, is to render him a very equivocal service. And not to him alone, but to the reader also, for whom the most beautiful passage is thereby made, if God will, very intelligible, but at the same time admirably frigid.

This is the purpose, and the error, of a famous English work. Spence wrote his *Polymetis*[66] with much classical erudition and a very intimate acquaintance with the surviving works of ancient art. His design of explaining by these the Roman poets, and, on the other hand, of deriving from the poets elucidations for ancient works of art hitherto unexplained, he often accomplished very happily. But nevertheless I contend that his book is altogether intolerable to any reader of taste.

It is natural that, when Valerius Flaccus describes the Winged Lightning upon the Roman shields –

> Nec primus radios, miles Romane, corusci
> Fulminis et rutilas scutis diffuderis alas,[67]

this description becomes to me far clearer when I perceive the representation of such a shield upon an ancient monument. It may be that Mars, hovering exactly as Addison fancied he saw him hovering, over the head of Rhea upon a coin, was also represented by the ancient armourers on shields and helmets, and that Juvenal had such a shield or helmet in mind when he alluded to it in a single word which, until Addison, remained a riddle for all the commentators.[68] For my part, I think that the passage of Ovid where the exhausted Cephalus calls to the cooling breezes:

> Aura...venias...
> Meque juves, intresque sinus, gratissima, nostros![69]

and his Procris takes this Aura for the name of a rival – that to me, I say, this passage appears more natural when I gather from the works of ancient artists that they actually personified the soft breezes and worshipped a kind of female sylphs under the name of Aurae. I grant you, that when Juvenal styles a distinguished good-for-nothing a Hermes-statue,[70] one could hardly find the likeness in the comparison without seeing such a statue, without knowing that it is a miserable pillar, which bears merely the head, or at most the torso, of the god, and, because we perceive thereon neither hands nor feet, awakens the conception of slothfulness. Illustrations of this sort are not to be despised, although, in fact, they are neither always necessary nor always adequate. The poet had the work of art in view as a thing existing for itself, and not as an imitation; or with both artist and poet certain conceptions of an identical kind were taken for granted, in consequence of which a further agreement in their representations must appear, from which, again, we can reason back to the generally accepted nature of these conceptions.

But when Tibullus[71] describes the form of Apollo, as he appeared to him in a dream – the most beautiful of youths, his temples bound about with the modest laurel; Syrian odours exhaling from the golden hair that flows about his neck; a gleaming white and rosy red mingled on the whole body, as on the tender cheek of the bride as she is led to her beloved – why must these features be borrowed from famous old pictures? Echion's[72] *nova nupta verecundia notabilis*[73] may have been seen in Rome, may have been copied a thousand times. Had then the bridal blush itself vanished from the world? Since the painter had seen it, was it no longer to be seen by a poet save in the painter's imitation? Or if another poet speaks of the exhausted Vulcan, or calls his face heated before the forge a red and fiery countenance, must he needs learn first from the work of a painter that labour wearies and heat reddens?[74] Or when Lucretius describes the changes of the seasons and causes them to pass before us in their natural order with the entire succession of their effects in earth and sky, was Lucretius an ephemeron?[75] Had he not lived through a whole year himself to witness all these transformations, but must depict them after a procession in which their statues were carried around? Must he first learn from these statues the old poetic artifice whereby abstract notions are turned into actual beings? Or Virgil's *pontem indignatus Araxes*, that splendid poetic picture of a stream overflowing its banks and tearing down the bridge thrown over it, does it not lose all its beauty if the poet is there alluding merely to a work of art in which this river-god is represented as actually breaking down a bridge?[76] What do we want with these commentaries which in the clearest passages supplant the poet in order to let the suggestion of an artist glimmer through?

I lament that so useful a book as *Polymetis* might otherwise have been has, by reason of this tasteless crotchet of foisting upon the ancient poets in place of their own proper fancy an acquaintance with another's, been made so offensive and so much more damaging to the classic authors than the watery expositions of the shallowest philologist could ever have been. I regret yet more that in this matter Spence should have been preceded by Addision himself, who, from a passionate desire to exalt the works of ancient art into a means of interpretation, has just as little distinguished between the cases in which it is becoming in a poet to imitate the artist and those in which it is disparaging.[77]

VIII

Of the likeness which poetry and painting bear to each other Spence has the most singular conceptions possible. He believes the two arts in ancient times to have been so closely united that they always went hand in hand, that the poet constantly kept the painter in view, and the painter the poet. That poetry is the more comprehensive art, that beauties are at her command which painting can never attain, that she may frequently have reason to prefer unpicturesque beauties to picturesque – of this he does not appear to have a notion, and therefore the smallest difference which he detects between poets and artists of the old world puts him in a difficulty, and he resorts to the most extraordinary subterfuges to escape from his embarrassment.

The ancient poets generally endow Bacchus with horns. It is quite wonderful, then, says Spence, that we find these horns so seldom on his statues. He lights on this explanation and on that: on the uncertainty of the antiquaries, on the smallness of the horns themselves, which might have crept into concealment under the grapes and ivy-leaves, the unfailing headcovering of the god. He winds around and about the true reason without ever suspecting it. The horns of Bacchus were not natural horns, such as we see on the fauns and satyrs. They were but a garnishment of the brow, which he could assume and lay aside at will.

Tibi, cum sine cornibus adstas,
Virgineum caput est –[78]

so runs the solemn invocation of Bacchus in Ovid. He could thus show himself also without horns, and did so when he would appear in his virginal beauty. The artists certainly would also wish so to represent him, and would therefore avoid every less pleasing adjunct. Such an adjunct the horns would have been if attached to the diadem, as we may see them on a head in the royal cabinet at Berlin. Such an adjunct was the diadem itself, hiding the beautiful brow, and for this reason it occurs on the statues of Bacchus just as rarely as the horns, although indeed it was dispensed with just as often by the poets, both in the representations of Bacchus and in those of his great progenitor. The horns and the diadem prompted the poet's allusions to the deeds and the character of the god; to the artist, on the contrary, they were hindrances to the exhibition of greater beauties, and if Bacchus, as I believe, for that very reason had the surname *Biformis*, Δίμορφος,[79] because he could show himself in a fair and in a terrible aspect, then it was quite natural for the artists greatly to prefer that one of his forms which best answered the purpose of their art.

Minerva and Juno in the Roman poets often dart forth lightning. 'Then why not also in their images?' asks Spence.[80] He replies, 'It was an especial privilege of these two goddesses, the grounds of which were perhaps only to be learned in the Samothracian mysteries; artists, moreover, were regarded by the ancient Romans as common people, were therefore seldom admitted to those mysteries, and so doubtless knew nothing of them, and what they did not know they could not depict.' I might in return ask Spence, did these common people work out their own notions, or work at the command of more distinguished persons who might have been instructed in the mysteries? Were artists among the Greeks regarded with a like contempt? Were the Roman artists not for the greater part born Greeks? And so on.

Statius[81] and Valerius Flaccus[82] depict an angry Venus, and with features so terrible that at the moment we should rather take her for one of the Furies than for the Goddess of Love. Spence looks round in vain amongst the works of ancient art for such a Venus. And what is his conclusion? That more is permitted to the poet than to the sculptor or the painter? That is the conclusion he ought to have drawn, but he has accepted the principle once for all, that in a poetic description nothing is good which would be unsuitable to be represented in a painting or a statue.[83] Consequently, the poets must have erred. 'Statius and Valerius belong to an age when Roman poetry was in its decline. They show in this particular also their corrupt taste and their faulty judgement. With the poets of a better time one will not find these offences against graphic expression.'[84]

To speak in this way betrays a very poor faculty of discrimination. All the same, I do not intend to take up the cudgels for either Statius or Valerius, but will confine myself to but one general observation. The gods and sacred persons, as the artist represents them, are not entirely the same beings which the poet knows. With the artist they are personified abstractions which must constantly retain the selfsame characterisation, if they are to be recognisable. With the poet, on the other hand, they are actual persons who live and act, who possess beyond their general character other qualities and emotions, which will stand out above it according to occasion and circumstances. Venus to the sculptor is nothing but Love; he must therefore endow her with the modest, blushful beauty and all the gracious charms that delight us in beloved objects and that we therefore combine in the abstract conception of Love. Deviate however slightly from this ideal, and we shall fail to recognise the picture. Beauty, but with more majesty than modesty, is at once no Venus, but a Juno. Charms, but commanding, masculine, rather than gracious charms, give us a Minerva in place of a Venus. In reality, an angry Venus, a Venus moved by revenge and rage, is to the sculptor a contradiction in terms; for Love as Love is never angry, never revengeful. To the poet, on the other hand, Venus certainly is Love, but she is more: she is the Goddess of Love, who beyond this character has an individuality of her own, and consequently must be just as capable of the impulse of aversion as of inclination. What wonder, then, that to him she blazes in rage or anger, especially when it is injured love that so transforms her?

Certainly it is true that the artist also in composition may just as well as the poet introduce Venus or any other divinity, out of her character, as a being actually living and acting. But in that case her actions must at least not contradict her character, even if they are not direct consequences of it. Venus commits to her son's charge her divine weapons; this action the artist can represent as well as the poet. Here nothing hinders him from giving to Venus all the grace and beauty that appertain to her as the Goddess of Love; rather, indeed, will she thereby be so much the more recognisable in his work. But when Venus would avenge herself on her contemners, the men of Lemnos; when in magnified and savage form, with stained cheeks and disordered hair, she seizes the torch, throws around her a black vesture and stormily plunges down on a gloomy cloud; surely that is not a moment for the artist, because in such a moment he cannot by any means make her distinguishable. It is purely a moment for the poet, since to him the privilege is granted of so closely and exactly uniting with it another aspect, in which the goddess is wholly Venus, that we do not lose sight of her even in the Fury. This Flaccus does:

> Neque enim alma videri
> Jam tumet, aut tereti crinem subnectitur auro
> Sidereos diffusa sinus. Eadem effera et ingens
> Et maculis suffecta genas, pinumque sonantem
> Virginibus Stygiis, nigramque simillima pallam.[85]

Statius does just the same:

> Illa Paphon veterem centumque altaria linquens,
> Nec vultu nec crine prior, solvisse jugalem
> Ceston, et Idalias procul ablegasse volucres
> Fertur. Erant certe, media qui noctis in umbra
> Divam alios ignes majoraque tela gerentem,
> Tartarias inter thalamis volitasse sorores
> Vulgarent: utque implicitis arcana domorum
> Anguibus et saeva formidine cuncta replerit
> Limina. —[86]

Or we might say, to the poet alone belongs the art of depicting with negative traits, and by mixing them with positive to bring two images into one. No longer the gracious Venus, no longer the hair fastened with golden clasps, floated about by no azure vesture, but without her girdle, armed with other flames, with greater arrows, companioned by like Furies. But because the artist is obliged to dispense with such an artifice, must the poet too in his turn abstain from using it? If painting will be the sister of poesy, let not the younger forbid to the elder all the garniture and bravery which she herself cannot put on.

IX

If in individual cases we wish to compare the painter and the poet with one another, the first and most important point is to observe whether both of them have had complete freedom, whether they have, in the absence of any outward compulsion, been able to aim at the highest effect of their art.

Religion was often an outward compulsion of this kind for the ancient artist. His work, designed for reverence and worship, could not always be as perfect as if he had had a single eye to the pleasure of the beholder. Superstition overloaded the gods with symbols, and the most beautiful of them were not everywhere worshipped for their beauty. In his temple at Lemnos, from which the pious Hypsipyle rescued her father under the shape of the god,[87] Bacchus stood horned, and so doubtless he appeared in all his temples, for the horns were a symbol that indicated his essential nature. Only the free artist who wrought his Bacchus for no holy shrine left this symbol out; and if amongst the statues of him still extant we find all without horns, this is perhaps a proof that they are not of the consecrated forms in which he was actually worshipped. Apart from this, it is highly probable that it was upon these last that the rage of the pious iconoclasts in the first centuries of Christianity chiefly fell, their fury sparing only here and there a work of art which had not been defiled by idolatrous worship.

As, however, works of both kinds are still found amongst antiquities in excavation, I should like the name of 'works of art' to be reserved for those alone in which the artist could show himself actually as artist, in which beauty has been his first and last object. All the rest, in which too evident traces of religious ritual appear, are unworthy of the name, because Art here has not wrought on her own account, but has been an auxiliary of religion, looking in the material representations which she made of it more to the significant than to the beautiful; although I do not mean by this that she did not often put great significance into the beauty, or, out of indulgence to the art and finer taste of the age, remitted her attention to the former so much that the latter alone might appear to predominate.

If we make no such distinction, then the connoisseur and the antiquary will be constantly at strife because they do not understand each other. If the former, with his insight into the aims of art, contends that this or that work was never made by the ancient artist – that is to say, not as artist, not voluntarily – then the latter will assert that neither religion nor any other cause lying outside the region of art has caused the artist to make it – the artist, that is to say, as workman. He will suppose that he can refute the connoisseur with the first figure that comes to hand, which the other without scruple, but to the great annoyance of the learned world, will condemn to the rubbish-heap once more from which it has been drawn.[88]

Yet, on the other hand, it is possible to exaggerate the influence of religion upon art. Spence affords a singular example of that tendency. He found that Vesta was not worshipped in her temple under any personal image, and this he deemed enough to warrant the conclusion that no statues of this goddess ever existed, and that every one so considered really represented not Vesta, but a vestal.[89] Strange inference! Did the artist, then, lose his right to personify a being to whom the poets give a distinct personality, whom they make the daughter of Saturnus and Ops, whom they expose to the danger of ill-usage at the hands of Priapus, and all else they relate of her – did he lose his right,

I ask, to personify this being in his own way, because she was worshipped in one temple merely under the symbol of fire? For Spence here falls into this further error: that what Ovid[90] says only of a certain temple of Vesta – namely, of that at Rome – he extends to all temples of the goddess without distinction and to her worship in general. She was not everywhere worshipped as she was worshipped in this temple at Rome, nor even in Italy itself before Numa[91] built it. Numa desired to see no divinity represented in human or animal form; and without doubt the reform which he introduced in the service of Vesta consisted in this, that he banished from it all personal representation. Ovid himself teaches us that before Numa's time there were statues of Vesta in her temple, which when her priestess Sylvia became a mother raised their maiden hands in shame before their eyes.[92] That even in the temples which the goddess had in the Roman provinces outside the city her worship was not wholly of the kind which Numa prescribed, various ancient inscriptions appear to prove, where mention is made of a 'Pontificus Vestae'.[93] At Corinth also there was a temple of Vesta without any statues, with a mere altar whereon offerings were made to the goddess. But had the Greeks therefore no statues of Vesta? At Athens there was one in the Prytaneum, beside the statue of Peace. The people of Iasos boasted of one, which stood in their city under the open sky, that neither snow nor rain fell upon it. Pliny mentions a sitting figure from the hand of Scopas which in his time was to be seen in the Servilian Gardens at Rome.[94] Granted that it is difficult for us now to distinguish a mere vestal from Vesta herself, does this prove that the ancients could not distinguish them, or indeed did not wish to distinguish them? Notoriously, certain characteristics indicate rather the one than the other. Only in the hands of the goddess can we expect to find the sceptre, the torch, the palladium.[95] The tympanum[96] which Codinus[97] associates with her belongs to her perhaps only as the Earth, or Codinus did not recognise very well what he saw.

X

I notice another expression of surprise in Spence which shows plainly how little he can have reflected on the limits of Poetry and Painting. 'As for what concerns the Muses in general,' he says, 'it is certainly singular that the poets are so sparing in the description of them – more sparing by far than we should expect with goddesses to whom they owe such great obligations.'[98]

What is this, but to wonder that when the poets speak of them they do not use the dumb language of the painter? Urania is for the poets the Muse of Astronomy; from her name, from her functions, we recognise her office. The artist in order to make it distinguishable must exhibit her with a pointer and a celestial globe; this wand, this celestial globe, this attitude of hers are his alphabet from which he helps us to put together the name Urania. But when the poet would say that Urania had long ago foretold his death by the stars:

Ipsa diu positis lethum praedixerat astris Uranie. –[99]

why should he, thinking of the painter, add thereto, Urania, the pointer in her hand, the celestial globe before her? Would it not be as if a man who can and may speak aloud should at the same time still make use of the signs which the mutes in the Turk's seraglio have invented for lack of utterance?

The very same surprise Spence again expresses concerning the personified moralities, or those divinities whom the ancients set over the virtues and the conduct of human life. 'It is worthy of remark,' says he, 'that the Roman poets say far less of the best of these personified moralities than we should expect. The artists in this respect are much richer, and he who would learn the particular aspect and attire of each need only consult the coins of the Roman Emperors: the poets speak of these beings frequently, indeed, as of persons; in general, however, they say very little of their attributes, their attire and the rest of their outward appearance.'[100]

When the poet personifies abstract qualities, these are sufficiently characterised by their names and by what they do. To the artist these means are wanting. He must therefore attach symbols to his personifications by which they can be distinguished. By these symbols, because they are something different and mean something different, they become allegorical figures. A woman with a bridle in her hand, another leaning on a pillar, are in art allegorical beings. But Temperance and Steadfastness are to the poet allegorical beings, and merely personified abstractions. The symbols, in the artist's representation, necessity has invented. For in no other way can he make plain what this or that figure signifies. But what the artist is driven to by necessity, why should the poet force on himself when no such necessity is laid upon him?

What surprises Spence so much deserves to be prescribed to the poets as a law. They must not make painting's indigence the rule of their wealth. They must not regard the means which Art has invented in order to follow poetry as if they were perfections which they have reason to envy. When the artist adorns a figure with symbols, he raises a mere figure to a superior being. But when the poet makes use of these plastic bedizenments, he makes of a superior being a mere lay-figure.

And just as this rule is authenticated by its observance amongst the ancient poets, so is its deliberate violation a favourite weakness amongst their successors. All their creatures of imagination go in masquerade, and those who understand this masquerade best generally understand least the chief thing of all, which is to let their creatures act and to distinguish and characterise them by their actions.

Yet amongst the attributes with which the artists distinguish their abstract personalities there is one sort which is more susceptible and more worthy of poetic employment. I mean those which properly have nothing allegorical in their nature, but are to be regarded as implements of which the being to whom they are assigned would or might make use when acting as real persons. The bridle in the hand of Temperance, the pillar on which Steadfastness leans, are purely allegorical, and thus of no use to the poet. The scales in the hand of

Justice are certainly less purely allegorical, because the right use of the scales is really a part of justice. But the lyre or flute in the hand of a Muse, the spear in the hand of Mars, hammer and tongs in the hands of Vulcan, are not symbols at all, but mere instruments, without which these beings could not effect the achievements we ascribe to them. Of this kind are the attributes which the ancient poets did sometimes weave into their descriptions, and which I on that ground, distinguishing them from the allegorical, would call the poetic. The latter signify the thing itself, the former only some likeness of it.[101]

XI

Count Caylus, again, appears to require that the poet shall embellish the creatures of his imagination with allegorical attributes.[102] The Count was more at home with painting than with poetry. In the work, nevertheless, where he expresses this requirement I have found the suggestion of more important considerations, the most essential of which, for the better judging of them, I will mention here.

The artist, according to the Count's view, should make himself very thoroughly acquainted with the greatest of descriptive poets, with Homer, with this 'second Nature'. He shows him what rich and still unused material for most admirable pictures is offered by the story handled by the Greek, and how much more perfect his delineations will prove the more closely he clings to the very smallest circumstances noticed by the poet.

Now in this proposition we see a mingling of the two kinds of imitation which we have separated above. The painter is not only to imitate what the poet has imitated, but he is further to imitate it with the self-same features; he is to use the poet not as narrator only, but as poet.

This second species of imitation, however, which detracts so much from the poet's merit, why is it not equally disparaging to the artist? If before Homer such a succession of pictures as Count Caylus cites from his pages had been extant, and we were aware that the poet had based his work on them, would he not lose unspeakably in our estimation? How comes it that we withdraw from the artist no whit of our esteem even though he does nothing more than translate the words of the poet into figures and colours?

The reason appears to be this. With the artist we deem the execution more difficult than the invention; with the poet, again, it is the contrary, and we deem the execution, as compared with the invention, the lighter task. Had Virgil taken from the sculptured group the entangling of Laocoon and his children, the merit in his picture which we consider the greater and the harder of attainment would be lost, and only the smaller would remain. For to shape this entangling by the power of imagination is far more important than to express it in words. Had, on the other hand, the artist borrowed this entangling from the poet, he would still, in our minds, retain sufficient merit, although the merit of invention is withdrawn. For expression in marble is more difficult by far than expression in words; and when we weigh invention and representation against each other we are always inclined to abate our demands on the artist for the one, in proportion to the excess we feel that we have received of the other.

There are two cases in which it is a greater merit for the artist to copy Nature through the medium of the poet's imitation than without it. The painter who represents a lovely landscape according to the description of a Thomson[103] has done more than he who copies it direct from Nature. The latter has his model before him; the former must first of all strain his imagination to the point that enables him to see it before him. The one makes a thing of beauty out of lively sensuous impressions, the other from weak and wavering descriptions of arbitrary signs.

But natural as the readiness may be to abate in our demands on the artist for the particular merit of invention, it is equally so on his part, for like reasons, to be indifferent to it. For when he sees that invention can never become his more shining merit, that his greatest praise depends on execution, it becomes all one to him whether the former is old or new, used once or times without number, and whether it belongs to himself or to another. He remains within the narrow range of a few designs, become familiar both to him and to everybody, and directs his inventive faculty merely to changes in the already known and to new combinations of old subjects. That, too, is actually the idea which the manuals of painting connect with the word *Invention*. For although certainly they divide into the pictorial and the poetic, yet the poetic is not made to consist in the production of the design itself, but purely in the arrangement or the expression. It is invention, but not invention of the whole, only of separate parts and their position in relation to each other. It is invention, but of that lower type which Horace recommended to his tragic poet:—

> ...Tuque
> Rectius Iliacum carmen deducis in actus
> Quam si proferres ignota indictaque primus.[104]

Recommended, I say, but not commanded. Recommended, as easier for him, more fitting, more advantageous; but not commanded as better and nobler in itself.

In fact the poet has a great advantage who treats a well-known story and familiar characters. A hundred indifferent trifles which otherwise would be indispensable to the understanding of the whole he can pass by; and the more quickly he becomes intelligible to his hearers, the more quickly he can interest them. This advantage the painter also has if his theme is not strange to us, if we make out at the first glance the purpose and meaning of his entire composition, if we at once not merely see his characters speaking, but hear also what they speak. It is on the first glance that the main effect depends, and if this forces on us troublesome reflection and conjecture, our inclination to be moved grows cold; in order to be avenged on the unintelligible artist, we harden ourselves against the expression, and woe betide him if he has sacrificed beauty to expression! We then find nothing whatever that can charm us to tarry before his work; what we see does not please us; and what we are to think concerning it we are left uninstructed.

Now let us consider these two things together; first, that the invention or novelty of the theme is far from being the principal thing that we desire of the painter; secondly, that a well-known theme furthers and facilitates the effect of his art; and I judge that the reason why he so seldom attempts new themes we need not, with Count Caylus, seek in his convenience, his ignorance, or the difficulty of the mechanical part of art, demanding all his time and diligence; but we shall find it more deeply founded, and it may be that what at first appears to be the limitations of art and the spoiling of our pleasure we shall be inclined to praise as a restraint wise in itself and useful to ourselves. Nor am I afraid that experience will confute me. The painters will thank the Count for his goodwill, but hardly follow his counsels so generally as he expects. If they should, in another hundred years a new Caylus would be wanted who should bring again to remembrance the old themes and reconduct the artist into the field where others before him have gathered immortal laurels. Or do we desire that the public shall be as learned as the connoisseur with his books? That to the public all scenes of history or fable which might suggest a beautiful picture shall become known and familiar? I grant that the artists would have done better if since Raphael's day they had made Homer instead of Ovid their manual. But as that in fact has not happened, let us leave the public in their old rut, and not make their pleasure harder to attain than a pleasure must be in order to be what it should.

Protogenes[105] had painted the mother of Aristotle. I don't know how much the philosopher paid him for the picture. But, either instead of payment or in addition thereto, he gave him counsel that was worth more than the payment. For I cannot imagine that his counsel was a mere flattery. But chiefly because he considered the need of art – to be intelligible – he advised him to paint the achievements of Alexander, achievements of which at that time all the world was speaking, and of which he could foresee that they would be memorable also to posterity. Yet Protogenes had not discernment enough to follow this counsel; *impetus animi*, says Pliny, *et quaedam artis libido*,[106] a certain arrogance of art, a certain lust for the strange and the unknown, attracted him to quite other subjects. He preferred to paint the story of a Ialysus, of a Cydippe[107] and the like, of which today one cannot even guess what they represented.

XII

Homer treats of a twofold order of beings and actions: visible and invisible. This distinction it is not possible for painting to suggest; with it all is visible, and visible in one particular way. When, therefore, Count Caylus lets the pictures of the invisible actions run on in unbroken sequence with the visible;

when in the pictures of mingled actions, in which visible and invisible things take part, he does not, and perhaps cannot, suggest how the latter, which only we who contemplate the picture should discover therein, are so to be introduced that the persons in the picture do not see them, or at least must appear not necessarily to see them; it is inevitable that the entire composition, as well as many a separate portion of it, becomes confused, inconceivable, and self-contradictory.

Yet, with the book in one's hand, there might be some remedy for this error. The worst of it is simply this, that by the abrogation of the difference between the visible and invisible things all the characteristic features are at once lost by which the higher are raised above the inferior species. For example, when at last the divided gods come to blows among themselves over the fate of the Trojans, the whole struggle passes with the poet invisibly, and this invisibility permits the imagination to enlarge the stage, and leaves it free play to conceive the persons of the gods and their actions as great, and elevated as far above common humanity as ever it pleases. But painting must assume a visible stage the various necessary parts of which become the scale for the persons acting on it, a scale which the eye has immediately before it, and whose disproportion, as regards the higher beings, turns these higher beings, who were so great in the poet's delineation, into sheer monsters on the canvas of the artist.

Minerva, on whom in this struggle Mars ventures the first assault, steps back and snatches up from the ground with powerful hand a black, rough, massive stone, which in ancient days many hands of men together had rolled thither as a landmark –

'Η δ' ἀναχασσαμένη λίθον εἵλετο χειρὶ παχείῃ,
Κείμενον ἐν πεδίῳ, μέλανα τρηχύν τε, μέγαν τε,
Τὸν ῥ' ἄνδρες πρότεροι θέσαν ἔμμεναι οὖρον ἀρούρης.[108]

In order to estimate adequately the size of this stone, let us bear in mind that Homer makes his heroes as strong again as the strongest men of his time, and represents these, too, as far excelled in strength by the men whom Nestor had known in his youth. Now, I ask, if Minerva flings a stone which not one man, but several men of Nestor's youth had set for a landmark, if Minerva flings such a stone at Mars, of what stature is the goddess to be? If her stature is in proportion to the size of the stone, the marvellous vanishes. A man who is three times bigger than I must naturally also be able to fling a three-times bigger stone. But if the stature of the goddess is not in keeping with the size of the stone, there is imported into the picture an obvious improbability, the offence of which is not removed by the cold reflection that a goddess must have superhuman strength. Where I see a greater effect I would also see a greater instrument. And Mars, struck down by this mighty stone –

'Επτὰ δ' ἔπεσχε πέλεθρα...

'covered three hides of land'. It is impossible that the painter can give the god this monstrous bulk. Yet if he does not, then Mars does not lie upon the ground, not the Homeric Mars, but only a common warrior.

Longinus[109] remarks that it often appeared to him as if Homer wished to elevate his men to gods and to degrade his gods to men. Painting carries out this degradation. In painting everything vanishes completely which with the poet sets the gods yet higher than godlike men. Stature, strength, swiftness – of which Homer has in store a higher and more wonderful degree for his gods than he bestows on his most pre-eminent heroes – must in picture sink down to the common measure of humanity, and Jupiter and Agamemnon, Apollo and Achilles, Ajax and Mars, become the same kind of beings, to be recognised no otherwise than by stipulated outward signs.

The means of which painting makes use to indicate that in her compositions this or that must be regarded as invisible, is a thin cloud in which she covers it from the view of the persons concerned. This cloud seems to have been borrowed from Homer himself. For when in the tumult of the battle one of the greater heroes comes into danger from which only heavenly power can deliver him, the poet causes him to be enveloped by the tutelary deity in a thick cloud or in actual night, and thus to be withdrawn from the place; as Paris was by Venus, Idäus by Neptune, Hector by Apollo. And this mist, this cloud Caylus never forgets heartily to commend to the artist when he is sketching for him a picture of such events. But who does not perceive that with the poet the enveloping in mist and darkness is nothing but a poetical way of saying invisible? It has, on this account, always surprised me to find this poetical expression realised and an actual cloud introduced into the picture, behind which the hero, as behind a screen, stands hidden from his enemy. That was not the poet's intention. That is to transgress the limits of painting; for this cloud is here a true hieroglyph, a mere symbolic sign, that does not make the rescued hero invisible, but calls out to the beholder, 'You must regard him as invisible to you.' This is no better than the inscribed labels which issue from the mouths of the persons in ancient Gothic pictures.

It is true Homer makes Achilles, when Apollo snatches away Hector from him, strike yet three times at the thick vapour with his spear: τρὶς δ' ἠέρα τύψε βαθεῖαν.[110] But even that, in the poet's language, means no more than that Achilles became so enraged that he struck yet thrice before he noticed that he no longer had his foe in front of him. An actual mist Achilles did not see, and the whole artifice by which the gods made things invisible consisted not at all in the cloud, but in the swift snatching. Only, in order to show at the same time that no human eye could follow the body thus snatched away, the poet first of all envelops it beforehand in vapour; not that instead of the body withdrawn a fog was seen, but that whatever is under fog we think of as not visible. Therefore at times he inverts the order of things, and, instead of making the object invisible, causes the subject to be struck with blindness. Thus Neptune darkens the eyes of Achilles to save Aeneas from his murderous hands, removing him in a moment from out the tumult of the rearguard. In fact, however, the eyes of Achilles are here just as little darkened as in the other case the withdrawn heroes were enveloped in fog; the poet merely adds the one thing and the other, in order thereby to make more perceptible the extreme swiftness of the withdrawal which we call the vanishing.

The Homeric mist, however, the painters have made their own not merely in the cases where Homer himself uses or would have used it – in actual invisibilities or vanishings – but everywhere when the beholder is to recognise something in the picture which the persons in it, either altogether or in part, do not recognise. Minerva became visible to Achilles alone when she held him back from assaulting Agamemnon. 'To express this,' says Caylus, 'I know no other way than to veil her in a cloud from the rest of the council.' This is quite contrary to the spirit of the poet. To be invisible is the natural condition of his gods: no blinding, no cutting-off of the light, was needed in order that they should not be seen, but an illumination, a heightening of mortal vision, was necessary if they were to be seen. It is not enough, therefore, that the cloud is an arbitrary and unnatural sign with the painters; this arbitrary sign has not at all the positive significance which it might have as such, for they use it as frequently to make the visible invisible as they do the reverse.

XIII

If Homer's works were entirely lost, and nothing was left of his *Iliad* and *Odyssey* save a succession of pictures such as Caylus has suggested might be drawn from them, should we from these pictures, even from the hand of the most perfect master, be able to form the conception we now have, I do not say of the poet's whole endowment, but even of his pictorial talent alone? Let us try the experiment with the first passage that occurs to us – the picture of the pestilence.[111] What do we perceive on the canvas of the artist? Dead corpses, flaming funeral pyres, dying men busy with the dead, the angry god upon a cloud letting fly his arrows. The greatest riches of this picture is, compared with the poet, mere poverty. For if we were to replace Homer from the picture, what could we make him say? 'Then did Apollo become enraged and shot his arrows amongst the Grecian host. Many Greeks died and their corpses were burned.' Now let us turn to Homer himself:–

Βῆ δὲ κατ' Οὐλύμποιο καρήνων | χωόμενος κῆρ,|
Τόξ' ὤμοισιν ἔχων | ἀμφηρεφέα τε φαρέτρην·
Ἔκλαγξαν δ' ἄρ' ὀϊστοὶ ἐπ' ὤμων χωομένοιο,
Αὐτοῦ κινηθέντος· ὁ δ' ἤϊε νυκτὶ ἐοικώς|.
Ἔζετ' ἔπειτ' ἀπάνευθε νεῶν, μετὰ | δ' ἰὸν ἔηκε·
Δεινὴ δὲ κλαγγὴ γένετ' ἀργυρέοιο βιοῖο·
Οὐρῆας μὲν πρῶτον ἐπῴχετο | καὶ κύνας ἀργούς,
Αὐτὰρ ἔπειτ' αὐτοῖσι | βέλος ἐχεπευκὲς ἐφιεὶς
Βάλλ'· αἰεὶ δὲ πυραὶ | νεκύων | καίοντο θαμειαί.[112]

Just as far as life is above painting, the poet here is above the painter. With his bow and quiver the enraged Apollo descends from the rocky peak of Olympus. I do not merely see him descend, I hear him. At every step the arrows rattle about the shoulders of the wrathful god. He glides along like night. And now he sits opposite the ships – fearfully twangs the silver bow – he darts the first arrow at the mules and dogs. And then, with a more poisonous shaft, he strikes the men themselves; and everywhere without cessation break into flame the corpse-encumbered pyres. The musical painting which we hear in the words of the poet it is not possible to translate into another language. It is just as impossible to gather it from the material picture, although it is only a very trivial advantage which the poetic picture possesses. The chief advantage is that what the material painting drawn from him exhibits, the poet leads us up to through a whole gallery of pictures.

But, then, perhaps the pestilence is not an advantageous subject for painting. Here is another having more charms for the eye – the gods taking counsel together over their wine. A golden palace open to the sky, arbitrary groups of the most beautiful and the most worshipful forms, their cups in their hands, waited on by Hebe, the image of eternal youth. What architecture, what masses of light and shade, what contrasts, what manifold expression! Where can I begin, and where leave off, to feast my eyes? If the painter so enchants me, how much more will the poet! I turn to his pages, and find – that I am deceived. Four simple lines only, such as might serve for the inscription of a picture; the material for a picture is there, but they themselves do not make a picture :-

Οἱ δὲ θεοὶ πὰρ Ζηνὶ καθήμενοι ἠγορόωντο
Χρυσέῳ ἐν δαπέδῳ, μετὰ δέ σφισι πότνια "Ηβη
Νέκταρ ἐῳνοχόει· τοὶ δὲ χρυσέοις δεπάεσσι
Δειδέχατ’ ἀλλήλους, Τρώων πόλιν εἰσορόωντες.[113]

This an Apollonius[114] or an even more mediocre poet would have said equally well; and Homer here stands just as far below the painter as in the former case the painter stood below him.

Yet more, Caylus finds in the whole of the Fourth Book of the *Iliad* no other picture, not one, than in these four lines. 'However much', he remarks, 'the Fourth Book is marked by manifold encouragements to the attempt, owing to the abundance of brilliant and contrasted characters and to the art with which the poet shows us the entire multitude whom he will set in action – yet it is perfectly unusable for painting.' He might have added, rich as it is otherwise in that which we call poetic picture. For truly these are for number and perfection as remarkable as in any other Book. Where is there a more finished or more striking picture than that of Pandarus, as, on the incitement of Minerva, he breaks the truce and lets fly his arrow at Menelaus? Or that of the approach of the Grecian host? Or that of the two-sided, simultaneous onset? Or that of Ulysses' deed by which he avenges the death of his Leucus?

What, then, follows from the fact that not a few of the finest descriptions in Homer afford no picture for the artist, and that the artist can draw pictures

from him where he himself has none? That those which he has and the artist
can use would be very poverty-stricken pictures if they did not show more than
can be shown by the artist? What else do they, but give a negative to my former
question? That from the material paintings for which the poems of Homer
provide the subjects, however numerous they may be and however excellent,
nothing can be concluded as to the pictorial talent of the poet.

XIV

But if it is so, and if one poem may yield very happy results for the painter
yet itself be not pictorial; if, again, another in its turn may be very pictorial
and yet offer nothing to the painter; this is enough to dispose of Count Caylus'
notion, which would make this kind of utility the criterion or test of the poets
and settle their rank by the number of pictures which they provide for the
artist.[115]

Far be it from us, even if only by our silence, to allow this notion to gain
the authority of a rule. Milton would fall the first innocent sacrifice to it. For
it seems really that the contemptuous verdict which Caylus passes upon him
was not mere national prejudice, but rather a consequence of his supposed
principle. 'The loss of sight', he says, 'may well be the nearest resemblance
Milton bore to Homer.' True, Milton can fill no galleries. But if, so long as
I had the bodily eye, its sphere must also be the sphere of my inward eye, then
would I, in order to be free of this limitation, set a great value on the loss of
the former. The *Paradise Lost* is not less the first epic poem since Homer on the
ground of its providing few pictures, than the story of Christ's Passion is a poem
because we can hardly put the point of a needle into it without touching a
passage that might have employed a multitude of the greatest artists. The
Evangelists relate the facts with all the dry simplicity possible, and the artist
uses the manifold parts of the story without their having shown on their side
the smallest spark of pictorial genius. There are paintable and unpaintable
facts, and the historian can relate the most paintable in just as unpictorial a
fashion as the poet can represent the least paintable pictorially.

We are merely misled by the ambiguity of words if we take the matter
otherwise. A poetic picture is not necessarily that which can be transmuted
into a material painting; but every feature, every combination of features by
means of which the poet makes his subject so perceptible that we are more
clearly conscious of this subject than of his words is called pictorial, is styled
a picture, because it brings us nearer to the degree of illusion of which the
material painting is specially capable and which can most readily and most
easily be drawn from the material painting.

XV

Now the poet, as experience shows, can raise to this degree of illusion the representations even of other than visible objects. Consequently the artist must necessarily be denied whole classes of pictures in which the poet has the advantage over him. Dryden's Ode on St Cecilia's Day is full of musical pictures that cannot be touched by the paint-brush. But I will not lose myself in instances of the kind, from which in the end we learn nothing more than that colours are not tones and that eyes are not ears.

I will confine myself to the pictures of purely visible objects which are common to the poet and the painter. How comes it that many poetical pictures of this kind cannot be used by the painter, and, *vice versa*, many actual pictures lose the best part of their effect in the hands of the poet?

Examples may help us. I repeat it – the picture of Pandarus in the Fourth Book of the *Iliad* is one of the most finished and most striking in all Homer. From the seizing of the bow to the very flight of the arrow every moment is depicted, and all these moments are kept so close together, and yet so distinctly separate, that if we did not know how a bow was to be managed we might learn it from this picture alone.[116] Pandarus draws forth his bow, fixes the bowstring, opens his quiver, chooses a yet unused, well-feathered shaft, sets the arrow on the string, draws back both string and arrow down to the notch, the string is brought near to his breast and the iron head of the arrow to the bow; back flies the great bent bow with a twang, the bowstring whirs, off springs the arrow flying eager for its mark.

This admirable picture Caylus cannot have overlooked. What, then, did he find in it to render it incapable of employing his artist? And for what reason did he consider fitter for this purpose the assembly of the carousing gods in council? In the one, as in the other, we find visible subjects, and what more does the painter want than visible subjects in order to fill his canvas? The solution of the problem must be this. Although both subjects, as being visible, are alike capable of actual painting, yet there exists the essential distinction between them, that the former is a visible continuous action, the different parts of which occur step by step in succession of time, the latter, on the other hand, is a visible arrested action, the different parts of which develop side by side in space. But now, if painting, in virtue of her signs or the methods of her imitation, which she can combine only in space, must wholly renounce time, then continuous actions as such cannot be reckoned amongst her subjects; but she must content herself with actions set side by side, or with mere bodies which by their attitudes can be supposed an action. Poetry, on the other hand –

XVI

But I will turn to the foundations and try to argue the matter from first principles.[117]

My conclusion is this. If it is true that painting employs in its imitations quite other means or signs than poetry employs, the former – that is to say, figures and colours in space – but the latter articulate sounds in time; as, unquestionably, the signs used must have a definite relation to the thing signified, it follows that signs arranged together side by side can express only subjects which, or the various parts of which, exist thus side by side, whilst signs which succeed each other can express only subjects which, or the various parts of which, succeed each other.

Subjects which, or the various parts of which, exist side by side, may be called *bodies*. Consequently, bodies with their visible properties form the proper subjects of painting.

Subjects which or the various parts of which succeed each other may in general be called *actions*. Consequently, actions form the proper subjects of poetry.

Yet all bodies exist not in space alone, but also in time. They continue, and may appear differently at every moment and stand in different relations. Every one of these momentary appearances and combinations is the effect of one preceding and can be the cause of one following, and accordingly be likewise the central point of an action. Consequently, painting can also imitate actions, but only by way of suggestion through bodies.

On the other hand, actions cannot subsist for themselves, but must attach to certain things or persons. Now in so far as these things are bodies or are regarded as bodies, poetry too depicts bodies, but only by way of suggestion through actions.

Painting, in her co-existing compositions, can use only one single moment of the action, and must therefore choose the most pregnant, from which what precedes and follows will be most easily apprehended.

Just in the same manner poetry also can use, in her continuous imitations, only one single property of the bodies, and must therefore choose that one which calls up the most living picture of the body on that side from which she is regarding it. Here, indeed, we find the origin of the rule which insists on the unity and consistency of descriptive epithets, and on economy in the delineations of bodily subjects.

This is a dry chain of reasoning, and I should put less trust in it if I did not find it completely confirmed by Homer's practice, or if, rather, it were not Homer's practice itself which had led me to it. Only by these principles can the great manner of the Greeks be settled and explained, and its rightness established against the opposite manner of so many modern poets, who would emulate the painter in a department where they must necessarily be outdone by him.

Homer, I find, paints nothing but continuous actions, and all bodies, all single things, he paints only by their share in those actions, and in general only by one feature. What wonder, then, that the painter, where Homer himself paints, finds little or nothing for him to do, his harvest arising only there where the story brings together a multitude of beautiful bodies, in beautiful attitudes, in a place favourable to art, the poet himself painting these bodies, attitudes, places, just as little as he chooses? Let the reader run through the whole succession of pictures piece by piece, as Caylus suggests, and he will discover in every one of them evidence for our contention.

Here, then, I leave the Count, who wishes to make the painter's palette the touchstone of the poet, that I may expound in closer detail the manner of Homer.

For one thing, I say, Homer commonly names one feature only. A ship is to him now the black ship, now the hollow ship, now the swift ship, at most the well-rowed black ship. Beyond that he does not enter on a picture of the ship. But certainly of the navigating, the putting to sea, the disembarking of the ship, he makes a detailed picture, one from which the painter must make five or six separate pictures if he would get it in its entirety upon his canvas.

If indeed special circumstances compel Homer to fix our glance for a while on some single corporeal object, in spite of this no picture is made of it which the painter could follow with his brush; for Homer knows how, by innumerable artifices, to set this object in a succession of moments, at each of which it assumes a different appearance, and in the last of which the painter must await it in order to show us, fully arisen, what in the poet we see arising. For instance, if Homer wishes to let us see the chariot of Juno, then Hebe must put it together piece by piece before our eyes. We see the wheels, the axles, the seat, the pole and straps and traces, not so much as it is when complete, but as it comes together under the hands of Hebe. On the wheels alone does the poet expend more than one feature, showing us the brazen spokes, the golden rims, the tyres of bronze, the silver hub, in fullest detail. We might suggest that as there were more wheels than one, so in the description just as much more time must be given to them as their separate putting-on would actually itself require.

> Ἥβη δ' ἀμφ' ὀχέεσσι θοῶς βάλε καμπύλα κύκλα,
> Χάλκεα ὀκτάκνημα, σιδηρέῳ ἄξονι ἀμφίς.
> Τῶν ἤτοι χρυσέη ἴτυς ἄφθιτος, αὐτὰρ ὕπερθεν
> Χάλκε' ἐπίσσωτρα προσαρηρότα, θαῦμα ἰδέσθαι·
> Πλῆμναι δ' ἀργύρου εἰσὶ περίδρομοι ἀμφοτέρωθεν·
> Δίφρος δὲ χρυσέοισι καὶ ἀργυρέοισιν ἱμᾶσιν
> Ἐντέταται, δοιαὶ δὲ περίδρομοι ἄντυγές εἰσι.
> Τοῦ δ' ἐξ ἀργύρεος ῥυμὸς πέλεν· αὐτὰρ ἐπ' ἄκρῳ
> Δῆσε χρύσειον καλὸν ζυγόν, ἐν δὲ λέπαδνα
> Κάλ' ἔβαλε, χρύσεια.[118]

If Homer would show us how Agamemnon was dressed, then the King must put on his whole attire piece by piece before our eyes: the soft undervest, the great mantle, the fine laced boots, the sword; and now he is ready and grasps the sceptre. We see the attire as the poet paints the action of attiring; another would have described the garments down to the smallest ribbon, and we should have seen nothing of the action.

Μαλακὸν δ' ἔνδυνε χιτῶνα,
Καλὸν, νηγάτεον, περὶ δ' αὖ μέγα βάλλετο φᾶρος·
Ποσσὶ δ' ὑπαὶ λιπαροῖσιν ἐδήσατο καλὰ πέδιλα,
'Αμφὶ δ' ἄρ' ὤμοισιν βάλετο ξίφος ἀργυρόηλον·
Εἵλετο δὲ σκῆπτρον πατρώϊον, ἄφθιτον αἰεί.[119]

And of this sceptre which here is called merely the paternal, ancestral sceptre, as in another place he calls a similar one merely χρυσείοις ἥλοισι πεπαρμένον – that is, the sceptre mounted with studs of gold – if, I say, of this mighty sceptre we are to have a fuller and exacter picture, what, then, does Homer? Does he paint for us, besides the golden nails, the wood also and the carved knob? Perhaps he might if the description were intended for a book of heraldry, so that in after times one like to it might be made precisely to pattern. And yet I am certain that many a modern poet would have made just such a heraldic description, with the naive idea that he has himself so painted it because the painter may possibly follow him. But what does Homer care how far he leaves the painter behind? Instead of an image he gives us the story of the sceptre: first, it is being wrought by Vulcan; then it gleams in the hands of Jupiter; again, it marks the office of Mercury; once more, it is the marshal's baton of the warlike Pelops, and yet again, the shepherd's crook of peace-loving Atreus.

Σκῆπτρον ἔχων, τὸ μὲν Ἥφαιστος κάμε τεύχων.
Ἥφαιστος μὲν δῶκε Διὶ Κρονίωνι ἄνακτι,
Αὐτὰρ ἄρα Ζεὺς δῶκε διακτόρῳ 'Αργεϊφόντῃ·
Ἑρμείας δὲ ἄναξ δῶκεν Πέλοπι πληξίππῳ,
Αὐτὰρ ὁ αὖτε Πέλοψ δῶκ' 'Ατρέϊ, ποιμένι λαῶν·
'Ατρεὺς δὲ θνῄσχων ἔλιπε πολύαρνι Θυέστῃ,
Αὐτὰρ ὁ αὖτε Θυέστ' 'Αγαμέμνονι λεῖπε φορῆναι,
Πολλῇσι νήσοισι καὶ 'Αργεϊ παντὶ ἀνάσσειν.[120]

And so in the end I know this sceptre better than if a painter had laid it before my eyes or a second Vulcan delivered it into my hands. It would not surprise me if I found that one of the old commentators of Homer had admired this passage as the most perfect allegory of the origin, progress, establishment, and hereditary succession of the royal power amongst mankind. True, I should smile if I were to read that Vulcan, the maker of this sceptre, as fire, as the most indispensable thing for the preservation of mankind, represented in general the satisfaction of those wants which moved the first men to subject themselves to the rule of an individual monarch; that the first king, a son of Time (Ζεὺς Κρονίων),[121] was an honest ancient who wished to share his power with, or wholly transfer it to, a wise and eloquent man, a Mercury (Διακτόρῳ 'Αργεϊφόντῃ);[122] that the wily orator, at the time when the infant State was threatened by foreign foes, resigned his supreme power to the bravest warrior (Πέλοπι πληξίππῳ);[123] that the brave warrior, when he had quelled the aggressors and made the realm secure, was able to hand it over to his son, who, as a peace-loving ruler, as a benevolent shepherd of his people (ποιμὴν λαῶν),[124] made them acquainted with luxury and abundance, whereby after his death the wealthiest of his relations (πολύαρνι Θυέστη)[125] had the way opened to him for attracting to himself by presents and bribes that which hitherto only confidence had conferred and which merit had considered more a burden than an honour, and to secure it to his family for the future as a kind of purchased estate. I should smile, but nevertheless should be confirmed in my esteem for the poet to whom so much meaning can be attributed. – This, however, is a digression, and I am now regarding the story of the sceptre merely as an artifice to make us tarry over the one particular object without being drawn into the tedious description of its parts. Even when Achilles swears by his sceptre to avenge the contempt with which Agamemnon has treated him, Homer gives us the history of this sceptre. We see it growing green upon the mountains, the axe cutting it from the trunk, stripping it of leaves and bark and making it fit to serve the judges of the people for a symbol of their godlike dignity.

Ναὶ μὰ τόδε σκῆπτρον, τὸ μὲν οὔποτε φύλλα καὶ ὄζους
Φύσει, ἐπεὶ δὴ πρῶτα τομὴν ἐν ὄρεσσι λέλοιπεν,
Οὐδ' ἀναθηλήσει· περὶ γάρ ῥά ἑ χαλκὸς ἔλεψε
Φύλλα τε καὶ φλοιόν· νῦν αὖτέ μιν υἷες 'Αχαιῶν
'Εν παλάμῃς φορέουσι δικασπόλοι, οἵ τε θέμιστας
Πρὸς Διὸς εἰρύαται...[126]

It was not so much incumbent upon Homer to depict two staves of different material and shape as to furnish us with a symbol of the difference in the powers of which these staves were the sign. The former a work of Vulcan, the latter carved by an unknown hand in the mountains; the former the ancient property of a noble house, the latter intended for any fist that can grasp it; the former extended by a monarch over all Argos and many an isle besides, the latter borne by any one out of the midst of the Grecian hosts, one to whom with others the guarding of the laws had been committed. Such was actually the distance that separated Agamemnon from Achilles, a distance which Achilles himself, in all the blindness of his wrath, could not help admitting.

Yet not in those cases alone where Homer combines with his descriptions this kind of ulterior purpose, but even where he has to do with nothing but the picture, he will distribute this picture in a sort of story of the object, in order to let its parts, which we see side by side in Nature, follow in his painting after each other and as it were keep step with the flow of the narrative. For instance, he would paint for us the bow of Pandarus – a bow of horn, of such and such a length, well polished, and mounted with gold plate at the extremities. How does he manage it? Does he count out before us all these properties dryly one after the other? Not at all; that would be to sketch, to make a copy of such a bow, but not to paint it. He begins with the chase of the deer, from the horns of which the bow was made; Pandarus had waylaid and killed it amongst the crags; the horns were of extraordinary length, and so he destined them for a bow; they are wrought, the maker joins them, mounts them, polishes them. And thus, as we have already said, with the poet we see arising what with the painter we can only see as already arisen.

Τόξον ἐΰξοον ἰξάλου αἰγὸς
'Αγρίου, ὃν ῥά ποτ' αὐτὸς ὑπὸ στέρνοιο τυχήσας
Πέτρης ἐκβαίνοντα δεδεγμένος ἐν προδοκῇσι,
Βεβλήκει πρὸς στῆθος· ὁ δ' ὕπτιος ἔμπεσε πέτρῃ.
Τοῦ κέρα ἐκ κεφαλῆς ἐκκαιδεκάδωρα πεφύκει·
Καὶ τὰ μὲν ἀσκήσας κεραοξόος ἤραρε τέκτων,
Πᾶν δ' ἐῢ λειήνας χρυσέην ἐπέθηκε κορώνην.[127]

I should never have done, if I were to cite all the instances of this kind. A multitude of them will occur to everyone who knows his Homer.

XVII

But, some will object, the signs or characters which poetry employs are not solely such as succeed each other; they may be also arbitrary;[128] and, as arbitrary signs, they are certainly capable of representing bodies just as they exist in space. We find instances of this in Homer himself, for we have only to remember his Shield of Achilles in order to have the most decisive example in how detailed and yet poetical a manner some single thing can be depicted, with its various parts side by side.

I will reply to this twofold objection. I call it twofold, because a just conclusion must prevail even without examples, and, on the other hand, the example of Homer weighs with me even if I know not how to justify it by any argument. It is true, as the signs of speech are arbitrary, so it is perfectly possible that by it we can make the parts of a body follow each other just as truly as in actuality they are found existing side by side. Only this is a property of speech and its signs in general, but not in so far as it suits best the purposes of poetry. The poet is not concerned merely to be intelligible, his representations should not merely be clear and plain, though this may satisfy the prose writer. He desires rather to make the ideas awakened by him within us living things, so that for the moment we realise the true sensuous impressions of the objects he describes, and cease in this moment of illusion to be conscious of the means – namely, his words – which he employs for his purpose. This is the substance of what we have already said of the poetic picture. But the poet should always paint; and now let us see how far bodies with their parts set side by side are suitable for this kind of painting.

How do we arrive at the distinct representation of a thing in space? First we regard its parts singly, then the combination of these parts, and finally the whole. Our senses perform these various operations with so astonishing a swiftness that they seem to us but one, and this swiftness is imperatively necessary if we are to arrive at a conception of the whole, which is nothing more than the result of the conceptions of the parts and their combination. Provided, then, the poet leads us in the most beautiful order from one part of the object to another; provided he knows also how to make the combination of those parts equally clear – how much time does he need for that? What the eye sees at a glance, he counts out to us gradually, with a perceptible slowness, and often it happens that when we come to the last feature we have already forgotten the first. Nevertheless, we have to frame a whole from those features; to the eye the parts beheld remain constantly present, and it can run over them again and again; for the ear, on the contrary, the parts heard are lost if they do not abide in the memory. And if they so abide, what trouble, what effort it costs to renew their impressions, all of them in their due order, so vividly, to think of them together with even a moderate swiftness, and thus to arrive at an eventual conception of the whole. Let us try it by an example which may be called a masterpiece of its kind:–[129]

> Dort ragt das hohe Haupt vom edeln Enziane
> Weit übern niedern Chor der Pöbelkräuter hin,
> Ein ganzes Blumenvolk dient unter seiner Fahne,
> Sein blauer Bruder selbst bückt sich und ehret ihn.
> Der Blumen helles Gold, in Strahlen umgebogen,
> Thürmt sich am Stengel auf, und krönt sein grau Gewand,
> Der Blätter glattes Weiß, mit tiefem Grün durchzogen,
> Strahlt von dem bunten Blitz von feuchtem Diamant.
> Gerechtestes Gesetz! daß Kraft sich Zier vermähle,
> In einem schönen Leib wohnt eine schönre Seele.
>
> Hier kriecht ein niedrig Kraut, gleich einem grauen Nebel,
> Dem die Natur sein Blatt im Kreuze hingelegt;
> Die holde Blume zeigt die zwei vergöldten Schnäbel,
> Die ein von Amethyst gebildter Vogel trägt.
> Dort wirft ein glänzend Blatt, in Finger ausgekerbt,
> Auf einen hellen Bach den grünen Widerschein;
> Der Blumen zarten Schnee, den matter Purpur färbet,
> Schließt ein gestreifter Stern in weiße Strahlen ein.
> Smaragd und Rosen blühn auch auf zertretner Heide,
> Und Felsen decken sich mit einem Purpurkleide.

Here are weeds and flowers which the learned poet paints with much art and fidelity to Nature. Paints, but without any illusion whatever. I will not say that out of this picture he who has never seen these weeds and flowers can make no idea of them, or as good as none. It may be that all poetic pictures require some preliminary acquaintance with their subjects. Neither will I deny that for one who possesses such an acquaintance here the poet may not have awakened a more vivid idea of some parts. I only ask him, how does it stand with the conception of the whole? If this also is to be more vivid, then no single parts must stand out, but the higher light must appear divided equally amongst them all, our imagination must be able to run over them all with equal swiftness, in order to unite in one from them that which in Nature we see united in one. Is this the case here? And if it is not the case, how could anyone maintain 'that the most perfect drawing of a painter must be entirely lifeless and dark compared with this poetic portrayal'?[130] It remains infinitely below that which lines and colours on canvas can express, and the critic who bestows on it this exaggerated praise must have regarded it from an utterly false point of view: he must have looked rather at the ornaments which the poet has woven into it, at the heightening of the subject above the mere vegetative life, at the development of the inner perfection to which the outward beauty serves merely as a shell, than at the beauty itself and at the degree of life and resemblance in the picture which the painter and which the poet can assure to us from it. Nevertheless, we are concerned here purely with the latter, and whoever says that the mere lines:–

> Der Blumen helles Gold, in Strahlen umgebogen,
> Thürmt sich am Stengel auf, und krönt sein grün Gewand,
> Der Blätter glattes Weiß, mit tiefem Grün durchzogen,
> Strahlt von dem bunten Blitz von feuchtem Diamant

– that these lines in respect of their impression can compete with the imitation of a Huysum,[131] can never have interrogated his feelings, or must be deliberately denying them. They may, indeed, if we have the flower itself in our hands, be recited concerning it with excellent effect; but in themselves alone they say little or nothing. I hear in every word the toiling poet, and am far enough from seeing the thing itself.

Once more, then; I do not deny to speech in general the power of portraying a bodily whole by its parts: speech can do so, because its signs or characters, although they follow one another consecutively, are nevertheless arbitrary signs; but I do deny it to speech as the medium of poetry, because such verbal delineations of bodies fail of the illusion on which poetry particularly depends, and this illusion, I contend, must fail them for the reason that the *co-existence* of the physical object comes into collision with the *consecutiveness* of speech, and the former being resolved into the latter, the dismemberment of the whole into its parts is certainly made easier, but the final reunion of those parts into a whole is made uncommonly difficult and not seldom impossible.

Wherever, then, illusion does not come into the question, where one has only to do with the understanding of one's readers and aims only at plain and as far as possible complete concepts, those delineations of bodies (which we have excluded from poetry) may quite well find their place, and not the prose-writer alone, but the didactic poet (for where he dogmatises he is not a poet) can employ them with much advantage. So Virgil, for instance, in his poem on agriculture, delineates a cow suitable for breeding from:–

> ...Optima torvae
> Forma bovis, cui turpe caput, cui plurima cervix,
> Et crurum tenus a mento palearia pendent;
> Tum longo nullus lateri modus: omnia magna,
> Pes etiam, et camuris hirtae sub cornibus aures.
> Nec mihi displiceat maculis insignis et albo,
> Aut juga detractans interdumque aspera cornu
> Et faciem tauro propior, quaeque ardua tota,
> Et gradiens ima verrit vestigia cauda.[132]

Or a beautiful foal:—

> ... Illi ardua cervix
> Argutumque caput, brevis alvus, obesaque terga,
> Luxuriatque toris animosum pectus, etc.[133]

For who does not see that here the poet is concerned rather with the setting forth of the parts than with the whole? He wants to reckon up for us the characteristics of a fine foal and of a well-formed cow, in order to enable us, when we have more or less taken note of these, to judge of the excellence of the one or the other; whether, however, all these characteristics can be easily gathered together into one living picture or not, that might be to him a matter of indifference.

Beyond such performances as these, the detailed pictures of physical objects, barring the above-mentioned Homeric artifice of changing the Co-existing into an actual Successive, has always been recognised by the best judges as a frigid kind of sport for which little or nothing of genius is demanded. 'When the poetic dabbler', says Horace, 'can do nothing more, he begins to paint a hedge, an altar, a brook winding through pleasant meads, a brawling stream, or a rainbow:—

> ... Lucus et ara Dianae
> Et properantis aquae per amoenos ambitus agros,
> Aut flumen Rhenum, aut pluvius describitur arcus.'[134]

Pope, in his manhood, looked back on the pictorial efforts of his poetic childhood with great contempt. He expressly required that whosoever would not unworthily bear the name of poet should as early as possible renounce the lust for description, and declared a merely descriptive poem to be a dinner of nothing but soup.[135] Of Herr von Kleist I can avow that he was far from proud of his 'Spring': had he lived longer, he would have given it an entirely different shape.[136] He thought of putting some design into it, and mused on means by which that multitude of pictures which he seemed to have snatched haphazard, now here, now there, from the limitless field of rejuvenated Nature, might be made to arise in a natural order before his eyes and follow each other in a natural succession. He would at the same time have done what Marmontel,[137] doubtless on the occasion of his Eclogues,[138] recommended to several German poets; from a series of pictures but sparingly interspersed with sensations he would have made a succession of sensations but sparingly interspersed with pictures.

XVIII

And yet may not Homer himself sometimes have lapsed into these frigid delineations of physical objects?

I will hope that there are only a few passages to which in this case appeal can be made; and I am assured that even these few are of such a kind as rather to confirm the rule from which they seem to be exceptions. It still holds good;

succession in time is the sphere of the poet, as space is that of the painter. To bring two necessarily distant points of time into one and the same picture, as Fr. Mazzuoli[139] has done with the Rape of the Sabine Women and their reconciling their husbands to their kinsfolk, or as Titian with the whole story of the Prodigal Son, his dissolute life, his misery, and his repentance, is nothing but an invasion of the poet's sphere by the painter, which good taste can never sanction. The several parts or things which in Nature I must needs take in at a glance if they are to produce a whole – to reckon these up one by one to the reader, in order to form for him a picture of the whole, is nothing but an invasion of the painter's sphere by the poet, who expends thereby a great deal of imagination to no purpose. Still, as two friendly, reasonable neighbours will not at all permit that one of them shall make too free with the most intimate concerns of the other, yet will exercise in things of less importance a mutual forbearance and on either side condone trifling interferences with one's strict rights to which circumstances may give occasion, so it is with Painting and Poetry.

It is unnecessary here for my purpose to point out that in great historical pictures the single moment is almost always amplified to some extent, and that there is perhaps no single composition very rich in figures where every figure has completely the movement and posture which at the moment of the main action it ought to have; one is earlier, another later, than historical truth would require. This is a liberty which the master must make good by certain niceties of arrangement, by the position or distance of his *personae*, such as will permit them to take a greater or a smaller share in what is passing at the moment. Let me here avail myself of but one remark which Herr Mengs has made concerning the drapery of Raphael.[140] 'All folds', he says, 'have with him their reasons, it may be from their own weight or by the pulling of the limbs. We can often see from them how they have been at an earlier moment; even in this Raphael seeks significance. One sees from the folds whether a leg or an arm, before the moment depicted, has stood in front or behind, whether the limb has moved from curvature to extension, or after being stretched out is now bending.' It is undeniable that the artist in this case brings two different moments into one. For as the foot which has rested behind and now moves forward is immediately followed by the part of the dress resting upon it, unless the dress be of very stiff material and for that very reason is altogether inconvenient to paint, so there is no moment in which the dress makes a fold different in the slightest from that which the present position of the limb demands; but if we permit it to make another fold, then we have the previous moment of the dress and the present moment of the limb. Nevertheless, who will be so particular with the artist who finds his advantage in showing us these two moments together? Who will not rather praise him for having the intelligence and the courage to commit a fault so trifling in order to attain a greater perfection of expression?

The poet is entitled to equal indulgence. His progressive imitation properly allows him to touch but one single side, one single property of his physical subject at a time. But if the happy construction of his language permits him to do this with a single word, why should he not also venture now and then to add a second such word? Why not even, if it is worth the trouble, a third? Or, indeed, perhaps a fourth? I have said that to Homer a ship was either the black ship, or the hollow ship, or the swift ship, or at most the well-rowed black ship. This is to be understood of his manner in general. Here and there a passage occurs where he adds the third descriptive epithet: Καμπύλα κύκλα, χάλκεα, ὀκτάκνημα, round, brazen, eight-spoked wheels.[141] Even the fourth: ἀσπίδα πάντοσε ἴσην, καλήν, χαλκείην, ἐξήλατον, a completely polished, beautiful, brazen, chased shield.[142] Who will blame him for that? Who will not rather owe him thanks for this little exuberance, when he feels what an excellent effect it may have in a suitable place?

I am unwilling, however, to argue the poet's or the painter's proper justification from the simile I have employed, of the two friendly neighbours. A mere simile proves and justifies nothing. But they must be justified in this way: just as in the one case, with the painter, the two distinct moments touch each other so closely and immediately that they may without offence count as but one, so also in the other case, with the poet, the several strokes for the different parts and properties in space succeed each other so quickly, in such a crowded moment, that we can believe we hear all of them at once.

And in this, I may remark, his splendid language served Homer marvellously. It allowed him not merely all possible freedom in the combining and heaping-up of epithets, but it had, too, for their heaped-up epithets an order so happy as quite to remedy the disadvantage arising from the suspension of their application. In one or several of these facilities the modern languages are universally lacking. Those, like the French, which, to give an example, for καμπύλα κύκλα, χάλκεα, ὀκτάκνημα, must use the circumlocution 'the round wheels which were of brass and had eight spokes', express the sense, but destroy the picture. The sense, moreover, is here nothing, and the picture everything; and the former without the latter makes the most vivid poet the most tedious babbler – a fate that has frequently befallen our good Homer under the pen of the conscientious Madame Dacier.[143] Our German tongue, again, can, it is true, generally translate the Homeric epithets by epithets equivalent and just as terse, but in the advantageous order of them it cannot match the Greek. We say, indeed, 'Die runden, ehernen, achtspeichigten';[144] but 'Räder'[145] trails behind. Who does not feel that three different predicates, before we know the subject, can make but a vague and confused picture? The Greek joins the subject and the first predicate immediately, and lets the other follow after; he says, 'Runde Räder, eherne, achtspeichigte'. So we know at once of what he is speaking, and are made acquainted, in consonance with the natural order of thought, first with the thing and then with its accidents. This advantage our language does not possess. Or, shall I say, possesses it and can only very seldom use it without ambiguity? The two things are one. For when we would place the epithets after, they must stand *in statu absoluto*; we must say, '*Runde Räder, ehern und achtspeichigt*'. But in this *status* our adjectives are exactly like adverbs, and must, if we attach them as such to the next verb which is predicated of the thing, produce a meaning not seldom wholly false, and, at best, invariably ambiguous.

But here I am dwelling on trifles, and seem to have forgotten the Shield – Achilles' Shield, that famous picture in respect of which especially Homer was from of old regarded as a teacher of painting. A shield, people will say – that is surely a single physical object, the description of which and its parts ranged side by side is not permissible to a poet? And this particular Shield, in its material, in its form, in all the figures that covered the vast surface of it, Homer has described in more than a hundred splendid verses, with such exactness and detail that it has been easy for modern artists to make a replica of it alike in every feature.

To this special objection I reply, that I have replied to it already. Homer, that is to say, paints the Shield not as a finished and complete thing, but as a thing in process. Here once more he has availed himself of the famous artifice, turning the *co-existing* of his design into a *consecutive*, and thereby making of the tedious painting of a physical object the living picture of an action. We see not the Shield, but the divine artificer at work upon it. He steps up with hammer and tongs to his anvil, and after he has forged the plates from the rough ore, the pictures which he has selected for its adornment stand out one after another before our eyes under his artistic chiselling. Nor do we lose sight of him again until all is finished. When it is complete, we are amazed at the work, but it is with the believing amazement of an eye-witness who has seen it in the making.

The same cannot be said of the Shield of Aeneas in Virgil. The Roman poet either did not realise the subtlety of his model here, or the things that he wanted to put upon his Shield appeared to him to be of a kind that could not well admit of being shown in execution. They were prophecies, which could not have been uttered by the god in our presence as plainly as the poet afterwards expounds them. Prophecies, as such, demand an obscurer language, in which the actual names of persons yet-to-be may not fitly be pronounced. Yet these veritable names, to all appearance, were the most important things of all to the poet and courtier. If, however, this excuses him, it does not remove the unhappy effect of his deviation from the Homeric way. Readers of any delicacy of taste will justify me here. The preparations which Vulcan makes for his labour are almost the same in Virgil as in Homer. But instead of what we see in Homer – that is to say, not merely the preparations for the work, but also the work itself – Virgil after he has given us a general view of the busy god with his Cyclops:–

> Ingentem clypeum informant...
> ...Alii ventosis follibus auras
> Accipiunt redduntque, alii stridentia tingunt

Aera lacu. Gemit impositis incudibus antrum.
Illi inter sese multa vi brachia tollunt
In numerum, versantque tenaci forcipe massam —[146]

drops the curtain at once and transports us to another scene, bringing us
gradually into the valley where Venus arrives at Aeneas' side with the armour
that has meanwhile been completed. She leans the weapons against the trunk
of an oak-tree, and when the hero has sufficiently gazed at, and admired, and
touched and tested them, the description of the pictures on the Shield begins,
and, with the everlasting: 'Here is', 'and there is', 'near by stands', and 'not
far off one sees', becomes so frigid and tedious that all the poetic ornament
which Virgil could give it was needed to prevent us finding it unendurable.
Moreover, as this picture is not drawn by Aeneas as one who rejoices in the
mere figures and knows nothing of their significance:—

...rerumque ignarus imagine gaudet;[147]

nor even by Venus, although conceivably she must know just as much of the
future fortunes of her dear grandchildren as her obliging husband;[148] but
proceeds from the poet's own mouth. The progress of the action meanwhile
is obviously at a standstill. No single one of his characters takes any share in
it; nor does anything represented on the Shield have any influence, even the
smallest, on what is to follow; the witty courtier shines out everywhere,
trimming up his matter with every kind of flattering allusion, but not the great
genius, depending on the proper inner vitality of his work and despising all
extraneous expedients for lending it interest. The Shield of Aeneas is consequently a sheer interpolation, simply and only intended to flatter the
national pride of the Romans, a foreign tributary which the poet leads into
his main stream in order to give it a livelier motion. The Shield of Achilles,
on the other hand, is a rich natural outgrowth of the fertile soil from which
it springs; for a Shield had to be made, and as the needful thing never comes
bare and without grace from the hands of the divinity, the Shield had also to
be embellished. But the art was, to treat these embellishments merely as such,
to inweave them into the stuff, in order to show them to us only by means of
the latter; and this could only be done by Homer's method. Homer lets Vulcan
elaborate ornaments because he is to make a Shield that is worthy of himself. Virgil, on the other hand, appears to let him make the Shield for the
sake of its ornaments, considering them important enough to be particularly
described, after the Shield itself has long been finished.

XIX

The objections which the elder Scaliger, Perrault, Terrasson, and others make
to the Shield in Homer are well known. Equally well known is the reply which
Dacier, Boivin, and Pope made to them.[149] In my judgement, however, the

latter go too far, and, relying on their good cause, introduce arguments that are not only indefensible, but contribute little to the poet's justification.

In order to meet the main objection – that Homer has crowded the Shield with a multitude of figures such as could not possibly find room within its circumference – Boivin undertook to have it drawn, with a note of the necessary dimensions. His notion of the various concentric circles is very ingenious, although the words of the poet give not the slightest suggestion of it, whilst, furthermore, not a trace of proof is to be found that the ancients possessed shields divided off in this manner. Seeing that Homer himself calls it σάκος πάντοσε δεδαιδαλμένον – 'a shield artfully wrought upon all sides' – I would rather, in order to reserve more room, have taken in aid the concave surface; for it is well known that the ancient artists did not leave this vacant, as the Shield of Minerva by Phidias proves.[150] Yet it was not even enough for Boivin to decline availing himself of this advantage; he further increased without necessity the representations themselves for which he was obliged to provide room in the space thus diminished by half, separating into two or three distinct pictures what in the poet is obviously a single picture only. I know very well what moved him to do so, but it ought not to have moved him; instead of troubling himself to give satisfaction to the demands of his opponents, he should have shown them that their demands were illegitimate.

I shall be able to make my meaning clearer by an example. When Homer says of the one City:–

Λαοὶ δ' εἰν ἀγορῇ ἔσαν ἀθρόοι· ἔνθα δὲ νεῖκος
Ὠρώρει, δύο δ' ἄνδρες ἐνείκεον εἵνεκα ποινῆς
Ἀνδρὸς ἀποφθιμένου· ὁ μὲν εὔχετο πάντ' ἀποδοῦναι
Δήμῳ πιφαύσκων, ὁ δ' ἀναίνετο μηδὲν ἑλέσθαι·
Ἄμφω δ' ἱέσθην ἐπὶ ἴστορι πεῖραρ ἑλέσθαι.
Λαοὶ δ' ἀμφοτέροισιν ἐπήπυον, ἀμφὶς ἀρωγοί·
Κήρυκες δ' ἄρα λαὸν ἐρήτυον· οἱ δὲ γέροντες
Εἵατ' ἐπὶ ξεστοῖσι λίθοις ἱερῷ ἐνὶ κύκλῳ,
Σκῆπτρα δὲ κηρύκων ἐν χέρσ' ἔχον ἠεροφώνων·
Τοῖσιν ἔπειτ' ἤϊσσον, ἀμοιβηδὶς δὲ δίκαζον.
Κεῖτο δ' ἄρ' ἐν μέσσοισι δύω χρυσοῖο τάλαντα –[151]

he is not then, in my view, trying to sketch more than a single picture – the picture of a public lawsuit on the questionable satisfaction of a heavy fine for the striking of a death-blow. The artist who would carry out this sketch cannot in any single effort avail himself of more than a single moment of the same; either the moment of the arraignment, or of the examination of witnesses, or of the sentence, or whatever other moment, before or after, he considers the most suitable. This single moment he makes as pregnant as possible, and endows it with all the illusions which art commands (art, rather than poetry) in the representation of visible objects. Surpassed so greatly on this side, what can the poet who is to paint this very design in words, and has no wish entirely to suffer shipwreck – what can he do but in like manner avail himself of his own peculiar advantages? And what are these? The liberty to enlarge on what has preceded and what follows the single moment of the work of art, and the power thus to show us not only that which the artist has shown, but also that which he can only leave us to guess. By this liberty and this power alone the poet draws level with the artist, and their works are then likest to each other when the effect of each is equally vivid; and not when the one conveys to the soul through the ear neither more nor less than the other can represent to the eye. This is the principle that should have guided Boivin in judging this passage in Homer; he would then not so much have made distinct pictures out of it as have observed in it distinct moments of time. True, he could not well have united in a single picture all that Homer tells us; the accusation and the defence, the production of witnesses, the acclamations of the divided people, the effort of the heralds to allay the tumult, and the decisions of the judge, are things which follow each other and cannot subsist side by side. Yet what, in the language of the schools, was not *actu* contained in the picture lay in it *virtute*,[152] and the only true way of copying in words a material painting is this – to unite the latter with the actually visible, and refuse to be bound by the limits of art, within which the poet can indeed enumerate the *data* for a picture, but never produce the picture itself.

Just so is it when Boivin divides the picture of the besieged city[153] into three different tableaux. He might just as well have divided it into twelve as into three. For as he did not at all grasp the spirit of the poet, and required him to be subject to the unities of the material painting, he might have found far more violations of these unities, so that it had almost been necessary to assign to every separate stroke of the poet a separate section of the Shield. But, in my opinion, Homer has not altogether more than ten distinct pictures upon the entire Shield, every one of which he introduces with the phrases ἐν μὲν ἔτευξε, *or* ἐν δὲ ποίησε, *or* ἐν δ᾽ ἐτίθει, *or* ἐν δὲ ποίκιλλε ᾽Αμφιγυήεις.[154] Where these introductory words do not occur one has no right to suppose a separate picture; on the contrary, all which they unite must be regarded as a single picture to which there is merely wanting the arbitrary concentration in a single point of time – a thing the poet was in nowise constrained to indicate. Much rather, had he indicated it, had he confined himself strictly to it, had he not admitted the smallest feature which in the actual execution could not be combined with it – in a word, had he managed the matter exactly as his critics demand, it is true that then these gentlemen would have found nothing to set down against him, but indeed neither would a man of taste have found anything to admire.

Pope was not only pleased with Boivin's plan of dividing and designing, but thought of doing something else of his own, by now further showing that each of these dismembered pictures was planned according to the strictest rules of painting as it is practised today. Contrast, perspective, the three unities – all these he found observed in the best manner possible. And this, although he certainly was well aware that, according to the testimony of quite trustworthy witnesses, painting in the time of the Trojan War was still in its cradle; so that either Homer must, by virtue of his god-like genius, not so much have adhered to what painting then or in his own time could perform, as, rather, have divined what painting in general was capable of performing; or even those witnesses themselves cannot be so trustworthy that they should be preferred to the ocular demonstration of the artistic Shield itself. The former anyone may believe who will; of the latter at least no one can be persuaded who knows something more of the history of art than the mere data of historians. For, that painting in Homer's day was still in its infancy, he believes not merely because a Pliny or such another says so, but above all because he judges, from the works of art which the ancients esteemed, that many centuries later they had not got much further; he knows, for instance, that the paintings of Polygnotus are far from standing the test which Pope believes would be passed by the pictures on the Shield of Homer. The two great works at Delphi of the master just mentioned, of : hich Pausanias has left us so circumstantial a description,[155] are obviously without any perspective. This aspect of art was entirely unknown to the ancients, and what Pope adduces in order to prove that Homer had already some conception of it, proves nothing more than that Pope's own conception of it was extremely imperfect. 'That Homer', he says, 'was not a stranger to aerial perspective, appears in his expressly marking the distance of object from object: he tells us, for instance, that the two spies lay a little remote from the other figures; and that the oak, under which was spread the banquet of the reapers, stood *apart*: what he says of the valley sprinkled all over with cottages and flocks, appears to be a description of a large country in perspective. And indeed, a general argument for this may be drawn from the number of figures on the shield; which could not be all expressed in their full magnitude: and this is therefore a sort of proof that the art of lessening them according to perspective was known at that time.'[156] The mere observation of the optical experience that a thing appears smaller at a distance than close at hand, is far indeed from giving perspective to a picture. Perspective demands a single viewpoint, a definite natural field of vision, and it was this that was wanting in ancient paintings. The base in the pictures of Polygnotus was not horizontal, but towards the background raised so prodigiously that the figures which should appear to stand behind one another appeared to stand above one another. And if this arrangement of the different figures and their groups were general, as may be inferred from the ancient bas-reliefs, where the hindmost always stand higher than the foremost and look over their heads, then it is natural that we should take it for granted also in Homer's description, and not separate unnecessarily those of his pictures that can be combined in one picture. The twofold scene of the peaceful city through whose streets went the joyous crowd of a wedding-party, whilst in the market-place a great lawsuit was being decided, demands according to this no twofold picture, and Homer certainly was able to consider it a single one, representing to himself the entire city from so high a point of vision that it gave him a free and simultaneous prospect both of the streets and the market-place.

I am of the opinion that the knowledge of true perspective in painting was only arrived at incidentally in the painting of scenery,[157] and also that when this was already in its perfection, it yet cannot have been so easy to apply its rules to a single canvas, seeing that we still find in later paintings amongst the antiquities of Herculaneum many and diverse faults of perspective such as we should nowadays hardly forgive to a schoolboy.

But I absolve myself from the trouble of collecting my scattered notes concerning a point on which I may hope to receive the fullest satisfaction in Herr Winckelmann's promised history of art.[158]

XX

I rather turn gladly to my own road, if a rambler can be said to have a road.

What I have said of physical objects in general is even more pertinent to beautiful physical objects. Physical beauty arises from the harmonious effect of manifold parts that can be taken in at one view. It demands also that these parts shall subsist side by side; and as things whose parts subsist side by side are the proper subject of painting, so it, and it alone, can imitate physical beauty. The poet, who can only show the elements of beauty one after another, in succession, does on that very account forbear altogether the description of physical beauty, as beauty. He recognises that those elements, arranged in succession, cannot possibly have the effect which they have when placed side by side; that the concentrating gaze which we would direct upon them immediately after their enumeration still affords us no harmonious picture; that it passes the human imagination to represent to itself what kind of effect this mouth, and this nose, and these eyes together have if one cannot recall from Nature or art a similar composition of such features.

Here, too, Homer is the pattern of all patterns. He says: 'Nireus was beautiful; Achilles was more beautiful still; Helen possessed a divine beauty.' But nowhere does he enter upon the more circumstantial delineation of those beauties. For all that, the poem is based on the beauty of Helen. How greatly would a modern poet have luxuriated in the theme!

True, a certain Constantinus Manasses tried to adorn his bald chronicle with a picture of Helen.[159] I must thank him for the attempt. For really I should hardly know where else I could get hold of an example from which it might more obviously appear how foolish it is to venture something which Homer has so wisely forborne. When I read in him, for example:–

> Ἦν ἡ γυνὴ περικαλλής, εὔοφρυς, εὐχρουστάτη,
> Εὐπάρειος, εὐπρόσωπος, βοῶπις, χιονόχρους,
> Ἑλικοβλέφαρος, ἁβρά, χαρίτων γέμον ἄλσος,
> Λευκοβραχίων, τρυφερά, κάλλος ἄντικρυς ἔμπνουν,
> Τὸ πρόσωπον κατάλευκον, ἡ παρειὰ ῥοδόχρους,

Τὸ πρόσωπον ἐπίχαρι, τὸ βλέφαρον ὡραῖον,
Κάλλος ἀνεπιτήδευτον, ἀβάπτιστον, αὐτόχρουν,
Ἔβαπτε τὴν λευκότητα ῥοδόχροια πυρίνη,
Ὡς εἴ τις τὸν ἐλέφαντα βάψει λαμπρᾷ πορφύρᾳ.
Δειρὴ μακρά, κατάλευκος, ὅθεν ἐμυθουργήθη
Κυκνογενῆ τὴν εὔοπτον Ἑλένην χρηματίζειν —160

then I imagine I see stones rolling up a mountain, from which at the top a splendid picture is to be constructed, the stones, however, all rolling down of themselves on the other side. What kind of picture does it leave behind – this torrent of words? What was Helen like, then? Will not, if a thousand men read this, every man of the thousand make for himself his own conception of her?

Still, it is certain the political verses[161] of a monk are not poetry. Let us therefore hear Ariosto, when he describes his enchanting Alcina:—[162]

> Di persona era tanto ben formata,
> Quanto mai finger san pittori industri:
> Con bionda chioma, lunga e annodata,
> Oro non è, che piu risplenda, e lustri,
> Spargeasi per la guancia delicata
> Misto color di rose e di ligustri
> Di terso avorio era la fronte lieta,
> Che lo spazio finia con giusta meta.
>
> Sotto due negri, e sottilissimi archi
> Son due negri occhi, anzi due chiari soli,
> Pietosi à riguardar, à mover parchi,
> Intorno à cui par ch' Amor scherzi, e voli,
> E ch' indi tutta la faretra scarchi,
> E che visibilmente i cori involi.
> Quindi il naso per mezo il viso scende
> Che non trova l'invidia ove l'emende.
>
> Sotto quel sta, quasi fra due valette,
> La bocca sparsa di natio cinabro,
> Quivi due filze son di perle elette,
> Che chiude, ed apre un bello e dolce labro;
> Quindi escon le cortesi parolette,
> Da render molle ogni cor rozo e scabro;
> Quivi si forma quel soave riso
> Ch' apre a sua posta in terra il paradiso.
>
> Bianca neve è il bel collo, e'l petto latte,
> Il collo è tondo, il petto colmo e largo;
> Due pome acerbe, e pur d'avorio fatte,
> Vengono e van, come onda al primo margo,
> Quando piacevole aura il mar combatte.
> Non potria l'altre parti veder Argo,
> Ben si può guidicar, che corrisponde,
> A quel ch' appar di fuor, quel che s'asconde.

> Mostran le braccia sua misura giusta,
> Et la candida man spesso si vede,
> Lunghetta alquanto, e di larghezza angusta,
> Dove nè nodo appar, nè vena eccede.
> Si vede al fin de la persona augusta
> Il breve, asciutto e ritondetto piede.
> Gli angelici sembianti nati in cielo
> Non si ponno celar sotto alcun velo.

Milton says of the building of Pandemonium: 'the work some praise, and some the architect'.[163] The praise of the one, then, is not always the praise of the other. A work of art may deserve all applause while nothing very special redounds from it to the credit of the artist. On the other hand, an artist may justly claim our admiration even when his work does not completely satisfy us. If we do not forget this, quite contradictory verdicts may often be reconciled. The present case is an instance. Dolce in his dialogue on Painting[164] puts in Aretino's mouth an extravagant eulogy of Ariosto on the strength of these stanzas just cited; and I, on the contrary, choose them as an example of a picture that is no picture. We are both right. Dolce admires in it the knowledge which the poet displays of physical beauty; but I look merely to the effect which this knowledge, expressed in words, produces on my imagination. Dolce argues, from that knowledge, that good poets are also good painters; and I, from the effect, that what painters can by line and colour best express can only be badly expressed by words. Dolce commends Ariosto's delineation to all painters as the most perfect model of a beautiful woman; and I commend it to all poets as the most instructive warning against attempting even more unfortunately what failed in the hands of an Ariosto. It may be that, when Ariosto says:–

> Di persona era tanto ben formata,
> Quanto mai finger san pittori industri –[165]

he proves thereby that he perfectly understood the theory of proportions as only the most diligent artist can gather it from Nature and from antiquity. He may, who knows? in the mere words:–

> Spargeasi per la guancia delicata
> Misto color di rose e di ligustri –[166]

show himself the most perfect of colourists, a very Titian. One might also, from the fact that he only compares Alcina's hair with gold but does not call it golden hair, argue as cogently that he disapproves the use of actual gold in laying on the colour. One may even find in his 'descending nose':–

> Quindi il naso per mezzo il viso scende –[167]

the profile of those ancient Greek noses, copied also by Roman artists from the Greeks. What good is all this erudition and insight to us his readers who want to have the picture of a beautiful woman, who want to feel something of the soft excitement of the blood which accompanies the actual sight of beauty? If the poet is aware what conditions constitute a beautiful form, do we too, therefore, share his knowledge? And if we did also know it, does he here make us aware of those conditions? Or does he in the least lighten for us the difficulty of recalling them in a vividly perceptible manner? A brow in its most graceful lines and limits:

> ...la fronte
> Che lo spazio finia con giusta meta;[168]

a rose in which envy itself can find nothing to improve:–

> Che non trova l'invidia ove l'emende;[169]

a hand somewhat long and rather slender:–

> Lunghetta alquanto, e di larghezza angusta:[170]

what kind of picture do we gather from these general formulas? In the mouth of a drawing-master who is calling his pupils' attention to the beauties of the school model they might perhaps be useful; for by a glance at the model they perceive the pleasing lines of the delightful brow, the exquisite modelling of the nose, the slenderness of the dainty hand. But in the poet I see nothing, and feel with vexation how vain is my best effort to see what he is describing.

In this particular, where Virgil can best imitate Homer by forbearing action altogether, Virgil, too, has been rather happy. His Dido also is to him nothing further than *pulcherrima Dido*.[171] If indeed he describes anything of her more circumstantially, it is her rich jewellery, her splendid attire:–

> Tandem progreditur...
> Sidoniam picto chlamydem circumdata limbo:
> Cui pharetra ex auro, crines nodantur in aurum,
> Aurea purpuream subnectit fibula vestem.[172]

If we on that account would apply to him what the ancient artist said to a pupil who had painted a Helen in elaborate finery – 'As you are not able to paint her beautiful, you have painted her rich' – then Virgil would answer, 'It is no fault of mine that I cannot paint her beautiful; the blame rests on the limits of my art; be mine the praise, to have remained within those limits.'

I must not forget here the two songs of Anacreon in which he analyses for us the beauty of his beloved and of his Bathyllus.[173] The turn he gives it there makes everything right. He imagines a painter before him, and sets him to work under his eye. So, he says, fashion me the hair, so the brow, so the eyes, so the mouth, so neck and bosom, so the hips and hands! Of what the artist can put together only part by part the poet can only set a copy in the same way. His purpose is not that we shall recognise and feel in this verbal instruction of the painter the whole beauty of the beloved subject; he himself feels the insufficiency of the verbal expression, and for this very reason calls to his aid the expressive power of art, the illusion of which he so greatly heightens that the whole song appears to be more a hymn to Art than to his beloved. He does

not see the image, he sees herself and believes that she is just about to open
her lips in speech:—

> Ἀπέχει· βλέπω γὰρ αὐτήν,
> Τάχα, κηρέ, καὶ λαλήσεις.[174]

In the sketch, too, of Bathyllus the praise of the beautiful boy is so inwoven
with praise of art and the artist that it is doubtful for whose honour Anacreon
really intended the poem. He collects the most beautiful parts from various
paintings in which the particular beauty of these parts was its characteristic
feature; the neck he takes from an Adonis, breast and hands from a Mercury,
the hips from a Pollux, the abdomen from a Bacchus; till he sees the whole
Bathyllus in a perfect Apollo:—

> Μετὰ δὲ πρόσωπον ἔστω,
> Τὸν Ἀδώνιδος παρελθών,
> Ἐλεφάντινος τράχηλος·
> Μεταμάζιον δὲ ποίει
> Διδύμας τε χεῖρας Ἑρμοῦ,
> Πολυδεύκεος δὲ μηρούς,
> Διονυσίην δὲ νηδὺν...
> Τὸν Ἀπόλλωνα δὲ τοῦτον
> Καθελὼν ποίει Βάθυλλον.[175]

Similarly also Lucian does not know how to give us a conception of the beauty
of Panthea except by reference to the finest female statues of ancient artists.[176]
And what is this but to confess that language by itself is here powerless, that
poetry stammers and eloquence is dumb where Art does not in some measure
serve them as interpreter?

XXI

But does not Poetry lose too much if we take from her all pictures of physical
beauty? Who wishes to do so? If we seek to close to her one single road, on
which she hopes to achieve such pictures by following in the footsteps of a sister
art, where she stumbles painfully without ever attaining the same goal, do we,
then, at the same time close to her every other road, where Art in her turn
can but follow at a distance?

Even Homer, who with evident intention refrains from all piecemeal
delineation of physical beauties, from whom we can scarcely once learn in
passing that Helen had white arms and beautiful hair – even he knows how,
nevertheless, to give us such a conception of her beauty as far outpasses all that
Art in this respect can offer. Let us recall the passage where Helen steps into
the assembly of the Elders of the Trojan people. The venerable old men looked
on her, and one said to the other:—

> Οὐ νέμεσις Τρῶας καὶ ἐϋκνήμιδας Ἀχαιούς
> Τοιῆδ᾽ ἀμφὶ γυναικὶ πολὺν χρόνον ἄλγεα πάσχειν·
> Αἰνῶς ἀθανάτῃσι θεῇς εἰς ὦπα ἔοικεν.[177]

What can convey a more vivid idea of Beauty than to have frigid age confessing her well worth the war that has cost so much blood and so many tears? What Homer could not describe in its component parts, he makes us feel in its working. Paint us, then, poet, the satisfaction, the affection, the love, the delight, which beauty produces, and you have painted beauty itself. Who can imagine as ill-favoured the beloved object of Sappho,[178] the very sight of whom she confesses robbed her of her senses and her reason? Who does not fancy he beholds with his own eyes the fairest, most perfect form, as soon as he sympathises with the feeling which nothing but such a form can awaken? Not because Ovid shows us the beautiful body of his Lesbia part by part:

> Quos humeros, quales vidi tetigique lacertos!
> Forma papillarum quam fuit apta premi!
> Quam castigato planus sub pectore venter!
> Quantum et quale latus! quam juvenile femur! —[179]

but because he does so with the voluptuous intoxication in which it is so easy to awaken our longing, we imagine ourselves enjoying the same sight of exquisite beauty which he enjoyed.

Another way in which poetry in its turn overtakes art in delineation of physical beauty is by transmuting beauty into grace. Grace is beauty in motion, and just for that reason less suitable to the painter than to the poet. The painter can only help us to guess the motion, but in fact his figures are motionless. Consequently grace with him is turned into grimace. But in poetry it remains what it is – a transitory beauty which we want to see again and again. It comes and goes; and as we can generally recall a movement more easily and more vividly than mere forms and colours, grace can in such a case work more powerfully on us than beauty. All that still pleases and touches us in the picture of Alcina is grace. The impression her eyes make does not come from the fact that they are dark and passionate, but rather that they:–

> Pietosi à riguardar, à mover parchi –

'look round her graciously and slowly turn'; that Love flutters about them and from them empties all his quiver. Her mouth delights us, not because lips tinted with cinnobar enclose two rows of choicest pearls; but because there the lovely smile is shaped which in itself seems to open up an earthly paradise; because from it the friendly words come forth that soften the most savage breast. Her bosom enchants us, less because milk and ivory and apples typify its whiteness and delicate forms than because we see it softly rise and fall, like the waves at the margin of the shore when a playful zephyr contends with the ocean:–

> Due pome acerbi, e pur d'avorio fatte,
> Vengono e van, come onda al primo margo,
> Quando piacevole aura il mar combatte.[180]

I am sure such features of grace by themselves, condensed into one or two stanzas, will do more than all the five into which Ariosto has spun them out, inweaving them with frigid details of the fair form, far too erudite for our appreciation.

Even Anacreon himself would rather fall into the apparent impropriety of demanding impossibilities from the painter than leave the picture of his beloved untouched with grace:–

Τρυφεροῦ δ' ἔσω γενείου,
Περὶ λυγδίνῳ τραχήλῳ
Χάριτες πέτοιντο πᾶσαι.[181]

Her chin of softness, her neck of marble – let all the Graces hover round them, he bids the artist. And how? In the exact and literal sense? That is not capable of any pictorial realisation. The painter could give the chin the most exquisite curve, the prettiest dimple, *Amoris digitulo impressum*[182] (for the ἔσω appears to me to signify a dimple); he could give the neck the most beautiful carnation; but he can do no more. The turning of this fair neck, the play of the muscles, by which that dimple is now more visible, now less, the peculiar grace, all are beyond his powers. The poet said the utmost by which his art could make beauty real to us, so that the painter also might strive for the utmost expression in his art. A fresh example of the principle already affirmed – that the poet even when he speaks of works of art is not bound in his descriptions to confine himself within the limits of art.

XXII

Zeuxis[183] painted a Helen and had the courage to set under it those famous lines of Homer in which the enchanted Elders confess their emotions. Never were painting and poetry drawn into a more equal contest. The victory remained undecided, and both deserved to be crowned. For, just as the wise poet showed beauty merely in its effect, which he felt he could not delineate in its component parts, so did the no less wise painter show us beauty by nothing else than its component parts and hold it unbecoming to his art to resort to any other method. His picture consisted in the single figure of Helen, standing in naked beauty. For it is probable that it was the very Helen which he painted for the people of Crotona.[184]

Let us compare with this, for wonder's sake, the painting which Caylus sketches from Homer's lines for the benefit of a modern artist: 'Helen, covered with a white veil, appears in the midst of an assemblage of old men, in whose ranks Priam also is to be found, recognisable by the signs of his royal dignity. It must be the artist's business to make evident to us the triumph of beauty in the eager gaze and in the expression of amazed admiration on the faces of the sober greybeards. The scene is by one of the gates of the city. The background of the painting thus can lose itself in the open sky or against the city's lofty walls; the former were the bolder conception, but one is as fitting as the other.'

Let us imagine this picture carried out by the greatest master of our time and place it against the work of Zeuxis. Which will show the real triumph of beauty? That in which I myself feel it, or this where I must argue it from the grimaces of the susceptible greybeards? *Turpe senilis amor*;[185] a lustful look makes the most venerable countenance ridiculous; an old man who betrays youthful passions is really a loathsome object. This objection cannot be made to the Homeric elders; for the emotion they feel is a momentary spark which their wisdom extinguishes immediately; intended only to do honour to Helen, but not to disgrace themselves. They confess their feeling and forthwith add:–

> Ἀλλὰ καὶ ὣς, τοίη περ ἐοῦσ᾽, ἐν νηυσὶ νεέσθω,
> Μηδ᾽ ἡμῖν τεκέεσσί τ᾽ ὀπίσσω πῆμα λίποιτο.[186]

Without this resolution they would be old coxcombs, which, indeed, they appear in the picture of Caylus. And on what, then, do they direct their greedy glances? On a masked and veiled figure! That is Helen, is it? Inconceivable to me how Caylus here can leave the veil. Homer, indeed, gives it her expressly:

> Αὐτίκα δ᾽ ἀργεννῆσι καλυψαμένη ὀθόνησιν
> Ὡρμᾶτ᾽ ἐκ θαλάμοιο...[187]

but it is to cross the streets in it; and if indeed with Homer the elders already betray their admiration before she appears to have again taken off or thrown back the veil, it was not then the first time the old men saw her; their confession therefore might not arise from the present momentary view: they may have already often felt what on this occasion they first confessed themselves to feel. In the painting nothing like this occurs. If I see here enchanted old men, I wish at the same time to see what it is that charms them; and I am surprised in the extreme when I perceive nothing further than, as we have said, a masked and veiled figure on which they are passionately gazing. What is here of Helen? Her white veil and something of her well-proportioned outline so far as outline can become visible beneath raiment. Yet perhaps it was not the Count's intention that her face should be covered, and he names the veil merely as a part of her attire. If this is so – his words, indeed, are hardly capable of such an interpretation: '*Hélène couverte d'un voile blanc*'[188] – then another surprise awaits me; he is so particular in commending to the artist the expression on the faces of the elders, but on the beauty of Helen's face he does not expend a syllable. This modest beauty, in her eyes the dewy shimmer of a remorseful tear, approaching timidly! What! Is supreme beauty something so familiar to our artists that they do not need to be reminded of it? Or is expression more than beauty? And are we in pictures, too, accustomed, as on the stage, to let the ugliest actress pass for a charming princess, if only her prince declares warmly enough the love he bears her?

In truth, Caylus' picture would bear the same relation to that of Zeuxis as burlesque does to the loftiest poetry.

Homer was, without doubt, read in former times more diligently than today. Yet one finds ever so many pictures unmentioned which the ancient artists would have drawn from his pages. Only of the poet's hint at particular physical beauties they do appear to have made diligent use; these they did paint, and in such subjects alone, they understood well enough, it was granted them to compete with the poet. Besides Helen, Zeuxis also painted Penelope, and the Diana of Apelles was the Homeric Diana in company of her nymphs. I may here call to mind that the passage of Pliny in which the latter is mentioned requires an emendation.[189] But to paint actions from Homer simply because they offer a rich composition, excellent contrasts, artistic lights, seemed to the ancient artists not to be their *métier*, nor could it be so long as art remained within the narrower limits of her own high vocation. Instead, they nourished themselves on the spirit of the poet; they filled their imagination with his most exalted characteristics; the fire of his enthusiasm kindled their own; they saw and felt like him; and so their works became copies of the Homeric, not in the relation of a portrait to its original, but in that of a son to his father – like, yet different. The resemblance often lies only in a single feature, the rest having amongst them all nothing alike except that they harmonise with the resembling feature in the one case as well as in the other.

As, moreover, the Homeric masterpieces in poetry were older than any masterpiece of art, as Homer had observed Nature with a painter's eye earlier than a Phidias[190] or an Apelles, it is not to be wondered at that various observations of particular use to them the artists found already made in Homer before they themselves had had the opportunity of making them in Nature. These they eagerly seized on, in order to imitate Nature through Homer. Phidias confessed that the lines:–

῏Η, καὶ κυανέῃσιν ἐπ᾿ ὀφρύσι νεῦσε Κρονίων·
᾿Αμβρόσιαι δ᾿ ἄρα χαῖται ἐπερρώσαντο ἄνακτος
Κρατὸς ἀπ᾿ ἀθανάτοιο· μέγαν δ᾿ ἐλέλιξεν ῎Ολυμπον[191]

served him as a model in his Olympian Jupiter, and that only by their aid did he achieve a divine countenance, *propemodum ex ipso caelo petitum*.[192] Whosoever considers this to mean nothing more than that the fancy of the artist was fired by the poet's exalted picture, and thereby became capable of representations just as exalted – he, it seems to me, overlooks the most essential point, and contents himself with something quite general where, for a far more complete satisfaction, something very special is demanded. In my view Phidias confesses here also that in this passage he first noticed how much expression lies in the eyebrows, *quanta pars animi*[193] is shown in them. Perhaps also it induced him to devote more attention to the hair, in order to express in some measure what Homer means by 'ambrosial' locks. For it is certain that the ancient artists before the days of Phidias little understood what was significant and speaking in the countenance, and almost invariably neglected the hair. Even Myron was faulty in both these particulars, as Pliny has remarked, and after him Pythagoras Leontinus was the first who distinguished himself by the elegance of coiffure.[194] What Phidias learned from Homer, other artists learned from the works of Phidias.

Another example of this kind I may specify which has always very much pleased me. Let us recall what Hogarth has noted concerning the Apollo Belvedere. 'This Apollo', he says,

and the Antinous are both to be seen in the same palace at Rome. If, however, the Antinous fills the spectator with admiration, the Apollo amazes him, and, indeed, as travellers have remarked, by an aspect above humanity which usually they are not capable of describing. And this effect, they say, is all the more wonderful because when one examines it, the disproportionate in it is obvious even to a common eye. One of the best sculptors we have in England, who recently went there on purpose to see this statue, corroborated what has just been said, and in particular that the feet and legs in relation to the upper part are too long and too broad. And Andrea Sacchi, one of the greatest Italian painters, seems to have been of the same opinion, otherwise he would hardly (in a famous picture now in England) have given to his Apollo, crowning the musician Pasquilini, exactly the proportions of Antinous, seeing that in other respects it appears to be actually a copy of the Apollo. Although we frequently see in very great works some small part handled carelessly, this cannot be the case here. For in a beautiful statue correct proportion is one of the most essential beauties. We must conclude, therefore, that these limbs must have been purposely lengthened, otherwise it would have been easy to avoid it. If we therefore examine the beauties of this figure thoroughly, we shall with reason conclude that what we have hitherto considered indescribably excellent in its general aspect has proceeded from that which appeared to be a fault in one of its parts.   (Hogarth, *Analysis of Beauty*)[195]

All this is very illuminating, and I will add that in fact Homer has felt it and has pointed out that it gives a stately appearance, arising purely from this addition of size in the measurements of feet and legs. For when Antenor would compare the figure of Ulysses with that of Menelaus, he makes him say:–

Στάντων μὲν Μενέλαος ὑπείρεχεν εὐρέας ὤμους,
Ἄμφω δ' ἑζομένω γεραρώτερος ἦεν Ὀδυσσεύς.[196]

('When both stood, then Menelaus stood the higher with his broad shoulders; but when both sat, Ulysses was the statelier.') As Ulysses therefore gained stateliness in sitting, which Menelaus in sitting lost, the proportion is easy to determine which the upper body had in each to feet and legs. Ulysses was the larger in the proportions of the former, Menelaus in the proportions of the latter.

XXIII

A single defective part can destroy the harmonious working of many parts towards beauty. Yet the object does not necessarily therefore become ugly. Even ugliness demands several defective parts which likewise must be seen at one view if we are to feel by it the contrary of that with which beauty inspires us.

Accordingly, ugliness also in its essential nature would not be a reproach to poetry; and yet Homer has depicted the extremest ugliness in Thersites, and depicted it, moreover, in its elements set side by side.[197] Why was that permitted to him with ugliness which in the case of beauty he renounced with so fine a discernment? Is the effect of ugliness not just as much hindered by the successive enumeration of its elements as the effect of beauty is nullified by the like enumeration of its elements? To be sure it is, but herein lies also Homer's justification. Just because ugliness becomes in the poet's delineation a less repulsive vision of physical imperfection, and so far as effect is concerned ceases as it were to be ugliness, it becomes usable to the poet; and what he cannot use for its own sake, he uses as an ingredient in order to produce or intensify certain mixed states of feeling with which he must entertain us in default of feelings purely pleasurable.

These mixed feelings are awakened by the laughable and the terrible. Homer makes Thersites ugly in order to make him laughable. It is not, however, merely by his ugliness that he becomes so; for ugliness is imperfection and for the laughable a contrast is required of perfection and imperfection. This is the declaration of my friend Mendelssohn,[198] to which I should like to add that this contrast must not be too sharp or too glaring, that the *opposita* (to continue in painter's language) must be of the kind that can melt into each other. The wise and honest Aesop, even if one assigns him the ugliness of Thersites, does not thereby become laughable.[199] It was a ridiculous monastic whim to wish the γέλοιον[200] of his instructive tales transferred to his own person by the help of its deformity. For a misshapen body and a beautiful soul are like oil and vinegar, which, even when they are thoroughly mixed, still remain completely separated to the palate. They afford us no *tertium quid*; the body excites disgust, the soul satisfaction, each its own for itself. Only when the misshapen body is at the same time frail and sickly, when it hinders the soul in her operations, when it becomes the source of hurtful prepossessions against her – then indeed disgust and satisfaction mingle and flow together, but the new apparition arising therefrom is not laughter, but pity, and the object which we otherwise should merely have esteemed becomes interesting. The misshapen and sickly Pope must have been far more interesting to his friends than the sound and handsome Wycherley.[201] – But, however little would Thersites have been made laughable by mere ugliness, just as little would he have become laughable without it. The ugliness; the harmony of this ugliness with his character; the contradiction which both make to the idea he entertains of his own importance; the harmless effect of his malicious chatter, humiliating only to himself – all must work together to this end. The last-named particular is the οὐ φθαρτικόν[202] which Aristotle makes indispensable to the laughable; just as also my friend makes it a necessary condition that such contrast must be of no moment and must interest us but little. For let us only suppose that Thersites' malicious belittling of Agamemnon had come to cost him dear, that instead of a couple of bloody weals he must pay for it with his life – then certainly we should cease to laugh at him. For this monster of a man is yet a man, whose destruction will always seem a greater evil than all his frailties and vices. This we can learn by experience if we read his end in Quintus Calaber.[203] Achilles laments having killed Penthesilea; the beautiful woman in her blood, so bravely poured out, commands the esteem and pity of the hero, and esteem and pity turn to love. But the slanderous Thersites makes that love a crime. He declaims against the lewdness that betrays even the worthiest man to folly:–

> …ἥτ' ἄφρονα φῶτα τίθησι
> Καὶ πινυτόν περ ἐόντα.…[204]

Achilles gets into a rage, and without replying a word strikes him so roughly between cheek and ear that teeth and blood and soul together gush from his throat. Horrible unspeakably! The passionate, murderous Achilles becomes more hateful to me than the spiteful, snarling Thersites; the jubilant cry which the Greeks raise over the deed offends me. I take part with Diomedes, who draws his sword forthwith to avenge his kinsman on the murderer: for I feel, too, that Thersites is my kinsman, a human being.

But grant only that Thersites' incitements had broken out in sedition, that the mutinous people had actually taken ship and traitorously forsaken their captains, that the captains had thus fallen into the hands of a revengeful enemy, and that a divine judgement had brought utter destruction to both fleet and people: in such a case how would the ugliness of Thersites appear? If harmless ugliness can be laughable, a mischievous ugliness is always terrible. I do not know how to illustrate this better than by a couple of excellent passages of Shakespeare. Edmund, the bastard son of the Earl of Gloucester in *King Lear*, is no less a villain than Richard, Duke of Gloucester, who paved his way by the most detestable crimes to the throne which he ascended under the name of Richard III. How comes it, then, that the former excites far less shuddering and horror than the latter? When I hear the Bastard say:–

> Thou, Nature, art my goddess, to thy law
> My services are bound; wherefore should I
> Stand in the plague of custom, and permit
> The curiosity of nations to deprive me,
> For that I am some twelve or fourteen moonshines
> Lag of a brother? Why bastard? Wherefore base?
> When my dimensions are as well compact,
> My mind as generous, and my shape as true
> As honest Madam's issue? Why brand they thus
> With base? with baseness? bastardy? base, base?
> Who in the lusty stealth of Nature take
> More composition and fierce quality
> Than doth, within a dull, stale, tired bed,
> Go to creating a whole tribe of fops
> Got 'tween asleep and wake? –[205]

in this I hear a devil, but I see him in the form of an angel of light. When,
on the other hand, I hear the Duke of Gloucester say:–

> But I, that am not shaped for sportive tricks
> Nor made to court an amorous looking-glass,
> I, that am rudely stamped and want Love's majesty,
> To strut before a wanton ambling nymph;
> I, that am curtailed of this fair proportion,
> Cheated of feature by dissembling Nature,
> Deformed, unfinished, sent before my time
> Into this breathing world scarce half made up,
> And that so lamely and unfashionably
> That dogs bark at me as I halt by them;
> Why, I (in this weak piping time of peace)
> Have no delight to pass away the time;
> Unless to spy my shadow in the sun
> And descant on mine own deformity.
> And therefore, since I cannot prove a lover
> To entertain these fair, well-spoken days,
> I am determined to prove a villain![206]

then I hear a devil and see a devil in a shape that only the Devil should have.

XXIV

It is thus the poet uses the ugliness of forms; what use of them is permitted
to the painter? Painting, as imitative dexterity, can express ugliness; but
painting, as beautiful art, will not express it. To her, as the former, all visible
objects belong; but, as the latter, she confines herself solely to those visible
objects which awaken agreeable sensations.

But do not even the disagreeable sensations please in the imitation of them?
Not all. A sagacious critic has already made the remark concerning the
sensation of disgust. 'The representations of fear,' he says,

of sadness, of terror, of pity and so on, can only excite discomfort in so far as we take
the evil to be actual. These, therefore, can be resolved into pleasant sensations by the
recollection that it is but an artistic deceit. The unpleasant sensation of disgust, however,
in virtue of the laws of the imagination, ensues on the mere representation in the mind
whether the subject be considered as actual or not. Of what use is it, therefore, to the
offended soul if Art betrays herself merely as imitation? Her discomfort arose not from
the knowledge that the evil was actual but from the mere presentation of the same,
and this *is* actual. The sensations of disgust are therefore always nature, never
imitation.[207]

The same principle holds good of the ugliness of forms. This ugliness offends
our sight, is repugnant to our taste for order and harmony, and awakens
aversion without respect to the actual existence of the subject in which we
perceive it. We do not want to see Thersites, either in Nature or in picture,

and if in fact his picture displeases us less, this happens not for the reason that the ugliness of his form ceases in the imitation to be ugliness, but because we have the power of abstracting our attention from this ugliness and satisfying ourselves merely with the art of the painter. Yet even this satisfaction will every moment be interrupted by the reflection how ill the art has been bestowed, and this reflection will seldom fail to be accompanied by contempt for the artist.

Aristotle suggests another reason why things on which we look in Nature with repugnance do yet afford us pleasure even in the most faithful copy – namely, the universal curiosity of mankind.[208] We are glad if we either can learn from the copy τί ἕκαστον, 'what anything is', or if we can conclude from it ὅτι οὗτος ἐκεῖνος, 'that it is this or that'. But even from this there follows no advantage to ugliness in imitation. The pleasure that arises from the satisfaction of our curiosity is momentary, and merely accidental to the subject from which it arises; the dissatisfaction, on the contrary, that accompanies the sight of ugliness is permanent, and essential to the subject that excites it. How, then, can the former balance the latter? Still less can the momentary agreeable amusement which the showing of a likeness gives us overcome the disagreeable effect of ugliness. The more closely I compare the ugly copy with the ugly original, the more do I expose myself to this effect, so that the pleasure of comparison vanishes very quickly, and there remains to me nothing more than the untoward impression of the twofold ugliness. To judge by the examples given by Aristotle, it appears as if he himself had been unwilling to reckon the ugliness of forms as amongst the unpleasing subjects which might yet please in imitation. These subjects are corpses and ravening beasts. Ravening wild beasts excite terror even though they are not ugly; and this terror, and not their ugliness, it is that is resolved into pleasant sensations by imitation. So, too, with corpses: the keener feeling of pity, the terrible reminder of our own annihilation makes a corpse in Nature a repulsive subject to us; in the imitation, however, that pity loses its sharper edge by the conviction of the illusion, and from the fatal reminder an alloy of flattering circumstances can either entirely divert us, or unite so inseparably with it that we seem to find in it more of the desirable than the terrible.

As, therefore, the ugliness of forms cannot by and for itself be a theme of painting as fine art, because the feeling which it excites, while unpleasing, is not of that sort of unpleasing sensations which may be transformed into pleasing ones by imitation; yet the question might still be asked whether it could not to painting as well as to poetry be useful as an ingredient, for the intensifying of other sensations. May painting, then, avail itself of ugly forms to evoke the laughable and the terrible?

I will not venture to give this question a point-blank negative. It is undeniable that harmless ugliness can even in painting be made laughable, especially when there is combined with it an affectation of charm and dignity. It is just as incontestable that mischievous ugliness does in painting, just as in

Nature, excite horror, and that this laughable and this horrible element, which in themselves are mingled feelings, attain by imitation a new degree of attractiveness and pleasure.

I must at the same time point out that, nevertheless, painting is not here completely in the same case with poetry. In poetry, as I have already remarked, the ugliness of forms does by the transmutation of their co-existing parts into successive parts lose its unpleasant effect almost entirely; from this point of view it ceases, as it were, to be ugliness, and can therefore ally itself more intimately with other appearances in order to produce a new and distinct effect. In painting, on the contrary, the uglinesss has all its forces at hand, and works almost as strongly as in Nature itself. Consequently, harmless ugliness cannot well remain laughable for long; the unpleasant sensation gains the upper hand, and what was farcical to begin with becomes later merely disgusting. Nor is it otherwise with mischievous ugliness; the terrible is gradually lost and the monstrous remains alone and unchangeable.

Keeping this in view, Count Caylus was perfectly right to leave the episode of Thersites out of the list of his Homeric pictures. But are we therefore right, too, in wishing them cut out of Homer's own work? I am sorry to find that a scholar of otherwise just and fine taste is of this opinion.[209] A fuller exposition of my own views on the matter I postpone to another opportunity.

XXV

The second distinction also, which the critic just quoted[210] draws between disgust and other unpleasant emotions of the soul, is concerned with the aversion awakened within us by the ugliness of physical forms.

'Other unpleasant emotions', he says, 'can often, not just in imitation but also in Nature itself, gratify the mind, inasmuch as they never excite unmixed aversion, but in every case mingle their bitterness with pleasure. Our fear is seldom denuded of all hope; terror animates all our powers to evade the danger; anger is bound up with the desire to avenge ourselves, as sadness is with the agreeable representation of the happiness that preceded it, whilst pity is inseparable from the tender feelings of love and affection. The soul is permitted to dwell now on the pleasurable, and now on the afflicting, parts of an emotion, and to make for itself a mixture of pleasure and its opposite which is more attractive than pleasure without admixture. Only a very little attention to what goes on within is needed to observe frequent instances of the kind; what else would account for the fact that to the angry man his anger, to the melancholy man his dejection, is dearer than any pleasing representations by which it is sought to quiet or cheer him? Quite otherwise is it in the case of disgust and the feelings associated with it. In that the soul recognises no noticeable admixture of pleasure. Distaste gains the upper hand, and there is therefore no situation that we can imagine either in Nature or in imitation in which the mind would not recoil with repugnance from such representations.'

Perfectly true! but as the critic himself recognises yet other sensations akin to disgust which likewise produce nothing but aversion, what can be nearer akin to it than the feeling of the ugly in physical forms? This sensation also is, in Nature, without the slightest admixture of delight, and as it is just as little capable of it in imitation, so there is no situation in the latter in which the mind would not recoil with repugnance from the representation of it.

Indeed, this repugnance, if I have studied my feelings with sufficient care, is wholly of the nature of disgust. The sensation which accompanies ugliness of form is disgust, only somewhat fainter in degree. This conflicts, indeed, with another note of the critic, according to which he thinks that only the *blind* senses – taste, smell, and touch – are sensitive to disgust. 'The two former', he says, 'by an excessive sweetness and the third by an excessive softness of bodies that do not sufficiently resist the fibres that touch them. Such objects then become unendurable even to sight, but merely through the association of ideas that recall to us the repugnance to which they give rise in the taste, or smell, or touch. For, properly speaking, there are no objects of disgust for the vision.' Yet, in my opinion, things of the kind can be named. A scar in the face, a hare-lip, a flattened nose with prominent nostrils, an entire absence of eyebrows, are uglinesses which are not offensive either to smell, taste, or touch. At the same time it is certain that these things produce a sensation that certainly comes much nearer to disgust than what we feel at the sight of other deformities of body – a crooked foot, or a high shoulder; the more delicate our temperament, the more do they cause us those inward sensations that precede sickness. Only, these sensations very soon disappear, and actual sickness can scarcely result; the reason of which is certainly to be found in this fact, that they are objects of sight, which simultaneously perceives in them and with them a multitude of circumstances through the pleasant presentation of which those unpleasing things are so tempered and obscured that they can have no noticeable effect on the body. The blind senses, on the other hand – taste, smell, and touch – cannot, when they are affected by something unpleasant, likewise take cognisance of such other circumstances; the disagreeable, consequently, works by itself and in its whole energy, and cannot but be accompanied in the body by a far more violent shock.

Moreover, the disgusting is related to imitation in precisely the same way as the ugly. Indeed, as its unpleasant effect is more violent, it can even less than the ugly be made in and for itself a subject either of poetry or painting. Only because it also is greatly modified by verbal expression, I venture still to contend that the poet might be able to use at least some features of disgust as an ingredient for the mingled sensations of which we have spoken, which he intensifies so successfully by what is ugly.

The disgusting can add to the laughable; or representations of dignity and decorum, set in contrast with the disgusting, become laughable. Instances of this kind abound in Aristophanes. The weasel[211] occurs to me which interrupted the good Socrates in his astronomical observations:–

ΜΑΘ. Πρώην δέ γε γνώμην μεγάλην ἀφῃρέθη
'Υπ' ἀσκαλαβώτου. ΣΤ. Τίνα τρόπον; κάτειπέ μοι.
ΜΑΘ. Ζητοῦντος αὐτοῦ τῆς σελήνης τὰς ὁδοὺς
Καὶ τὰς περιφοράς, εἶτ' ἄνω κεχηνότος
'Απὸ τῆς ὀροφῆς νύκτωρ γαλεώτης κατέχεσεν.
ΣΤ. ῞Ησθην γαλεώτῃ καταχέσαντι Σωκράτους.[212]

Suppose that not to be disgusting which falls into his open mouth, and the
laughable vanishes. The drollest strokes of this kind occur in the Hottentot tale,
Tquassouw and Knonmquaiha in the *Connoisseur*, an English weekly magazine
full of humour, ascribed to Lord Chesterfield.[213] Everyone knows how filthy
the Hottentots are and how many things they consider beautiful and elegant
and sacred which with us awaken disgust and aversion. A flattened cartilage
of a nose, flabby breasts hanging down to the navel, the whole body smeared
with a cosmetic of goat's fat and soot gone rotten in the sun, the hair dripping
with grease, arms and legs bound about with fresh entrails – let one think of
this as the object of an ardent, reverent, tender love; let one hear this uttered
in the exalted language of gravity and admiration and refrain from laughter!

With the terrible it seems possible for the disgusting to be still more
intimately mingled. What we call the horrible is nothing but the disgusting
and terrible in one. Longinus,[214] it is true, is displeased with the τῆς ἐκ μὲν ῥινῶν
μύξαι ῥέον in Hesiod's description of melancholy;[215] but, in my opinion, not
so much because it is a disgusting trait as because it is merely a disgusting trait
contributing nothing to the terrible. For the long nails extending beyond the
fingers (μακροὶ δ' ὄνυχες χείρεσσιν ὑπῆσαν) he does not appear to find fault
with. Yet long nails are not less disgusting than a running nose. But the long
nails are at the same time terrible, for it is they that lacerate the cheeks until
the blood runs down upon the ground:–

            ...'Εκ δὲ παρειῶν
      Αἷμ' ἀπελείβετ' ἔραζε...[216]

A running nose, on the contrary, is nothing more than a running nose, and
I only advise Melancholy to keep her mouth closed. Let one read in Sophocles
the description of the vacant, barren den of the unhappy Philoctetes. There
is nothing to be seen of the necessaries or the conveniences of life beyond a
trodden matting of withered leaves, a misshapen bowl of wood, and a fireplace.
The whole wealth of the sick, forsaken man! How does the poet complete the
sad and fearful picture? With an addition of disgust. 'Ha!' exclaims
Neoptolemus, recoiling – 'torn rags drying in the wind, full of blood and
matter!'

ΝΕ. 'Ορῶ κενὴν οἴκησιν, ἀνθρώπων δίχα.
ΟΔ. Οὐδ' ἔνδον οἰκοποιός ἐστί τις τροφή;
ΝΕ. Στιπτή γε φυλλὰς ὡς ἐναυλίζοντί τῳ.
ΟΔ. Τὰ δ' ἄλλ' ἔρημα, κοὐδέν ἐσθ' ὑπόστεγον;
ΝΕ. Αὐτόξυλόν γ' ἔκπωμα, φλαυρουργοῦ τινὸς
    Τεχνήματ' ἀνδρός, καὶ πυρεῖ' ὁμοῦ τάδε.

ΟΔ. Κείνου τὸ θησαύρισμα σημαίνεις τόδε.
ΝΕ. 'Ιοὺ ἰού· καὶ ταῦτά γ' ἄλλα θάλπεται
'Ράκη, βαρείας τοῦ νοσηλείας πλέα.²¹⁷

And, similarly, in Homer dead Hector, dragged along, his countenance disfigured with blood and dust and clotted hair:

> Squalentem barbam et concretos sanguine crines²¹⁸

(as Virgil expresses it), a disgusting object, but all the more terrible on that account and all the more moving. Who can think of the torture of Marsyas in Ovid without a sensation of disgust?

> Clamanti cutis est summos derepta per artus,
> Nec quidquam nisi vulnus erat. Cruor undique manat,
> Detectique patent nervi, trepidaeque sine ulla
> Pelle micant venae: salientia viscera possis
> Et perlucentes numerare in pectore fibras.²¹⁹

But who does not feel at the same time that the disgusting is here in place? It makes the terrible horrible; and the horrible itself in Nature, when our pity is engaged, is not wholly disagreeable; how much less in the imitation! I will not heap up instances. But one thing I must still note: that there is a variety of the terrible, the poet's way to which stands open simply and solely through the disgusting – this is the terrible of *hunger*. Even in common life it is impossible to express the extremity of hunger otherwise than by the narration of all the innutritious, unwholesome, and especially all the loathsome things, with which the appetite must be appeased. As the imitation can awaken in us nothing of the feeling of hunger itself, it resorts to another unpleasant feeling which in the case of the fiercest hunger we recognise as the smaller of two great evils. This feeling it seeks to excite within us in order that we may from the discomfort conclude how fearful must be that other discomfort under which this becomes of no account. Ovid says of the oread whom Ceres sent off to starve:–

> Hanc (Famem) procul ut vidit ...
> ...Refert mandata deae, paulumque morata,
> Quanquam aberat longe, quanquam modo venerat illuc,
> Visa tamen sensisse Famem....²²⁰

An unnatural exaggeration! The sight of one who hungers, were it even Hunger herself, has not this infectious power; pity and horror and disgust it may make us feel, but not hunger. This horror Ovid has not spared us in his picture of famine, and in the hunger of Erysichthon, both in Ovid's description and that of Callimachus,²²¹ the loathsome features are the strongest. After Erysichthon had devoured everything, not sparing even the beast which his mother had reared to be a burnt-offering for Vesta, Callimachus makes him fall upon horses and cats, and beg upon the streets for the crusts and filthy fragments from strange tables:–

Καὶ τὰν βῶν ἔφαγεν, τὰν 'Εστίᾳ ἔτρεφε μάτηρ,
Καὶ τὸν ἀεθλοφόρον καὶ τὸν πολεμήϊον ἵππον,
Καὶ τὰν αἴλουρον, τὰν ἔτρεμε θηρία μικκά –
Καὶ τόθ' ὁ τῶ βασιλῆος ἐνὶ τριόδοισι καθῆστο
Αἰτίζων ἀκόλως τε καὶ ἔκβολα λύματα δαιτός –[222]

And Ovid makes him finally put his teeth into his own limbs, to nourish his
body with his own flesh:–

> Vis tamen illa mali postquam consumserat omnem
> Materiam...
> Ipse suos artus lacero divellere morsu
> Coepit, et infelix minuendo corpus alebat.[223]

For that very reason were the repulsive Harpies[224] made so noisome, so filthy,
that the hunger which their snatching of the viands was to produce should be
so much more terrible. Listen to the lament of Phineus in Apollonius:–

Τυτθὸν δ' ἦν ἄρα δή ποτ' ἐδητύος ἄμμι λίπωσι,
Πνεῖ τόδε μυδαλέον τε καὶ οὐ τλητὸν μένος ὀδμῆς.
Οὔ κέ τις οὐδὲ μίνυνθα βροτῶν ἀνσχοιτο πελάσσας
Οὐδ' εἴ οἱ ἀδάμαντος ἐληλαμένον κέαρ εἴη.
'Αλλά με πικρὴ δῆτά κε δαιτὸς ἐπίσχει ἀνάγκη
Μίμνειν, καὶ μίμνοντα κακῇ ἐν γαστέρι θέσθαι.[225]

I would from this point of view gladly excuse the loathsome introduction of
the Harpies in Virgil;[226] but it is no actual present hunger which they cause,
but only an impending one which they prophesy, and, furthermore, the whole
prophecy is resolved in the end into a play upon words. Dante, too, prepares
us not only for the story of the starvation of Ugolino by the most loathsome
and horrible situation in which he places him in hell with his aforetime
persecutor;[227] but the starvation itself also is not without elements of disgust,
which more particularly overcomes us at the point where the sons offer
themselves as food to their father. There is in a drama of Beaumont and
Fletcher a passage which I might cite here in place of all other examples were
I not obliged to think it somewhat overdone.[228]

I turn to the question of disgusting subjects in painting. If it were quite
incontestable that, properly speaking, there are no disgusting subjects whatever
for sight, of which it might be assumed that painting, as fine art, would refuse
them: all the same, she must avoid disgusting subjects in general, because the
association of ideas makes them disgusting to sight also. Pordenone in a picture
of Christ's burial makes one of the onlookers hold his nose.[229] Richardson
condemns this on the ground that Christ was not yet so long dead that his
body could have suffered corruption.[230] In the Resurrection of Lazarus, on the
other hand, he thinks it might be permitted to the painter to show by such
an indication what the story expressly asserts – that his body was already
corrupt. In my view this representation is unendurable in this case also; for
not only the actual stench, but the mere idea of it awakens disgust. We flee

offensive places even if we actually have a cold. Yet painting accepts the disgusting not for disgust's sake: she accepts it, as poetry does, in order to intensify by it the laughable and the terrible. But at her own risk! What, however, I have in this case noted of the ugly holds yet more certainly of the disgusting. It loses in a *visible* imitation incomparably less of its effect than in an *audible* one; and therefore can mingle less intimately with the laughable and terrible elements in the former case than in the latter; as soon as the first surprise is past, as soon as the first eager glance is satisfied, it isolates itself in its turn completely and lies there in all its crudeness.[231]

Letter to Nicolai, 26 May 1769[1]

Translated by Joyce P. Crick.
German text in *Sämtliche Schriften*, edited by Lachmann and Muncker (1886–1924), XVII, 289–92.

I can be well satisfied with the review of my *Laocoon* in the last issue of your *Bibliothek*.[2] And I think I know the name of the reviewer. But what do I care about names? After all, I shall not make the acquaintance of the person. If he goes on to read the continuation of my book,[3] he will probably find that his strictures do not apply. I grant, there are various things in it which are not sufficiently precise; but how can they be, when I have barely begun to consider the one distinction between poetry and painting which arises from the different use of their representational signs, insofar as the signs of the one exist in time, and of the other in space. Both can be either natural or arbitrary; consequently there must be two sorts of painting and two sorts of poetry, a higher and a lower kind. Painting requires co-existing signs, which are either natural or arbitrary; and this same distinction is also to be found in the consecutive signs of poetry. For it is not true that painting uses only natural signs, just as it is not true that poetry uses only arbitrary signs. But one thing is certain: the more painting departs from natural signs, or employs natural and arbitrary signs mixed together, the further it departs from its true perfection; just as conversely poetry draws all the closer to its true perfection, the closer it makes its arbitrary signs approach the natural. Consequently the higher kind of painting is that which employs only natural signs in space, and the higher kind of poetry is that which employs only natural signs in time. Consequently, neither historical nor allegorical painting can belong to the higher kind, for they can be understood only by means of their additional arbitrary signs. By arbitrary signs in painting I do not only mean the costuming and all that pertains to it, but also much of the bodily expressiveness itself. It is true that these things are not really arbitrary in painting; their signs in painting are also natural signs; but they are still *natural* signs of *arbitrary* things, which could not possibly produce that general understanding, that swift and immediate effect which *natural* signs of *natural* things can produce. Now if in this latter case the highest law is the law of beauty, and if my reviewer himself admits that the painter is in fact most fully painter when this is so, then we are in agreement, and, as I said, his strictures do not touch my argument. For everything I said about painting applied only to the effect of painting on the viewer at its highest and most painterly. I have never denied that it can also produce effects enough quite apart from this; I only wanted to deny that the name of painting was any the less appropriate then. I have never doubted the effect produced by historical and allegorical painting, still less wanted to banish these kinds from the world. I said only that in this respect the painter is less of a painter than in paintings where his sole end and purpose is beauty. And does the reviewer concede me that? And now a word more about poetry, so that you do not misunderstand what I have just said. Poetry must endeavour absolutely to elevate its arbitrary signs into natural ones, for only thereby is it distinguished from prose and becomes poetry. The means it employs to do this are tone, choice of words, arrangement of words, metre, figures of speech, tropes, metaphors and so forth. All these things cause the arbitrary signs to approximate more closely to the natural; but they do not make them natural signs; consequently all the kinds of poetry that employ only these means are to be regarded as the lower kinds of poetry; and the highest kind of poetry is the one that turns the arbitrary signs wholly into natural signs.[4] Now that is dramatic poetry, for in drama the words cease to be arbitrary signs, and become the *natural* signs of arbitrary things. Aristotle already declared that dramatic poetry is the highest, indeed the only poetry, and he puts epic poetry into second place only insofar as it is, or can be, to a large extent dramatic. The reason he gives for this is not mine, it is true; but it can be reduced to mine, and only reducing it to mine ensures it against being applied falsely.

If you happen to have a half hour's conversation with Herr Moses[5] about it, pray let me know what he has to say. The third part of my *Laokoon* will constitute a further development of these ideas.[6]

Part 3

Hamann

Johann Georg Hamann

(1730–88)

Hamann was born at Königsberg in East Prussia. He studied theology and law at Königsberg University, and then, like Winckelmann, eked out his living for a time as a private tutor. He subsequently found employment in commerce, and was sent in 1757 on a business trip to London. This became the decisive experience of his life. Months spent in idleness and disreputable company were succeeded by a sudden religious conversion, which in turn led to a burst of literary activity. Hamann's conversion to a mystical and evangelical form of Christianity fuelled his literary output for the rest of his life.

His first major work was the *Socratic Memorabilia* (1759), in which he rebuffed the attempts of various friends, including the young philosopher Kant, to reconvert him to the rationalism of the Enlightenment. In it, he reinterpreted the figure of Socrates, an idol of the eighteenth-century rationalists, in a radically anti-rationalist manner (see Introduction, pp. 12 f.). This work, along with his miscellany *Crusades of the Philologist* (1762), the main item in which is the *Aesthetica in nuce*, were the basis of his reputation among the *Sturm und Drang* writers of the 1770s, by whom he was regarded as something of a guru. His Christianity passed most of them by; but his rehabilitation of the senses and emotions, of primitive poetry and pre-rational inspiration, had a peculiar appeal to this pre-Romantic generation.

Hamann was an eccentric and anomalous figure in the Age of Reason. He rejected the Enlightenment and everything it stood for, in philosophy, theology, and literature. The *Aesthetica in nuce*, which contains his most important pronouncements on poetry and literature, is directed partly against rational theology (as represented by Johann David Michaelis), partly against neo-classicism (Winckelmann), partly against rationalistic literary criticism and modern secular literature (Mendelssohn, Nicolai, Lessing). His common-law marriage to an uneducated peasant girl, although a happy one, accentuated his outsiderdom in the eyes of his contemporaries.

Many of Hamann's later works are concerned with language. His *Metacritique on the Purism of Reason* (1781), written as a reply to Kant's *Critique of Pure Reason*, maintains that all thought-processes are rooted in, and relative to, language. In so doing, it points to an area seriously neglected by Kant and anticipates certain arguments of modern linguistic philosophy. As to Hamann's own use of language, he could write a lucid and elegant German when he chose, but he usually chose not to. His notoriously difficult and at times impenetrable style was cultivated in deliberate defiance of rationalism; it has been a major obstacle to the appreciation of his thought ever since.

Further reading

The standard edition of Hamann's works is that of Nadler (1949–57); the correspondence is edited by Ziesemer and Henkel (1955–79). Very little has been translated into English, but O'Flaherty's edition (1967) of the *Socratic Memorabilia* is an invaluable exception. The fullest German account of Hamann's achievement is that of Unger (1911), but Nadler (1949) is less dated. General accounts in English include those by Alexander (1966) and O'Flaherty (1979).

Aesthetica in nuce[1]
A Rhapsody in Cabbalistic Prose
1762

Translated by Joyce P. Crick, with modifications by the editor.
German text in *Sämtliche Werke*, edited by Nadler (1949–57), II, 195–217

Judges v, 30

A prey of divers colours in needlework, meet for the necks of them that take the spoil.

Elihu in the Book of Job, XXXII, 19–22

Behold, my belly is as wine which hath no vent; it is ready to burst like new bottles.

I will speak, that I may be refreshed: I will open my lips and answer.

Let me not, I pray you, accept any man's person, neither let me give flattering titles unto man.

For I know not to give flattering titles; in so doing my maker would soon take me away.[2]

Horace

The uninitiate crowd I ban and spurn!
Come ye, but guard your tongues! A song that's new
    I, priest of the Muses, sing for you
        Fair maids and youths to learn!

Kings o'er their several flocks bear sway. O'er kings
Like sway hath Jove, famed to have overthrown
    The Giants, by his nod alone
        Guiding created things.[3]

Not a lyre! Nor a painter's brush! A winnowing-fan for my Muse, to clear the threshing-floor of holy literature! Praise to the Archangel on the remains of Canaan's tongue![4] – on white asses[a] he is victorious in the contest, but the wise idiot of Greece[5] borrows Euthyphro's[b] proud stallions for the philological dispute.

Poetry is the mother-tongue of the human race; even as the garden is older than the ploughed field, painting than script; as song is more ancient than declamation; parables older than reasoning;[c] barter than trade. A deep sleep was the repose of our farthest ancestors; and their movement a frenzied dance. Seven days they would sit in the silence of deep thought or wonder; – and would open their mouths to utter winged sentences.

The senses and passions speak and understand nothing but images. The entire store of human knowledge and happiness consists in images. The first outburst of Creation, and the first impression of its recording scribe; – the first manifestation and the first enjoyment of Nature are united in the words: Let there be Light! Here beginneth the feeling for the presence of things.[d]

Finally GOD crowned the revelation of His spendour to the senses with His masterpiece – with man. He created man in divine form – in the image of God created He him. This decision of our prime originator unravels the most complex knots of human nature and its destiny. Blind heathens have recognised the invisibility which man has in common with GOD. The veiled figure of the body, the countenance of the head, and the extremities of the arms are the visible schematic form in which we wander the earth; but in truth they are nothing but a finger pointing to the hidden man within us.

Each man is a counterpart of God in miniature.[e]

The first nourishment came from the realm of plants; wine – the milk of the ancients; the oldest poetry was called botanical[f] by its learned commentator[6] (to judge from the tales of Jotham and of Joash);[g] and man's first apparel was a rhapsody of fig-leaves.

But the LORD GOD made coats of skins and clothed them – our ancestors, whom the knowledge of good and evil had taught shame. If necessity is the mother of invention, and made the arts and conveniences, then we have good cause to wonder with Goguet first how the fashion of clothing ourselves could have arisen in Eastern lands, and second why it should have been in the skins of beasts.[7] Let me risk a conjecture which seems to me at least ingenious. I place the origin of this costume in the universal constancy of animal characters,[8] familiar to Adam from consorting with the ancient poet (known as Abaddon in the language of Canaan, but called Apollyon in the Hellenistic tongue).[9] This moved primal man to hand on to posterity beneath this borrowed skin an intuitive knowledge of past and future events...

Speak, that I may see Thee! This wish was answered by the Creation, which is an utterance to created things through created things, for day speaketh unto day, and night proclaimeth unto night. Its word traverses every clime to the ends of the earth, and its voice can be heard in every dialect. The fault may

lie where it will (outside us or within us): all we have left in nature for our
use is fragmentary verse and *disjecta membra poetae*.[10] To collect these together
is the scholar's modest part; the philosopher's to interpret them; to imitate
them,[h] or – bolder still – to adapt them, the poet's.

To speak is to translate – from the tongue of angels into the tongue of men,
that is, to translate thoughts into words – things into names – images into signs;
which can be poetic or cyriological,[i] historic or symbolic or hieroglyphic – and
philosophical or characteristic.[j] This kind of translation (I mean, speech)
resembles more than ought else the wrong side of a tapestry:

And shows the stuff, but not the workman's skill;[13]

or it can be compared with an eclipse of the sun, which can be looked at in
a vessel of water.[k]

Moses's torch illumines even the intellectual world, which also has its heaven
and its earth. Hence Bacon compares the sciences with the waters above and
below the vault of our vaporous globe.[17] The former are a glassy sea,[18] like unto
crystal with fire; the latter, by contrast, are clouds from the ocean, no bigger
than a man's hand.[19]

But the creation of the setting bears the same relation to the creation of man
as epic to dramatic poetry. The one takes place by means of the word, the other
by means of action. Heart, be like unto a tranquil sea! Hear this counsel: let
us make men in our image, after our likeness, and let them have dominion! –
Behold the deed: and the LORD GOD formed man of the dust of the ground –
Compare word and deed: worship the mighty speaker with the Psalmist;[l] adore
the supposed gardener[m] with her who bore the news to the disciples; honour
the free potter[n] with the Apostle to the Hellenistic scribes and philosophers of
the Talmud![20]

The hieroglyphic Adam is the history of the entire race in the symbolic
wheel:– the character of Eve is the original of Nature's beauty and of
systematic economy, which is not flaunted as a sacred method, but is formed
beneath the earth and lies hidden in the bowels, in the very reins of things.

Virtuosos of the present aeon, cast by the LORD GOD into a deep trance of
sleep! Ye noble few! Take advantage of this sleep, and make from this
Endymion's rib[21] the newest version of the human soul, which the bard of
midnight songs[22] beheld in his morning dream[o] – but not from close at hand.
The next aeon will awake like a giant from a drunken sleep to embrace your
muse and rejoice and bear witness: Yea, that is bone of my bone and flesh of
my flesh!

If some modern literary Levite[24] were to take passing note of this rhapsody,
I know in advance that he will bless himself like Saint Peter[p] at the vision of
the great sheet knit at the four corners, upon which he fastened his eyes and
saw four-footed beasts of the earth, and wild beasts, and creeping things, and
fowls of the air...'Oh no, thou one possessed, thou Samaritan' – (that is how
he will scold the philologist in his heart) – 'for readers of orthodox tastes, low
expressions and unclean vessels[25] are not proper' – *Impossibilissimum est,*

communia proprie dicere[26] – Behold, that is why an author whose taste is but eight days old, but who is circumcised,[27] will foul his swaddling clothes with white gentian[28] – to the honour of human excrement! The old Phrygian's fabled ugliness[29] was never so dazzling as the aesthetic beauty of Aesop the younger.[30] Today, Horace's typical ode to Aristus[q] is fulfilled, that the poet who sings the praises of sweet-smiling Lalage, whose kiss is still sweeter than her laughter, has made dandies out of Sabine, Apuline, and Mauretanian monsters.[31] True, one can be a man without finding it necessary to become an author. But whoever expects his good friends to think of the writer apart from the man, is more inclined to poetic than to philosophical abstractions.[32] Therefore do not venture into the metaphysics of the fine arts without being initiated into the orgies[r] and Eleusinian mysteries. But the senses belong to Ceres, and to Bacchus the passions, the ancient foster-parents of Nature the beautiful:

> Come to us, Bacchus, with the sweet grape cluster hanging
> From thy horns, and, Ceres, wreathe thy temples with the corn ears![s]

If this rhapsody might even be honoured by the judgement of a Master in Israel,[34] then let us go to meet him in holy prosopopoeia,[t] which is as welcome in the realm of the dead as it is in the realm of the living[35] (. . .si NUX modo ponor in illis):[36]

Most Worthy and Learned Rabbi!

'The postilion of the Holy Roman Empire, who bears the motto *Relata refero* on the shield of his escutcheon,[37] has made me desirous of the second half of the homilies *da sacra poesi*.[38] I yearn for them, and have waited in vain until this day, even as the mother of the Hazorite captain looked out of a window for her son's chariot and cried through the lattice[39] – so do not think ill of me if I speak to you like the ghost in *Hamlet*, with signs and beckonings, until I have a proper occasion to declare myself in *sermones fideles*.[u][40] Will you believe without proof that *Orbis pictus*,[41] the book by that renowned fanatic, schoolmaster, and philologist Amos Comenius,[v] and the *Exercitia* of Muzelius[42] are both far too learned for children still pract-is-ing their spell-ing, and verily, verily, we must become even as little children if we are to receive the spirit of truth which passeth the world's understanding, for it seeth it not, and (even if it were to see it) knoweth it not – – Ascribe the fault to the foolishness of my way of writing, which accords so ill with the original mathematical sin of your oldest writings, and still less with the witty rebirth of your most recent works, if I borrow an example from the spelling-book which doubtless may be older than the Bible. Do the elements of the ABC lose their natural meaning, if in their infinite combinations into arbitrary signs they remind us of ideas which dwell, if not in heaven, then in our brains? But if we raise up the whole deserving righteousness of a scribe upon the dead body of the letter, what sayeth the spirit to that? Shall he be but a groom of the chamber to the dead letter, or perhaps a mere esquire to the deadening letter? God forbid!

According to your copious insight into physical things,[43] you know better than I can remind you that the wind bloweth where it listeth – regardless of whether one hears it blowing; so one looks to the fickle weather-cock to find out where it comes from, or rather, whither it is going.'

> O outrageous crime! Shall the precious work be destroyed?
> Rather let the venerable power of the laws be infringed.
> Bacchus and sweet Ceres, come to our aid!...[w][44]

The opinions of the philosophers are variant readings of Nature, and the precepts of the theologians variants of the Scriptures. The author is the best interpreter of his own words. He may speak through created things and through events – or through blood and fire and vapour of smoke,[x] for these constitute the sacramental language.

The Book of Creation contains examples of general concepts which GOD wished to reveal to His creatures through His Creation. The Books of the Covenant contain examples of secret articles which GOD wished to reveal to man through man. The unity of the great Author is mirrored even in the dialect of his works – in all of them a tone of immeasurable height and depth! A proof of the most splendid majesty and of total self-divesting! A miracle of such infinite stillness that makes GOD resemble Nothingness, so that in all conscience one would have to deny His existence, or else be a beast.[y] But at the same time a miracle of such infinite power, which fulfils all in all, that we cannot escape the intensity of His affection!

If it is a question of the good taste of the devotions, which are constituted by the philosophical spirit and poetic truth, and if it is a matter of the statecraft[z] of the versification, can we present a more credible witness than the immortal Voltaire, who virtually declares religion to be the cornerstone of epic poetry and whose greatest lament is that his religion[aa] is the reverse of mythology?

Bacon represented mythology as a winged boy of Aeolus, the sun at his back, and with clouds for his footstool, fleeting away the time piping on a Grecian flute.[bb]

But Voltaire, High Priest in the Temple of Taste, can draw conclusions as compellingly as Caiaphas,[cc] and thinks more fruitfully than Herod.[dd] For if our theology is not worth as much as mythology, then it is simply impossible for us to match the poetry of the Heathens, let alone excel it[54] – which would be most appropriate to our duty and to our vanity. But if our poetry is worthless, our history will look leaner than Pharaoh's kine; but fairy-tales and court gazettes will take the place of our historians. And it is not worth the trouble of thinking of philosophy; all the more systematic calendars instead! – more than spider-webs in a ruined castle. Every idle fellow who can just about manage dog-Latin or Switzer-German, but whose name is stamped by the whole number M or half the number of the academic beast[55] is a blatant liar, and the benches and the clods sitting on them would have to cry 'outrage!' if the former only had ears, and the latter, ironically called listeners, only exercised their ears to listen with –

Where is Euthyphro's whip, timid jade?
So that my cart does not get stuck...

Mythology here, mythology there![ee] Poetry is an imitation of Nature the beautiful – and the revelations of Nieuwentyt,[56] Newton, and Buffon will surely be able to replace a tasteless mythology? Indeed they should, and they would too, if they could. So why does it not happen? – Because it is impossible, say your poets.

Nature works through the senses and the passions. But whoso maims these instruments, how can he feel? Are crippled sinews fit for movement?

Your lying, murderous philosophy has cleared Nature out of the way, and why do you demand that we should imitate her? – So that you can renew the pleasure by murdering the young students of Nature too.

Verily, you delicate critics of art, go on asking what is truth, and make for the door, because you cannot wait for an answer to this question. Your hands are always washed, whether you are about to eat bread, or whether you have just pronounced a death-sentence. Do you not also ask: what means did you employ to clear Nature out of the way? Bacon accuses you of flaying her with your abstractions. If Bacon is a witness to the truth, well then, stone him – and cast clods of earth or snowballs at his shade – – –

If one single truth, like the sun, prevaileth, it is day. But if you behold instead of this One truth, as many as the sands of the seashore; and here close by, a little light[ff] which excels in brightness[gg] a whole host of suns; that is a night beloved of poets and thieves. The poet[hh] at the beginning of days is the same as the thief[ii] at the end of days.

All the colours of the most beautiful world grow pale if once you extinguish that light, the firstborn of Creation. If the belly is your god, then even the hairs on your head are under his guardianship. Every created thing becomes alternately your sacrifice and your idol. Cast down against its will, but hoping still, it groans beneath your yoke, or at your vanity; it does its best to escape your tyranny, and longs even in the most passionate embrace for that freedom with which the beasts paid Adam homage, when GOD brought them unto man to see what he would call them; for whatsoever man would call them, that was the name thereof.

This analogy of man to the Creator endows all creatures with their imprint and their stamp, on which faithfulness and faith in all Nature depends. The more vividly this idea of the image of the invisible GOD[jj] dwells in our heart, the more able we are to perceive his loving-kindness in his creatures; and to taste, and see it and grasp it with our hands. Every impression of Nature in man is not only a memorial, but also a warrant of fundamental truth: who is the LORD. Every counter-effect of man in GOD's created world is charter and seal that we partake of the divine nature,[kk] and that we are his offspring.[ll]

Oh for a muse like a refiner's fire, and like a fuller's soap![mm] – – She will dare to purify the natural use of the senses from the unnatural use of abstractions,[nn] which distorts our concepts of things, even as it suppresses the name of the Creator and blasphemes against Him. I speak with you, o ye Greeks, for you deem yourselves wiser than the chamberlains with the gnostic key; go on and try to read the *Iliad* if you have first, with your abstractions, sifted out the two vowels alpha and omega, and then give me your opinion of the poet's sense and sound!

Sing, – G–ddess, the wr–th –f Peleus's s–n –chilles[57]

Behold, the scribes of worldly wisdom, great and small, have overwhelmed the text of Nature, like the Great Flood. Were not all its beauties and riches bound to turn into water? But you perform far greater miracles than ever delighted the gods,[oo] with oak-trees[pp] and pillars of salt, with petrifactions, alchemical transformations and fables, to convince the human race. You make Nature blind, that she might be your guide! Or rather, you have with your Epicureanism[58] put out the light of your own eyes, that you might be taken for prophets who spin your inspirations and expositions out of your own heads. Oh, you would have dominion over Nature, and you bind your own hands and feet with your Stoicism,[59] that you may warble all the more movingly in your Poetic Miscellanies at the diamond fetters of fate.

If the passions are limbs of dishonour, do they therefore cease to be weapons of virility? Have you a wiser understanding of the letter of reason than that allegorical chamberlain of the Alexandrian Church had of the letter of the Scriptures when he castrated himself in order to reach heaven?[60] The prince of this aeon takes his favourites from among the greatest offenders against themselves; his court fools are the worst enemies of Nature in her beauty; true, she has Corybants and Gauls as her pot-bellied priests, but *esprits forts* as her true worshippers.[61]

A philosopher such as Saul[qq] sets up laws for celibates – passion alone gives hands, feet, and wings to abstractions and hypotheses, and to pictures and signs gives spirit, life, and tongue. Where will you find a swifter syllogism? Where is the rolling thunder of eloquence begotten? And where its companion, the single-syllabled lightning-flash?[rr]

Why should I paraphrase *one* word for you with an infinity of them, you readers whose estate, honour, and dignity make you so ignorant? For they can observe for themselves the phenomena of passion everywhere in human society; even as everything, however remote, can touch our hearts in a particular direction; even as each individual feeling extends over the range of all external objects;[ss] even as we can make the most general instances our own by applying them to ourselves personally, and expand any private circumstance into the public spectacle of heaven and earth. Each individual truth grows into the foundation of a design more miraculously than the fabled cow-hide grew into the extent of a state, and a plan greater than the hemisphere comes together in the focus of perception. In short, the perfection of the design, the strength of the execution – the conception and birth of new ideas and new expressions – the labour and the rest of the wise man, the consolation and the loathing he finds in them, lie hidden from our senses in the fruitful womb of the passions.

'The philologist's public, his world of readers, seems to resemble that lecture-hall which Plato filled by himself.'[tt] Antimachus continued confidently, as it is written:

like the leech which does not drop off the skin until it is sated.[63]

Just as if our learning were a mere remembering, our attention is constantly being drawn to the monuments of the ancients, to shape our minds through memory. But why stop at the fountain of the Greeks, all riddled with holes as it is, and abandon the most living sources of antiquity? Perhaps we do not really know ourselves what it is in the Greeks and Romans that we admire even to idolatry.[64] This is where that accursed lying[uu] in our symbolic textbooks comes from, for to this day they are daintily bound in sheep's parchment, but within, verily, within they are whited sepulchres and full of hypo-critical wickedness.[vv]

We treat the ancients like a man who gazes on his visible face in a looking-glass, but who, having looked upon it, straightway goes and forgets how he was formed. A painter sits for his self-portrait in a wholly different spirit. Narcissus (the bulbous plant of *beaux esprits*) loves his picture more than his life.[ww]

Salvation comes from the Jews.[66] I had not yet seen their philosophical writings, but I was certain of finding sounder concepts in them – to your shame, Christians! Yet you feel the sting of that worthy name by which ye are called[xx] as little as you feel the honour GOD did himself in taking the vile name of Son of Man.

Nature and Scripture then are the materials of the beautiful spirit which creates and imitates – Bacon compares matter with Penelope. Her importunate suitors are the scribes and philosophers.[67] The tale of the beggar who appeared at the court of Ithaca you know, for has not Homer translated it into Greek, and Pope into English verse?

But how are we to raise the defunct language of Nature from the dead? By making pilgrimages to the fortunate lands of Arabia,[68] and by going on crusades to the East, and by restoring their magic art. To steal it, we must employ old women's cunning, for that is the best sort. Cast your eyes down, ye idle bellies, and read what Bacon has to say about the magic art.[yy] Silken feet in dancing shoes will not bear you on such a weary journey, so be ready to accept guidance from this hyperbole.[zz]

O Thou who tearest the heavens and camest down from them, before whose arrival the mountains melt as hot water boils on a bright fire, that Thy name shall be proclaimed among its enemies, who nevertheless call themselves by it; and that anointed heathens may learn to tremble before the wonders that Thou doest, which are beyond their understanding. Let new false lights rise in the Orient! Let the pert cleverness of their magi be roused by new stars into bearing their treasures in person to our country. Myrrh, frankincense, and their gold, which mean more to us than their magic art! Let kings be gulled by it, and their philosophical muse rage at children and children's lore;[69] but let not Rachel weep in vain! – –

Why should we swallow death from the pots,[70] to make the garnish palatable for the children of the prophets? And how shall we appease the vexed spirit[71] of the Scripture: 'Will I eat the flesh of bulls, or drink the blood of goats?'[72] Neither the dogmatic thoroughness of the orthodox Pharisees nor the poetic extravagance of the free-thinking Sadducees will renew the mission of the spirit which inspired GOD's holy men (in season or out of season) to speak and write. That dearly loved disciple of GOD's only-begotten Son, which is in the bosom of the Father, has declared it to us:[73] that the spirit of prophecy liveth in the testimony of the name of the ONE GOD, who alone maketh us blessed and through whom alone we may inherit the promise of this and the next life; the name which no one knows except he who receives it, the name which is above all names, that all things which dwell in Heaven and upon the earth and beneath the earth should bow their knee in the name of JESUS; and that all tongues should confess that JESUS CHRIST is the LORD to the glory of GOD the creator, to whom be praise in all eternity, Amen!

Thus the testimony of JESUS is the spirit of prophecy,[aaa] and the first sign by which He reveals the majesty of His humble figure transforms the holy books of the covenant into fine old wine, which deceives the steward's judgement[74] and strengthens the weak stomach of the critics. 'If you read the prophetic books without understanding Christ', says the Punic[bbb] Father of the Church, 'what insipidity and foolishness you will find! If you understand Christ in them, then what you read will not only be to your taste, but will also intoxicate you.'[80] – 'But to put a curb on the proud and wicked spirits here, Adam must surely have been dead before he would suffer this thing and drink the strong wine. Therefore have a care that you drink no wine while you are still a suckling child; every doctrine has its measure, time, and age.[ccc]

After GOD had grown weary of speaking to us through Nature and Scripture, through created things and prophets, through reasonings and figures, through poets and seers, and had grown short of breath, He spoke to us at last in the evening of days through His Son – yesterday and today! – until the promise of His coming, no longer as a servant, shall be fulfilled –

> Thou art the King of Glory, O Christ,
> Thou art the everlasting Son of the Father,
> Thou didst not abhor the Virgin's womb.[ddd 82]

We would pass a judgement for slander if we were to call our clever sophists fools and idiots when they describe the Law-Giver of the Jews as an ass's head and when they compare the proverbs of their great singers to dove's dung.[84] But the day of the LORD, a Sabbath darker than the midnight in which indomitable armadas are but as a stubble-field – the gentlest zephyr, herald of the last Thunderstorm – as poetical as the LORD of Hosts could think and express it – will drown the blasts of even the sturdiest trumpeter – – Abraham's joy shall reach its pinnacle – his cup shall run over, then with his own hand GOD shall wipe away Abraham's last tear, more precious than all the pearls wantonly wasted by the last Queen of Egypt;[85] the last tear shed over the last ashes of Sodom and the fate of the last martyr[eee] GOD will wipe from the eye of Abraham, from the father of the faithful.

That day of the LORD, which gives the Christian courage to preach the LORD's death, will publish and make known the most stupid village idiots among all the angels for whom the fires of hell are waiting. The devils believe and tremble! But your senses, crazed by the cunning of reason, tremble not. You laugh when Adam the sinner chokes on the apple, and Anacreon the wise man on the grape-pip. Do ye not laugh when the geese fill the Capitol with alarm, and the ravens feed the lover of his country, whose spirit was Israel's artillery and cavalry? You congratulate yourselves secretly on your blindness when GOD on the cross is numbered among the criminals, and when some outrage in Geneva or Rome, in the opera or the mosque,[86] reaches its apotheosis or purgation.

> Paint two snakes! Consecrated ground, my lads:
> Not the place for a piss! I take my leave...[87]   (Persius)

The birth of a genius will be celebrated, as usual, to the accompanying martyrdom of innocents – I take the liberty of comparing rhyme and metre to innocent children, for our most recent poetry seems to put them in mortal danger.

If rhyme belongs to the same genus as paronomasia and word-play,[fff] then its origins must be almost as old as the nature of language and our sense-impressions. The poet who finds the yoke of rhyme too heavy to bear is not therefore justified in denigrating its talents.[ggg] The failed rhyme might otherwise have given this frivolous pen as much occasion for a satire as Plato may have had to immortalise Aristophanes's hiccups in *The Symposium*, or Scarron his own hiccups in a sonnet.[90]

The free structure which that great restorer of lyric song, Klopstock, has allowed himself is, I would guess, an archaism, a happy imitation of the mysterious workings of sacred poetry among the ancient Hebrews.[91] And, as the most thorough critics of our time[hhh] shrewdly observe, what we apprehend in it is nothing but 'an artificial prose whose periods have been broken down into their elements, each one of which can be read as a single line in a particular metre; and the reflections and feelings of the most ancient and holy poets seem of their own accord' (perhaps just as randomly as Epicurus's cosmic atoms) 'to have arranged themselves into symmetrical lines which are full of harmony, although they have no (prescribed or mandatory) metre'.[92]

Homer's monotonous metre ought to seem at least as paradoxical to us as the free rhythms of our German Pindar.[iii] My admiration or ignorance of the causes for the Greek poet's use of the same metre throughout was modified when I made a journey through Courland and Lithuania. In certain parts of these regions, you can hear the Lettish or non-German people at work, singing only a single cadence of a few notes, which greatly resembles a poetic metre.[96] If a poet were to emerge among them, it would be quite natural for him to tailor all his lines to this measure initiated by their voices. To place this small detail in the appropriate light ('perhaps to please the foolish – who wish to burn it with their curling irons'),[97] compare it with several other phenomena, trace their causes, and develop their fruitful consequences would take too much time.

> Surely enough of snow and icy showers
> From the stern north Jove hath in vengeance called,
> Striking with red right hand his sacred towers,
> And Rome appalled –
>
> Ay, the whole earth – lest should return the time
> Of Pyrrha's blank amaze at sights most strange,
> When Proteus drove his finny herd to climb
> The mountain range.   Horace[98]

Gloss

As the oldest reader of this Rhapsody in cabbalistic prose, I feel obliged by the right of primogeniture to bequeath to my younger brethren who will come after, one more example of a merciful judgement, as follows:

Everything in this aesthetic nutshell tastes of vanity, vanity! The Rhapsodist[jjj] has read, observed, reflected, sought and found agreeable words, quoted faithfully, gone round about like a merchant ship and brought his far-fetched cargo home. He has calculated sentence for sentence as arrows are counted on a battle-field;[kkk] and circumscribed his figures as stakes are measured for a tent. Instead of stakes and arrows he has, with the amateurs and pedants of his time, ... written obelisks and asterisks.[lll]

Let us now hear the sum total of his newest aesthetic, which is the oldest:

Fear GOD, *and give glory to Him; for the time of His judgement is come; and worship Him that made heaven, and earth, and the sea, and the fountains of waters!*[100]

Part 4
Herder

Johann Gottfried Herder

(1744–1803)

Herder was born in Mohrungen in East Prussia, and grew up in humble circumstances. He studied theology at Königsberg University from 1762 to 1764, and attended the lectures of the young Immanuel Kant, who had not yet emancipated himself from post-Cartesian rationalism and was keenly interested in the sciences. At the same time, he became friendly with the deeply religious Hamann.

Herder taught at a school in Riga for several years, and thereafter occupied posts of increasing seniority within the Lutheran church, at Riga (1767–9), Bückeburg (1771–6), and Weimar (1776–1803). He was a polymath and prolific writer from an early age. His early works deal mainly with literary and aesthetic theory, and are indebted to, among others, Lessing, Winckelmann, and Hamann. His prize-essay *On the Origin of Language* (1771) applied naturalistic, psychological methods to the problem of linguistic origins, and the essays on Ossian and on Shakespeare (1773) display a degree of imaginative historical understanding hitherto unprecedented in the German Enlightenment. The historical relativism already apparent in these essays is extended to history as a whole in his (ironically entitled) *Yet Another Philosophy of History* (1774), in which the then fashionable optimism of progress is rejected in favour of a more sympathetic view of primitive societies and of the Middle Ages.

After a series of theological works, some of them close in spirit to Hamann and often concerned with the poetic aspects of the Bible, Herder returned to history with his greatest work, the *Ideas on the Philosophy of History* of 1784–91. Human history is now placed in the context of the physical universe as a whole, and the determining influence of climate and geography is emphasised. Herder's earlier relativism is now modified by a belief in rational laws in both nature and human history. His late works, mainly collections of essays in periodical form, show an increasingly secular spirit. *God, a Series of Dialogues* (1787) expounds a form of nature pantheism strongly influenced by Spinoza, and anticipates the *Naturphilosophie* of Schelling. His last years were embittered by a feud with his former teacher Kant, whose critical philosophy seemed to Herder a new form of scholasticism divorced from experience, and by a breach in his long friendship with Goethe.

Herder was an unsystematic and eclectic thinker, but his fertile mind generated ideas which others, including Goethe, Schiller, Schelling, and Alexander von Humboldt, were to develop further. Perhaps his greatest contribution to German thought is his historical relativism, which taught his successors to assess each age and culture on its own terms and helped to discredit the linear and progressive model of history favoured by the rationalists of the *Aufklärung*.

Further reading

The standard edition of the works is that of Suphan (1877–1913), and the new edition of the letters by Hahn (1977–) is nearly completed. Barnard (1969) contains a useful selection of English translations from the works, and there are complete translations of *On the Origin of Language* by Moran and Gode (1967), *God* by Burkhardt (new edition, 1962), and the *Outlines of a Philosophy of History* (= *Ideas on the Philosophy of History*) by Churchill (new edition, 1966). The standard biography is that of Haym (new edition, 1954), and there are shorter (Gillies, 1945) and longer (Clark, 1955) biographies in English. Berlin (1976) assesses Herder's stimulus to Romanticism, Wells (1959) and Barnard (1965) deal with social and political aspects, and Nisbet (1970) examines Herder's relationship with the sciences.

Extract from a Correspondence on Ossian and the Songs of Ancient Peoples[1]

1773

Translated by Joyce P. Crick, with modifications by the editor.
German text in *Sämtliche Werke*, edited by Suphan (1877–1913), V, 159–207.

My friend,[2] I share your delight at the translation of Ossian[3] for our language and our nation; it has pleased me as much as an original epic. A poet so full of the grandeur, innocence, simplicity, activity, and bliss of human life must assuredly make an impact – if we do not *in faece Romuli*[4] entirely despair of the effectiveness of good books – and move all those hearts which likewise would dwell in a poor Highland cottage and consecrate their houses to a cottage celebration. And Denis's translation shows such taste, such industry, partly a happy liveliness in the images, partly the vigour of the German language, that I too promptly ranged it among the favourite books in my library, and congratulated Germany on a bard of its own who has but been awakened by the Scottish bard. You used to be so obstinately sceptical of the Scottish Ossian's authenticity,[5] but listen to me now, who once defended him, not obstinately doubting, but nevertheless maintaining that despite all the taste and industry and liveliness and vigour of the German translation, our Ossian is assuredly not the true Ossian any more. I have not enough space to prove it here, so I can only offer my assertion as the Turkish Mufti utters his dictum, and here the name of the Mufti...[6]

My arguments against the German Ossian are not, as you kindly imagine, merely a general animus against the German hexameter; for what kind of feeling, of tone or harmony of soul do you credit me with, if I were to have no feeling for Ewald von Kleist's use of the hexameter, for example, or

Klopstock's?[7] But – since you have yourself brought it up – what is Klopstock's hexameter doing in Ossian's poetry? *Hinc illae lacrimae*[8] indeed! If only Herr Denis had listened to Ossian's true style with his inner ear as well – Ossian so short and sharp, so strong, so virile, so abrupt in images and feelings; Klopstock's manner so leisurely, so admirable in the way it pours out feelings at length, making them advance in waves, break and die and advance again, letting the words and expressive combinations flow out. What a difference! And what is Ossian, when presented to us in Klopstock's hexameter? In Klopstock's style? I cannot think of two more different poets, even if Ossian were regarded as being a true writer of epics.

But he is not. – But I wanted to do no more than mention that, for I think some critical journal has already discussed this topic, and that has nothing to do with me.[9] What I wanted to do was to remind you that Ossian's poems are songs, songs of the people, folksongs, the songs of an unsophisticated people living close to the senses, songs which have been long handed down by oral tradition. And is that what they are when clad in our fine epic form? How could they possibly be? My friend, my first argument against your obstinate scepticism towards Ossian's originality relied above all upon an inner witness, the spirit of the work itself, which told us with prophetic voice that Macpherson could not possibly have invented something of this kind. Poetry of this kind could not possibly be composed in this century. And now, with that self-same inner witness I cry just as loudly: 'It is really impossible to sing that, impossible for a barbarous mountain people to sing it, hand it on, preserve it in a form such as this! Consequently it is not Ossian, the singer, whose songs were handed down.' What do you say to my inner proof? Next time I shall perhaps send you pages on this!

...I did not believe you would cling so wilfully to your German Ossian, nor try with your detailed comparisons and analyses to force me to admit 'that he is certainly as good as the English Ossian'. As far as sheer immediate feeling is concerned, what cannot be analysed out of it! What cannot be proved by a brooding dissection – which at the very least is not the aforementioned immediate feeling. Have you considered in this case what you are usually very sensible of: what a different tone the discourse acquires from the omission of a word, the addition of another, the paraphrase or repetition of a third, from a different accent, glance, or voice? The sense may remain the same, but what of the tone, the colour, the immediate feeling of the individuality of place and purpose? And does not all the beauty of the poem, all the spirit and strength of the discourse depend upon these factors? I grant you that our Ossian, as a work of poetry, is as good as the English, indeed better – but just because it is such a beautiful poetic work, it is no longer Ossian the ancient bard. That is what I wanted to say.[10]

* * *

Know then, that the more barbarous a people is – that is, the more alive, the more freely acting (for that is what the word means) – the more barbarous, that is, the more alive, the more free, the closer to the senses, the more lyrically dynamic its songs will be, if songs it has. The more remote a people is from an artificial, scientific manner of thinking, speaking, and writing, the less its songs are made for paper and print, the less its verses are written for the dead letter. The purpose, the nature, the miraculous power of these songs as the delight, the driving-force, the traditional chant and everlasting joy of the people – all this depends on the lyrical, living, dance-like quality of the song, on the living presence of the images, and the coherence and, as it were, compulsion of the content, the feelings; on the symmetry of the words and syllables, and sometimes even of the letters, on the flow of the melody, and on a hundred other things which belong to the living world, to the gnomic song of the nation, and vanish with it. These are the arrows of this barbarous Apollo with which he pierces our hearts and transfixes soul and memory. The longer the song is to last, the stronger and more attached to the senses these arousers of the soul must be to defy the power of time and the changes of the centuries – so which way does my argument turn now?

The Scandinavians, as we find them throughout Ossian too, were certainly a wilder, ruder people than the mild idealised Scots. I do not know of any Scandinavian song where a gentle feeling flows. They tread on rock and ice and frozen earth, and with regard to such treatment and culture, I do not know any Scandinavian poem that can be compared with Ossian's. But if once you look at their poems in the editions of Worm, Bartholin, Peringskiöld, or Verel[11] – how many kinds of metre! how exactly each one is determined by the ear's immediate susceptibility to rhythm! alliterative syllables symmetrically arranged within the lines like signals for the metrical beat, marching-orders to the warrior-band. Alliterative sounds as a call to arms, for the bardic song to resound against the shields. Distichs and lines corresponding! Vowels alike! Syllables harmonising – truly a rhythmical pulse to the line so skilful, rapid, and exact that we study-bound readers have difficulty apprehending it with our eyes alone. But those peoples in all their vitality who did not read it from the page but heard it, heard it from childhood on and joined in singing it and adapted their ear to it – do not imagine that they had any difficulty with the rhythm! Nothing becomes habituated more strongly and enduringly, more rapidly and delicately than the ear. Once it has grasped a thing, how durably it retains it! Once apprehended in our youth with stumbling speech, how vividly it returns to us, and in swift association with every aspect of the living world, how richly and powerfully it returns! If I were minded to psychologise, I could relate you many a strange phenomenon from the realms of music, song and speech![12]

* * *

And another thing. Read through Ossian's poems. In all the characteristics of bardic song they resemble another nation which still lives and sings and acts on earth today, and in whose history I have more than once recognised without illusion or prejudice the living story of Ossian and his forebears. They are the five Indian nations of North America: war-cry and lament, battle-song and funeral dirge, historical paeans on their forefathers and to their forefathers – all this is common to Ossian's bards and the North American savages alike. I make an exception of the Indians' songs promising torture and revenge; instead the gentle Caledonians coloured their songs with the tender blood of love. Now look at how all the travellers, Charlevoix and Lafiteau, Roger and Cadwallader Colden have described the tone, the rhythm, the power of these songs even for strangers' ears.[13] Examine how all the reports agree on how much these songs depend for their effect upon living movement, melody, gesture, and mime. And when travellers acquainted with the Scots who have also lived for long periods among the American Indians – Captain Timberlake,[14] for example – acknowledge the obvious similarity between the lays of both nations – you can draw your own conclusions. With Denis's translation our feet are firmly planted on dull earth: we can hear something of the content and meaning conveyed in our own decently poetic idiom; but not a sound, not a tone resembling all the barbarous tribes, not a single living breath from the Caledonian hills to raise our hearts and set our pulses racing and bring us the living sound of their songs. We sit and read with our feet firmly on dull earth.

I once hoped deep in my heart that I might some day travel to England. Dear friend, you cannot imagine how I counted on visiting these Scots too! First an insight, I thought, into the spirit of this nation, into its public institutions, into the English stage and the vast living drama of the English people to clarify my ideas about the history, philosophy, politics, and peculiarities of this marvellous nation which are so often obscure and confused in the mind of the foreigner. And then the great change of scenery – to the Scots, to Macpherson! There I wanted to hear a living performance of a living people's songs, see them in all their effectiveness, see the places that are so alive in all their poems, study in their customs the remains of that ancient world, become for a while an ancient Caledonian myself – and then back to England to increase my acquaintance with the living monuments of her literature, art collections, and the finer points of her national character – how much I looked forward to fulfilling this plan! And as a translator I would certainly have set about my task in a completely different way from Denis. For him, even the example of the original Gaelic offered by Macpherson was printed in vain.

. . . You mock my enthusiasm for these savages almost as Voltaire scoffed at Rousseau for wanting to go on all fours:[15] but do not think that this makes me despise the advantages of our own morals and manners, whatever they may be. The human race is destined to develop through a series of scenes in culture and customs; alas for the man who mislikes the scene on which he has to make his entrance, do his deeds, and live his life! But alas too for the philosopher of mankind and culture who thinks that his scene is the only one, and misjudges the primal scene to be the worst and the most primitive! If they all belong

together as part of the great drama of history, then each one displays a new
and remarkable aspect of humanity – and take care that I do not shortly afflict
you with a psychology based on Ossian's poems! The ideas for one, at least,
are stirring alive and deep in my heart, and would make very strange
reading![16]

* * *

You know from travellers' accounts how vigorously and clearly savages
always express themselves. Always with a sharp, vivid eye on the thing they
want to say, using their senses, feeling the purpose of their utterance immediately
and exactly, not distracted by shadowy concepts, half-ideas, and symbolic
letter-understanding (the words of their language are innocent of this, for they
have virtually no abstract terms); still less corrupted by artifices, slavish
expectations, timid creeping politics, and confusing pre-meditation – blissfully
ignorant of all these debilitations of the mind, they comprehend the thought
as a whole with the whole word, and the word with the thought. Either they
are silent, or they speak at the moment of involvement with an unpre-
meditated soundness, sureness, and beauty, which learned Europeans of all
times could not but admire – and were bound to leave untouched. Our
pedants who have to clobber everything together in advance and learn it by
rote before they can stammer it out with might and method; our schoolmasters,
sextons, apothecaries and all the tribe of the little-learned who raid the
scholar's house and come out empty-handed until finally, like Shakespeare's
gravediggers, his Lancelot or his Dogberry, they speak in the uncertain
inauthentic tones of decline and death – compare these learned fellows with
the savages! If you are seeking traces of their firm clarity in our own time, do
not go looking for it among the pedants. Unspoiled children, women, folk of
a sound natural sense, minds formed less by speculation than by activity –
these, if what I have been describing is true eloquence, are the finest, nay the
only orators of our time.

But in ancient times, it was the poets, the skalds, the scholars who best knew
how to wed this sureness and clarity of expression to dignity, sonority, and
beauty. And as they had thus united soul and voice and a firm bond, not to
confound each other but to be a support and an helpmeet, thus it was that
those (to us) half-miraculous works were composed by the ἀοίδοις,[17] singers,
bards, minstrels – for that is what the greatest poets of ancient times were.
Homer's rhapsodies and Ossian's songs were as it were impromptus, for at that
time oratory was known only in impromptu delivery. Ossian was followed,
though faintly and at a distance, by the minstrels, but still they did follow him,
until finally Art arrived and extinguished Nature. From our youth we have
tormented ourselves learning foreign languages and spelling out the syllabic
quantity of their verses, to which our ear and nature can no longer respond;
working according to rules virtually none of which a genius would acknowledge as rules of Nature; composing poetry about subject-matter that gives us
nothing to think about, still less to *sense*, and even less to imagine; feigning

passions we do not feel; imitating faculties of the soul we do not possess – until finally it all turned false, insipid, and artificial. Even the best minds were confounded, and lost their sureness of eye and hand, their certainty of thought and expression and with them their true vitality and truth and urgency – everything was lost. Poetry, which should have been the most passionate, confident daughter of the human soul, became the most insecure, weak and hesitant, and poems turned into schoolboys' exercises for correction. And if that is the way our time thinks, then of course we will admire Art rather than Nature in these ancient poems; we will find too much or too little Art in them, according to our predisposition, and we will rarely have ears to hear the voice that sings in them: the voice of Nature. I am sure that if Homer and Ossian were to come back to earth and hear their works read and praised, they would all too often be astonished at what we add to them and take away from them, at the artifices we apply to them, and at our lack of any immediate feeling for them.

Of course our hearts and minds have been formed differently from theirs by our education from youth and by the long intervening generations. We scarcely see and feel any longer: we only think and brood. Our poetry does not emerge from a living world, nor exist in the storm and confluence of such objects and feelings. Instead we force either our theme or our treatment or both, and we have done so for so long and so often and from our tenderest years that if we attempted any free development, it would scarcely prosper; for how can a cripple get up and walk? That is why so many of our recent poems lack that certainty, that exactness, that full contour which comes only from the first spontaneous draft, not from any elaborate later revisions. Our ridiculous versifying would have appeared to Homer and Ossian as the weak scribbles of an apprentice would have appeared to Raphael, or to Apelles,[18] whose barest sketch revealed his mastery.

...What I said recently about the first spontaneous draft of a poem in no way justifies the careless and bungling efforts of our young would-be poets. For what deficiency is more obvious in their work than the very indefiniteness of their thoughts and words? They themselves never know what they want or ought to say. But if someone lacks even that knowledge, how can any corrections ever teach him it? Can anyone make a marble statue of Apollo out of a kitchen skewer?

It seems to me, given the state of our poetry at present, that two main possibilities are open to us. If a poet recognises that the mental faculties which are required partly by his subject and by the poetic genre he has chosen, and which also happen to be predominant within him, are the representational and cognitive faculties – he must reflect thoroughly on the content of his poem, comprehend it, turn it over, and order it clearly and distinctly until every letter is, as it were, engraved upon his soul, and his poem need only reproduce this in a complete and honest manner. But if his poem requires an outpouring of

passion and feeling, or if this class of faculties supplies the most active and
habitual kind of motivation he needs for his work – then he will abandon
himself to the inspiration of the happy hour, and will write and enchant us.[19]

*   *   *

...You think that we Germans too probably had poems like the Scottish ballad
I quoted.[20] I do not merely think so; I know it for certain. I know of folksongs,
dialect songs, peasant-songs from more than one province which certainly yield
nothing in the way of rhythm and liveliness, simplicity and vigour of language,
to many such ballads. But who is there to collect them? to care about them?
to care about the songs of the people, from the streets and alleys and
fishmarkets? about the unsophisticated roundelays of country folk? about songs
which often do not scan, whose rhymes are often false? who would take the
trouble to collect them – who would bother to print them for our critics who
are so clever at scansion and syllable-counting? We would rather read our
prettily printed modern poets – just to pass the time, of course. Let the French
collect their old *chansons*! Let the English publish their ancient songs and
ballads and romances in splendid volumes! Let Lessing be the only one in
Germany to bother about Logau and Scultetus and the old bardic lays![21] Our
recent poets, of course, are better printed and more agreeable to read; at most
we print extracts from Opitz, Fleming, and Gryphius.[22] Let the remnants of
the old, true folk poetry vanish entirely with the daily advance of our so-called
culture, just as many such treasures have already vanished – after all, we have
metaphysics and dogmatics and bureaucratics – and we dream peacefully on –
      And yet, believe me, if we were to go in search of our local songs, each one
of us, in our own province, we might well gather poems together, perhaps half
as many as in Percy's *Reliques*, but almost their equal in value! How often
have I been reminded as I read poems from his collection, particularly the best
Scottish pieces, of German customs and German poems, some of which I have
heard myself. If you have friends in Alsace, in Switzerland, in the Tyrol, in
Franconia or Swabia, then beg of them – first that they should not be ashamed
of these poems – for the sturdy Englishmen were not ashamed of theirs, nor
did they need to be.[23]
                              *   *   *

All the songs of these savage peoples move around objects, actions, events,
around a living world! How rich and various are the details, incidents,
immediate features! And the eye has seen it all, the mind has imagined it all.
This implies leaps and gaps and sudden transitions. There is the same
connection between the sections of these songs as there is between the trees and
bushes of the forest; the same between the cliffs and grottoes of the wilderness
as there is between the scenes of the event itself. When the Greenlander tells
of the seal-hunt, he does not speak; he paints all the details with words and
gestures, for they are all part of the picture in his mind. When he holds a
graveside eulogy and sings a funeral dirge for his departed, he does not praise

or lament, but paints, and the dead man's life, vividly portrayed with all the sudden leaps of the imagination, cannot but speak and cry.[24]

*   *   *

Look at the overloaded artificial Gothick style of the recent so-called philosophical and pindaric odes by the English poets Gray, Akenside, Mason,[25] etc., which they regard as masterpieces! Does the content or the metre or the wording produce the least effect of an ode? Look at the artificial Horatian style we Germans have fallen into at times – Ossian, the songs of the savage tribes and the old Norse skalds, romances, dialect poems could show us a better path, but only if we are ready to learn more than the form, the wording, or the language. But unfortunately this is only our starting-point, and if we stay there, we will get nowhere. Am I wrong, or is it not true that the most beautiful lyric poems we have now – and long have had – are consonant with this virile, firm, vigorous German tone, or at least approach it – so what can we not hope from the awakening of more of that kind![26]

Shakespeare[1]

1773

Translated by Joyce P. Crick, with modifications by the editor.
German text in *Sämtliche Werke*, edited by Suphan (1877–1913), v, 208–31.

If there is any man to conjure up in our minds that tremendous image of one 'seated high on the craggy hilltop, storm, tempest, and the roaring sea at his feet, but with the radiance of the heavens about his head',[2] that man is Shakespeare. Only with the addition that below him, at the foot of his rocky throne, there murmur the masses who explain him, apologise for him, condemn him, excuse him, worship, calumniate, translate, and traduce him – and to all of whom he is deaf!

What a library of books has already been written about him, for him, against him! And I have no wish to add to it. I would rather that no one in the small circle of my readers would ever again dream of writing about him, for him, against him, excusing him or slandering him; but would rather explain him, feel him as he is, use him, and – if possible – make him alive for us in Germany. May this essay help in the task.

Shakespeare's boldest enemies have, in so many guises, mocked at him and declared that though he may be a great poet, he is not a good dramatist; and even if he is a good dramatist, he is incapable of the great classical tragedies of Sophocles, Euripides, Corneille, and Voltaire, who have taken this art to its furthest limits. And Shakespeare's boldest friends have mostly been satisfied with finding excuses and making apologies for him, always treating his beauties as compensations for his transgressions against the rules, uttering an *Absolvo te* over the accused and then idolising his greatness the more extravagantly, the more they are obliged to shrug their shoulders at his flaws. This is still the case with his most recent editors and commentators.[3] I hope these pages will change the perspective and throw a fuller light upon his image.

But is this not too bold, too presumptuous a hope, when so many of the great have written about him? I think not. If I can demonstrate that both sides have been building on prejudice, on illusion, on nothing; if I have only to draw a cloud from their eyes or at most adjust the image without in the least altering anything in either eye or image, then perhaps I can ascribe it to my time or even to chance that I should have found the place on which to position my reader: here is the place to stand, else you will see nothing but caricature. But if we go on winding and unwinding at the great tangle of pedantry without ever getting any further, what a grievous destiny we shall weave!

It is from Greece that we have inherited the words drama, tragedy, comedy. And as the lettered culture of the human race has, in a narrow region of the world, made its way solely through tradition, a certain store of rules which seemed inseparable from its teaching has naturally been carried everywhere with it as in its womb and in its language. Since of course it is impossible to educate a child by way of reason, but only by way of authority, impression, and the divinity of example and of habit, so also entire nations are to an even greater extent children in all that they learn. The kernel will not grow without the husk, and they will never harvest the kernel without the husk, even if they have no use for it. That is the case with Greek and northern drama.

In Greece drama developed in a way in which it could not develop in the north. In Greece it was what it could not be in the north. Therefore in the north it is not and cannot be what it was in Greece. Thus Sophocles's drama and Shakespeare's drama are two things which in a certain respect have scarcely the name in common. I believe I can demonstrate these propositions from Greece itself and thereby decipher in no small measure the nature of northern drama and of the greatest northern dramatist, Shakespeare. We will perceive the origins of the one by means of the other, but at the same time see it transformed, so that it does not remain the same thing.

Greek tragedy developed as it were out of *one* scene, out of the impromptu dithyramb, the mimed dance, the chorus. This underwent accretions, adaptations: instead of one acting figure, Aeschylus introduced two on to the stage, invented the concept of the protagonist, and reduced the choric element. Sophocles added the third figure, invented the stage – out of such origins, but relatively late, Greek tragedy rose to its great heights, became a masterpiece of the human spirit, the summit of poetry which Aristotle honours so highly, and we, looking at Sophocles and Euripides, cannot admire deeply enough.

But at the same time we see that certain things can be explained in terms of these origins which, if we were to look upon them as dead rules, we would be bound to misjudge dreadfully. That simplicity of the Greek plot, that austerity of Greek manners, that sustained, buskined quality of expression, the music, the stage, the unity of place and time – all this lay so fundamentally and naturally, without any art or magic, in the origins of Greek tragedy – that it could come into being only in the sublimation of all these characteristics. They were the husk in which the fruit grew.

Go back to the childhood of that time: simplicity of plot really was so deeply embedded in what was called the deeds of ancient times, republican, patriotic, religious, heroic action, that the poet's difficulty lay in discerning parts in this simple whole, in introducing a dramatic beginning, middle, and end, rather than in forcing them apart, lopping them off, or in shaping a whole out of disparate events. Any reader of Aeschylus or Sophocles would see nothing incomprehensible in that. In Aeschylus's drama, what is tragedy often but an allegorical, mythological, semi-epic tableau, almost without sequence of scenes, story, feelings? It was, as the Ancients said, nothing but chorus, with a certain amount of story in between. Could there be the least labour or art expended on simplicity of plot in such a case? And was it any different in most of Sophocles's plays? His *Philoctetes*, *Ajax*, *Oedipus Coloneus*, etc. are all still very close to the uniform nature of their origin: the dramatic tableau surrounded by the chorus. No doubt about it! This is the genesis of the Greek stage!

Now see how much follows from this simple observation. Nothing less than: 'the artificiality of their rules was – not artifice at all! it was Nature!' Unity of plot was unity of the action before them which, according to the circumstances of their time, country, religion, manners, could not be other than single and simple. Unity of place – was unity of place; for the one brief solemn act took place only in one location, in the temple, the palace, as it were in the nation's market-place. There it first admitted only mimed enactments and narrated interpolations; then at last the entrances and exits and the separate scenes were added – but of course it was still but one scene, where everything was held together by the chorus, where in the nature of things the stage could never remain empty, and so on. And now what child needs to have it spelt out that the natural accompaniment and consequence of all this is unity of time? All these elements lay in the very nature of things, so for all his skill, without them the poet could do nothing!

So it is also obvious that the art of the Greek poets took a path completely opposite to the one which we have had ascribed to them nowadays. They did not simplify, I think, but they complicated.[4] Aeschylus made the chorus more complex. Sophocles elaborated on Aeschylus. And if we compare Sophocles's most cunning dramas and his masterpiece *Oedipus Rex* with Aeschylus's *Prometheus Bound* or with what information we have of the ancient dithyrambs, we shall perceive the astonishing art which he succeeded in bringing to them. But it was never the art of making many into one, but really the art of turning simplicity into a multiplicity, into a beautiful labyrinth of scenes. And his greatest care was still, when he had reached the most complicated point of the labyrinth, to transform his spectators' perception back into the illusion of that earlier simplicity, and to unwind the tangled knot of their feelings so gently and gradually as to make them feel that they had never lost it, that previous dithyrambic feeling of oneness. That is why he separated out the scenes for them, at the same time retaining the choruses and making them the points of rest for the action. That is why, with every individual word, he did not let them lose sight of the whole, in the expectation, in the illusion of development and of completion (all these things the ingenious Euripides, when the stage had scarcely been established, promptly failed to do!). In short, Sophocles gave the action *grandeur* (which is something that has been terribly misunderstood).[5]

And anyone who reads him with clear eyes and from the point of view of Sophocles's own time will appreciate how highly Aristotle valued the genius of his art, and will realise that everything he says was virtually the opposite of what modern times have been pleased to make of it. The very fact that Aristotle moved away from Thespis and Aeschylus and based himself on the complexity of Sophocles's poetry; that he took this innovation as his starting-point and located the essence of the new poetic genre there; that it became his dearest wish to develop a new Homer of the drama and compare him to his advantage with the first; that he omitted not the slightest detail that might in performance support his conception of the action of scale and grandeur – all this shows that the great philosopher too was theorising according to the great tendency of his time, and that he is in no way to blame for the restrictive and childish follies which have turned him into the paper scaffolding of our modern stage![6] In his excellent chapter on the nature of the plot,[7] he clearly knew and recognised no other rule than the eye of the spectator, soul, illusion, and expressly stated that limitations of length, still less of kind or time or place of the structure, do not admit of being determined by any other rules. Oh, if Aristotle were alive today and saw the false, perverted use of his rules in dramas of a wholly different kind! But we had better stick to calm and dispassionate inquiry!

As everything in the world changes, so the Nature which was the true creator of Greek drama was bound to change also. Their view of the world, their customs, the state of the republics, the tradition of the heroic age, religion, even music, expression, and the degrees of illusion changed. And in the natural course of things the material for plots vanished, the opportunity for their use, the incentive for using them. True, poets could work on old material and even take over their material from other nations and dress it in the accustomed manner. But that did not achieve the effect. In consequence it lacked the soul. In consequence it was no longer (why should we mince our words) the thing itself. Puppet, imitation, ape, image, in which only the most blinkered devotee could find the moving spirit which once filled the statue with life. Let us turn straight away (for the Romans were too stupid, or too clever, or too savage and immoderate to create a totally hellenising theatre) to the new Athenians[8] of Europe, and the matter will, I think, become obvious.

There is no doubt: everything that makes for this stuffed likeness of the Greek theatre has scarcely been more perfectly conceived and produced than in France. I do not only mean the rules of the theatre, so-called, which are laid at the good Aristotle's door: unity of time, place, action, connection between scenes, verisimilitude of setting, and so on. What I really want to ask is whether there is anything in the world possible beyond that glib classical thing that Corneille, Racine, and Voltaire have produced, beyond that sequence of beautiful scenes, of dialogue, of lines and rhymes with their measure, their decorum, their polish? The writer of this essay not only doubts it, but all the admirers of Voltaire and the French, especially those noble Athenians themselves, will deny it outright – they have done so often enough in the past, they are still at it, and they will go on doing so: 'There is nothing above it; it cannot be bettered!' And in the light of this general agreement, with that stuffed and stilted image there on the stage, they are right, and are bound to become more so, the more all the countries of Europe lose their heads to this glib smoothness and continue to ape it.

But all the time there is that oppressive, incontrovertible feeling: 'This is not Greek tragedy, not in purpose, effect, kind, or nature', and the most partial admirer of the French cannot deny this, once he has experienced the Greeks. I will not even attempt to inquire whether they observe their Aristotle's rules as much as they claim, for Lessing has recently raised the most terrible doubts about the loudest pretensions.[9] But granted all that, the drama is not the same, because it has nothing in common with Greek drama at its very heart: neither action, nor customs, nor language, nor purpose – nothing. So what is the point of all these externals, this scrupulously preserved uniformity? Does anybody believe that a single one of the great Corneille's heroes is a Roman or a French hero? Spanish heroes! Heroes out of Seneca! Gallant heroes; adventurous, brave, magnanimous, amorous heroes, cruel heroes – dramatic fictions who outside the theatre would be called fools and who even then, at least in France, were almost as alien as they are now – that is what they are. Racine speaks the language of sensibility – and it is widely agreed that, in this respect, he is unrivalled. But even so, I would not know where sensibility ever spoke such a language as this. These are pictures of sensibility at third hand; they are never, or but rarely, the first, immediate, naked emotions, groping for words and then finding them at last. Is not Voltaire's beautiful poetic line – its mould, content, treatment of imagery, brilliance, wit, philosophy – a beautiful line indeed? Of course! The most beautiful you could imagine; and if I were a Frenchman, I would despair of writing a single line after Voltaire – but beautiful or not, it is not *theatrical* verse, appropriate to the action, language, morals, passions, purpose of a *drama* (other than French drama); it is false, pedantic balderdash! And the ultimate aim and end of it all? Certainly not a Greek end, certainly not a tragic aim and purpose. To stage a beautiful play – as long as it is a beautiful action as well – to have a number of ladies and gentlemen of elegant dress and deportment utter fine speeches and recite philosophy both sweet and useful in beautiful verse, to put them all into a story which gives an illusion of reality and holds our attention, finally to have it all performed by a cast of well-rehearsed ladies and gentlemen who go to great lengths to win our applause and approval with their declamation, the stilted gait of the sentiments, and the externalities of feeling – all this might serve most excellently as a living textbook, as an exercise in expression, deportment, and decorum, as a pattern of good, even heroic, behaviour, and even as a complete academy of national wisdom and propriety in matters of living and dying (quite apart from all secondary purposes). Beautiful, instructive, educative, most excellent it may be – but it contains not a hint of the aim and purpose of the Greek theatre.

And what was this aim? According to Aristotle (and there has been enough dispute about it ever since), it is no more nor less than a certain convulsion of the heart, an agitation of the soul to a certain degree and in certain aspects – in short, a specific kind of illusion which, believe me, no French play has yet achieved, or will achieve. And consequently, whatever splendid or useful name it may bear, it is not Greek drama! it is not Sophoclean tragedy! It resembles Greek drama as an effigy might! The effigy lacks spirit, life, nature, truth – that is, all the elements that move us; that is, the tragic purpose and the achievement of that purpose – so how can it be the same thing?

This in itself proves nothing as to its merit or lack of merit, but only raises the question of difference, which I think my previous remarks have established beyond doubt. And now I leave it to the reader to decide for himself whether a copy of foreign ages, customs, and actions which is only half true, with the entertaining purpose of adapting them to a two-hour performance on a wooden stage, could compare with, let alone be regarded as greater than, an imitation which in a certain sense was the epitome of a country's national identity? I leave it to the reader to judge (and a Frenchman will have to do his best to get round this one) whether a poetic drama which really has no purpose at all as a whole – for according to the best thinkers its greatest virtue lies only in the selection of detail – whether this can be compared with a national institution in which each minute particular has its effect and is the bearer of the richest, deepest culture. Whether finally a time was not bound to come when, with most of Corneille's most artificial plays already forgotten, we will regard Crébillon[10] and Voltaire with the same admiration with which we now look on d'Urfé's *Astrea*[11] and all the *Clelias*[12] and *Aspasias*[13] from the times of chivalry: 'So clever, so wise, so inventive and well-made, there might be so much to learn from them, but what a pity it is in *Astrea* and *Clelia*.' Their entire art is unnatural, extravagant, tedious! We would be fortunate if our taste for truth had already reached that stage! The entire French repertory would have been transformed into a collection of pretty lines, maxims, and sentiments – but the great Sophocles would still stand where he is now!

So let us now assume a nation which, on account of circumstances which we will not pursue, had no desire to ape ancient drama and run off with the walnut-shell, but rather wanted to create its own drama. Then, I think, our first question would still be: when, where, under what conditions, out of what materials should it do so? And it needs no proof that its creation can and will be the result of these questions. If it does not develop its drama out of the chorus and the dithyramb, then it will not have any trace of a choric, dithyrambic character. If its world did not offer such simplicity in its history, traditions, domestic, political, and religious conditions, then of course it will not display it either. If possible, it will create its drama out of its own history, the spirit of its age, customs, views, language, national attitudes, traditions, and pastimes, even if they are carnival farces or puppet-plays (just as the Greeks did from the chorus) – and what they create will be drama, as long as it achieves the true purpose of drama among this nation. Clearly, I am referring to the

toto divisis ab orbe Britannis[14]

and their great Shakespeare.

That this was not Greece, neither then nor earlier, will not be denied by any *pullulus Aristotelis*,[15] and so to demand that Greek drama should develop naturally then and there (I am not speaking of mere imitation) is worse than expecting a sheep to give birth to lion-cubs. Our first and last question is solely: what is the soil like? what harvest has it been prepared for? what has been sown in it? what is its most suitable produce? And great heavens, how far we are from Greece! History, tradition, customs, religion, the spirit of the time, of the nation, of emotion, of language – how far from Greece! Whether the reader knows both periods well or but a little, he will not for a moment confuse things that have nothing in common. And if in this different time – changed for good or ill, but changed – there happened to be an age, a genius who might create a dramatic œuvre out of this raw material as naturally, impressively, and originally as the Greeks did from theirs; and if this creation were to attain the same end, though taking very different paths; and if it were essentially a far more complexly simple and simply complex entity, that is (according to all the metaphysical definitions) a perfect whole – then what fool would compare and condemn because this latter was not the former? For its very nature, virtue, and perfection consist in the fact that it is not the same as the first; that out of the soil of the age there grew a different plant.

Shakespeare's age offered him anything but the simplicity of national customs, deeds, inclinations, and historical traditions which shaped Greek drama. And since, according to the first maxim in metaphysics, nothing will come of nothing, not only, if it were left to the philosophers, would there be no Greek drama, but, if nothing else existed besides, there would and could no longer be any drama at all. But since it is well known that genius is more than philosophy, and creation a very different thing from analysis, there came a mortal man, endowed with divine powers, who conjured out of utterly different material and with a wholly different approach the self-same effect: *fear* and *pity*! and both to a degree which the earlier treatment and material could scarcely produce. How the gods favoured his venture! It was the very freshness, innovation, and difference that demonstrated the primal power of his vocation.

Shakespeare did not have a chorus to start from, but he did have puppet-plays and popular historical dramas; so out of the inferior clay of these dramas and puppet-plays he shaped the splendid creation that lives and moves before us! He found nothing like the simplicity of the Greek national character, but a multiplicity of estates, ways of life, attitudes, nations, and styles of speech. To grieve for the former would be labour lost; so he concentrated the estates and the individuals, the different peoples and styles of speech, the kings and fools, fools and kings, into a splendid poetic whole! He found no such simple spirit of history, story, action: he took history as he found it, and his creative spirit combined the most various stuff into a marvellous whole; and though we cannot call it plot in the Greek sense, we could refer to it by the middle-period term 'action', or by the modern term 'event' (*événement*), 'great occurrence' – O Aristotle, if you were to appear now, what Homeric odes you would sing to the new Sophocles! You would invent a theory to fit him, such as his fellow countrymen Home[16] and Hurd,[17] Pope and Johnson have not yet created! You would rejoice to draw lines for each of your plays on plot, character, sentiments, expression, stage, as it were from the two points at the base of a triangle to meet above at the point of destination – perfection! You would say to Sophocles: 'Paint the sacred panel of this altar; and thou, northern bard, paint all the sides and walls of this temple with thy immortal fresco!'

Let me continue expounding and rhapsodising, for I am closer to Shakespeare than to the Greek. Whereas in Sophocles's drama the unity of a single action is dominant, Shakespeare aims at the entirety of an event, an occurrence. Whereas Sophocles makes a single tone predominate in his characters, Shakespeare uses all the characters, estates, walks of life he requires to produce the concerted sound of his drama. Whereas in Sophocles a single ethereal diction sings as it were in the Empyrean, Shakespeare speaks the language of all ages, of all sorts and conditions of men; he is the interpreter of Nature in all her tongues – and in such different ways can they both be the familiars of the same Divinity? And if Sophocles represented and taught and moved and educated Greeks, Shakespeare taught and moved and educated northern men! When I read him, it seems to me as if theatre, actors, scenery all vanish! Single leaves from the book of events, providence, the world, blowing in the storm of history. Individual impressions of nations, classes, souls, all the most various and disparate machines, all the ignorant blind instruments – which is what we ourselves are in the hand of the creator of the world – which combine to form a whole theatrical image, a grand event whose totality only the poet can survey. Who can imagine a greater poet of mankind in the northern world, and a greater poet of his age?

Step then before his stage, as before an ocean of events, where wave thunders upon wave. Scenes from nature come and go before our eyes; however disparate they seem, they are dynamically related; they create and destroy one another so that the intention of their creator, who seems to have put them together according to a crazy and disorderly plan, may be fulfilled – dark little symbols that form the silhouette of a divine theodicy. Lear, the rash, hot-headed old man, noble in his weakness as he stands before his map giving away crowns and tearing countries apart – the very first scene already bears within its seed the harvest of his fate in the dark future. Behold, soon we shall see the generous spendthrift, the hasty tyrant, the childish father even in his daughters' antechambers, pleading, praying, begging, cursing, raving, blessing – o Heavens, and presaging madness! Then he will soon go bare-headed in the thunder and lightning, cast down to the lowest of the low, in the company of a fool, in a crazy beggar's cave, almost calling down madness from above. And now see him as he is, in all the light-yoked majesty of the poor abandoned wretch; and now restored to himself, illumined by the last rays of hope only for them to be extinguished for ever! Imprisoned, dead in his arms the child and daughter who had comforted and forgiven him; dying over her body; and his faithful servant dying after the old king! O God, what vicissitudes of times, circumstances, tempests, climes, and ages! And all of it not merely a single story, a heroic political action, if you will, moving from a single beginning to a single end according to Aristotle's strictest rule;[18] but draw nearer and feel too the human spirit which integrated every person and age and character, down to the smallest secondary thing, into the picture. Two old fathers and all their very different children. The son of the one, grateful in his misfortune towards his deceived father; the other hideously ungrateful towards his affectionate father, even in his abominable good fortune. One father against his daughters, his daughters against him, their husbands, suitors, and all their accomplices in fortune and misfortune! Blind Gloucester supported by his unrecognised son, and mad Lear at the feet of his rejected daughter! And now the moment at the cross-roads of fortune, when Gloucester dies beneath his tree, and the trumpet calls, all the incidental circumstances, motives, characters, and situations concentrated into the poetic work, all in a world of fiction, all developing into a whole, a whole made up of fathers, children, kings and fools, beggars and misery, but throughout which the soul of the great event breathes even in the most disparate scenes, in which places, times, circumstances, even, I would say, the pagan philosophy of fate and the stars which reigns throughout, all belong so essentially to the whole that I could change nothing, move nothing, nor transfer parts from other plays, or to other plays. And that is not a drama? Shakespeare is not a dramatic poet? The poet who embraces a hundred scenes of a world event in his arms, composes them with his glance, breathes into them an all-animating soul, and enraptures us, our attention, our heart, all our passions, our entire soul from beginning to end – if not more, then let father Aristotle be witness: 'the scale of the living creature must allow it to be comprehended with *one* glance'[19] – and here – great Heavens! How Shakespeare feels the whole course of events in the depths of his soul and draws them to a close! A world of dramatic history, as great and as profound as Nature; but it is the creator who gives us the eye and perspective to see its greatness and profundity.

In *Othello*, the Moor, what a world! what a whole! the living history of how the passion of this noble, unhappy man emerges, develops, erupts, and comes to its sad end. And what richness and complexity in the mechanism that goes to make *one* drama! How this Iago, this devil in human form, has to view the world in a certain way and treat everyone around him as his playthings; and how the other figures, Cassio and Roderigo, Othello and Desdemona, with their susceptibilities as tinder to his diabolical flame, have to be grouped around him; how all are caught in his net and exploited by him, and everything hastens to its sorrowful end. If an angel of providence were to weigh human passions against one another, and compose groups of souls and characters, and endow them with occasions for each to act in the illusion of free will, while he led them by this illusion, as if by the chain of fate, towards his controlling idea – this is how the human mind which conceived this work devised, pondered, planned, and guided its course.

It should not be necessary to point out that time and place are as essential to the action as husk is to kernel, and yet these are what provoke the loudest outcry. If Shakespeare discovered the godlike art of conceiving an entire world of the most disparate scenes as one great event, then of course it was part of the truth of his events also to idealise time and place for each scene in such a way that they too contributed to the illusion. Is there anyone in the world who is indifferent to the time and place of even trivial events in his life? And are they not particularly important in matters where the entire soul is moved, formed, and transformed? In our youth, in scenes of passion, in all the decisive actions of our lives! Is it not place and time and the fullness of external circumstances which endow the whole story with its direction, duration, and existence? And can one remove from a child, a youth, a lover, a man in the field of action, a single localising circumstance, a single how? where? or when?, without prejudicing our whole grasp of his personality? In this respect, Shakespeare is the greatest master, simply because he is only and always the servant of Nature. When he created the events in his dramas and pondered them in his mind, he pondered times and places too. From out of all the scenes and conjunctures in the world, Shakespeare chose, as though by some law of fatality, just those which are the most powerful, the most appropriate to the feeling of the action; in which the strangest, boldest circumstances best support the illusion of truth; in which the changes of time and place over which the poet rules, proclaim most loudly: 'This is not a poet, but a creator! Here is the history of the world!'

For example, when the poet was turning over in his mind as a fact of creation the terrible regicide, the tragedy called *Macbeth* – if then, dear reader, you were too timid to enter into the feeling of place and setting in any scene, then alas for Shakespeare, and for the withered page in your hand! For you will have felt nothing of its opening, with the witches on the blasted heath, nothing of the scene with the bloody man bringing the news of Macbeth's deeds, nothing of the king's tidings to him; you will have felt nothing of the change of scene when Macbeth is ready to listen to the witches' prophetic spirit and identifies their greeting with Duncan's previous message. You will not have seen his wife walking the castle with that fateful letter, nor how she will walk there later so terribly transformed. Nor finally will you have enjoyed with the gentle king the sweet evening air where fearlessly the martlet breeds and haunts, while you, King Duncan – this lies in the workings of the invisible – are drawing near your murderous grave. The house in a bustle, making ready for guests, and Macbeth making ready for murder! Banquo's preparatory scene at night with torches and sword! The dagger, the terrible dagger in the vision! The bell – the deed has scarcely been done when there comes that knocking on the door! The discovery – the assembled guests – you may travel all ages and places and you will find that the intention behind this creation could not have been realised other than there and in this way. The scene of Banquo's murder in the forest, the nocturnal banquet and Banquo's ghost – then again on the witches' heath (for his terrible and fateful deed is done!). Then the witches' cavern, spells, prophecies, rage, despair! The death of Macduff's children, with only their mother to shelter them beneath her wing! and the two outlaws beneath the tree, and then the frightful queen sleep-walking in the castle, and the marvellous fulfilment of the prophecy – Birnam Wood drawing near – Macbeth's death at the sword of one not of woman born – I would have to enumerate all the scenes, all of them, to give a local habitation to the ineffable whole, a world of magic and regicide and destiny which is the soul of the play and breathes life into it right down to the smallest detail of time, place, and apparently wayward interlude. I would have to enumerate them so that I could summon it all before the soul as a terrible, indissoluble whole – and yet withal I would say nothing.

The individual quality of each drama, of each separate universe, pulses through place and time and composition in all the plays. Lessing compared certain aspects of *Hamlet* with that theatrical queen Semiramis.[20] How the spirit of the place fills the entire drama from beginning to end! The castle platform and the bitter cold – the watch relieved, tales told in the night, disbelief and credulity, the star, and then it appears! Is there anyone who does not sense art and nature in every word and detail! And so it proceeds. All ghostly and human guises exhausted! The cock crows and the drum rolls, the silent beckoning and the nearby hill, speech and silence – what a setting! what a profound revelation of the truth! See how the frightened king kneels, and Hamlet strays past his father's picture in his mother's chamber! And now the other scene! Hamlet at Ophelia's grave! The touching good fellow in all his dealings with Horatio, Ophelia, Laertes, Fortinbras! the young man's playing with action, which runs through the play and almost until the end never becomes action – if for one moment you feel and look for the boards of a stage and a series of decorous versified speeches upon them, neither Shakespeare nor Sophocles nor any true poet in the world has written for you.

Oh, if only I had words for the one main feeling prevailing in each drama, pulsing through it like a world soul. As it does in *Othello*, belonging as an essential part to the drama, as in his searching for Desdemona at night, as in their fabulous love, the sea-crossing, the tempest, as in Othello's raging passion, in Desdemona's manner of death, which has been so much derided, singing her willow-song as she undresses, while the wind knocks; as in the nature of the sin and passion itself, his entrance, his address to the candle – if only it were possible to comprehend all this in words, to express how it all belongs deeply and organically to *one* world, one great tragic event – but it is not possible. Words cannot describe or reproduce the merest most miserable painting, so how can they render the feeling of a living world in all the scenes, circumstances, and enchantments of Nature? Peruse what you will, gentle reader, *Lear* or the *Henries*, *Caesar* or the two *Richards*, even the magical plays and the interludes; *Romeo* in particular, the sweet drama of love, a romance indeed in every detail of time and place and dream and poetry – attempt to remove something of its quality, to change it, even to simplify it for the French stage – a living world in all the authenticity of its truth transformed into this wooden nullity – a fine metamorphosis! Deprive this plant of its soil, juices, and vigour, and plant it in the air, deprive this human being of place, time, individuality – you have robbed them of breath and soul, and you have a mere image of the living creature.

For Shakespeare is Sophocles's brother, precisely where he seems to be so dissimilar, and inwardly he is wholly like him. His whole dramatic illusion is attained by means of this authenticity, truth, and historical creativity. Without it, not merely would illusion be left unachieved, but nothing of Shakespeare's drama and dramatic spirit would remain – or else I have written in vain. Hence the entire world is but the body to this great spirit. All the scenes of Nature are the limbs of this body, even as all the characters and styles of thought are the features of this spirit – and the whole might well bear the name of Spinoza's giant god: Pan! Universum![21] Sophocles was true to Nature when he treated of *one* action in *one* place and at *one* time. Shakespeare could only be true to Nature when he rolled his great world events and human destinies through all the places and times – where they took place. And woe betide the frivolous Frenchman who arrives in time for Shakespeare's fifth act, expecting it will provide him with the quintessence of the play's touching sentiment. This may be true of many French plays, where everything is versified and paraded in scenes only for immediate theatrical effect. But here, he would go home empty-handed. For the great world-event would already be over. He would witness but its last and least important consequences, men falling like flies. He would leave the theatre and scoff: Shakespeare is an affront to him, and his drama the merest foolishness.

The whole tangled question of time and place would long ago have been unravelled if some philosophical mind had only taken the trouble to ask what time and place really mean in drama.[22] If the place is the stage and the length of time that of a *divertissement au théâtre*, then the only people in the world to have observed the unity of place and the measure of time and scenes are – the French. The Greeks, with a degree of illusion higher than we can conceive, whose stage was a public institution and whose theatre was a temple of worship, never gave the unities a thought. What kind of illusion is experienced by a spectator who looks at his watch at the end of every scene to check whether such an action could take place in such a span of time, and whose chief delight it is that the poet has not cheated him out of a second, but has showed him on the stage only what would take the same length of time in the snail's pace of his own life? What kind of creature could find this his greatest pleasure? And what kind of poet would regard this as his chiefest end, and pride himself on this nonsense of rules? 'How much pretty performance I have crammed so neatly into the narrow space of this pit made of boards, called *le théâtre français*; how elegantly I have fitted it all into the prescribed length of time of a polite visit! How I have sewed and stitched, polished and patched!' – miserable master of ceremonies, a theatrical posturer, not a creator, poet, god of the drama! The clock does not strike on tower or temple for you if you are a true dramatic poet, for you create your own space and time; and if you are capable of creating a world which can only exist in the categories of time and space, behold, your measure of space and duration is there within you, and you must conjure all your spectators to accept it, and urge it upon them – or else you are, as I have said, anything but a true dramatic poet.

Is there anyone in the world who needs to have it demonstrated that space and time are in themselves nothing, that in respect of being, action, passion, sequence of thought, and degree of attention within and without the soul, they are utterly relative? Has there never been any occasion in your life, good time-keeper of the drama, when hours seemed to you moments, and days seemed hours; and conversely times when hours turned into days and the watches of the night into years? Have you never known situations in your life when your soul dwelt sometimes outside you? Here, in your beloved's romantic chamber? there, gazing upon that frozen corpse? again, in the oppression of external shame and distress – or occasions when your soul fled far beyond world and time, overleaping the places and regions of the earth, unmindful of itself, to inhabit heaven, or the soul, the heart of the one whose being you feel so deeply? And if something of this kind is possible in your slow and sluggish, vermiculate and vegetable life, where there are roots enough to hold you fast to the dead ground, and each slow length you drag along is measure enough for your snail's pace, then imagine yourself for just one moment into another, poetic world, transpose yourself into a dream. Have you never perceived how in dreams space and time vanish? What insignificant things they are, what *shadows* they must be in comparison with action, with the working of the soul? Have you never observed how the soul creates its own space, world, and tempo as and where it will? And if you had experienced that only once in your life, and wakened after a mere quarter of an hour, the dark remnants of your actions in the dream would cause you to swear that you had slept and dreamed and acted whole nights away, and Mahomet's dream would not for one moment seem absurd to you.[23] And is it not the first and sole duty of every genius, of every poet, above all of the dramatic poet, to carry you off into such a dream? And now think what worlds you would be throwing into disarray if you were to show the poet your pocket-watch or your drawing-room, and ask him to teach you to dream according to their prescriptions!

The poet's space and time lie in the movement of his great event, in the *ordine successivorum et simultaneorum*[24] of *his* world. How and where does he transport you? As long as he sees to it that you are transported, you are in his world. However quickly or slowly he causes the course of time to pass, it is he who makes it pass; it is he who impresses its sequence upon you: that is his measure of time. And what a master Shakespeare is in this respect too! His grand events begin slowly and ponderously in his nature, as they do in Nature itself, for it is this which he renders, but on a smaller scale. How laborious his presentation, before the springs of action are set in motion! But once they are, how the scenes race by, how fleeting the speeches, how winged the souls, the passion, the action, and how powerful then the hastening movement, the pell-mell interjection of single words when time has run out for everyone. And finally, when the reader is entirely caught up in the illusion he has created, and is lost in the dark abyss of his world and his passion, how bold he becomes, what trains of events he commands! Lear dies after Cordelia! And Kent after Lear! It is virtually the end of his world; the Last Judgement is upon us, when everything, the Heavens included, lurches and collapses, and the mountains fall! The measure of time is no more. Not for our merry clock-watcher, of course, who turns up unscathed for the fifth act to measure by his time-piece how many died and how long it took. But Great Heavens, if that is supposed to be criticism, theatre, illusion – so much the worse for criticism, theatre, illusion! What do all these empty words mean?

At this point the heart of my inquiry might begin: what art, what creator's skills did Shakespeare employ to turn some base romance or tale or fabulous history into such a living poetic whole? What laws of historical, philosophical, or dramatic art are revealed in all his doings, in all the secrets of his craft?

What an inquiry! How much it could contribute to our reading of history, our philosophy of the human soul, our drama! But I am not a member of all our academies of history and philosophy and the fine arts, where in any case they turn their minds to anything but such a question. Even Shakespeare's own countrymen do not consider it. What historical errors his commentators have so often castigated him for, what beautiful historical passages have been faulted – for example in that bulky edition by Warburton![25] And has it occurred to the author of the most recent essay on him[26] to raise my fundamental question: 'how did Shakespeare turn tales and romances into poetic drama?'? Hardly. Just as it scarcely occurred to the Aristotle of this British Sophocles, Lord Home.[27]

So just a nod in the direction of the usual classifications of his plays. Not long ago a writer who certainly had a deep feeling for his Shakespeare had the bright idea of making that fishmonger of a courtier with his grey beard and wrinkled face, his eyes purging thick amber and his plentiful lack of wit together with weak hams, of making the childish Polonius, I say, into his Aristotle, and suggesting that the string of ...als and ...cals he splutters out should be taken seriously as the basis of classification for all of Shakespeare's plays.[28] I doubt it. True, it is Shakespeare's mischievous habit to put into the mouths of children and fools all those empty commonplaces, moral sentiments, and classifications which, when applied to a hundred instances, are appropriate to all and to none. And a new Stobaeus or *Florilegium* or *cornucopia* of Shakespeare's wisdom, such as the English already possess and we Germans, praise be, are supposed to have had of late,[29] would give the greatest pleasure precisely to figures like Polonius and Lancelot, the fools and harlequins, poor Dickon or bombastic king of knights,[30] because all the sane and sensible human beings in Shakespeare do not have any more to say than the moment requires. But even here I still have my doubts. It is probable that in this passage Polonius is intended to be just a great baby who takes clouds to be camels and camels to be bass-viols and in his youth once enacted Julius Caesar and was accounted a good actor and was killed by Brutus and knows very well

Why Day is Day, Night Night and Time is Time[31]

– spinning a top of theatrical words here too. But who would want to build a theory upon that? And what virtue lies in the distinctions Tragedy, Comedy, History, Pastoral, Tragical-Historical or Historical-Pastoral, Pastoral-Comical or Comical-Historical-Pastoral? And were we to shuffle those ...cals a hundred times, what insight would we have in the end? Not one single play would be a Greek tragedy, Comedy or Pastoral, nor should it be. Every play is History in the widest sense, which of course from time to time shades off in varying degrees into tragedy, comedy, etc., but the colours are so infinitely nuanced that in the last resort each play remains and cannot but remain – what it is: History! the heroic drama of the nation's destiny conjuring the illusion of the Middle Ages or (with the exception of a few plays which are really entertainments and interludes) a great and entire enactment of a world event, of a human destiny.

Sadder and more important is the thought that even this great creator of history and the world soul grows older himself, that the words and customs and categories of the age fall into the sere and yellow leaf, and that we ourselves are already so remote from these great ruins of the days of chivalry that even Garrick,[32] who has revived Shakespeare and been the guardian angel of his grave, has had to change, cut, and mutilate his works so much. And soon perhaps, as everything gets blurred and tends in different directions, even his drama will become incapable of living performance, and will become the fragment of a Colossus, an Egyptian pyramid which everyone gazes at in amazement and no one understands. Happy am I that, though time is running out, I still live at a time when it is possible for me to understand him; and when you, my friend,[33] who feel and recognise yourself in reading his dramas, and whom I have embraced more than once before his sacred image, can still dream the sweet dream worthy of your powers, that one day you will raise a monument to him here in our degenerate country, drawn from our age of chivalry and written in our language.[34] I envy you that dream. May your noble German powers not flag until the garland hangs aloft. And should you too in later times perceive how the ground shakes beneath your feet, and the rabble round about stand still and gape or jeer, and the everlasting pyramids cannot re-awaken the spirit of ancient Egypt – your work will stand. And a faithful successor will seek out your grave and write with pious hand the words that have summed up the lives of almost all the worthies in the world:

Voluit! quiescit![35]

Part 5

Schiller

Friedrich Schiller

(1759–1805)

Schiller was born at Marbach in the Duchy of Württemberg, where his father held a commission in the Duke's army. From 1773 to 1780, he studied at the Military Academy in nearby Stuttgart, in whose running the despotic Duke Karl Eugen took a personal interest. After graduating in medicine, Schiller became a regimental physician. The Duke disapproved of the young Schiller's literary activities, and Schiller fled his domains in 1782 to Mannheim, at whose theatre his first drama, *The Robbers*, had already been successfully performed.

Schiller's early work, particularly *The Robbers* and his early tragedy *Intrigue and Love* (*Kabale und Liebe*, 1784), is characterised by social and political protest, in which the influences of Rousseau and of the *Sturm und Drang* movement of the 1770s are apparent. His historical tragedy *Don Carlos* (1787) defends the rights of the Dutch people under Spanish oppression, and Schiller's work on it prepared the way for his *History of the Revolt of the Netherlands* (1788), a work which gained him the Chair of History at Jena University. His *History of the Thirty Years War* followed in 1791–3.

In 1793, Schiller embarked on intensive studies of Kant, and wrote a series of essays on ethical and aesthetic subjects, several of them dealing with the theory of tragedy. Central to them is the concept of tragic sublimity, which is achieved by voluntary acceptance of suffering in the interests of a moral end. His *Aesthetic Letters* (1794–5) deal with the educative effects of aesthetic experience in promoting a balanced state of mind and an integral personality. This work, and *On Naive and Sentimental Poetry* (1795–6), in which Schiller distinguishes two basic types of poetry and poet (ancient and modern, spontaneous and reflective), benefited from his friendship with Goethe, which began in 1794.

Schiller's greatest historical tragedy, the trilogy *Wallenstein* (1797–8), was followed in quick succession by *Maria Stuart* (1800), *The Maid of Orleans* (1801), *The Bride of Messina* (1803), and *Wilhelm Tell* (1804). All are in verse, and all aspire to a universally representative or 'classical' character at the expense of merely local or contemporary relevance. (*The Bride of Messina* even employs a Greek chorus.)

As a critic, Schiller was much indebted to Kant's philosophy. But whereas Kant's moral rigorism could readily be accommodated to the theory of tragedy, Schiller felt the need to modify Kant's uncompromising dualism in presenting art as a means of harmonising conflicting impulses within the human psyche and restoring it to wholeness. The ideal of wholeness is again fundamental in *On Naive and Sentimental Poetry*, which adopts a historical approach to the problem. Schiller defines and justifies the distinctive character of modern, as opposed to ancient, poetry; but he contends that the modern, reflective poet must ultimately overcome, by his own self-conscious methods, that division between ideal and reality which did not exist for the 'naive' poet of antiquity.

Further reading

The *Nationalausgabe* of the collected works (1943–) is still incomplete, but the edition by Fricke and Göpfert (1958–9) contains the principal writings. The letters have been collected by Jonas (1892–6). Biographical studies include those of Minor (1890) and the more modern account by von Wiese (fourth edition, 1978). Most of the plays have been translated into English, and Lamport's versions of *Maria Stuart* (1969) and of *The Robbers* and *Wallenstein* (1979) can be recommended. The bilingual edition of the *Aesthetic Letters* by Wilkinson and Willoughby (1967) is excellent. General studies in English include Garland (1949) and Witte (1949). Kerry (1961) deals specifically with the aesthetic writings.

On Naive and Sentimental Poetry[1]

1795–6

Translated by Julius A. Elias (slightly modified).
German text in *Schillers Werke. Nationalausgabe*, edited by Petersen and others (1943–), xx, 413–503.

There are moments in our lives when we dedicate a kind of love and tender respect to nature in plants, minerals, animals, and landscapes, as well as to human nature in children, in the customs of country folk, and to the primitive world, not because it gratifies our senses, nor yet because it satisfies our understanding or taste (the very opposite can occur in both instances), rather, simply *because it is nature*. Every person of a finer cast who is not totally lacking in feeling experiences this when he wanders in the open air, when he stays in the country, or lingers before the monuments of ancient times; in short, whenever he is surprised in the midst of artificial circumstances and situations by the sight of simple nature. It is this interest, not infrequently elevated into a need, which underlies much of our fondness for flowers and animals, for simple gardens, for strolls, for the country and its inhabitants, for many an artifact of remote antiquity, and the like; provided that neither affectation nor any other fortuitous interest plays a role. However, this kind of interest in nature can take place only under two conditions. First, it is absolutely necessary that the object which inspires it should be *nature* or at least be taken by us as such; second, that it be *naive* (in the broadest meaning of the word), i.e., that nature stand in contrast to art and put it to shame. As soon as the latter is joined with the former, not before, nature becomes naive.

Nature, considered in this wise, is for us nothing but the voluntary presence, the subsistence of things on their own, their existence in accordance with their own immutable laws.

This representation is absolutely necessary if we are to take an interest in such appearances. If one were able by the most consummate deception to give an artificial flower the similitude of nature, if one were able to induce the highest illusion of the naive in human behaviour by imitating it, the discovery that it was imitation would completely destroy the feeling of which we spoke.[a] From this it is clear that this kind of satisfaction in nature is not aesthetic but moral; for it is mediated by an idea, not produced immediately by observation; nor is it in any way dependent upon beauty of form. For what could a modest flower, a stream, a mossy stone, the chirping of birds, the humming of bees, etc., possess in themselves so pleasing to us? What could give them a claim even upon our love? It is not these objects, it is an idea represented by them which we love in them. We love in them the tacitly creative life, the serene spontaneity of their activity, existence in accordance with their own laws, the inner necessity, the eternal unity with themselves.

They are what we were; they are what *we should once again become*. We were nature just as they, and our culture, by means of reason and freedom, should lead us back to nature. They are, therefore, not only the representation of our lost childhood, which eternally remains most dear to us, so that they fill us with a certain melancholy. But they are also representations of our highest fulfilment in the ideal, thus evoking in us a sublime tenderness.

Yet their perfection is not to their credit, because it is not the product of their choice. They accord us then, the quite unique delight of being our example without putting us to shame. They surround us like a continuous divine phenomenon, but more exhilarating than blinding. What determines their character is precisely what is lacking for the perfection of our own; what distinguishes us from them, is precisely what they themselves lack for divinity. We are free, they are necessary; we change, they remain a unity. But only if both are joined one with the other – if the will freely obeys the law of necessity, and reason asserts its rule through all the flux of imagination, does the ideal or the divine come to the fore. *In them*, then, we see eternally that which escapes us, but for which we are challenged to strive, and which, even if we never attain to it, we may still hope to approach in endless progress. *In ourselves* we observe an advantage which they lack, and in which they can either never participate at all (as in the case of the irrational) or only insofar as they proceed by *our* path (as with childhood). They afford us, therefore, the sweetest enjoyment of our humanity as idea, even though they must perforce humiliate us with reference to any particular condition of our humanity.

Since this interest in nature is based upon an idea, it can manifest itself only in minds which are receptive to ideas, i.e., in moral minds. By far the majority of people merely affect this state, and the universality of this sentimental taste in our times as expressed, particularly since the appearance of certain writings,[3] in the form of sentimental journeys, pleasure gardens, walks, and other delights of this sort, is by no means a proof of the universality of this mode of feeling. Yet nature will always have something of this effect even upon the most unfeeling, if only because that tendency toward the moral common to all men is sufficient for the purpose, and we are all without distinction, regardless of the distance between our actions and the simplicity and truth of nature, impelled to it in idea. Particularly powerfully and most universally this sensitivity to nature is given expression at the instance of such objects as stand in close connection with us, affording a retrospective view of ourselves and revealing more closely the unnatural in us, as, for example, in children and childlike folk. One is in error to suppose that it is only the notion of helplessness which overcomes us with tenderness at certain moments when we are together with children. That may perhaps be the case with those who in the presence of weakness are accustomed only to feeling their own superiority. But the feeling of which I speak (it occurs only in specifically moral moods and is not to be confused with the emotion that is excited in us by the happy activity of children) is humiliating rather than favourable to self-love; and even if an advantage were to be drawn from it, this would certainly not be on our side. We are touched not because we look down upon the child from the height of our strength and perfection, but rather because we *look upward* from the *limitation* of our condition, which is inseparable from the *determination* which we have attained, to the unlimited *determinability*[4] of the child and to its pure innocence; and our emotion at such a moment is too transparently mixed with a certain melancholy for its source to be mistaken. In the child *disposition* and *determination*[5] are represented; in us that *fulfilment* that forever remains far short of those. The child is therefore a lively representation to us of the ideal, not indeed as it is fulfilled, but as it is enjoined; hence we are in no sense moved by the notion of its poverty and limitation, but rather by the opposite: the notion of its pure and free strength, its integrity, its infinity. To a moral and sensitive person a child will be a *sacred* object on this account; an object, in fact, which by the greatness of an idea destroys all empirical greatness; one which, whatever else it may lose in the judgement of the understanding, it regains in ample measure in the judgement of reason.[6]

It is from just this contradiction between the judgement of reason and the understanding that the quite extraordinary phenomenon arises of those mixed feelings which the *naive* mode of thought excites in us. It connects *childlike* simplicity with the *childish*; through the latter it exposes its weakness to the understanding and causes that smile by which we betray our (*theoretical*) superiority. But as soon as we have cause to believe that childish simplicity is at the same time childlike, that in consequence not lack of understanding, not incapacity, but rather a higher (*practical*)[7] strength, a heart full of innocence and truth, is the source of that which out of its inner greatness scorns the aid of art, then that triumph of the understanding is set aside, and mockery of ingenuousness yields to admiration of simplicity. We feel ourselves obliged to respect the object at which we formerly smiled, and since we at the same time cast our glance upon ourselves, bemoan the fact that we are not likewise endowed. Thus arises the entirely unique phenomenon of a feeling in which joyous mockery, respect, and melancholy are compounded.[b]

To be naive it is necessary that nature be victorious over art,[c] whether this occur counter to the knowledge or will of the individual or with his full awareness. In the first case this is the naive of *surprise* and amuses us; in the second, it is the naive of *temperament* and touches us.

With the naive of surprise the individual must be *morally* capable of denying nature; with the naive of temperament this may not be the case, but we must not be able to think him *physically* incapable of doing so if it is to affect us as being naive. The actions and speech of children thus give us a pure impression of the naive only so long as we do not recall their incapacity for art and in any case only take into consideration the contrast between their naturalness and the artificiality in ourselves. The naive is *childlikeness where it is no longer expected*, and precisely on this account cannot be ascribed to actual childhood in the most rigorous sense.

But in both cases, in the naive of surprise just as in the naive of temperament, nature must be in the right where art is in the wrong.

Only by this last provision is the concept of the naive completed. The affect[9] is also nature, and the rule of propriety is something artificial; yet the victory of the affect over propriety is anything but naive. If, on the other hand, the same affect should triumph over artifice, over false modesty, over deceit, then we do not hesitate to call it naive.[d] Hence it is necessary that nature should triumph over art not by her blind violence as *dynamic greatness*, but by her form as *moral greatness*, in brief, not as *compulsion*, but as *inner necessity*. It is not the inadequacy of art but its invalidity that must have assured the victory of nature; for inadequacy is a shortcoming, and nothing that derives from a shortcoming can inspire respect. It is indeed the case with the naive of surprise that the superior power of the affect and a lack of awareness reveal nature; but this lack and the superior power by no means constitute the naive, rather they simply provide the opportunity for nature to obey unimpeded her moral character, i.e., the law of harmony.

The naive of surprise can apply only to a human being, and then only insofar as in this moment he is no longer pure and innocent nature. It presupposes a will that is not in harmony with nature's own acts. Such a person, when brought to awareness, will take fright at himself; the naive *temperament*, on the other hand, will marvel at people and at their astonishment. But since, in the naive of surprise, the truth is revealed not by the personal and moral character, but by the natural character as revealed through the affect, we cannot attribute any merit to the individual for his sincerity, and our laughter is mockery deserved, which will not be restrained by any personal esteem for the individual. But since even in this case it is the sincerity of nature that breaks through the veil of falsity, a satisfaction of a higher order will be joined with the malicious joy at having caught somebody out; for nature in contrast with deceit must always engender respect. We therefore experience a truly moral pleasure even at the expense of the naive of surprise, although not at the expense of moral character.[e]

In the naive of surprise we do indeed always respect nature because we are obliged to respect truth; in the naive of temperament, on the other hand, we respect the person and hence enjoy not only a moral pleasure but a moral object. In both cases nature is in the *right* in that it speaks truth; but in the latter case not only is nature in the right, but the individual also possesses *honour*. In the first case the sincerity of nature accrues to the shame of the individual because it is involuntary; in the second it always accrues to his credit, even if whatever he said should put him to shame.

We ascribe a naive temperament to a person if he, in his judgement of things, overlooks their artificial and contrived aspects and heeds only their simple nature. We demand of him whatever can be judged about things within healthy nature, and absolutely ignore whatever presupposes any detachment from nature, whether due to thought or feeling, or any knowledge thereof.

If a father tells his child that some man or other is expiring from poverty, and the child goes and gives the poor man his father's purse, such an action is naive; for healthy nature is acting through the child, and in a world in which healthy nature were predominant he would be entirely right to act so. He sees only the distress and the means nearest at hand to alleviate it; such a development of property rights as permits a portion of humanity to perish has no basis in simple nature. The child's act, therefore, puts the world to shame, and this our hearts also confess by the satisfaction they derive from such an act.

If a man without knowledge of the world, but otherwise sound of understanding, tells his secrets to another who is deceiving him, but who is able skilfully to conceal his motives, and so, by his own sincerity, lends the other the means with which to harm him, this we find naive. We laugh at him, yet we cannot refrain from esteeming him. For his trust in the other man springs from the uprightness of his own temperament; at least he is naive only insofar as this is the case.

The naive mode of thought can therefore never be a characteristic of depraved men, rather it can be attributed only to children and to those of a childlike temperament. These latter often act and think naively in the midst of the artificial circumstances of fashionable society; they forget in their own beautiful humanity that they have to do with a depraved world, and comport themselves even at the courts of kings with the same ingenuousness and innocence that one would find only in a pastoral society.

It is, incidentally, not at all easy to distinguish always between childish and childlike innocence, since there are actions which hover on the extreme boundary between both, and where we are left absolutely in doubt whether we should laugh at their simplemindedness or esteem their noble simplicity. There is a very remarkable example of this type in the history of the reign of

Pope Adrian VI which has been described for us by Herr Schröckh with his customary punctiliousness and factual accuracy.[10] This pope, a Dutchman by birth, occupied the Holy See at one of the most critical times for the hierarchy, when an embittered faction was exposing the shortcomings of the Roman Church without mercy, and the opposing faction was interested in the highest degree in concealing them. What the truly naive character, if indeed such a one should ever stray upon the seat of St Peter, should have done in this case, is not the question; rather, it is how far such naivety of temperament might be compatible with the role of the pope. This it was, however, that placed the predecessors and successors of Adrian in the extremest embarrassment. They uniformly followed the established Roman system of making no admissions whatever. But Adrian truly possessed the upright character of his nation and the innocence of his former station. From the narrow sphere of the scholar he was translated to his supreme position, and even upon the heights of his new office had not become untrue to that simple character. The abuses in the Church disturbed him, and he was far too straightforward to dissimulate publicly what he privately admitted to himself. In accordance with this manner of thinking he allowed himself in the instructions he sent with his legate to Germany to be betrayed into admissions which had never been heard of from any pope, and which ran directly counter to the principles of this Court. 'We well know', they read in part, 'that for many years much that is abominable has issued from this Holy See; no wonder, then, if the diseased condition has been transmitted from the head to the limbs, from the pope to the prelates. We have all fallen by the way, and it has already been long since one of us has done any good thing, not even one.' Elsewhere he instructs the legate to declare in his name that he, Adrian, was not to be blamed for anything that had been done by the popes before him, and that such excesses, even when he was still living in a lowly estate, had always displeased him, and so forth. One can easily imagine how such naivety on the part of the pope must have been received by the Roman clergy; the least that was laid to his charge was that he had betrayed the Church to the heretics. This most impolitic measure by the pope would, nevertheless, be worthy of our entire respect and admiration, if we could only convince ourselves that he was really naive, that is, that it had been elicited from him solely by the natural candour of his character without any consideration for the possible consequences, and that he would have done no less had he been aware of the whole extent of the imprudence involved. But we have some reason to believe that he took this course to be by no means so impolitic, and went so far in his innocence as to hope by his complaisance to have won from his adversaries something very important to the advantage of his Church. He not only imagined that as a man of honour he was obliged to take this step, but also that he could justify it as pope; but, since he forgot that the most artificial of all institutions could be maintained only by a continued denial of the truth,[11] he committed the inexcusable error of applying rules of conduct which might have proven correct under natural circumstances in an entirely opposite situation. This perforce much alters our judgement; and even if we cannot withhold our respect for the uprightness of the heart from which that action flowed, yet it is not a little diminished by the consideration that here nature had too weak an opponent in art, and the heart in the head.

Every true genius must be naive, or it is not genius. Only its naivety makes for its genius, and what it is intellectually and aesthetically it cannot disavow morally. Unacquainted with the rules, those crutches for weakness and taskmasters of awkwardness, led only by nature or by instinct, its guardian angel, it goes calmly and surely through all the snares of false taste in which, if it is not shrewd enough to avoid them from afar, the nongenius must inevitably be entrapped. Only to genius is it given to be at home beyond the accustomed and to *extend* nature without *going beyond* her. It is true that sometimes the latter befalls even the greatest geniuses, but only because even they have their moments of fantasy in which protective nature abandons them either because they are engrossed by the power of example, or because the perverted taste of their times misleads them.

The genius must solve the most complex tasks with unpretentious simplicity and facility; the egg of Columbus appears in every decision of genius. And only thus does genius identify itself as such, by triumphing over the complications of art by simplicity. It proceeds not by the accepted principles, but by flashes of insight and feeling; but its insights are the inspirations of a god (everything done by healthy nature is divine), its feelings are laws for all ages and for all races of men.

The childlike character that the genius imposes upon his works he likewise displays in his private life and morals. He is *chaste*, for this nature always is; but he is not *prudish*, for only decadence is prudish. He is *intelligent*, for nature can never be otherwise; but he is not *cunning*, for only art can be so. He is *true* to his character and his inclinations, but not so much because he possesses principles as because nature, despite all fluctuations, always returns to its former state, always revives the old necessity. He is *modest*, even shy, because genius always remains a mystery to itself; but he is not fearful, because he does not know the dangers of the path he travels. We know little of the private lives of the greatest geniuses, but even the little that is preserved, for example, of Sophocles, Archimedes, Hippocrates, and, in more recent times, of Ariosto, Dante, and Tasso, of Raphael, of Albrecht Dürer, Cervantes, Shakespeare, of Fielding, Sterne, etc., confirms this assertion.

Indeed, and this seems to present much more difficulty, even great statesmen and generals, if their greatness is due to their genius, will display a naive character. Among the ancients I cite only Epaminondas and Julius Caesar, among moderns only Henry IV of France, Gustavus Adolphus of Sweden, and Czar Peter the Great. The Duke of Marlborough, Turenne, and Vendôme all display this character. It is to the opposite sex that nature has assigned the naive character in its highest perfection. Woman's desire to please manifests itself nowhere so much as in seeking the *appearance of naivety*; proof enough, even if one had no other, that the greatest power of the sex depends upon this characteristic. But since the leading principles of feminine education are in perpetual conflict with this character, it is as difficult for a woman morally as it is for a man intellectually to preserve this magnificent gift of nature intact along with the advantages of a good education; and the *woman* who combines naivety of manner with a demeanour appropriate for society, is as worthy of the highest esteem as the scholar who joins the genius's freedom of thought with all the rigours of the schools.

From the naive mode of thought there necessarily follows naive expression in word as well as in gesture, and this is the most important element in gracefulness. By this naive grace genius expresses its most sublime and profound thought; the utterances of a god in the mouth of a child. The understanding of the schools, always fearful of error, crucifies its words and its concepts upon the cross of grammar and logic, and is severe and stiff to avoid uncertainty at all costs, employs many words to be quite sure of not saying too much, and deprives its thoughts of their strength and edge so that they may not cut the unwary. But genius delineates its own thoughts at a single felicitous stroke of the brush with an eternally determined, firm, and yet absolutely free outline. If to the former the sign remains forever heterogeneous and alien to the thing signified, to the latter language springs as by some inner necessity out of thought, and is so at one with it that even beneath the corporeal frame the spirit appears as if laid bare. It is precisely this mode of expression in which the sign disappears completely in the thing signified, and in which language, while giving expression to a thought, yet leaves it exposed (whereas the other mode cannot represent it without simultaneously concealing it); and this it is we generally call a gifted style displaying genius.

As freely and naturally as genius expresses itself in its works of the spirit, its innocence of heart is expressed in its social intercourse. Because we have fallen as far from simplicity and strict truth of expression in life in society as from simplicity of temperament, our easily wounded guilt, as well as our easily seduced powers of imagination, have made a timid propriety necessary. Without being false, one often speaks otherwise than one thinks; one is forced into periphrasis in order to say things which could cause pain only to a sick egotism or danger to a perverted fantasy. Ignorance of these conventional rules combined with natural sincerity that despises all deviousness and every trace of falsity (not crudity, which violates the rules because it finds them oppressive), produces a naivety of expression in society that consists of calling things which one may mention either only in some artificial manner, or not at all, by their true names and in the most succinct fashion. Of this sort are the customary expressions of children. They arouse laughter by their contrast with the usages, but one must always confess in one's heart that the child is right.

The naive temperament, strictly speaking, can indeed be ascribed only to the human being as a being not absolutely subject to nature, even though only insofar as pure nature actually still is active within him; but by an effect of the poetic imagination it is often transferred from the rational to the irrational. Thus we often attribute a naive character to an animal, a landscape, a building, even to nature in general, in opposition to the caprice and the fantastic concepts of men. But this always demands that we assign a will to the involuntary in our thoughts and insist on its rigorous consequence according to the law of necessity. The dissatisfaction at our own badly abused moral freedom and at the moral harmony we sense is lacking in our actions easily induces a mood in which we address the non-rational as a person, making a virtue of its eternal uniformity, and envying its calm bearing, as though there were really some temptation to be otherwise which it had resisted. At such a moment it suits us well to take the prerogative of our reason as a curse and an evil and, in our lively apprehension of the imperfection of our actual performance, to pass unfair judgement on our predisposition and determination.

Then we see in irrational nature only a happier sister who remained in our mother's house, out of which we impetuously fled abroad in the arrogance of our freedom. With painful nostalgia we yearn to return as soon as we have begun to experience the pressure of civilisation and hear in the remote lands of art our mother's tender voice. As long as we were children of nature merely, we enjoyed happiness and perfection; we became free, and lost both. Thence arises a dual and very unequal longing for nature, a longing for her *happiness*, a longing for her *perfection*. The sensuous man bemoans the loss of the first; only the moral man can grieve at the loss of the other.

Then ask of yourself, sensitive friend of nature, whether your lassitude craves her peace, your injured morality her harmony? Ask yourself, when art revolts you and the abuses in society drive you to lifeless nature in loneliness, whether it is society's deprivations, its burdens, its tedium, or whether it is its moral anarchy, its arbitrariness, its disorders that you despise in it? In the former your courage must joyfully rush in, and your compensation must be the freedom whence these evils derive. You may indeed retain the calm happiness of nature as your distant object, but only as one which is the reward of your worthiness. Then no more of complaints at the difficulties of life, of the inequality of stations, of the pressure of circumstances, of the uncertainty of possession, of ingratitude, oppression, persecution; with free resignation, you must subject yourself to all the *ills* of civilisation, respect them as the natural conditions of the only good; only its *evil* you must mourn, but not with vain tears alone. Rather, take heed that beneath that mire you remain pure, beneath that serfdom, free; constant in that capricious flux, acting lawfully in that anarchy. Be not afraid of the confusion around you, only of the confusion within you; strive after unity, but do not seek conformity; strive after calm, but through the equilibrium, not the cessation of your activity. That nature which you envy in the non-rational is worthy of no respect, no longing. It lies behind you, and must lie eternally behind you. Abandoned by the ladder that supported you, no other choice now lies open to you, but with free consciousness and will to grasp the law, or fall without hope of rescue into a bottomless pit.

But when you are consoled at the lost *happiness* of nature then let her *perfection* be your heart's example. If you march out toward her from your artificial environment she will stand before you in her great calm, in her naive beauty, in her childlike innocence and simplicity – then linger at this image, cultivate this emotion; this is worthy of your sublimest humanity. Let it no longer occur to you to want to exchange with her, but take her up within yourself and strive to wed her infinite advantage with your infinite prerogative,[12] and from both produce the divine. Let her surround you like an enchanting idyll in which you can always find yourself safe from the waywardness of art, and in which you accumulate courage and new confidence for the race, and which lights anew in your heart the flame of the ideal which is so easily extinguished in the storms of life.

If one recalls the beautiful nature that surrounded the ancient Greeks; if one ponders how familiarly this people could live with free nature beneath their fortunate skies, how very much closer their outlook, their manner of perception, their morals, were to simple nature, and what a faithful copy of this their poetry is, then the observation must be displeasing that one finds so little trace among them of the *sentimental* interest with which we moderns are attached to the scenes and characters of nature. The Greek is indeed to the highest degree precise, faithful, and circumstantial in describing them, yet simply no more so and with no more preferential involvement of his heart than he displays in the description of a tunic, a shield, a suit of armour, some domestic article, or any mechanical product. In his love of an object, he does not seem to make any distinction between those which appear of themselves, and those which arise as a result of art or the human will. Nature seems to interest his understanding and craving for knowledge more than his moral feeling; he does not cling to her with fervour, with sentimentality, with sweet melancholy, as we moderns do. Indeed, by hypostatising nature's individual phenomena, treating them as gods, and their effects as the acts of free beings, the Greek eliminates that calm necessity of nature precisely in virtue of which she is so attractive to us. His impatient fantasy leads him beyond nature to the drama of human life. Only the live and free, only characters, acts, destinies, and customs satisfy him, and if, *we*, in certain moral moods of the mind, might wish to surrender the advantage of our freedom of will, which exposes us to so much conflict within ourselves, to so much unrest and errant bypaths, to the choiceless but calm necessity of the non-rational, the fantasy of the Greek, in direct opposition to this, is engaged in rooting human nature in the inanimate world and assigning influence to the will where blind necessity reigns.

Whence derive these different spirits? How is it that we, who are in everything which is nature so boundlessly inferior to the ancients, offer tribute to nature just in this regard to such a higher degree, cling to her with fervour, and embrace even the inanimate world with the warmest sensibility? It is *because* nature in us has disappeared from humanity and we rediscover her in her truth only outside it, in the inanimate world. Not our greater *accord with nature*, but quite the contrary, the *unnaturalness* of our situation, conditions, and manners forces us to procure a satisfaction in the physical world (since none is to be hoped for in the moral) for the incipient impulse for truth and simplicity which, like the moral tendency whence it derives, lies incorruptible and inalienable in every human heart. For this reason the feeling by which we are attached to nature is so closely related to the feeling with which we mourn the lost age of childhood and childlike innocence. Our childhood is the only undisfigured nature that we still encounter in civilised mankind, hence it is no wonder if every trace of the nature outside us leads us back to our childhood.

It was quite otherwise with the ancient Greeks.[f] With them civilisation did not manifest itself to such an extent that nature was abandoned in consequence. The whole structure of their social life was founded on perceptions, not on a contrivance of art; their theology itself was the inspiration of a naive feeling, the child of a joyous imaginative power, not of brooding reason like the religious beliefs of modern nations; since, then, the Greek had not lost nature in his humanity, he could not be surprised by her outside it either and thus feel a pressing need for objects in which he might find her again. At one with himself and happy in the sense of his humanity he was obliged to remain with it as his maximum and assimilate all else to it; whereas *we*, not at one with ourselves and unhappy in our experience of mankind, possess no more urgent interest than to escape from it and cast from our view so unsuccessful a form.

The feeling of which we here speak is therefore not that which the ancients possessed; it is rather identical with that which *we have for the ancients*. They felt naturally; we feel the natural. Without a doubt the feeling that filled Homer's soul as he made his divine swineherd regale Ulysses was quite different from that which moved young Werther's soul as he read this song after an irritating evening in society.[14] Our feeling for nature is like the feeling of an invalid for health.

Just as nature began gradually to disappear from human life as *experience* and as the (active and perceiving) *subject*, so we see her arise in the world of poetry as *idea* and *object*. The nation that had brought this to the extremest degree both in unnaturalness and in reflection thereon must have been the first to be most moved by the phenomenon of the naive and to give it a name. This nation was, as far as I know, the French. But the feeling of the naive and interest in it is naturally much older and goes back even before the beginning of moral and aesthetic corruption. This change in the mode of perception is, for example, extremely obvious in Euripides, if one compares him with his predecessors, notably with Aeschylus, and yet the later poet was the favourite of his age. The same revolution can likewise be documented among the old historians. Horace, the poet of a cultivated and corrupt era, praises serene happiness in Tibur,[15] and one could call him the founder of this sentimental mode of poetry as well as a still unexcelled model of it. In Propertius, too, and Virgil, among others, one finds traces of this mode of perception, less so in Ovid, in whom the requisite fullness of heart was lacking and who in exile in Tomi painfully missed the happiness that Horace in Tibur so gladly dispensed with.

The poets are everywhere, by their very definition, the *guardians* of nature. Where they can no longer quite be so and have already felt within themselves the destructive influence of arbitrary and artificial forms or have had to struggle with them, then they will appear as the *witnesses* and *avengers* of nature. They will either *be* nature, or they will *seek* lost nature. From this arise two entirely different modes of poetry which, between them, exhaust and divide the whole range of poetry. All poets who are truly so will belong, according to the temper of the times in which they flourish, or according to the influence upon their general education or passing states of mind by fortuitous circumstances, either to the *naive* or to the *sentimental* poets.

The poet of a naive and bright youthful world, like the poet who in ages of artificial civilisation is closest to him, is severe and modest like virginal Diana in her forests; without intimacy he flees the heart that seeks his, flees the desire that would embrace him. The dry truth with which he deals with the object seems not infrequently like insensitivity. The object possesses him entirely, his heart does not lie like a tawdry alloy immediately beneath the surface, but like gold waits to be sought in the depths. Like the divinity behind the world's structure he stands behind his work; *he* is the work, and the work is *he*; to ask only for *him* is to be unworthy of it, inadequate to it, or sated with it.

Thus, for example, Homer among the ancients and Shakespeare among the moderns reveal themselves; two vastly different natures separated by the immeasurable distance of the years, but *one* in precisely this trait of character. When, at a very early age I first made the acquaintance of the latter poet, I was incensed by his coldness, the insensitivity which permitted him to jest in the midst of the highest pathos, to interrupt the heartrending scenes in *Hamlet*, in *King Lear*, in *Macbeth*, etc., with a Fool; restraining himself now where my sympathies rushed on, then coldbloodedly tearing himself away where my heart would have gladly lingered. Misled by acquaintance with more recent poets into looking first for the poet in his work, to find *his* heart, to reflect in unison with *him* on his subject matter, in short, to observe the object in the subject, it was intolerable to me that here there was no way to lay hold of the poet, and nowhere to confront him. I studied him and he possessed my complete admiration for many years before I learned to love him as an individual. I was not yet prepared to understand nature at first hand. I could only support her image reflected in understanding and regulated by a rule, and for this purpose the sentimental poets of the French, and the Germans, too, of the period from 1750 to about 1780, were just the right subjects. However, I am not ashamed of this youthful judgement, since the old-established criticism had promulgated a similar one and was naive enough to publish it in the world.[16]

The same occurred to me with Homer also, whom I learned to know only at a later period. I recall now the curious point in the sixth book of the *Iliad* where Glaucus and Diomedes come face to face in the battle and, having recognised one another as guest-friends, afterwards exchange gifts. This touching depiction of the piety with which the rules of *hospitality* were observed even in battle can be compared with an account of the *knightly sense of nobility* in Ariosto, when two knights and rivals, Ferraù and Rinaldo, the latter a Christian, the former a Saracen, covered with wounds after a violent duel, make peace and in order to overtake the fleeing Angelica, mount the same horse. Both examples, as different as they may be otherwise, are almost alike in their effect upon our hearts, because both depict the beautiful victory of morals over passion and touch us by the naivety of their attitudes. But how differently the poets react in describing these similar actions. Ariosto, the citizen of a later world which had fallen from simplicity of manners, cannot, in recounting the occurrence, conceal his own wonderment and emotion. The feeling of the distance between those morals and those which characterised his own age overwhelms him. He abandons for a moment the portrait of the object and appears in his own person. This beautiful stanza is well known and has always been greatly admired:

> O nobility of ancient knightly mode!
> Who once were rivals, divided still
> In godly faith, bitter pain still suffered,
> Bodies torn in enmity's wild struggle,
> Free of suspicion, together rode
> Along the darkling crooked path.
> The steed, by four spurs driven, sped
> To where the road in twain divided.[17]

And now old Homer! Scarcely has Diomedes learned from the narrative of Glaucus, his antagonist, that the latter's forefathers were guest-friends of his family, than he thrusts his lance into the ground, speaks in a friendly tone with him and agrees with him that in future they will avoid one another in battle. Let us, however, hear Homer himself:

In me you will now have a good friend in Argos, and I shall have you in Lycia, if ever I visit that country. So let us avoid each other's spears, even in the melee, since there are plenty of the Trojans and their famous allies for me to kill, if I have the luck and speed to catch them, and plenty of Achaeans for you to slaughter, if you can. And let us exchange our armour, so that everyone may know that our grandfathers' friendship has made friends of us. With no more said, they leapt from their chariots, shook hands, and pledged each other.[18]

It would hardly be possible for a *modern* poet (at least, hardly one who is modern in the moral sense of the word) to have waited even this long before expressing his pleasure at this action. We would forgive him this all the more readily because, even in reading, our hearts pause, and gladly detach themselves from the object in order to look within. But of all this, not a trace in

Homer; as though he had reported something quite everyday; indeed, as though he possessed no heart in his bosom, he continues in his dry truthfulness:

But Zeus the son of Cronos must have robbed Glaucus of his wits, for he exchanged with Diomedes golden armour for bronze, a hundred oxen's worth for the value of nine.

Poets of this naive category are no longer at home in an artificial age. They are indeed scarcely even possible, at least in no other wise possible except they *run wild* in their own age, and are preserved by some favourable destiny from its crippling influence. From society itself they can never arise; but from outside it they still sometimes appear, but rather as strangers at whom one stares, and as uncouth sons of nature by whom one is irritated. As beneficent as such phenomena are for the artist who studies them and for the true connoisseur who is able to appreciate them, they yet elicit little joy on the whole and in their own century. The stamp of the conqueror is marked upon their brows; but we would rather be coddled and indulged by the Muses. By the critics, the true gamekeepers of taste, they are detested as trespassers whom one would prefer to suppress; for even Homer owes it only to the power of more than a thousand years of testimony that those who sit in judgement on taste permit him to stand; and it is unpleasant enough for them to maintain their rules against his example and his reputation against their rules.

The poet, I said, either *is* nature or he will *seek* her. The former is the naive, the latter the sentimental poet.

The poetic spirit is immortal and inalienable in mankind, it cannot be lost except together with humanity or with the capacity for it. For even if man should separate himself by the freedom of his fantasy and his understanding from the simplicity, truth and necessity of nature, yet not only does the way back to her remain open always, but also a powerful and ineradicable impulse, the moral, drives him ceaselessly back to her, and it is precisely with this impulse that the poetic faculty stands in the most intimate relationship. For this faculty is not forfeited along with the lost simplicity of nature; it merely assumes a new direction.

Even now, nature is the sole flame at which the poetic spirit nourishes itself; from her alone it draws its whole power, to her alone it speaks even in the artificial man entoiled by civilisation. All other modes of expression are alien to the poetic spirit; hence, generally speaking, all so-called works of wit[19] are quite misnamed poetic; although, for long, misled by the reputation of French literature, we have mistaken them as such. It is still nature, I say, even now in the artificial condition of civilisation, in virtue of which the poetic spirit is powerful; but now it stands in quite another relation to nature.

So long as man is pure – not, of course, crude – nature, he functions as an undivided sensuous unity and as a harmonious whole. Sense and reason, passive and active faculties, are not separated in their activities, still less do they stand in conflict with one another. His perceptions are not the formless play of chance, his thoughts not the empty play of the faculty of representation;

the former proceed out of the law of *necessity*, the latter out of *actuality*. Once man has passed into the state of civilisation and art has laid her hand upon him, that *sensuous* harmony in him is withdrawn, and he can now express himself only as a *moral* unity, i.e., as striving after unity. The correspondence between his feeling and thought which in his first condition *actually* took place, exists now only *ideally*; it is no longer within him, but outside of him, as an idea still to be realised, no longer as a fact in his life. If one now applies the concept of poetry, which is nothing but *giving mankind its most complete possible expression*, to both conditions, the result in the earlier state of natural simplicity is the completest possible *imitation of actuality* – at that stage man still functions with all his powers simultaneously as a harmonious unity and hence the whole of his nature is expressed completely in actuality; whereas now, in the state of civilisation where that harmonious cooperation of his whole nature is only an idea, it is the elevation of actuality to the ideal or, amounting to the same thing, the *representation of the ideal*, that makes for the poet. And these two are likewise the only possible modes in which poetic genius can express itself at all. They are, as one can see, extremely different from one another, but there is a higher concept under which both can be subsumed, and there should be no surprise if this concept should coincide with the idea of humanity.

This is not the place further to pursue these thoughts, which can only be expounded in full measure in a separate disquisition. But anyone who is capable of making a comparison, based on the spirit and not just on the accidental forms, between ancient and modern poets,[g] will be able readily to convince himself of the truth of the matter. The former move us by nature, by sensuous truth, by living presence; the latter by ideas.

This path taken by the modern poets is, moreover, that along which man in general, the individual as well as the race, must pass. Nature sets him at one with himself, art divides and cleaves him in two, through the ideal he returns to unity. But because the ideal is an infinitude to which he never attains, the civilised man can never become perfect in *his* own wise, while the natural man can in his. He must therefore fall infinitely short of the latter in perfection, if one heeds only the relation in which each stands to his species and to his maximum capacity. But if one compares the species themselves with one another, it becomes evident that the goal to which man *strives* through culture is infinitely preferable to that which he *attains* through nature. For the one obtains its value by the absolute achievement of a finite, the other by approximation to an infinite greatness. But only the latter possesses *degrees* and displays a *progress*, hence the relative worth of a man who is involved in civilisation is in general never determinable, even though the same man considered as an individual necessarily finds himself at a disadvantage compared with one in whom nature functions in her utter perfection. But insofar as the ultimate object of mankind is not otherwise to be attained than by that progress, and the latter cannot progress other than by civilising himself and hence passing over into the former category, there cannot therefore be any question to which of the two the advantage accrues with reference to that ultimate object.

The very same as has been said of the two different forms of humanity can likewise be applied to those species of poet corresponding to them.

Perhaps on this account one should not compare ancient with modern – naive with sentimental – poets either at all, or only by reference to some higher concept common to both (there is in fact such a concept). For clearly, if one has first abstracted the concept of those species onesidedly from the ancient poets, nothing is easier, but nothing also more trivial, than to depreciate the moderns by comparison. If one calls poetry only that which in every age has affected simple nature uniformly, the result cannot be other than to deny the modern poets their title just where they achieve their most characteristic and sublimest beauty, since precisely here they speak only to the adherent of civilisation and have nothing to say to simple nature.[h] Anyone whose temperament is not already prepared to pass beyond actuality into the realm of ideas will find the richest content empty appearance, and the loftiest flights of the poet exaggeration. It would not occur to a reasonable person to want to compare any modern with Homer where Homer excels, and it sounds ridiculous enough to find Milton or Klopstock honoured with the title of a modern Homer. But just as little could any ancient poet, and least of all Homer, support the comparison with a modern poet in those aspects which most characteristically distinguish him. The former, I might put it, is powerful through the art of finitude; the latter by the art of the infinite.

And for the very reason that the strength of the ancient artist (for what has been said here of the poet can, allowing for self-evident qualifications, be extended to apply to the fine arts generally) subsists in finitude, the great advantage arises which the plastic art of antiquity maintains over that of modern times, and in general the unequal value relationship in which the modern art of poetry and modern plastic art stand to both species of art in antiquity. A work addressed to the eye can achieve perfection only in finitude; a work addressed to the imagination can achieve it also through the infinite.[21] In plastic works the modern is little aided by his superiority in ideas; here he is obliged to *determine in space in the most precise way* the representation of his imagination and hence to compete with the ancient artists in precisely that quality in which they indisputably excel. In poetic works it is otherwise, and even if the ancient poets are victorious too in the simplicity of forms and in whatever is sensuously representable and *corporeal*, the modern can nonetheless leave them behind in richness of material in whatever is insusceptible of representation and ineffable, in a word, in whatever in the work of art is called *spirit*.

Since the naive poet only follows simple nature and feeling, and limits himself solely to imitation of actuality, he can have only a single relationship to his subject and in *this* respect there is for him no choice in his treatment. The varied impression of naive poetry depends (provided that one puts out of mind everything which in it belongs to the content, and considers that impression only as the pure product of the poetic treatment), it depends, I say, solely upon the various degrees of one and the same mode of feeling; even the variety of external forms cannot effect any alteration in the quality of that aesthetic impression. The form may be lyric or epic, dramatic or narrative: we can indeed be moved to a weaker or stronger degree, but (as soon as the matter is abstracted) never heterogeneously. Our feeling is uniformly the same, entirely composed of *one* element, so that we cannot differentiate within it. Even the difference of language and era changes nothing in this regard, for just this pure unity of its origin and of its effect is a characteristic of naive poetry.

The case is quite otherwise with the sentimental poet. He *reflects* upon the impression that objects make upon him, and only in that reflection is the emotion grounded which he himself experiences and which he excites in us. The object here is referred to an idea and his poetic power is based solely upon this referral. The sentimental poet is thus always involved with two conflicting representations and perceptions – with actuality as a limit and with his idea as infinitude; and the mixed feelings that he excites will always testify to this dual source.[1] Since in this case there is a plurality of principles it depends which of the two will *predominate* in the perception of the poet and in his representation, and hence a variation in the treatment is possible. For now the question arises whether he will tend more toward actuality or toward the ideal – whether he will realise the former as an object of antipathy or the latter as an object of sympathy. His presentation will, therefore, be either *satirical* or it will be (in a broader connotation of the word which will become clearer later) *elegiac*; every sentimental poet will adhere to one of these two modes of perception.

The poet is satirical if he takes as his subject alienation from nature and the contradiction between actuality and the ideal (in their effect upon the mind both amount to the same thing). But this he can execute either seriously and with passion, or jokingly and with good humour, according as he dwells in the realm of will or the realm of understanding. The former is a function of punitive or pathetic satire, the latter of playful satire.

Strictly speaking, the poet's purpose is compatible neither with the accent of correction nor with that of amusement. The former is too solemn for that play which poetry should always be; the latter too frivolous for the solemnity which must underlie all poetic play. Moral contradictions necessarily interest our hearts and therefore deprive our minds of their freedom; yet every substantive interest, i.e., any reference to a necessity, should be banished from poetic emotion. Contradictions of the understanding, on the other hand, leave the heart indifferent, and yet the poet is concerned with the highest promptings of the heart, with nature, and with the ideal. Hence it is no small task for him in pathetic satire to avoid doing injury to the poetic form which subsists in freedom of play; and in playful satire not to fall short of the poetic content which must always be the infinite. This undertaking can be resolved only in a single manner. Punitive satire achieves poetic freedom by passing over into the sublime; playful satire obtains poetic content by treating its subject with beauty.

In satire, actuality is contrasted with the highest reality as falling short of the ideal. It is, moreover, quite unnecessary that this be articulated, provided only that the poet is able to intimate this to the mind; but this he absolutely must do or it will not function poetically at all. Actuality is here therefore a necessary object of antipathy; but – and this is all-important – this antipathy must itself necessarily arise out of the opposed ideal. For it could in fact have a sensuous origin and be grounded merely in *some inner need* with which actuality is in conflict; and often enough we feel moral indignation at the world, when it is only the conflict between the world and our inclination that embitters us. It is this material interest that the vulgar satirist exploits, and since he can hardly fail by this method to arouse our emotion, he believes he has conquered our hearts, and that he is a master of pathos. But any pathos deriving from this source is unworthy of the art of poetry, which may touch us only through ideas and approach our hearts only by the path of reason. In addition, this impure and material pathos will always reveal itself by an excess of passion and through a painful embarrassment of the intellect, whereas truly poetic pathos can be recognised by a predominance of spontaneity and by a freedom of spirit which still survives even in emotion. For if the emotion arises out of the ideal that confronts actuality, then all inhibiting feelings are lost in the sublimity of the former, and the greatness of the idea with which we are filled elevates us above all the limitations of experience. In the representation of offending actuality everything depends therefore upon necessity's being the basis on which the poet or narrator presents the actual, if he is to be able to attune our spirits to ideas. If only *we* remain lofty in our judgement nothing is lost if the subject remains base and far beneath us. When the historian Tacitus depicts for us the profound depravity of the Romans of the first century he is still a superior spirit who looks down upon the base, and our mood is truly poetic because only the height where he himself stands and to which he was able to elevate us makes his subject base.

Pathetic satire must, therefore, always derive from a temperament that is vigorously permeated by the ideal. Only a predominant impulse toward harmony can and may produce that profound sense of moral contradiction and that burning indignation against moral perversity which becomes the inspiration of a Juvenal, a Swift, a Rousseau, a Haller,[22] and others. These poets would and must have written with the same felicity also in the more moving and tender forms if fortuitous causes had not given this definite tendency to their temperaments at an early age; and this they have actually done to some extent. All those mentioned have lived either in a depraved era and saw before them a fearful spectacle of moral decay, or their own fates had sown bitterness in their souls. Even the philosophical spirit, since he separates with implacable rigour appearances from essence, and penetrates into the depths of things, inclines to that severity and austerity with which Rousseau, Haller, and others depict actuality. But these extraneous and coincidental influences which always have an inhibiting effect may at most determine the tendency only, never supply the content of inspiration. This must be the same in everyone and, free of every external constraint, must flow out of a burning impulse for the ideal which is absolutely the only true vocation for the satiric as for the sentimental poet in general.

If pathetic satire is appropriate only to sublime souls, playful satire will succeed only with a beautiful soul. For the first is already secured from frivolity by its serious subject; but the second, which may treat only a morally neutral subject, would lapse unavoidably into frivolity, and lose all poetic value if in this case the manner did not ennoble the matter and the poet's *personality* did not stand in place of his *theme*. But it is given only to the beautiful heart to impress a complete image of itself on all its utterances, independently of the subject of its activity. The sublime character can manifest itself only in discrete victories over the resistance of the senses, only in certain instants of impetus and momentary effort; but in the beautiful soul the ideal functions as nature, that is, uniformly, and hence can reveal itself even in a state of calm. The fathomless sea appears most sublime in its motion, the pellucid brook most beautiful in its serene flow.

It has frequently been disputed which of the two, tragedy or comedy, merits precedence over the other. If the question is merely which of the two treats of the more important subject matter, there can be no doubt that the first has the advantage; but if one would know which of the two demands the more significant poet, then the decision may rather fall to the latter. In tragedy much is already determined by the substance, in comedy nothing is determined by the substance and everything by the poet. Since in judgements of taste the content is never taken into account it follows naturally that the aesthetic value of these two artistic genres stands in inverse proportion to their substantive significance. The tragic poet is supported by his theme, the comic poet on the other hand must raise his to aesthetic height through his own person. The first may make a leap for which, however, not much is required; the other must remain himself, he must therefore already *be* there and be at home there where the first cannot attain without a starting leap. And it is precisely in this way that the beautiful character is distinguished from the sublime.[23] In the first, all the dimensions are already contained, flowing unconstrainedly and effortlessly from its nature and it is, according to its capacity, an infinitude at every point in its path; the other can elevate and exert itself to any dimension, by the power of its will it can tear itself out of any state of limitation. The latter is, then, only intermittently and with effort free, the former with facility and always.

To promote and nourish this freedom of temperament is the fair task of comedy, just as tragedy is destined to help to restore by aesthetic means the freedom of temperament when it has been violently disrupted by emotion. In tragedy, therefore, freedom of temperament must be artificially and experimentally disrupted, since it displays its poetic power in the restoration of that freedom; in comedy, on the other hand, care must be taken to assure that that disruption of the freedom of temperament should never occur. Hence the tragic poet always treats his subject practically, the comic poet always treats his theoretically,[24] even if the former should indulge the quirk (like Lessing in his *Nathan*)[25] of treating a theoretical subject, or the latter of treating a practical subject. Not the sphere from which the subject is drawn, but the forum before which the poet brings it makes it tragic or comic. The tragedian must beware of calm reasoning and always engage the heart; the comedian must beware of pathos and always entertain the understanding. The former thus displays his art by the constant excitement of passion, the latter by constant avoidance of it; and this art is naturally so much the greater on both sides the more the subject of one is of an abstract nature, and that of the other tends toward the pathetic.[j] Even if tragedy proceeds from a more significant point, one is obliged to concede, on the other hand, that comedy proceeds toward a more significant purpose and it would, were it to attain it, render all tragedy superfluous and impossible. Its purpose is uniform with the highest after which man has to struggle, to be free of passion, always clear, to look serenely about and within himself, to find everywhere more coincidence than fate, and rather to laugh at absurdity than to rage or weep at malice.

As in actual life, it often happens in poetic works also that mere frivolity, pleasing talent, amiable good humour, are confused with beauty of soul, and since the vulgar taste can never raise itself above the pleasant it is easy enough for such *lightsome* spirits to usurp the fame which is so difficult to earn. But there is an infallible test by means of which lightness of disposition can be distinguished from lightness of the ideal, as well as virtue of temperament from true morality of character, and this is when both confront a difficult and great theme. In such a case the precious genius inevitably collapses into the banal, as does virtue of temperament into the material; the truly beautiful soul, however, passes over as certainly into the sublime.

So long as Lucian[27] merely castigates absurdity, as in the *Wishes*, the *Lapithae*, in *Zeus Rants*, etc., he remains a mocker and delights us with his joyful humour; but he becomes quite another man in many passages of his *Nigrinus*, his *Timon*, his *Alexander*, in which his satire strikes also at moral decay. 'Unhappy wretch', he begins in his *Nigrinus*, the shocking picture of contemporary Rome, 'why did you leave the light of the sun, Greece, and that happy life of freedom, and come here into this turmoil of sumptuous servitude, of dancing attendance, of banquets, of sycophants, flatterers, poisoners, legacy-hunters, and false friends?' etc. On this and similar occasions is revealed the high solemnity of feeling that must underlie all play if it is to be poetic. Even in the malicious joke with which Lucian as well as Aristophanes abuses Socrates one perceives a serious reason which avenges truth upon the Sophist, and battles on behalf of an ideal that it does not always articulate. The first of these two, in his *Diogenes* and *Demonax*, has justified this character beyond all doubt; among moderns, what a great and noble character has Cervantes expressed on every worthy occasion in his *Don Quixote*! What a magnificent ideal must have dwelt in the soul of the poet who created a Tom Jones and a Sophia![28] How readily can laughing Yorick[29] touch our minds at will so loftily and so powerfully! In our own Wieland[30] also I recognise this seriousness of feeling; even the wanton play of his moods is ensouled and ennobled by grace of heart; even in the rhythm of his song its impress is manifest, and he never lacks the impetus to carry us, if the moment is apt, to the greatest heights.

No comparable judgement can be passed on Voltaire's satire. True enough, even with this writer it is still only the truth and simplicity of nature by which he sometimes moves us poetically, either because he really attains to it in a naive character, as frequently in his *Ingénu*, or because he seeks and defends it, as in *Candide*, etc. If neither of these two is the case then he may indeed amuse us as a witty fellow, but certainly not move us as a poet. Everywhere too little seriousness underlies his ridicule, and this justly brings his poetic vocation under suspicion. We perpetually encounter only his understanding, never his feeling. No ideal is manifest beneath that airy frame and scarcely anything absolutely fixed in that ceaseless motion. Far from displaying any evidence for the inner abundance of his spirit, his wonderful variety of external forms gives rather a dubious testimony to the opposite effect, for despite all those forms he has not found even *one* upon which to leave the impress of his heart. One must therefore almost fear that in this richly endowed genius it was only poverty of feeling that determined his satiric vocation. Had this been otherwise he must surely somewhere along his broad career have departed from this narrow way. But despite the tremendous variety of content and external form we see the endless recurrence of this inner form in all its indigent uniformity, and despite his massive career he never fulfilled in himself the cycle of humanity which one joyfully finds permeating the satirists mentioned above.

If the poet should set nature and art, the ideal and actuality, in such opposition that the representation of the first prevails and pleasure in it becomes the predominant feeling, then I call him *elegiac*. This category, too, like satire, comprehends two species. Either nature and the ideal are an object of sadness if the first is treated as lost and the second as unattained. Or both are an object of joy represented as actual. The first yields the *elegy* in the narrower sense, and the second the idyll in the broader sense.[k]

Just as indignation in the pathetic satire and mockery in the playful satire, so also should sadness in the elegy be derived only from an enthusiasm awakened by the ideal. Only thus does elegy receive poetic content, and every other source of it is beneath the dignity of the art of poetry. The elegiac poet seeks nature, but in her beauty, not merely in her pleasantness, in her correspondence with ideas, not just in her acquiescence in necessity. Sadness at lost joys, at the golden age now disappeared from the world, at the lost happiness of youth, love, and so forth, can only become the material of an elegiac poem if those states of sensuous satisfaction can also be construed as objects of moral harmony. Thus I cannot consider the lamentations of Ovid which he chanted from his place of exile on the Black Sea, moving as they are and containing so much that is poetic in individual passages, as being as a whole a poetic work. There is far too little energy, far too little spirit and nobility in his pain. Necessity, not inspiration, utters those laments; in them breathes, if not actually a vulgar soul, yet the vulgar mood of a finer spirit that has been crushed by its fate. Still, when we recall that it is Rome and the Rome of Augustus for which he sorrows, we forgive the son of pleasure his pain; but even magnificent Rome, with all its enchantments, is still (if the power of imagination has not first ennobled it) only a finite quantity, hence an unworthy object for the poetic art which, superior to everything that actuality has to offer, possesses the right to mourn only for the infinite.

The content of poetic lamentation can therefore never be an external object, it must always be only an ideal, inner one; even if it grieves over some loss in actuality, it must first be transformed into an ideal loss. In this assimilation of the finite to the infinite, poetic treatment in fact subsists. The external matter is, therefore, always indifferent in itself since the poetic art can never employ it as it occurs, but only by means of what poetry makes of it does it receive its poetic value. The elegiac poet seeks nature, but as an idea and in a perfection in which she has never existed, even if he bemourns her as something having existed and now lost. When Ossian tells of the days which are no more, and of the heroes who have disappeared, his poetic power has long since transformed those images of recollection into ideals, and those heroes into gods. The experience of a particular loss has been broadened into the idea of universal evanescence and the bard, affected and pursued by the image of omnipresent ruin, elevates himself to the skies to find there, in the cycle of the sun, an image of the immutable.[1]

I turn now to the modern poets of the elegiac category. Rousseau, both as poet and as philosopher, reveals no other tendency but either to seek nature or to revenge her on art. According as his feeling dwells on one or the other we find him sometimes elegiacally moved, sometimes inspired to Juvenalian satire, and sometimes, as in his *Julie*,[32] enraptured in the realm of the idyll. Unquestionably his poems possess poetic content, since they are concerned with an ideal; but he does not know how to exploit it in a poetic manner. His serious character never permits him, it is true, to sink to frivolity, but it does not permit him either to rise to poetic play. Sometimes, gripped by passion, sometimes by abstraction, he rarely or never achieves the aesthetic freedom which the poet must maintain in relation to his material and communicate to his listener. Either it is his unhealthy excess of feeling which overpowers him and renders his emotion painful; or it is his excess of thought that lays shackles upon his imagination, and by the rigour of his concepts destroys the grace of the depiction. Both characteristics, whose inner reciprocal workings and recon- ciliation in fact make for the poet, are present in this writer to an unusually high degree, and nothing is lacking except that they should manifest themselves in actual unison, that his intellectual activity should be combined with his feeling, and his sensitivity more combined with his thought. Hence, in the ideal that he established for humanity, too much emphasis is laid upon man's limitations and too little upon his capacities; and in it one observes everywhere a need for physical calm rather than for moral harmony. His passionate sensitivity is to blame for preferring to restore man to the spiritless uniformity of his first state in order simply to be rid of the conflict within him, rather than to look for the termination of that conflict in the spiritual harmony of a completely fulfilled education; he would rather that art had never begun than that he should await its consummation; in a word, he would rather set his aim lower and degrade his ideal only in order to attain to it the more quickly and more surely.

Among German poets of this order I will mention here only Haller, Kleist, and Klopstock.[33] The character of their poetry is sentimental; they touch us by ideas, not by sensuous truth; not so much because they are nature as because they are able to inspire enthusiasm in us for nature. Whatever, therefore, is true of the character of these as well as of all sentimental poets *in general* naturally does not by any means exclude the capacity *in particular* to move us by naive beauty; without this they would not be poets at all. But it is not their essential and predominant character to feel with serene, simple, and unencumbered senses and to present again what they have felt in like manner. Involuntarily imagination crowds out sense and thought feeling, and they close their eyes and ears to sink into internal reflection. The mind cannot tolerate any impression without at once observing its own activity and reflection, and yielding up in terms of itself whatever it has absorbed. In this mode we are never given the object, only what the reflective understanding has made of it, and even when the poet is himself the object, if he would describe his feeling to us, we never learn of his condition directly and at first hand, but rather how he has reflected it in his own mind, what he has thought about it as an observer of himself. When Haller is lamenting the death of his wife (in his well known poem), and begins as follows:

> Shall I sing of thy death?
> O Mariane, what a song!
> When sighs contest with words
> And one idea flees before the rest, etc.[34]

then we may indeed find this description exactly true, but we feel also that the poet has not actually communicated his feelings but his thoughts about them. He therefore moves us much more feebly also, because he must himself have been very much cooler to be an observer of his own emotion.

The predominantly supersensuous material alone of Haller's and, in part, of Klopstock's poetry excludes them from the naive category; hence, for that material to be poetically treated, it must (since it cannot assume any corporeal nature and in consequence cannot become an object of sensuous intuition) be translated into the infinite and be elevated into an object of spiritual intuition. Generally speaking, didactic poetry can only be conceived of without inner contradiction in this sense; for, to repeat this once again, the art of poetry comprehends these two realms only: either it must dwell in the world of sense or in the world of ideas, since it absolutely cannot flourish in the realm of concepts or in the world of the understanding.[35] I confess that I have yet to encounter the poem of this order either in ancient or modern literature that was able to lead the concept which it treated purely and completely either downward to individuality or upward to the idea. It is usually the case, when it is successful at all, that the poem fluctuates between both, while the abstract concept dominates, and imagination, which should be in command in the poetic realm, is simply subordinated to the service of the understanding. The didactic poem in which the thought is itself poetic and remains so has yet to be seen.

What has been said here in general about all didactic poetry applies in particular to Haller. The thought itself is not poetic, but the execution sometimes is, either by the employment of the images, or by its soaring to ideas. Only in this latter quality do they belong here. Strength and profundity and a pathetic seriousness characterise this poet. His spirit is kindled by an ideal and his glowing feeling for truth seeks in the still alpine valleys the innocence that has disappeared from the world. His lament is deeply moving: with energetic, almost bitter satire, he marks the distractions of understanding and heart, and with love the beautiful simplicity of nature. But the concept predominates everywhere in his descriptions, just as within himself understanding dominates over feeling. Hence, he *teaches* throughout more than he *represents*, and represents throughout more with powerful than with attractive strokes. He is great, daring, fiery, sublime; but he rarely, if ever, raises his work to beauty.

Kleist is far inferior to him in the content of his ideas and depth of spirit; in grace he may be superior to him if we do not, as sometimes happens, account his weakness in the one aspect as a strength in the other. Kleist's emotion-laden soul expands most at the spectacle of rural scenes and usages. Gladly he escapes from the empty turmoil of society and finds in the bosom of inanimate nature the harmony and peace that he misses in the moral world. How affecting is his longing for calm! How true and how felt when he sings:

> Aye, world, thou truly art the grave of life.
> Often am I urged by an impulse to virtue,
> And melancholy draws many a tear down my cheek,
> Example is victorious, and thou, oh fire of youth:
> Together drying up those noble tears.
> A true man must avoid his fellow men.[36]

Yet, if his poetic impulse has led him away from the constricting round of circumstances into the spiritual loneliness of nature, still he is pursued even this far by the anxious image of the age and unfortunately, too, by its fetters. What he flees lies within him, what he seeks is forever outside him; he can never overcome the bale influence of his century. Even if his heart is sufficiently afire, his fantasy energetic enough, to ensoul the dead configurations of his understanding by his composition, still cold thought as often deprives the living creation of his poetic powers of its soul, and reflection disrupts the secret labour of feeling. His poetry is indeed as bright and sparkling as the spring[37] that he celebrates in song, his fantasy is live and active; yet one must call it evanescent rather than rich, playful rather than creative, uneasily progressing rather than unifying and plastic. Rapidly and luxuriantly its features change, but without crystallising themselves into a whole, without becoming filled with life and rounding themselves into a unity. So long as he merely writes lyrically and merely dwells upon landscape images, partly the greater freedom of lyrical form, partly the more arbitrary quality of his material permits us to overlook this shortcoming, since in this case we always demand the representation of the poet's feelings rather than of the subject itself. But the mistake becomes only too obvious when he goes out of his way, as in his *Cissides and Paches* and his *Seneca*,[38] to depict human beings and human actions; for here the imaginative power finds itself hemmed in amid fixed and necessary limits, and the poetic effect can proceed only from the *object*. Here he becomes insipid, dull, thin, and all but insupportably cold: an admonition to anyone who tries without inner vocation to project himself from the field of musical into the realm of plastic poetry. A similar genius, Thomson,[39] fell victim to the same human weakness.

In the sentimental genus, and particularly in the elegiac species of it, few poets of modern times and fewer still of antiquity may be compared with our Klopstock. Whatever could be attained in the realm of ideality, outside the boundaries of living form and outside the sphere of individuality, has been achieved by this musical poet.[m] One would indeed do him a grave injustice if one were altogether to deny him that individual truth and vivacity with which the naive poet depicts his theme. Many of his odes, several individual features of his dramas and of his *Messiah* portray the object with striking veracity and with beautiful circumscription; particularly where the object is his own heart, he has not infrequently displayed a lofty nature, an enchanting naivety. But *his* strength does not lie in this, this characteristic is not to be fulfilled throughout the whole of his poetic range. As superb a creation as the *Messiah* is in the *musical* poetic sense as defined above, yet much is left to be desired from the *plastic* poetic point of view in which one expects specific forms and forms *specific for sensuous intuition*. The personages in this poem may perhaps be specific enough, but not for intuition; abstraction alone has created them, only abstraction can distinguish them. They are fine examples of concepts, but not individuals, not living figures. It is left much too much to the imagination, to which nonetheless the poet must return and which he should command by the thoroughgoing specificity of his forms, in what manner these men and angels, this God and Satan, this heaven and this hell shall embody themselves. An outline is given within which the understanding must necessarily conceive of them, but no firm boundary is set within which fantasy must necessarily portray them. What I say here of the characters applies to everything that is or should be life and action in this poem; and not just in this epic, but also in the dramatic works of our poet. For the understanding everything is finely delineated and delimited (I mention here only his Judas, his Pilate, his Philo,[40] his Solomon in the tragedy of that name),[41] but it is far too formless for the imagination and here, I freely confess, I find the poet entirely out of his sphere.

His sphere is always the realm of ideas, and he is able to transport everything he touches into the infinite. One might say he disembodies everything he touches so as to transform it into spirit, just as other poets endow everything spiritual with a body. Virtually every pleasure that his poetry affords must be gained by the exercise of thought; all the feelings, however fervent and powerful, that he is able to engender in us stream forth from supersensuous sources. Hence the seriousness, the power, the impetus, the depth that characterises everything that comes from him; hence also the perennial tension of the mind in which we are maintained in reading him. No poet (with the possible exception of Young,[42] who demands more in this respect than Klopstock but without compensating for it as he does) would seem to be less apt to become a favourite and companion through life than Klopstock, who always leads us only away from life, always summons up only the spirit, without vivifying the senses with the serene presence of an object. His poetical muse is chaste, supermundane, incorporeal, holy, like his religion, and one must confess with admiration that even though he may sometimes go astray on these heights, he still has never fallen from them. I admit, therefore, without reserve, that I am somewhat fearful for the sanity of anyone who really and without affectation can make this poet his favourite reading, the kind of reading by which one can attune oneself to any situation, to which one can return from any situation; also, it would seem to me, we have seen enough in Germany of the fruits of his dangerous domination. Only in certain exalted frames of mind can he be sought out and appreciated; for this reason, too, he is the idol of the young, if by far not their happiest choice. Youth, which always strives beyond the conditions of life, which escapes from all forms and finds any limitation too constricting, abandons itself with love and delight in the endless expanses opened up to it by this poet. But when the boy becomes a man and returns from the realm of ideas into the limitations of experience, then much is lost, very much of that enthusiastic love, but not of the respect which is due to so unique a phenomenon, to so extraordinary a genius, to such very ennobled feeling, a respect which the German owes to such high merit.

I called this poet great above all in the elegiac species, and it will hardly be necessary to justify this judgement in further detail. Equal to every effort and master of the entire range of sentimental poetry, he can now shake us with the highest pathos, now soothe us with celestially tender feelings; but above all his heart is inclined to a lofty spirit-filled melancholy and, as sublime as his harp, his lyre sounds, yet the melting tones of his lute[43] will still ring truer and more deeply and movingly. I appeal to every purely attuned feeling and ask whether it would not gladly abandon everything bold and powerful, every fiction, every superb description, every model of oratorical eloquence in the *Messiah*, all the glittering similes in which our poet is so outstandingly successful – whether it would not abandon all this for the sake of the tender feelings that are breathed forth in the elegy *To Ebert*, in the splendid poems *Bardale*, *Early Graves*, *Summer Night*, *Lake Zurich*, and many of this order. For as dear to me as the *Messiah* is as a treasure of elegiac feelings and ideal portrayals, it satisfies me less as the depiction of action or as an epic work.

Perhaps, before leaving this field, I should refer also to the merits of Uz, Denis, Geßner (in his *Death of Abel*), Jacobi, von Gerstenberg, of Hölty, von Göckingk,[44] and many others of this class, who all move us through ideas and, in the sense of the word defined above, have written as sentimental poets. But my purpose is not to write a history of German poetry, but to illustrate what has been said by a few examples out of our literature. It was the variety of the path that I wanted to show, by which ancient and modern, naive and sentimental poets proceed to the same goal – that if the former move us through nature, individuality, and living *sensuousness*, the latter, by ideas and lofty *spirituality*, manifest an equally great, if not so widespread, power over our minds.

From the previous examples it could be seen how the sentimental poetic spirit treats a natural theme; but one might also be interested in knowing how the naive poetic spirit proceeds with a sentimental theme. This task appears to be completely new and of a quite unique difficulty, for in the ancient and naive world a *theme* of this kind did not occur, whereas in the modern the *poet* would be lacking. Nevertheless, genius has accepted this task also and has resolved it in an admirably felicitous manner. A personality who embraces the ideal with burning feeling and abandons actuality in order to contend with an insubstantial infinitude, who seeks continuously outside himself for that which he continuously destroys within himself, to whom only his dreams are the real, his experiences perennial limitations, who in the end sees in his own existence only a limitation, and, as is reasonable, tears even this down in order to penetrate to the true reality – this dangerous extreme of the sentimental character has become the theme of a poet in whom nature functions more faithfully and purely than any other, and who, among modern poets, is perhaps least removed from the sensuous truth of things.[45]

It is interesting to note with what fortunate instinct everything that nourishes the sentimental character is concentrated in *Werther*: fanatically unhappy love, sensitivity to nature, feeling for religion, a spirit of philosophical contemplation; finally, so that nothing shall be forgotten, the gloomy, formless, melancholic Ossianic world. If one takes account with how little recommendation, even in how hostile a manner actuality is contrasted with it, and how everything external unites to drive the tortured youth back into his world of ideals, then one sees no possibility how such a character could have saved himself from such a cycle. In the same poet's *Tasso*[46] the same opposition occurs, albeit in quite different characters; even in his latest novel,[47] just as in that first one, the poetic spirit is set in opposition to plain common sense, the ideal over against the actual, the subjective mode of representation over against the objective – but with what a difference!; even in *Faust*[48] we encounter the same opposition, of course insofar as the theme requires it, very coarsened and materialised on both sides; it would be well worth the effort to attempt to analyse the psychological development of this personality as it is manifested in four such different ways.

It was observed earlier that the merely carefree and jovial type of mind, when it is not based on an inner wealth of ideas, fails to yield a vocation for playful satire as readily as popular opinion would assume this; just as little does merely tender effeminacy and melancholy provide a vocation for elegiac poetry. Both are lacking that principle of energy that belongs to the true poetic gift, and that must animate its subject matter in order to produce the truly beautiful. Products of this delicate sort can, therefore, only melt us and, without enlivening the heart and engaging the spirit, they merely flatter sensuousness. A continuous tendency to this mode of feeling must, at the last, necessarily enervate the character and depress it into a condition of passivity out of which no reality at all can proceed, either for the external or the inner life. It was, therefore, altogether warranted to pursue with implacable mockery that evil of *affected feeling*[n] and *lachrymose demeanour* which, as a result of the misunderstanding and aping of a few excellent works, began to gain the upper hand in Germany about eighteen years ago,[50] even though the indulgence which there is a tendency to display toward the scarcely better counterpart of that elegiac caricature, toward facetious manners, toward heartless satire and pointless caprices[o] makes it clear enough that they were not attacked for entirely pure reasons. In the scales of genuine taste the one must have as little effect as the other, for both lack the aesthetic content which is contained only in the inmost combination of spirit and matter, and in the unified relation of a work to the faculties of feeling and ideas.

Siegwart and his cloister story have been mocked,[52] and the *Journey to Southern France*[53] is admired; yet both works have an equal claim to a certain degree of appreciation; and an equally small one to unqualified praise. True, if extravagant, feeling makes for the value of the first novel, a delicate humour and a vivaciously fine understanding for that of the second; but just as the first is entirely lacking in appropriate sobriety of understanding, the second is lacking in aesthetic dignity. The first is a little ridiculous in the light of experience, the other virtually contemptible compared with the ideal. But since the truly beautiful must correspond on the one hand with nature and on the other with the ideal, the first can lay as little claim as the second to the name of a beautiful work. Nonetheless it is natural and reasonable, and I know from my own experience, that Thümmel's novel is read with great pleasure. Since he offends only against those demands that originate in the ideal, which in consequence are not imposed at all by the greatest number of his readers and never by the better ones if they are reading a novel, and he fulfils the remaining demands of the spirit – and in no mean degree of the body – so his must and will justifiably remain a favoured book of our and every age in which aesthetic works are written simply in order to please, and are read simply for pleasure.

But does not poetic literature possess even classical works which offend the lofty purity of the ideal in a like manner, and which seem by the materiality of their content to be very far removed from that spirituality which we here demand of every aesthetic work of art?[54] What even the poet, that chaste apostle of the muse, may permit himself, should that be denied to the novelist, who is only his half-brother and still so very much earthbound? I can all the less avoid this question here since there exist in the elegiac as well as in the satiric class masterpieces in which a quite other nature from that of which this essay treats is sought, recommended, and gives the appearance of being defended not against evil morals as much as against good morals. Hence, either these poetic works would have to be rejected, or the concept established here of elegiac poetry must be taken as much too arbitrary.

Whatever the poet may permit himself, we asked, should that be withheld from the prose narrator? The answer is already contained in the question: whatever is permitted the poet can prove nothing for one who is not a poet. In the concept itself of poet, and only in this, lies the ground of that freedom which is merely contemptible licence as soon as it is not derived from the highest and noblest that constitutes him.

The laws of propriety are alien to innocent nature; only the experience of corruption has given them their origin. But as soon as that experience has been undergone and natural innocence has disappeared from morals, then they become sacred laws which a moral feeling may not contravene. They apply in any artificial world with the same right as the laws of nature rule in the world of innocence. But it is precisely this that denotes the poet: that he revokes everything in himself that recalls an artificial world, that he is able to restore nature within himself to her original simplicity. But having done this, then he is by the same token exempted from all laws by which a corrupted heart is protected against itself. He is pure, he is innocent, and whatever is permitted to innocent nature is permitted him too; if you, who read or listen to him, are no longer guiltless, and if you cannot become so for the moment through his purifying presence, then it is *your* misfortune, not his; you are forsaking him, he has not sung for you.

The following, then, may be said with reference to liberties of this kind:

First: only *nature* can justify them. Hence they may not be the product of choice or of deliberate imitation; for we can never allow to the will, which is always directed according to moral laws, to favour sensuousness. They must therefore be *naivety*. In order, however, to convince us that they are truly so, we must see them supported and accompanied by all else that is likewise grounded in nature, for nature can only be recognised by the rigorous consequence, unity, and uniformity of her effects. Only to a heart that despises all artificiality outright, and hence also even if it is useful, do we permit its exemption where it represses and limits; only to a heart that subordinates itself to all the shackles of nature do we permit that it make use of her freedom. All other feelings of such a person must in consequence bear the impress of naturalness; he must be true, simple, free, candid, full of feeling, upright; all deception, cunning, all caprice, all petty selfishness must be banished from his character, every trace of them from his work.

Second: only *beautiful* nature can justify liberties of this sort. Therefore they may not be onesided manifestations of appetite; for everything that originates in crude necessity is contemptible. From the totality and from the richness of human nature these sensuous energies must likewise derive. They must be *humanity*. But in order to be able to judge that the whole of human nature demands them and not merely a onesided and vulgar exigency of sensuousness, we must see that whole depicted of which they represent a single feature. In itself the sensuous mode of feeling is something innocent and indifferent. It displeases us in a human being only because it is animal and testifies to a lack of a more truly perfect humanity in him: it offends us in a work of art only because such a work makes a claim to please us and hence assumes that *we* are also capable of such a lack. But if we surprise in a person humanity functioning in all its remaining aspects, if we find in the work in which liberties of this species have been exercised all the realities of mankind expressed, then that ground of our disapproval is removed and we can delight with unequivocal joy in the naive expression of true and beautiful nature. The same poet, therefore, who may allow himself to make us participants in such basely human feelings, must on the other hand be able to elevate us to all that is humanly great and beautiful and sublime.

This, then, would provide us with the criterion to which we could with certainty submit every poet who offends somewhat against propriety, and forces his freedom in the depiction of nature to this extreme. His work is vulgar and low, reprehensible without exception, if it is *cold*, if it is *empty*, for this reveals its origin in intention and in vulgar exigency, and is a heinous assault on our appetites. On the other hand, it is beautiful, noble, and worthy of applause despite all the objections of frosty decency, if it is naive and binds spirit and heart together.[p]

If I am told that, according to the criterion laid down here, most French narratives of this genre and their best imitations in Germany would not survive – that this would in part be the case with many a product of our most graceful and gifted poet,[56] not even excepting his masterpieces – to this I have no reply. The dictum itself is anything but new, and I only give here the grounds of a judgement which has already long been enunciated by every finer feeling on this subject. But these very principles which perhaps appear all too rigorous in connection with those writings may perhaps be found too liberal in connection with some other works; for I do not deny that the same grounds on which I find entirely inexcusable the seductive pictures of the Roman and German Ovid,[57] as well as of Crébillon,[58] Voltaire, Marmontel[59] (who calls himself a moral narrator), Laclos,[60] and many others, yet reconcile me to the elegies of the Roman and German Propertius,[61] even to some of the ill-reputed works of Diderot,[62] for the former are only witty, only prosaic, only lascivious, while the latter are poetic, human, and naive.[q]

Idyll

There remain only a few more words for me to say about this third species of sentimental poetry, because a more detailed development of them, which they surely require,[63] is reserved for another occasion.[r]

The poetic representation of innocent and contented mankind is the universal concept of this type of poetic composition. Since this innocence and this contentedness appear incompatible with the artificial conditions of society at large and with a certain degree of education and refinement, the poets have removed the location of idyll from the tumult of everyday life into the simple pastoral state and assigned its period before the *beginnings of civilisation* in the childlike age of man. But one can readily grasp that these designations are merely accidental, that they are not to be considered as the purpose of the idyll, simply as the most natural means to it. The purpose itself is invariably only to represent man in a state of innocence, i.e., in a condition of harmony and of peace with himself and with his environment.

But such a condition does not occur only before the beginnings of civilisation, rather it is also the condition which civilisation, if it can be said to have any particular tendency everywhere, aims at as its ultimate purpose. Only the idea of this condition and belief in its possible realisation can reconcile man to all the evils to which he is subjected in the course of civilisation, and were it merely a chimera the complaints of those would be justified who deplore society at large and the cultivation of the understanding simply as an evil, and assume that superseded state of nature to be the true purpose of mankind.[64] For the individual who is immersed in civilisation, infinitely much therefore depends upon his receiving a tangible assurance of the realisation of that idea in the world of sense, of the possible reality of that condition, and since actual experience, far from nourishing this belief, rather contradicts it constantly, here, as in so many cases, the faculty of poetic composition comes to the aid of reason in order to render that idea palpable to intuition and to realise it in individual cases.

That innocence of the pastoral state is indeed also a poetic conception, and hence imagination must already there have shown itself to be creative; but, apart from the solution of the task having been incomparably simpler and easier, experience itself provided the individual features which it had only to select and combine into a whole. Beneath the unclouded skies, in the simple conditions of the primitive state, and with limited knowledge nature is easily satisfied, and man does not become savage until dire need has frightened him. All peoples who possess a history have a paradise, a state of innocence, a golden age; indeed, every man has his paradise, his golden age, which he recalls, according as he has more or less of the poetic in his nature, with more or less inspiration. Experience itself therefore supplies features enough for the depiction of which the pastoral idyll treats. For this reason it remains always a beautiful, an elevating fiction, and the poetic power in representing it has truly worked on behalf of the ideal. For, to the man who has once deviated from the simplicity of nature and is delivered over to the dangerous guidance of his reason, it is of infinite importance to perceive once again nature's legislation in a pure exemplar, and in this faithful mirror to be able once again to purify himself of the corruption of civilisation. But in doing so, one circumstance is involved that very much reduces the aesthetic value of such poems. Set *before the beginnings of civilisation*, they exclude together with its disadvantages all its advantages, and by their very nature they find themselves necessarily in conflict with it. *Theoretically*, then, they lead us backwards, while *practically* they lead us forwards and ennoble us. Unhappily they place that purpose *behind* us, *toward* which they should, however, lead us, and hence they imbue us only with a sad feeling of loss, not with joyous feelings of hope. Since they can only attain their purpose by the denial of all art, and only by the simplification of human nature, they possess together with the utmost value for the *heart*, all too little for the *spirit*, and their narrow range is too soon exhausted. Therefore we can love them and seek them out only when we stand in need of peace, but not when our forces are striving for motion and activity. Only for the sick in spirit can they provide *healing*, but no *nourishment* for the healthy; they cannot vivify, only assuage. This shortcoming grounded in the essence of the pastoral idyll has been beyond the art of the poets to correct. This type of composition has not, indeed, been lacking in enthusiastic admirers, and there are readers enough who can prefer an *Amyntas* and a *Daphnis*[65] to the greatest masterpieces of the epic and dramatic muses; but with such readers it is not so much their taste as their private needs that judge of works of art; consequently their opinion cannot be considered here. The reader of spirit and perception does not, indeed, mistake the value of such poetry, but he feels himself more rarely drawn to it and sooner satiated. They function at the needful moment all the more powerfully; but the truly beautiful should not be obliged to wait for such a moment, but should rather produce it.

What I am here criticising in the bucolic idyll applies of course only to the sentimental; for the naive can never be lacking content since here it is already contained in the form itself. All poetry must indeed possess an infinite content, only through this is it poetry; but it can fulfil the requirement in two different ways. It can be infinite in accordance with its form, if it presents its subject with *all its limits*, by individualising it; it can be infinite according to its matter if it *removes all its limits* from the subject, by idealising it; hence either by an absolute representation or by the representation of an absolute. The naive poet takes the first way, the sentimental the second. The first cannot fall short of his content so long as he remains faithful to nature which is always radically limited, i.e., infinite in relation to its form. To the second, however, nature stands in opposition with her radical limitation, since he should place an absolute content in the subject. The sentimental poet, therefore, does not well understand the advantages when he *borrows his subjects* from the naive poet; in themselves they are completely indifferent and only become poetic by their treatment. In this way he imposes on himself the naive poet's limitations quite unnecessarily, without however being able to carry through the limitation completely, or to compete with him in absolute assurance of the representation; he should therefore rather remove himself in his subject from the naive poet, because he can only regain from him through the subject what the latter has to his advantage in the form.

In order to make the application from this to the bucolic idyll of the sentimental poets, it now becomes clear why these poems, despite every effort of genius and art, are not completely satisfactory either for the heart or for the spirit. They implement an ideal, and yet retain the narrower indigent pastoral world, whereas they should absolutely have chosen either another world for the ideal, or a different representation for the pastoral world. They are so far ideal that thereby the representation loses in individual truth, yet again they are so far individual that the ideal content suffers thereby. One of Geßner's shepherds, for example, cannot delight us as nature by the fidelity of imitation, since for this he is too ideal a being; he can as little satisfy us as an ideal by infinitude of thought since for this he is much too inadequate a creature. He will, indeed, satisfy all classes of readers without exception up to a certain point because he strives to unite the naive with the sentimental, and consequently discharges to a certain degree the two opposed demands that can be made on a poem; but because the poet, in the effort to unify both, fails to do justice to either one, and is neither wholly nature nor wholly ideal, he cannot for that very reason be quite acceptable to a rigorous taste that cannot forgive half-measures in aesthetic matters. It is extraordinary that this hybrid quality extends likewise to the language of the poet we have mentioned; he wavers undecided between poetry and prose, as though the poet were fearful of removing himself in metrical address too far from actual nature, and in nonmetrical address of losing his poetic impulse. A loftier satisfaction is aroused by Milton's superb representation of the first human couple and the state of innocence in paradise: the most beautiful idyll known to me of the sentimental type. Here nature is noble, spirited, at once full of range and depth, the highest meaning of humanity clothed in the most graceful form.

Hence here too, in the idyll, as in all other poetic types, one must make a choice once and for all between individuality and ideality; for to seek to satisfy both demands simultaneously is, so long as one has not reached the acme of perfection, the surest way of falling short of both. Should the modern feel within himself sufficient of the Greek spirit to compete, despite all the intractability of his material, with the Greek on his own ground, namely in the field of naive poetry, then let him do it wholly and exclusively, and liberate himself from every demand of the sentimental taste of the age. He may indeed reach his model with difficulty; between the original and the most successful epigone a perceptible interval will always remain open, but by these means he is nevertheless certain to produce a genuinely poetic work.[8] If he is driven, on the contrary, to the ideal by the sentimental poetic impulse, then let him pursue this wholly, in complete purity, and not rest content until he has reached the highest, without looking back to see whether actuality has borne him out. Let him despise the unworthy evasion of cheapening the meaning of the ideal in order to accommodate it to human inadequacy, or of excluding the spirit in order to make readier way with the heart. Let him not lead us backwards into our childhood in order to secure to us with the most precious acquisitions of the understanding a peace which cannot last longer than the slumber of our spiritual faculties, but rather lead us forward into our maturity in order to permit us to perceive that higher harmony which rewards the combatant and gratifies the conqueror. Let him undertake the task of idyll so as to display that pastoral innocence even in creatures of civilisation and under all the conditions of the most active and vigorous life, of expansive thought, of the subtlest art, the highest social refinement, which, in a word, leads man who cannot now go back to Arcady forward to Elysium.[67]

The concept of this idyll is the concept of a conflict fully reconciled not only in the individual, but in society, of a free uniting of inclination with the law, of a nature illuminated by the highest moral dignity, briefly, none other than the ideal of beauty applied to actual life. Its character thus subsists in the complete reconciliation of *all opposition between actuality and the ideal* which has supplied material for satirical and elegiac poetry, and therewith of all conflict in the feelings likewise. Calm would then be the predominant impression of such a poetic type, but calm of perfection, not of inertia; a calm that derives from the balance not the arresting of those powers, that springs from richness and not emptiness, and is accompanied by the feeling of an infinite capacity. But for the very reason that all resistance vanishes it will then be incomparably more difficult than in the two former types of poetry to represent *motion*, without which, however, no poetic effect whatsoever can be conceived. The highest unity must prevail; but not at the expense of variety; the mind must be satisfied, but not so that aspiration ceases on that account. The resolution of this question is in fact what the theory of the idyll has to supply.

The following has been established on the relation of both modes of poetry to one another and to the poetic ideal:

To the naive poet nature has granted the favour of functioning always as an undivided unity, to be at every instant an independent and complete whole, and to represent mankind, in all its significance, in actuality. Upon the sentimental poet she has conferred the power, or rather impressed a lively impulse, to restore out of himself that unity that has been disrupted by abstraction, to complete the humanity within himself, and from a limited condition to pass over into an infinite one.[t] But to give human nature its full expression is the common task of both, and without that they could not be called poets at all; the naive poet, however, always possesses the advantage of sensuous reality over the sentimental, since he implements as an actual fact what the other only strives to attain. And this it is too that everyone experiences in himself when he observes himself in the enjoyment of naive poetry. He feels all the powers of his humanity active in such a moment, he stands in need of nothing, he is a whole in himself; without distinguishing anything in his feeling, he is at once pleased with his spiritual activity and his sensuous life. It is quite another mood into which the sentimental poet casts him. Here he feels only a lively *impulse* to produce that harmony in himself which he there actually felt, to make a whole of himself, to give complete expression to the humanity within himself. Hence in the latter his mind is in motion, it is in tension, it wavers between conflicting feelings; whereas in the former it is calm, relaxed, at one with itself and completely satisfied.

But if the naive poet gains on the one hand in reality at the expense of the sentimental, and brings into actual existence what the latter can only arouse a lively impulse to attain, the latter for his part possesses the great advantage over the first that he can give the impulse a *greater object* than the former has supplied or could supply. All actuality, we know, falls short of the ideal; everything existing has its limits, but thought is boundless. From this limitation, to which everything sensuous is subjected, the naive poet therefore also suffers, whereas the unconditional freedom of the faculty of ideas accrues to the sentimental. The former therefore indeed fulfils his task, but the task itself is something limited; the latter indeed does not fulfil his, but his task is an infinite one. In this, too, everyone can learn from his own experience. From the naive poet one turns with facility and eagerness to the active environment; the sentimental will always for a few moments disaffect one for actual life. This is because our minds are here extended by the infinitude of the idea beyond their natural circumscription, so that nothing to hand can any longer be adequate to it. We fall back rather, lost in our thoughts, where we find nourishment for the impulse generated in the world of ideas instead of seeking outside ourselves, as with the former, for sensuous objects. Sentimental poetry is the offspring of retreat and quietude, and to them, too, it invites us; the naive is the child of life, and to life also it leads us back.

I have called naive poetry a *favour of nature* to underscore that reflection has no part in it. It is a lucky throw of the dice, standing in no need of improvement if successful, but equally incapable of any if it should fail. In his feeling the whole work of the naive genius is acquitted; here is his strength and his limit. If he has not at once *felt* poetically, i.e., not at once completely humanly, then this shortcoming can no longer be repaired by art. Criticism can only afford him an insight into his mistake, but it cannot supply any beauty in its place. By his nature the naive genius must do everything; by his freedom he can achieve little; and it will fulfil its essence so long as nature in him should operate according to an inner necessity. Now everything indeed is necessary that takes place by nature: this applies equally to every product of the naive genius (from whom nothing is farther removed than arbitrary action) be it never so successful; but the coercion of the moment is one thing, the inner necessity of the whole quite another. Considered as a whole, nature is independent and infinite; in any individual manifestation, however, she is dependent and limited. This, therefore, applies also to the nature of the poet. Even the most felicitous moment in which he can find himself is dependent upon a preceding one; hence, too, only a conditional necessity can be attributed to him. But now the poet is assigned the task of equating an individual state to the human whole, consequently to base that state absolutely and necessarily upon itself. Hence, every trace of temporal dependence must be removed from the moment of inspiration, and the subject itself, however limited it may be, may not limit the poet. It will be readily understood that this is possible only insofar as the poet brings to the subject absolute freedom and breadth of ability and as he is practised in embracing everything with his whole humanity. His practice, however, he can receive only from the world in which he lives and by which he is directly affected. The naive genius is thus dependent upon experience in a way unknown to the sentimental. The latter, we know, only begins his function where the former concludes his; his strength subsists in completing an inadequate subject *out of himself* and in transforming by his own power a limited condition into a condition of freedom. Thus the naive poetic genius requires assistance from without, whereas the sentimental nourishes and purifies himself from within; around him he must observe nature instinct with form, a poetic world, naive humanity, since he must complete his work in sense perception. If, however, this assistance from without is not forthcoming, and he finds himself surrounded by a spiritless matter, only two things then occur. Either he abandons his species if the genus predominates in him, and he becomes sentimental if only to remain poetic; or, if the characteristics of the species retain their predominance, he abandons his genus and becomes common nature if only to remain nature. The first may well be the case with the finest sentimental poets in the ancient Roman world and in more modern times. Had they been born in another age, transplanted beneath other skies, they, who now move us by ideas, would have enchanted us by individual truth and naive beauty. From the second the poet could only with difficulty protect himself if he cannot abandon nature in a vulgar world.

Actual nature, of course; but from this one cannot carefully enough distinguish true nature which is the *subject* of naive poetry. Actual nature exists everywhere, but true nature is all the rarer, for to it belongs an inner necessity of existence. Actual nature is every outburst of passion, however crude; it may even be true nature, but truly *human* it cannot be, for this requires some participation in every utterance of the independent faculties, the expression of which is dignity. Actual human nature includes every moral baseness, but it is to be hoped that true human nature does not; for the latter cannot be other than noble. The absurdities cannot be overlooked to which this confusion between actual and true human nature has misled criticism as well as practice: what trivialities have been permitted, even praised, in poetry because, alas! they are actual nature; how pleased one is to find caricatures which are ghastly enough in the actual world carefully transported into the poetic and counterfeited true to life. Certainly, the poet may imitate bad nature also, and indeed the very notion of satire involves this: but in this case his own beautiful nature must be conveyed with the subject, but the vulgar material must not drag the imitator down with it. If only he himself is true human nature at least in the moment of execution then it does not matter at all what he executes: but equally we can only accept a true picture of actuality from the hands of such a poet. Woe unto us readers, if the grotesque mirrors itself in the grotesque, if the scourge of satire falls into the hands of one whom nature intended should wield a much more serious lash, if men who, devoid of everything that one can call poetic spirit, possess only the apish talent of vulgar imitation and exercise it in a gruesome and frightful manner at the expense of our taste!

But even for the truly naive poet, I have noted, common nature can become dangerous; for in the final analysis that fine accord between feeling and thinking in which his character subsists, is still only an idea that is never entirely attained in actuality; and even in the most fortunate geniuses of this class, passive receptivity will always predominate somewhat over independent activity. But receptivity is always more or less dependent upon external impression and only a continuous agility of the productive faculties, which is not to be expected of human nature, would be able to prevent the material from exercising upon occasion its blind power over receptivity. Whenever this is the case, poetic feeling turns into the vulgar.[u]

No genius of the naive category, from Homer down to Bodmer,[70] has entirely avoided these reefs; but of course they are most dangerous to those who are obliged to defend themselves externally from vulgar nature, or whose inner cultivation is destroyed by a lack of discipline. The first is responsible for the fact that even cultivated writers do not always remain free of platitudes, and the second that many a fine talent is prevented from occupying the rank to which nature has called it. The comic poet, whose genius most of all is nourished by actual life, is for that very reason most exposed to platitude, as indeed the examples of Aristophanes and Plautus and of almost all the later poets show who have followed in their footsteps. How far does even the sublime Shakespeare let us sink sometimes; with what trivialities are we not tormented by Lope de Vega, Molière, Regnard,[71] Goldoni; into what mire are we not dragged down by Holberg?[72] Schlegel,[73] one of the most gifted poets of our fatherland, whose genius might have shone among the foremost in this category; Gellert,[74] a truly naive poet, as also Rabener,[75] even Lessing, the cultivated student of criticism and a so watchful judge of his own work – do they not all, more or less, pay for the insipid character of the nature they have selected as the material of their satire? I do not mention any of the most recent writers of this class since there are none that I can except.

And not enough that the naive poetic spirit is in danger of nourishing itself all too much with common reality – by the facility with which it expresses itself, and precisely by means of this greater assimilation to actual life it encourages the vulgar imitator to try his hand in the realm of poetry. Sentimental poetry, albeit dangerous enough from another point of view, as I shall later show, at least keeps *these* folk at a distance, because it is not everyone's forte to elevate himself to the idea; but naive poetry encourages the belief that it is mere feeling, mere humour, mere imitation of actual nature that makes for the poet. But nothing is more repellent than the banal individual who takes it into his head to be ingratiating and naive – he who should envelop himself in all the veils of art in order to conceal his loathsome nature. From this source, too, come the unspeakable platitudes which Germans love to hear in the form of naive and comic songs and with which they are wont to amuse themselves incessantly at a well-laden table. Granted the licence of whimsy, of feeling, these paltry things are tolerated – but this whimsy and this feeling cannot be too carefully suppressed. The muses on the Pleiße constitute a specially pitiful chorus in this respect, and they are answered in no better accords by the Camenae[76] of the Leine and Elbe.[v] These jokes are as insipid as the passion is pitiful that is heard upon our tragic stages and that, instead of imitating true nature, achieves only the spiritless and ignoble expression of the actual, so that after such a tearful dish we are in the same mood as if we had just paid a visit to a hospital or read Salzmann's *Human Misery*.[78] Matters are still worse with satiric poetry and particularly with the comic novel which simply by its nature is so close to common life and hence ought, like any frontier post, to be in the safest hands. That man is truly least called to be the *portrayer* of his time who is its *creature* and its *caricature*; but because it is so easy to conjure up some kind of comic character from one's own acquaintance, even if only *a fat man*,[79] and to get the grotesque down on paper with a crude pen, even the sworn enemies of everything in the poetic spirit sometimes feel the urge to founder in this style and delight a circle of worthy friends with the fair offspring. A purely attuned feeling would, of course, never be in danger of confusing these products of a vulgar nature with the gifted fruits of naive genius; but it is precisely this mode of pure feeling that is lacking, and in most cases the attempt is made only to gratify a desire without making any demands on the spirit. The so patently misunderstood notion, true enough in itself, that one finds *recreation* in works of *bel esprit*, contributes substantially to this indulgence, if one can indeed call it indulgence when nothing loftier is intimated and the reader profits by it in the same manner as the author. Common nature, in fact, when it is under tension, can recuperate only in emptiness, and even a high degree of understanding, if it is not supported by an equivalent cultivation of feeling, relaxes from its affairs only in insipid sensual enjoyment.

If the poetic genius must elevate itself by its free individual activity above all *accidental* limits that are inseparable from any *determined* condition in order to attain to human nature in its absolute capacity, it may not, on the other hand, go beyond the *necessary* limits which are involved in the concept of human nature; for the absolute (but only within humanity) is its task and its sphere. We have seen that the naive genius is not in fact in danger of surpassing this sphere, nor indeed of *exhausting it fully*, if it sets external necessity or the accidental exigency of the moment too much in the place of inner necessity. The sentimental genius, however, is exposed to the danger, due to the effort of removing all limitations from it, of suppressing human nature altogether, and not only, as it may and should, elevating or *idealising* itself above and beyond all determined and limited actuality to absolute possibility, but rather of going still further beyond possibility or otherwise falling into extravagant *enthusiasm*. This error of *overtension* is as much founded in the specific nature of its procedure as the opposed error of *indolence* is rooted in the idiosyncratic approach of the naive. For the naive genius permits nature to reign unrestrictedly within himself, and since nature in its individual temporal manifestations is always dependent and scanty, naive feeling will not always remain sufficiently *exalted* to be able to resist the accidental determinations of the moment. On the other hand, the sentimental genius abandons actuality in order to rise upward to ideas and to command his material with free spontaneity; but since reason, in accordance with its laws, always strives toward the unconditioned, the sentimental genius will not always remain sufficiently *dispassionate* to maintain himself uninterruptedly and uniformly within the conditions that are entailed in the concept of human nature and to which reason, even in its freest effects, must here always remain bound. This could take place only through a relative degree of receptivity which, however, in the sentimental spirit, is as far outweighed by spontaneity as in the naive it outweighs spontaneity. If one therefore sometimes misses the *spirit* in the creations of naive genius, one will frequently seek in vain in the products of the sentimental for the *matter*. Both, therefore, albeit in entirely opposed ways, fall into the error of *emptiness*; for matter without spirit, and a play of spirit without matter, are both a nullity in the aesthetic judgment.

All poets who draw their material too onesidedly from the world of thought and are driven more by an inner wealth of ideas than by stress of feeling to poetic creation are more or less in danger of falling into this bypath. In its creations reason draws too little upon this counsel of the limits of the sensuous world, and thought is always driven farther than experience can follow. If, however, thought is driven so far that not only could no particular experience correspond to it (for thus far the ideally beautiful may and must go), but that it also in fact contravenes the conditions of all possible experience and consequently, in order to make it actual, human nature would have to be totally and completely abandoned, then such a thought is no longer poetic but overstrained – provided, however, that it has declared itself as representable and poetic; for if it does not possess this it would still suffice if it only does not contradict itself. If it does contradict itself it is no longer overstrained, but *nonsense*; for that which does not exist at all can likewise not exceed its boundaries. If, however, it should not declare itself as an object for the imagination then, too, it is not overstrained; for mere thought is boundless, and whatever has no limits cannot surpass any. Hence only that can be called overstrained that outrages, not indeed logical, but sensuous truth, while still making claims upon it. If, then, a poet has the unhappy inspiration of choosing as a theme for depiction natures that are simply *superhuman* and which also *may* not be represented otherwise, he can only save himself from being overstrained by abandoning the poetic and by not even undertaking to execute his subject by means of the imagination. For if he were to do this, either the imagination would impose its own limits on the subject, and make of an absolute object a limited *human* one (as, for example, all the Greek gods are, and rightly so), or the subject would remove the limits set to imagination, i.e., it would suppress them, and in this precisely the overstrain subsists.

Overstrain in feeling must be distinguished from overstrain in representation; we are speaking here only of the first. The object of feeling can be unnatural, but the feeling itself is nature, and hence must speak the language of nature. If, therefore, overstrain in feeling can flow out of warmheartedness and a truly poetic disposition, then overstrain in representation testifies always to a cold heart, and very often to poetic incapacity. It is therefore not a mistake against which the sentimental poetic genius might have to be warned, but which threatens only his uninspired imitator, especially since he does not disdain the company of the banal, insipid, and even base. Overstrained feeling is by no means without truth, and as actual feeling it must also necessarily possess a real object. Because it is nature it also admits of simple expression and, coming from the heart, it cannot fail to reach the heart. Since its subject is not drawn from nature but is onesidedly and artificially advanced by the understanding, it also possesses a merely logical reality, and the feeling is therefore not purely human. It is not an illusion that Héloïse feels for Abélard, Petrarch for his Laura, St Preux for his Julie,[80] Werther for his Lotte, and what Agathon, Phanias, Peregrinus Proteus (Wieland's heroes, I mean) feel for their ideals.[81] The feeling is true, but its object is artificial and lies outside human nature. If their feeling had simply remained attached to the sensuous truth of its objects it would not have been able to assume that impetus; on the other hand a merely capricious play of fantasy without any inner meaning would likewise not have been able to touch our hearts, for the heart is touched only by reason. This overstrain, then, merits correction, not contempt, and whoever mocks at it should ask himself whether he is not perhaps so clever out of heartlessness, or so cautious out of lack of reason. Thus also the exaggerated tenderness in matters of gallantry and honour that characterises the knightly romances, particularly the Spanish, the scrupulous delicacy driven to the point of preciosity in the French and English sentimental novels (of the best kind) are not only subjectively true, but also, objectively considered, not without substance; they are genuine feelings actually derived from a moral source and are only objectionable because they surpass the bounds of human truth. Without that moral reality how would it be possible that they could be communicated with such power and fervour as we nonetheless find them in experience to be? The same applies also to moral and religious enthusiasm and to exalted love of freedom and fatherland. Since the objects of these feelings are always ideas and do not appear in external experience (for what affects the political enthusiast, for example, is not what he sees, but what he thinks), the spontaneous imagination possesses a dangerous freedom and cannot, as in other cases, be restored to its limits by the sensuous presence of its objects. But neither man in general nor the poet in particular may withdraw himself from the jurisdiction of nature other than to submit to the opposed jurisdiction of reason; only for the ideal may he abandon actuality, since by one of these two anchors freedom *must* be secured. But the path from experience to the ideal is long, and in between lies fantasy with its unbridled arbitrariness. It is therefore unavoidable that man in general, just as the poet in particular, if he should quit the domination of feeling for the freedom of his understanding without having been driven to it by the laws of reason, that is, if he leaves nature through caprice, then he will remain *without a law*, and is thus rendered a prey to the fantastic.

Experience shows that whole peoples as well as individuals who have withdrawn from the secure guidance of nature are actually in this state, and this too provides sufficient examples of an analogous deviation in the art of poetry. Because the genuine sentimental poetic impulse must, in order to elevate itself to the idea, pass beyond the limits of actual nature, the inauthentic goes beyond every limit whatever and persuades itself that the mere wild play of imagination is all that makes for poetic inspiration. To the true poetic genius, who abandons actuality only for the sake of the idea, this can either never happen, or only in those moments in which he has lost himself; for he, on the other hand, can be seduced by his own nature into an exaggerated mode of perception. He can, however, seduce others into the fantastic by his example, because readers of vivid fantasy and weak understanding take into account only the licence against actual nature which he permits himself, without being able to follow him as far as his lofty inner necessity. The same thing happens here to the sentimental genius that we have observed in the naive. Since the latter carries out by his nature everything that he does, the vulgar imitator prefers no worse guide than his own nature. Masterpieces of the naive category will, therefore, usually have as their sequel the most banal and sordid impressions of vulgar nature, and the chief works of the sentimental genre, a numerous host of fantastic productions; and this can easily be demonstrated in the literature of every people.

With reference to poetry, two principles are employed which in themselves are completely correct, but in the interpretation in which they are commonly taken, cancel one another out. Of the first: 'That the art of poetry serves for pleasure and recreation', we have already observed that it not a little favours emptiness and platitude in poetic depictions; by the second principle: 'That it serves for the moral ennoblement of man', the exaggerated finds protection. It is not superfluous to illuminate somewhat more closely both these principles, which are so often enunciated, so often incorrectly interpreted, and so clumsily applied.

By recreation we mean the transition from a constrained state to one which is natural to us. Everything here, of course, depends on what we posit our natural condition to be, and what we understand by a constrained one. If we posit the former exclusively as an unbridled play of the physical powers, and in liberty from every constraint, then all activity of reason (because it exercises resistance to sensuousness) becomes a violence done to us, and spiritual quietude combined with sensuous activity is the proper ideal of recreation, If, however, we posit our natural condition as an unlimited capacity for every human utterance, and the ability to exercise all our powers with equal freedom, then any separation and *isolation* of these powers is a constrained condition, and the ideal of recreation is the restoration of our whole nature after onesided tensions. The first ideal is therefore dictated solely by the needs of *sensuous* nature, the second by the independence of *human* nature. Which of these two types of recreation the art of poetry ought and must supply can scarcely be a question in theory; for no one would gladly give the appearance that he could be tempted to set the ideal of humanity beneath the ideal of animality. Nevertheless, the demands that one is accustomed in actual life to make of poetic works are drawn by preference from the sensuous ideal, and in most cases it is in accordance with it – not indeed that the *esteem* that one accords to these works is determined, but certainly that the *predilection* is decided and the *favourite* chosen. The state of mind of most people is on the one hand intensive and exhausting *labour*, on the other, enervating *indulgence*. The former, we know, renders the sensuous need for spiritual calm and for cessation of activity disproportionately more pressing than the moral need for harmony and for an absolute freedom of function, because above all else *nature* must be satisfied before the *mind* can make its demands; the latter confines and cripples the moral impulses themselves from which these demands should originate. Hence nothing is more disadvantageous for sensitivity to the truly beautiful than both these all-too-common frames of mind among men, and from this it becomes clear why so few, even among better men, possess correct judgement in aesthetic matters. Beauty is the product of accord between the mind and the senses; it addresses itself at once to all the faculties of man and can, therefore, be perceived and appreciated only under the condition that he employ all his powers fully and freely. One must assemble clear senses, a full heart, a fresh and unimpaired mind, one's whole nature must be collected, which is by no means the case with those who are divided in themselves by abstract thought, hemmed in by petty business formalities, or exhausted by strenuous concentration. These persons yearn indeed for sensuous matter, not in order to continue the play of their intellectual powers, but in order to stop it. They want to be free, but only from a burden that fatigues their lassitude, not from a barrier that blocks their activity.

Should one then still be amazed at the happiness of mediocrity and emptiness in aesthetic matters, or at the vengeance of weak minds upon the truly and actively beautiful? They expected recreation from it, but a recreation to meet their need and in accordance with their feeble notion, and they discover with dismay that they are now first expected to put out an effort of strength for which they might lack the capacity even in their best moments. There, on the contrary, they are welcome as they are; for as little strength as they bring with them, still they need very much less to exhaust the minds of their writers. Here they are at once relieved of the burden of thought; and nature relaxed can indulge itself upon the downy pillow of *platitude* in blessed enjoyment of nothingness. In the temple of Thalia and Melpomene,[82] as it is established among us, the beloved goddess sits enthroned receiving in her ample bosom the dull pedant and the tired businessman, and lulls the mind into a mesmeric sleep, thawing out the frigid senses and rocking the imagination in gentle motion.

And why should one not indulge vulgar individuals, when that is often enough done for the best ones? The relaxation that nature demands after every sustained effort and also takes without invitation (and only for such moments does one reserve the enjoyment of beautiful works), is so little favourable to aesthetic judgement that among those classes who are really occupied only extremely few will be found who can judge in matters of taste with certainty, and what is here more to the point, with consistency. Nothing is more usual than that scholars, in contrast to cultivated mundane individuals, reveal themselves in judgements of beauty in the most ridiculous light, and in particular the professional critics are the scorn of all connoisseurs. Their neglected, sometimes exaggerated, sometimes coarse, feeling leads them astray in most cases, and even if they have seized upon something in theory in defence of it, they can only formulate *technical* (concerning the purposiveness of a work) not *aesthetic* judgements, which must always comprehend the whole, and in which, therefore, feeling must decide. If they at last voluntarily renounce the latter and rest content with the former, they may yet be of sufficient use, since the poet in his inspiration and the perceptive reader at the moment of enjoyment may only too easily overlook details. But it is an all the more laughable spectacle if these crude natures who, with all their painstaking efforts, at best attain the cultivation of a single skill, set up their paltry personalities as representative of universal feeling, and in the sweat of their brows pass judgement upon the beautiful.

The concept of *recreation*, which poetry is to provide, is, as we have seen, usually beset by too narrow limits because one is accustomed to referring it too onesidedly to mere sensuous necessity. The notion of *ennoblement*, which the poet is supposed to aim at, is exactly the reverse; it is given too wide a scope because it is too onesidedly determined by the mere idea.

For, in accordance with the idea, ennoblement passes always into the infinite because reason in its demands is not bound by the necessary limits of the world of sense and does not stop short of the absolutely perfect. Nothing beyond which something still higher can be conceived can satisfy it; at its stern court no limitation of finite nature is acceptable in excuse; it acknowledges no other boundaries but those of thought, and of this we know that it soars beyond all the limits of space and time. Such an ideal of ennoblement which reason prescribes in its pure legislation may no more be established as his purpose by the poet as that base ideal of recreation which sensuousness sets up, since he should indeed liberate mankind from all accidental limitations, but without setting aside its concept or disrupting its necessary limitations. Whatever he allows himself beyond those limitations is exaggeration, and it is to just this that he is all too readily misled by a falsely construed concept of ennoblement. But the evil is that he can scarcely elevate himself to the true ideal of human ennoblement without in any case taking a few steps beyond it. For in order to attain to it he must abandon actuality, since he can draw upon it, as upon any ideal, only out of inner and moral sources. Not in the world that surrounds him nor in the tumult of everyday life, but only in his heart is it to be encountered, and only in the stillness of solitary contemplation can he find his heart. Yet this withdrawal from life will not only remove from his vision the accidental limitations of mankind – it will often remove the necessary and insurmountable limitations, and in seeking the pure form he stands in danger of losing the entire meaning. Reason will pursue its business much too isolated from experience, and whatever the contemplative spirit has discovered in the serene course of thought, the man of action will not be able to realise in the tempestuous course of daily life. Thus the very same produces the fanatic that was solely able to engender the sage, and the advantage of the latter may perhaps subsist less in that he did not become the former than in that he did not remain so.

It may therefore be left neither to the labouring classes of mankind to determine the concept of recreation in accordance with their needs, nor to the contemplative classes to determine the concept of ennoblement in accordance with their speculation, if the former concept is not to become too physical and too unworthy of poetry, nor the latter too hyperphysical and too extravagant for poetry. But since both these concepts, as experience shows, govern common opinion of poetry and poetic works we must, in order to interpret them, look for a class of men which, without toiling, is active, and is capable of formulating ideals without fanaticism; a class that unites within itself all the realities of life with its least possible limitations and is borne by the current of events without becoming its victim. Only such a class can preserve the beautiful unity of human nature that is destroyed for the moment by any particular task, and continuously by a life of such toil, and decide, in everything that is purely human, by their *feelings* the rule of common opinion. Whether such a class might actually exist, or whether that class which actually does exist under the external conditions described possesses the inner disposition corresponding to the concept, is another question which I am not concerned with here. If it does not correspond to it, then it has only itself to blame, since the contrasting labouring class has at least the satisfaction of considering itself a victim of its labour. In such a class of society (which, however, I offer here only as an idea and by no means wish to have taken as a fact) the naive character would be united with the sentimental so that each would preserve the other from its own extreme, and while the first would save the mind from exaggerations the second would secure it against inertia. For, in the final analysis, we must concede that neither the naive nor the sentimental character, each considered alone, quite exhausts that ideal of beautiful humanity that can only arise out of the intimate union of both.

For so long as one exalts both characters as far as the *poetic*, as we have thus far considered them, much of the limitation which adheres to them falls away, and their antithesis becomes all the less noticeable the higher the degree to which they become poetic; for the poetic mood is an independent whole in which all distinctions and all shortcomings vanish. But for the very reason that it is only the concept of the poetic in which both modes of perception can coincide, their mutual differences and limitations become in the same degree more noticeable the more they are divested of their poetic character; and this is the case in ordinary life. The more they descend to this, the more they lose of their generic character which brings them closer to one another, until finally in their caricatures only their specific character remains to oppose one to the other.

This leads me to a very remarkable psychological antagonism among men in a century that is civilising itself: an antagonism that because it is radical and based on inner mental dispositions is the cause of a worse division among men than any fortuitous clash of interests could ever provoke; one that deprives the artist and poet of all hope of pleasing and affecting universally, as is their task; which makes it impossible for the philosopher, even when he has done his utmost, to convince universally: yet the very concept of philosophy demands this; which, finally, will never permit a man in practical life to see his course of action universally approved – in a word, an antithesis that is to blame that no work of the spirit and no action of the heart can decisively satisfy one class without for that very reason bringing upon itself the damning judgement of the other. This antithesis is without doubt as old as the beginnings of civilisation and is scarcely to be overcome before its end other than in a few rare individuals who, it is to be hoped, always existed and always will; but among its effects is also this one, that it defeats every effort to overcome it because neither side can be induced to admit that there is any shortcoming on its part and any reality on the other; despite this, it still remains profitable enough to pursue so important a division back to its ultimate source and thereby to reduce the actual point of the conflict at least to a simpler formulation.

One can best discover the true concept of this antithesis, as I have just remarked, by abstracting from both the naive and the sentimental character what each possesses of the poetic. Of the first, then, nothing remains (from the theoretical point of view) but a sober spirit of observation and a fixed loyalty to the uniform testimony of the senses, and (from the practical point of view) a resigned submission to the necessity (but not the blind necessity) of nature: an accession thus to what is and what must be. Of the sentimental character nothing remains (theoretically) but a restless spirit of speculation that presses on to the unconditional in all its knowledge, and (practically) a moral rigorism that insists upon the unconditional in acts of the will. The member of the first class can be called a *realist* and of the other class an *idealist*; but these names should not recall either the good or bad senses which are connected with them in metaphysics.ʷ

Since the realist allows himself to be determined by the necessity of nature and the idealist by the necessity of reason, the same relation must obtain between them as is found between the effects of nature and the actions of reason. Nature, we know, although of infinite dimension as a whole, displays its dependence and indigence in every particular manifestation; only in the universe of its phenomena does it express an independently vast character. Every particular within it subsists only because something else exists; nothing arises out of itself, everything springs out of the antecedent moment in order to give rise to the following one. But it is just this reciprocal relation of phenomena to one another that assures to each its existence by the existence of the other, and its constancy and necessity is inseparable from the dependence of its manifestations. Nothing is free in nature, but nothing is arbitrary in her either.

And in just this way the realist also reveals himself in his *knowledge* as well as in his *actions*. The compass of his knowledge and functions extends to everything that exists conditionally; but he can never proceed beyond conditional cognition, and the rules which he formulates out of particular experience apply, in their strictest form, only once also; but should he elevate the rule of the moment into a universal law he will irremediably fall into error. If, therefore, the realist seeks to attain to something unconditional in his knowledge, he must attempt to do so along the very same path by which nature becomes an absolute, that is, by the path of totality and in the universe of experience. But since the sum of experience is never completely concluded, only a comparative totality is the highest to which the realist attains in his knowledge. He founds his insights upon the recurrence of similar instances, and will therefore judge correctly wherever the order remains unchanged; but in whatever presents itself for the first time, his wisdom returns to its beginnings.

Whatever applies to the realist's knowledge applies equally to his moral actions. His character possesses morality, but this lies, considered according to its concept, not in any particular act, but only in the whole sum of his life. In every particular case he will be determined by external causes and by external purposes; but those causes will not be accidental nor those purposes momentary, but will rather flow subjectively out of the whole of nature and will refer back objectively to it. Thus the impulses of his will are not, in the rigoristic sense, sufficiently free or morally pure enough, because they have as their cause something other than the pure will, and as their object something other than pure law; yet these are by no means blind and materialistic impulses since that other something is the absolute totality of nature, and therewith something independent and necessary. In this way common human understanding, the most distinctive feature of the realist, shows itself throughout his thought and conduct. From the individual case he draws the rule of his judgement, out of an inner perception the rule of his conduct; but by a happy instinct he is able to distinguish from both everything that is momentary and incidental. By this method he proceeds excellently on the whole, and will scarcely have to accuse himself of significant errors; but he will not be able to lay claim to greatness and dignity in any particular case. This is the prize only of independence and freedom and in his individual actions we see too few traces of these.

With the idealist the situation is quite different; he finds his cognitions and motives in himself and in pure reason. If nature always appears dependent and limited in her individual manifestations, reason on the other hand imposes the character of independence and perfection equally on every individual action. It draws everything out of itself, and to itself it refers everything. Whatever happens because of it happens only for its sake; every concept that it establishes is an absolute dimension, as is every decision that it formulates. And the idealist reveals himself in the same way, so far as he justly bears the name, in his knowledge as in his actions. Dissatisfied with cognitions that are valid only under certain presuppositions he seeks to penetrate to truths for which no presuppositions are necessary and which are the presuppositions of everything else. He is satisfied only by the philosophical insight that refers all conditional knowledge to the unconditional and attaches all experience to the necessity within the human spirit; those things to which the realist subordinates his thought, the idealist subordinates to his faculty of thought. And in this he proceeds with complete authority, for if the laws of the human spirit were not simultaneously the laws of the universe, if reason, in the last analysis, were subordinate to experience, then no experience would be possible either.

But he can have reached as far as absolute truths and yet still not be much furthered in knowledge thereby. For while it is true that everything is subject to necessary and universal laws, yet every individual matter is governed by accidental and particular rules; and in nature everything is individual. With his philosophical cognition he can therefore command the whole, while having gained nothing thereby for the particular or in practice: indeed, because he everywhere penetrates to the *remote* causes by which everything is possible, he can easily overlook the *proximate* causes whereby everything becomes actual; because he directs his attention in everything to the universal that finds the common factor in the most varied instances, he can easily neglect the particularity that differentiates them. He will, therefore, be able to *comprehend* very much by his knowledge and, perhaps for that very reason, *apprehend* very little, and often lose in insight what he gains in perspective. Thus it happens that if speculative understanding scorns common sense for its *narrowness*, common understanding derides the speculative for its *emptiness*; for cognitions always lose in specific content what they gain in range.

In moral judgements one will find in the idealist a purer morality in individual matters, but much less moral uniformity as a whole. He is called an idealist only insofar as he takes the grounds of his determinations from pure reason, but reason displays itself in each of its utterances absolutely, hence his individual actions, if they are moral at all, will bear the *whole* character of moral independence and freedom; and if in actual life a truly moral deed could be found at all which would remain so even in face of rigorous scrutiny, then it could only be executed by the idealist. But the purer the morality of his individual actions the more fortuitous it is too, since consistency and necessity are indeed the character of nature, but not of freedom. Not, of course, that idealism could ever be in conflict with morality (which would be a contradiction in terms), but because human nature is simply incapable of strict idealism. If the realist, even in his moral actions, calmly and uniformly submits to physical necessity, the idealist requires inspiration, he must for the moment exalt his nature, for he can do nothing unless he is inspired. But then, of course, he can do all the more and his behaviour will manifest a character of loftiness and grandeur which one looks for in vain in the actions of the realist. But actual life is by no means fitted to arouse that enthusiasm in him and still less so to maintain it uniformly. Set against the absolute greatness from which he always departs, the absolute smallness of the individual case to which he has to apply it makes far too great a contrast. Since his will in relation to form is always directed to the whole he is not prepared in relation to matter to direct it to the part, and yet in most cases the achievements are only trifling by which he can display his moral disposition. Thus it not infrequently happens that because of the limitless ideal he overlooks the application in the limited case, and, himself imbued by a maximum, loses sight of the minimum out of which, nevertheless, everything great arises in actuality.

In order to do justice to the realist, therefore, one must judge him according to the entire context of his life; for the idealist one must limit oneself to particular occurrences in it, but these must first be selected. Common opinion, which so gladly decides on the basis of individual cases, will therefore maintain an indifferent silence in regard to the realist because his individual actions provide as little occasion for praise as for blame; but in connection with the idealist, opinion will always be partial and divided between obloquy and admiration, because both his weakness and his strength lie in his individual acts.

It is unavoidable, because of so great a divergence of principles, that both parties will often be diametrically opposed in their judgements and that, even if they should agree as to facts and outcomes, their reasons will be opposed. The realist will ask what a thing is good *for*, and will appraise things according to their use; the idealist will ask *whether* they are good, and appraise them according to their worth. Whatever possesses its value and purpose in itself (with the exception, however, of the whole) the realist little knows or esteems; in matters of taste his criterion will be pleasure, in matters of morality it will be happiness, even if he does not make this the condition of moral action; in his religion, too, he does not gladly forget his *interest*, but he renders it noble and sacred by the ideal of the *greatest good*. Whatever he loves he will seek to make *happy*, where the idealist will seek to *ennoble* it. Whereas the realist aims, in his political tendencies, at *well-being* even if it should to some extent detract from the moral self-reliance of the people, the idealist will imperil well-being to make freedom his standard. To the first, independence *of condition* is his highest object; to the second, independence *from condition*, and this characteristic difference can be traced throughout their respective modes of thought and action. Thus the realist will always manifest his affection by *giving*, the idealist by *receiving*; and each reveals by what he sacrifices in his generosity what he prizes most highly. The idealist will pay for the shortcomings of his system with his own person and with his temporal condition, but he does not heed this sacrifice; the realist makes up for the shortcomings of his with his personal dignity, but he knows nothing of this sacrifice. His system holds good for everything about which he knows and for which he feels a need – why should he be bothered with goods of which he has no notion and in which he does not believe? It is enough for him that he is in possession, the earth is his, there is light in his understanding, and satisfaction in his breast. The idealist by no means enjoys so happy a fate. It is not enough that he often quarrels with happiness because he fails to make the moment his friend, he quarrels with himself too; he cannot be content either with his knowledge or with his actions. What he demands of himself is boundless; but everything that he achieves is limited. This rigour, which he applies to himself, he does not renounce in his behaviour towards others. He is indeed generous because in relations with others he does not remember his own individuality so much; but he is often unfair because he as easily overlooks the individuality of others. The realist, on the other hand, is less generous, but more fair-minded since he judges everything rather *in its limitation*. The vulgar, even the base in thought and action he can forgive, but never the arbitrary or eccentric; but the idealist is the sworn enemy of everything petty and jejune and will reconcile himself even with the extravagant and monstrous if it only testifies to a great potentiality. The former shows himself to be a philanthropist but simply without entertaining any very high idea of humanity; the latter thinks so highly of mankind that he thereby falls into the danger of despising man.

Left to himself the realist would never extend the compass of mankind beyond the borders of the world of sense, he would never seek to acquaint the human spirit with its independent greatness and freedom; for everything absolute in humanity is for him only a beautiful chimera and belief in it is not much better than fanaticism, because he never observes men in their pure potentiality, only in a determined and hence limited actuality. But the idealist left to himself would just as little seek to cultivate the sensuous faculties or to educate man as a natural being; yet this is an equally substantial part of man's vocation and the condition of all moral ennoblement. The striving of the idealist too far surpasses the sensuous life and the present moment; only for the whole, for eternity, does he want to sow and plant, and thereby forgets that the whole is only the consummated cycle of the individual, that eternity is only a totality of moments. The world, as the realist would construct it about himself, and in fact does, is a well-planned garden in which everything has its use, and merits its place and from which everything that does not bear fruit is banished; in the hands of the idealist the world is nature less utilised, but laid out on a grander scale. It does not occur to the first that man could exist for any other purpose than to live well and contentedly, and that he should put roots down only in order to thrust the plant into the skies. The latter does not understand that he must above all live well if only in order to think consistently well and nobly, and that the plant must wither if the roots are lacking.

If in a system something is left out for which an urgent and unavoidable need exists in nature, then nature can only be satisfied by some inconsistency in the system. Here both parties are guilty of such an inconsistency and this demonstrates, even if it could still have remained in doubt hitherto, both the onesidedness of the two systems and the richness of content of human nature. In regard to the idealist I do not have to supply any particular proof that he must necessarily depart from his system as soon as he aims at a particular effect: for all determined existence depends upon temporal conditions and follows empirical laws. With reference to the realist, however, it might seem doubtful whether he is not in fact able to do justice within his system to all the necessary demands of mankind. If one asks the realist: 'Why do you do what is right, and submit to what is necessary?' he will reply in the spirit of his system: 'Because this is entailed in nature, because that is how it must be.' But this by no means answers the question, because we are not speaking about what is involved in nature but about what men want, since they can certainly *not* want what must be. One can then ask him again: 'Why do you want what must be? Why do you submit your free will to this necessity of nature since it can just as well (even without success, which we are not discussing here) be opposed to her, and in millions of your fellow men is in fact opposed? You cannot say because all other natural beings submit to her, for you for one possess a will, and even feel that your submission should be a voluntary one. You submit, then, if you do so voluntarily, not to the necessity of nature itself, but to the *idea* of it; for the first merely compels you blindly as it compels the worm; but it has no power over your will, for you, even crushed by it, can still express another desire. But where do you take that idea of the necessity of nature from? Surely not from experience, which supplies you only with the discrete effects of nature but not with nature (as a whole), and only with discrete actualities but not with necessity. Thus you go beyond nature and determine yourself idealistically, each time you will to *act morally* or only not to *endure blindly*.' It is apparent, then, that the realist acts more worthily than, following his theory, he would allow, just as the idealist thinks more sublimely than he acts. Without admitting it to himself the first displays in the whole conduct of his life the self-reliance of human nature while the latter displays its poverty in his individual actions.

To the attentive and impartial reader I will not, following the account just given (the truth of which can be admitted even by anybody who does not accept the outcome), have first to demonstrate that the ideal of human nature is divided between both, but is not fully attained by either. Experience and reason each has its own prerogatives and neither can infringe upon the area of the other without inflicting serious consequences upon either the inner or external condition of man. Experience alone can teach us what is under certain conditions, what follows upon certain antecedent circumstances, and what must occur for a certain purpose. Reason alone, on the other hand, can teach us what is unconditionally valid and what must necessarily be so. If we should presume to decide anything by our pure reason about the external existence of things we should be engaged in a merely empty game, and the results would amount to nothing; for all existence is conditional and reason determines unconditionally. If, however, we should permit an accidental occurrence to decide about something that is already involved in the very concept of our own being, then we make of ourselves an empty game of chance, and our personality would amount to nothing. In the first case we relinquish the *value* (the temporal content) of our lives, in the second the *dignity* (the moral content).

In our account thus far we have indeed allowed a moral value to the realist and a measure of experience to the idealist, but only insofar as both do not proceed consistently, and nature operates in them more powerfully than their systems. Even though both do not entirely correspond to the ideal of perfect humanity, yet between them the important difference subsists that although the realist in no individual case does justice to the rational concept of mankind, he never contradicts its concept of the understanding; and although the idealist in individual cases approaches the highest concept of humanity, he not infrequently falls short of even its lowest concepts. But in practical life much more depends upon the whole being *uniformly* humanly good, than upon the particular being *accidentally* divine – and even if the idealist is a more appropriate subject to arouse in us a lofty notion of what is possible for mankind, and to imbue us with respect for its vocation, still only the realist can carry it out in practice with constancy and maintain the race within its eternal boundaries. The former is indeed a more noble, but a disproportionately less perfect being; the latter may appear generally less noble, but he is on the other hand all the more perfect; for nobility is already present in the manifestation of a great potentiality, but the perfect lies in the conduct of the whole and in the actual deed.

What is true of both characters in their most favourable interpretation is even more noticeable in their respective *caricatures*. True realism is beneficent in its effects and only less noble in its origin; false realism is contemptible in its origin and only slightly less pernicious in its effects. For the true realist submits himself to nature and to her necessity – but to nature as a whole, to her eternal and absolute necessity, not to her blind and momentary *compulsions*. He embraces and follows her law in freedom, and will always subordinate the particular to the universal; thus he cannot fail to agree with the genuine idealist in the final result, however different the path which each takes to that end. The vulgar empiricist, however, submits himself to nature as a force, and in indiscriminate blind surrender. His judgements, like his efforts, are limited to the particular; he believes and grasps only what he touches; he esteems only what advances him sensuously. He is, therefore, no more than external impressions chance to make him; his individuality is suppressed and, as a human being, he possesses absolutely no worth and no dignity. But as a thing he is still something, he can still serve some purpose. For that same nature to which he blindly abandons himself does not let him sink altogether; her eternal boundaries protect him, her inexhaustible assistance rescues him, if only he surrenders his freedom without reservation. Although in this condition he knows no laws, yet they govern him unacknowledged, and as much as his individual efforts might be in conflict with the whole, yet that whole will infallibly be able to overcome them. There are men enough, even whole peoples, who live in this lamentable condition, who survive solely by the grace of the law of nature, without individuality, and hence are good only *for something*; but that they even live and survive demonstrates that this condition is not entirely without meaning.

If, in contrast to this, true idealism is insecure and often dangerous in its effects, false idealism is appalling in its effects. The true idealist abandons nature and experience only because he does not find in it the immutable and unconditional necessity for which his reason prompts him to strive; the fantast abandons nature out of mere caprice, in order to indulge with all the less restraint the wantonness of his desires and the whims of his imagination. He bases his freedom not on independence from physical duress, but on emancipation from moral compulsion. Thus the fantast renounces not only human character – he renounces all character, he is completely lawless, hence nothing in himself and fit for nothing. But for the very reason that his phantasmagoria is not an aberration of nature but of freedom, and thus develops out of a capacity in itself estimable and infinitely perfectible, it leads likewise to an infinite fall into a bottomless abyss and can only terminate in complete destruction.

Part 6

Goethe

Johann Wolfgang von Goethe

(1749–1832)

Born in Frankfurt into a well-to-do bourgeois family, Goethe studied at Leipzig (1765–8) and Strasbourg (1770–1) Universities, taking a degree in Law at the latter. His meeting with Herder in Strasbourg provided the first major impetus in his literary career, introducing him to the folksong as a model for his own lyric poetry, and to Shakespeare, whose work inspired his historical drama *Götz von Berlichingen* (1773). Goethe became the leading figure of the *Sturm und Drang* movement, and his novel *The Sorrows of Werther* (1774) gave him a European reputation. His move to Weimar in 1775 led to his ennoblement (1782) and to high administrative office under Duke Karl August. His extended visit to Italy in 1786–8 completed his conversion, which had begun several years earlier, to classical ideals in art and literature, and allowed him to revise and complete his dramas *Iphigenie in Tauris* (1787), *Egmont* (1788), and *Torquato Tasso* (1790). His work on *Faust*, which he started before 1775, was not completed until 1831.

In the 1790s, Goethe devoted much time to his scientific studies; his chief publications in this area were *The Metamorphosis of Plants* (1790) and the *Theory of Colours* (1810). He also completed his novel *Wilhelm Meister's Apprenticeship* in 1795–6, the sequel to which (*Wilhelm Meister's Years of Wandering*) appeared in 1821. His friendship with Schiller from 1794 onwards led the two poets to formulate a joint scheme of classical values in poetry and art, which they defended against the young generation of Romantic poets and other non-classical tendencies in Germany. The essay *Winckelmann* (1805), written just before Schiller's death, marks the climax and end of this phase in Goethe's career.

The novel *The Elective Affinities* (1809) has some Romantic characteristics, in keeping with the older Goethe's increasing openness to multifarious literary influences, not all of them European ones. The *West-Eastern Divan* (1819), for example, is a collection of poems inspired by the fourteenth-century Persian poet Hafiz, and *Faust* embodies an encyclopaedic range of themes and forms of expression from the most disparate literary traditions.

Goethe's output was prodigious, and its diversity equally so. He tried his hand at almost every literary genre, and developed an enormous stylistic repertoire over his long career. He was less of a theorist than Schiller, and was temperamentally disinclined to philosophising. But his aesthetic principles carried the authority of the canonic works of literature in which he implemented them. The exemplary and historic significance which he attributes to Winckelmann in the essay which follows belongs in even greater measure to Goethe himself: he has overshadowed German literature for the last two hundred years.

Further reading

The standard edition of Goethe's works and letters is the Weimar edition in 133 volumes (1887–1919). The Hamburg edition, edited by Trunz (1948–64), is selective but includes a helpful critical apparatus. The conversations are assembled in volumes 22 to 24 of the Gedenkausgabe (1948–60). Most of the main works have been translated into English. Readers of the present volume may find the *Literary Essays* translated by Spingarn (1964), the *Italian Journey* translated by Auden and Mayer (1962), the *Conversations and Encounters* translated by Luke and Pick (1966), and Eckermann's *Conversations with Goethe* translated by Oxenford (1971) of particular interest. Staiger (1952–9) and Conrady (1982–3) are general biographical studies, and biographies in English include Fairley (1947) and Friedenthal (1965). Reed (1980) gives an excellent account of Weimar classicism as a whole. Wilkinson (1984) contains a substantial bibliography of works on Goethe in English.

Winckelmann

1805

Translated by H. B. Nisbet.
German text in *Goethes Werke*, edited by Trunz (1948–64), XII, 96–129.

Introduction

The memory of remarkable men, like the presence of major works of art, periodically stimulates the spirit of reflection. Both exist as legacies to every generation, the former in the shape of deeds and posthumous fame, the latter through their continued reality as ineffable creations. All men of insight know very well that the only worthwhile approach is to contemplate each as an individual whole; nevertheless, we repeatedly try to extract some meaning from them with the help of reflection and words.

We have a particular incentive to do so when new information comes to light on such subjects; and accordingly, our renewed reflections on Winckelmann, on his character and achievement, will not seem inappropriate at a time when the letters which have just been published[1] throw a clearer light on his outlook and circumstances.

Beginnings

Whereas nature does not withhold its priceless heritage from the common run of men – I mean that vital urge, from childhood onwards, to grasp the external world with enthusiasm, to establish a relationship with it, to unite with it to form a single whole – outstanding minds often have the peculiar characteristic of feeling a kind of timidity in relation to real life, of creating a world of their own within themselves, and of thereby attaining the highest excellence on a purely inward dimension.

If, on the other hand, particularly gifted individuals share that common need to search assiduously in the external world for counterparts to everything that nature has implanted in them, and thereby to raise their inner world to the status of a complete and definite whole, we may be certain that this attitude will likewise generate a life which will afford the greatest satisfaction to contemporaries and to posterity.

Winckelmann was a man of this kind. Nature had implanted in him everything that makes and enhances a human being. And in return, he spent his entire life looking for equivalent qualities outside him, for worth and excellence in human beings and in the kind of art which is pre-eminently concerned with humanity.

A lowly childhood, inadequate instruction in youth, disjointed and fragmented studies in early manhood, the pressure of a schoolteacher's duties, and the anxiety and tribulations which such a career brings with it – all this he had endured, as had many other young men in his position. He had reached the age of thirty without having once been smiled upon by fate; yet within him lay the seeds and potential of an enviable destiny.

Even in those miserable years we can detect signs of that urge – as yet dim and confused, but resolutely enough expressed – to convince himself at first hand of what the world might hold for him. Several ill-considered attempts to visit foreign countries ended in failure. He dreamed of a journey to Egypt; he set off for France: but unforeseen obstacles forced him to turn back. With better guidance from his guardian spirit, he at last resolved to make every effort to get to Rome. He realised just how congenial a period of residence there would be for him. And this was no longer merely an idea or a sudden fancy; it was a definite plan which he pursued with shrewdness and tenacity.

Antiquity

Man may achieve much through the purposeful application of isolated faculties, and he may achieve the extraordinary by combining several of his capacities; but he can accomplish the unique, the totally unexpected, only when all his resources are uniformly united within him. The latter was the happy lot of the ancients, especially of the Greeks in their best period; fate has assigned the two former possibilities to us moderns.

When the healthy nature of man functions as a totality, when he feels himself in the world as in a vast, beautiful, worthy, and valued whole, when a harmonious sense of well-being affords him pure and free delight – then the universe, if it were capable of sensation, would exult at having reached its goal, and marvel at the culmination of its own development and being. For what is the use of all the expenditure of suns and planets and moons, of stars and galaxies, of comets and nebulae, of completed and developing worlds, if at the end a happy man does not unconsciously rejoice in existence?

Whereas modern man – as our own example has just demonstrated – launches out into infinity almost every time he reflects, only to return eventually – if he is lucky – to a limited point, the ancients took a more direct route from the outset: they felt a characteristic need to remain firmly within the pleasant confines of the beautiful world. Here was their place, here their vocation, here was scope for their activity, and here were objects and food for their passions.

Why are their poets and historians the admiration of men of discernment and the despair of all who would emulate them? Simply because the persons whose actions they describe took so deep an interest in themselves, in the narrow circle of their fatherland, in the allotted course of their own and their fellow citizens' lives, and devoted all their senses, inclinations, and powers to acting upon the present; and for this reason, it was not difficult for a like-minded interpreter to render this present immortal.

Actual events were the only thing that mattered, whereas it is only what men have thought or felt that seems to hold any value for us today.

The ancient poet lived in the same way in his imagination as did the historian in the world of politics and the scientist in the natural world. All of them held fast to the immediate, the true, and the real, and even the products of their fancy have flesh and blood. Man and humanity were esteemed above all else, and all man's inner and outer relationships with the world were observed and depicted with the same breadth of vision. Feeling and reflection were not yet fragmented, that perhaps irreparable rift had not yet opened up within the healthy powers of man.[2]

But such natures as these were eminently equipped not only to enjoy happiness, but also to endure misfortune: for just as healthy fibres resist disease and rapidly recover from every attack of illness, so also can that healthy sense which distinguished the ancients recover quickly and easily from internal or external accidents. An antique nature of this kind – in so far as this can be said of any of our contemporaries – appeared once more in Winckelmann;[3] and it proved its mettle from the beginning by remaining unvanquished, unmoved, and unblunted by thirty years of abasement, malaise, and affliction. From the very moment when he won the freedom he required, he appeared whole and complete, entirely in the spirit of antiquity. Activity, enjoyment and privation, joy and sorrow, acquisition and loss, elevation and debasement – all of these were his lot; yet amidst these strange vicissitudes, he was always content with that happy earthly abode in which the whims of fate seek us out.

Just as he brought to his life a genuinely antique spirit, so also did it remain faithful to him in his studies. Yet whereas the ancients, in dealing with the sciences at large, already found themselves in a somewhat problematic situation – inasmuch as it is scarcely possible to comprehend the manifold objects of the extra-human world without a division of our powers and capacities, a fragmentation of the previous unity – modern man, in a similar situation, has an even more hazardous task. For when he looks in detail at the multifarious realm of the knowable, he runs the risk of dissipating his energies, of losing himself in disconnected facts, without being able, as the ancients were, to compensate for his shortcomings by the completeness of his own personality.[4]

However widely Winckelmann ranged over all possible and worthwhile knowledge, guided partly by love and desire, and partly by necessity, he always came back sooner or later to antiquity, and particularly to ancient Greece, with which he felt so close an affinity and with which he was to achieve so happy a union in his best years.

Paganism

The above description of the antique mentality and its concern with things of this world leads directly to the conclusion that the advantages it offered are compatible only with a pagan attitude.[5] That reliance of the ancients on the self, their concern with the present, their veneration of the gods as ancestors, their admiration for them, so to speak, only as works of art, their submission to an all-powerful fate, their high estimation of posthumous fame, which made even the future a function of this world – all of these factors are so essentially interrelated, form so indivisible a whole, and together constitute a human condition so clearly intended by nature itself, that we can detect, not only in the supreme moment of enjoyment but also in the darkest moment of self-sacrifice – or even extinction – an indestructible health.

This pagan mentality shines forth from Winckelmann's actions and writings, and is particularly evident in his early letters, when he is still embroiled in conflict with modern religious attitudes. This outlook of his, his remoteness from all Christian sentiments – indeed his revulsion against them – must be borne in mind when we come to assess his so-called religious conversion. The factions into which the Christian religion is divided were a matter of total indifference to him, for he did not by nature belong to any of the churches within it.

Friendship

But if, as we have claimed, the ancients were truly complete human beings who felt at one with themselves and with the world, they were also obliged to explore the whole range of human relationships; they could not deny themselves that rapturous pleasure which springs from the union of kindred natures.

Here again, a remarkable difference is apparent between ancient and modern times. Relations with women, which have become so tender and spiritualised in our era, scarcely rose in antiquity above the level of the most basic necessity. The relationship of parents to children seems to have been somewhat more affectionate. But more than all such sentiments, they valued friendship between members of the male sex (although Chloris and Thyia,[6] as females, also remained inseparable friends even in the underworld).

The passionate fulfilment of affectionate duties, the bliss of inseparability, the sacrifice of oneself for another, the explicit pledge of lifelong devotion, and the necessity of companionship even in death fill us with amazement when we encounter them in a relationship between two youths; we even feel ashamed when poets, historians, philosophers, and orators regale us with stories, events, sentiments, and attitudes of this variety.

Winckelmann felt he was born for this kind of friendship, for he was not only capable of it, but also eminently in need of it. He depended on friendship for his own self-awareness, and he could define his own identity only in relation to a whole for whose completion another person was necessary. At an early stage, he applied this idea to someone who may have been unworthy of it,[7] and dedicated himself to living and suffering for his sake; even in his poverty he found means to be generous towards his friend, to give and to sacrifice for him, and he did not hesitate to pledge to him his existence, indeed his life. Here it was that Winckelmann, even in the midst of oppression and privation, felt himself great, rich, generous, and happy, because he was able to do something for the person whom he loved above all else, and for whom he even had to make the supreme sacrifice of forgiving his ingratitude.

As time and circumstances changed, Winckelmann transformed all the worthy people who sought his company into friends on this model; and although many of the friendships he thereby created were easily and quickly dissolved, this admirable attitude won him the hearts of various excellent individuals, and he had the good fortune to enjoy the best of relations with the finest men of his age and circle.

Beauty

But while this profound need for friendship virtually creates and fashions its own object, the antique mentality can derive from it only a one-sided advantage of a moral variety; little is gained from the external world unless this need is happily complemented by a similar, related need which in turn finds an object to satisfy it; we mean by this the need for sensuous beauty, and sensuous beauty itself: for the ultimate product of nature, in its constant process of self-enhancement,[8] is human beauty. Admittedly, nature can only rarely succeed in producing it, for too many limiting factors run counter to its ideas, and even the omnipotence of nature is unable to hold on to perfection for long and to confer any permanence on the beauty it has created. For strictly speaking, the beautiful human being is beautiful only for a moment.

But this is where art comes in: for although man is the culmination of nature, he also sees himself as a complete nature which must in turn achieve its own culmination. He raises[9] himself to this level by asserting all his perfections and virtues, bringing discrimination, order, harmony, and significance into play, until he at last ascends to the production of the work of art, which occupies a magnificent place among his other deeds and achievements. Once it is created and stands before the world in its ideal reality, it produces an enduring effect, indeed the highest effect of all: for since it is the spiritual product of all man's faculties, it becomes the vessel of everything glorious, admirable, and amiable about him; and by breathing life into the human figure, it raises man above himself, completes the cycle of his life and actions, and deifies him for the present moment, in which the past and future are also contained. Those who saw the statue of Zeus at Olympia[10] were inspired by such sentiments, as is evident from the descriptions, reports, and testimonies of the ancients. The god had become man, so that man might be raised to the level of a god. The highest dignity was there for all to see, and it fired them with enthusiasm for the highest beauty. In this sense, we may well agree with those ancients who declared, with full conviction, that it was a misfortune to die without having seen this work.

Winckelmann had a natural ability to appreciate this beauty, and he first encountered it in the writings of the ancients; but it confronted him face to face in works of visual art, which alone give us the knowledge we need to recognise and appreciate it in the products of living nature.

If these two needs, for friendship and for beauty, are satisfied simultaneously by the same object, the happiness and gratitude of the man in question will seem boundless, and he will gladly give away all his possessions as inadequate tokens of his devotion and reverence.

Thus we often find Winckelmann in the company of beautiful young men, and at no time does he appear more animated and engaging than in these often all-too-fleeting moments.

Catholicism

With such attitudes, and with such needs and desires, Winckelmann was for long a slave to the interests of others. Nowhere around him could he see the slightest prospect of help and support.

Count Bünau,[11] who as a private individual need only have saved the expense of a single major book for his library in order to open the way to Rome for Winckelmann, and who as a minister of state had sufficient influence to relieve the excellent man of all embarrassment, doubtless did not wish to dispense with his active services, or had no perception of the great credit he might gain by introducing an able man to the world. The court at Dresden, which did offer the prospect of adequate support, professed the Catholic faith, and there was scarcely any other way of obtaining grace and favour than through the help of confessors and other members of the clergy.

A ruler's example exerts a powerful influence and, with imperceptible force, enjoins all citizens to emulate it in whatever actions are open to them in the private sphere (and hence above all in the sphere of ethics). The religion of the ruler will always be, in a certain sense, the dominant religion, and the Roman faith, like a whirlpool in constant motion, draws the peacefully passing wave towards it and into its own vortex.

At the same time, Winckelmann necessarily felt that, if one wished to be a

Roman in Rome, to be closely integrated with its life, and to enjoy friendly relations with its society, it was essential to join the Catholic community, to acknowledge its faith, and to adapt to its customs. And in the event, it later became obvious that he could not have fulfilled his ambition completely without this early decision; it was also made much easier for him by the fact that his baptism as a Protestant had not succeeded in Christianising his thoroughly pagan nature.

Nevertheless, his change of status was not won without an intense struggle.[12] After consulting our convictions and adequately pondering our motives, we may finally reach a decision which is wholly in harmony with our volition, desires, and needs, and which indeed seems inevitable if we are to preserve and further our existence and so become completely at one with ourselves. Yet such a decision may be quite at odds with current attitudes and with the convictions of many others; then a new conflict begins, and although it causes us no uncertainty, it does cause us uneasiness and an impatient annoyance when we are unable to reconcile the whole number within us with the fractions all around.

Thus Winckelmann too, having resolved upon his new step, appears concerned, anxious, sorrowful, and impassioned when he considers the effects of his undertaking, particularly on his first patron, the count. How impressive, profound, and honest his private utterances on this matter are!

For it is a fact that everyone who changes his religion bears a kind of stigma which seems impossible to remove. We can see from this that human beings prize steadfastness of purpose more than anything else, all the more so because they constantly have their own security and survival in mind, for they are themselves divided into separate factions. And this is a question neither of feeling nor of conviction. We are simply supposed to remain firmly in the place which fate rather than our own choice has allotted to us. To remain true to a nation, a city, a ruler, a friend, or a woman, to relate everything to this object, to base all one's actions on it, to suffer every privation for its sake, is regarded as admirable; desertion of a cause, on the other hand, is always hated, and vacillation seems merely ridiculous.

This, then, was the harsh and serious side of the matter; but seen from another angle, it takes on a lighter and more cheerful aspect. Certain human situations which we in no way approve of, certain moral shortcomings on the part of others, have a particular attraction for our imagination. If a simile is permitted, we might say that it is like eating game, which tastes much better to the trained palate with a slight hint of putrefaction than if it is cooked fresh. A divorced woman, or a renegade, makes a particularly piquant impression on us. People who would otherwise strike us as perhaps merely unusual or appealing now seem quite extraordinary; and it cannot be denied that Winckelmann's change of religion significantly enhances the romantic allure of his life and character for our imagination.

But for Winckelmann himself, the Catholic religion held no particular attraction. He saw in it merely a disguise which he had to adopt, and he has hard enough things to say about it. And later on, he seems not to have practised its observances with sufficient rigour, and perhaps even to have incurred the suspicion of zealots through careless talk; at least we can sometimes detect a slight fear of the Inquisition on his part.

Awareness of Greek art

To make the transition from the world of letters, and even from the highest manifestations of words and language, namely poetry and rhetoric, to the visual arts, is difficult and well-nigh impossible: for between them lies an enormous gulf which only a special natural aptitude can bridge. Sufficient documents are now available for us to assess how far Winckelmann succeeded in this task.

He was first drawn to great works of art by his love of pleasure; but in order to utilise and assess them, he still required artists as mediators. He was able to grasp, edit, and himself expound their more or less valid opinions, and these formed the basis of his essay *On the Imitation of the Painting and Sculpture of the Greeks*,[13] which was published while he was still in Dresden, and its two supplements.[14]

In these works, Winckelmann already seems to be on the right path: they contain some excellent central passages, and already accurately define the ultimate aim of art. Nevertheless, both in form and in content, they remain so wayward and eccentric that it would be futile to try to make any sense of them without prior knowledge of the personalities of the connoisseurs and critics who were congregated in Saxony at that time, and of their abilities, opinions, predilections, and idiosyncrasies; they will therefore remain a closed book to later generations unless some informed art-lovers who were alive nearer those times soon decide to undertake, or encourage others to provide, a description of the conditions which then prevailed – insofar as this is still possible.[15]

Lippert, Hagedorn, Oeser, Dietrich, Heinecken, and Österreich[16] were all in their own way amateurs, practitioners, or patrons of art. Their aims were limited, their maxims one-sided and often strange. Stories and anecdotes were in circulation, and their many applications were supposed not only to entertain society, but also to instruct it. It was from elements such as these that Winckelmann's early writings arose. He himself soon found these works inadequate, and made no secret of this fact to his friends.

But at last he embarked on his new course, without adequate preparation but at least with some previous training, and arrived in that country where a unique period of education begins for every receptive mind. Its influence extends to the whole personality, and its effects must be both real and harmonious if they are subsequently to provide a firm and enduring bond between highly different people.

Rome

Winckelmann was now in Rome, and who could be more worthy than he of feeling the effects which that great experience is capable of producing on a truly receptive nature? He saw his wishes fulfilled, his happiness assured, his hopes more than satisfied. He saw his ideas in corporeal form around him as he wandered in amazement through the ruins of a gigantic age; the greatest glories ever produced by art stood out in the open air; he could look up at such wonders of art as freely as at the stars in the heavens, and every private treasure-house opened its doors for a modest fee. The newcomer crept around unnoticed like a pilgrim, and visited the most splendid and sacred monuments in inconspicuous dress; he did not yet permit any individual impression to take hold of him, the whole acted upon him in infinitely varied ways, and he could already feel in anticipation that harmony which would eventually arise for him out of the many often seemingly hostile elements. He saw and contemplated everything, and, to complete his satisfaction, he was mistaken for an artist, a role in which all of us would at heart be happy to appear.

But in place of all further reflections, we may offer the reader a spirited account of the Roman experience and its powerful effects in the words of one of our friends:[17]

Rome is the place where, in our view, the whole of antiquity is fused into one, so that what we feel about the ancient poets or political constitutions seems, in Rome, more than just a feeling: we can see it with our own eyes. Just as Homer cannot be compared with other poets, so also is it impossible to compare Rome and its surroundings with any other place. It is true that most of this impression derives from ourselves rather than from the object; but it is not just the sentimental thought of standing where this or that great man once stood – it is as if we were powerfully transported into a past which, if only through a necessary illusion, strikes us as nobler and more sublime than the present. We cannot resist this force even if we wish to, because the derelict state in which the present inhabitants have left the country and the incredible mass of ruins themselves lead our eye in that direction. And since this past appears to the inner sense in a grandeur which is beyond the reach of envy, and in which one is more than happy to participate, if only in the imagination (for we cannot conceivably do so in any other way), and since at the same time the loveliness of the forms, the grandeur and simplicity of the figures, the richness of the vegetation (which is not, however, as luxuriant as in regions further south), the definition of the outlines in the translucent medium, and the beauty of the colours transport the outer sense into a realm of universal clarity – our enjoyment of nature here is a pure aesthetic pleasure without a trace of desire. Everywhere else, it is coupled with contrasting ideas, and our pleasure becomes elegiac or satirical.[18] But of course this is only our subjective impression. Tibur[19] seemed more modern to Horace than Tivoli does to us, as his *Beatus ille, qui procul negotiis*[20] proves. But it is also merely an illusion if we ourselves wish we were citizens of Athens or Rome. For we must view antiquity only from a distance, purged of base reality, purely as something of the past. This, at least, is how one of my friends and I feel about the ruins: we are always angry when a half-buried building is excavated; it is at most a gain for scholarship at the expense of the imagination. I can myself conceive of only two comparable calamities: if the Campagna di Roma were to be cultivated, and Rome made into a policed city where men no longer carried knives. If ever an order-loving pope should come forward with such proposals – and may the seventy-two cardinals ensure that he does not – I shall leave the country. Only while so divine an anarchy prevails in Rome and so heavenly a wilderness surrounds it will room be left for those shades of antiquity of which a single one is worth more than this entire generation.

Mengs

But Winckelmann would have had to grope his way around the vast collections of ancient relics for a long time before he discovered the best and most rewarding examples if he had not at the beginning had the good fortune to meet Mengs.[21] This artist, whose own considerable talent took its direction from ancient art (particularly the most beautiful items) immediately introduced his friend to the finest of those works which are worthy of inspection. Here, Winckelmann grew familiar with the beauty of forms and their execution, and at once felt inspired to compose an essay *On the Taste of the Greek Artists*.[22]

One cannot, however, study works of art attentively for long without discovering that they are not only the product of different artists, but also of different eras, and that their place of origin, date, and individual merit must all be considered simultaneously. Thus Winckelmann, with his usual directness, found that this was the axis around which all art history revolves. He at first concentrated on the highest phase of Greek art, which he planned to describe in a treatise *On the Style of Sculpture in the Age of Phidias*.[23] But he soon rose above such details to conceive the idea of a history of art, and discovered, like a new Columbus, a new territory whose existence had long been suspected, hinted at, and discussed – one might even say a land which had once been known, but was subsequently lost from view.

It is always sad to reflect how mankind, first through the Romans and later through the incursions of the northern peoples and the confusion which followed, reached a position where the progress of all true and authentic culture was for long obstructed, and indeed almost extinguished for the future.

In whatever art or science we care to name, the direct and accurate perception of ancient observers had already discovered much which, through the barbarous age which followed and the barbarous methods that were used to escape from it, became and remained a mystery, and will long continue to be a mystery for the mass of mankind (for the higher culture of the modern age can only gradually become universal).

This does not apply to technology, which the human race fortunately makes use of without asking where it comes from or where it leads to.

These reflections are prompted by some passages in the ancient authors in which we can already detect inklings, or even suggestions, concerning the possibility and necessity of a history of art.

Velleius Paterculus[24] comments with great interest on the parallel rise and decline of all the arts. As a man of the world, he was particularly exercised by the thought that they can sustain themselves only for a short time at the highest peak of their achievement. He was not in a position to view all art as a living thing (ζωόν) which, like all other organisms (apart from the fact that it includes many individuals), necessarily has imperceptible beginnings, a slow growth, a glorious moment of fulfilment, and a gradual decline. He therefore offers only moral explanations – which cannot, of course, be ruled out as contributory factors; but they do not satisfy his acute perception, because he is well aware that a necessity is at work here which cannot simply be the sum total of freely operating causes. As he puts it:

Anyone who examines the evidence of the past will find that the same applies to grammarians, painters, and sculptors as to orators; artistic excellence is invariably confined to a very limited period. I constantly ask myself why it is that several like-minded and able men should all appear around the same time and jointly pursue and promote one particular art; but I cannot discover what I could confidently describe as the true causes. Among the likely causes, I consider the following to be the most important. Emulation fosters talent; sometimes it is envy, sometimes admiration, which provides the incentive for the imitator, and the art which has been so diligently cultivated quickly rises to its highest expression. But it is difficult to sustain perfection for long, and what cannot move forward moves backward. And thus we at first try to catch up with the leaders; but when we despair of surpassing or equalling them, our diligence diminishes with our hope, and we no longer pursue what we cannot attain. We no longer strive to possess what others have already appropriated, but look for something new; and so we abandon the sphere in which we cannot excel, and seek another goal for our aspirations. This inconstancy of purpose, it seems to me, is the greatest obstacle to the production of any perfect work.

There is also a passage in Quintilian[25] which contains a convincing outline of the history of ancient art, and which deserves particular mention as a major milestone in this subject.

In his conversations with art-lovers in Rome, Quintilian may also have noticed a striking similarity in character between the Greek artists and the Roman orators, and accordingly made further inquiries among connoisseurs and amateurs. As a result, in his comparative survey, in which the character of each age coincides with the character of its art, he was compelled, without wishing or realising it, to sketch out a history of art himself. He writes as follows:

It is said that the first famous painters whose works are admired not just because of their antiquity are Polygnotus and Aglaophon. Their simple colouring still finds keen advocates, who – somewhat oddly, in my view – prefer such crude efforts and rudimentary stages of art to the greatest masters of the subsequent age.

Then Zeuxis and Parrhasius, who lived near each other, greatly furthered the development of art around the time of the Peloponnesian War. The former is said to have invented the laws of light and shade, whereas the latter apparently made precise studies of lines. Zeuxis, moreover, gave the limbs of his figures more substance, and made them fuller and more imposing. It is thought that he was following the example of Homer, who favours powerful proportions even in his female figures. But Parrhasius defined everything with such precision that he was known as the lawgiver, for the prototypes of gods and heroes which he gave to posterity have been taken as authoritative and adhered to by others.

Thus painting flourished from around the time of Philip to the time of Alexander's successors, albeit among artists of varying talents. For Protogenes is unrivalled in meticulousness, Pamphilus and Melanthius in studied composition, Antiphilus in lightness of touch, Theon of Samos in the invention of strange and fantastic forms, and Apelles in spirit and grace. Euphranor is admired because he must be reckoned among the best artists by any standards, and because he excelled both as a painter and sculptor.

Similar phases can also be distinguished in sculpture. For Callon and Hegesias worked in a more severe, almost Tuscan manner, whereas Calamis is more relaxed, and Myron's manner is softer still.

Polycleitus leads all others in painstaking workmanship and delicacy. Many would accord him the highest place of all; but in case he should appear faultless, his work is said to be lacking in weight. For since he made the human form more delicate than it is in nature, he does not seem to have done full justice to the dignity of the gods; indeed, it is even said that he shunned the gravity of age and did not venture beyond the smooth cheeks of youth.

But what Polycleitus lacks, Phidias and Alcamenes are acknowledged to possess. Phidias is said to have created the most perfect models of gods and men, and to have far surpassed his rival with his work in ivory. This judgement would stand even if he had created only the statue of Minerva at Athens or the Olympian Zeus at Elis, whose beauty, it is said, served the established religion well – so closely did the majesty of the work approach that of the god himself.

By common consent, Lysippus and Praxiteles came closest to reality in their work; but Demetrius is censured for having gone too far in this direction: he gave verisimilitude precedence over beauty.

Literary career

Few men are fortunate enough to have their advanced education paid for by a totally unselfish patron. Even if the latter has the best of intentions, he can support only what he knows and likes, and more readily still what he finds useful. It was accordingly Winckelmann's literary and bibliographical training which commended him first to Count Bünau and later to Cardinal Passionei.[26] An expert on books is welcome everywhere, and Winckelmann was even more welcome at a time when the vogue for collecting rare and unusual books was more flourishing and the library trade more self-contained than today. A major German library looked much like its Roman equivalent, and they were able to compete with each other in the matter of acquisitions. The librarian of a German count was a desirable member of a cardinal's household, and he could at once feel at home in it. The libraries were real treasure-houses, whereas nowadays, with the rapid advance of knowledge and the purposeful (and purposeless) accumulation of printed material, they must rather be regarded as useful storehouses, and at the same time as useless lumber-rooms. A librarian today has more reason than ever before to acquaint himself with the progress of scholarship and the worth (or worthlessness) of publications, and a German librarian must possess knowledge which would be useless to him abroad.

But Winckelmann stuck to his purely literary activities only for a short time – only for as long as was necessary for him to attain a reasonable income; accordingly, he soon lost interest in everything connected with critical scholarship, and had no wish to collate manuscripts or to answer miscellaneous inquiries from German scholars.

But his knowledge had already insured him a favourable reception in Italy. The private lives of the Italians, and of the Romans in particular, have for various reasons a mysterious quality about them. This secrecy, one might even say this segregation, extended even to literature. Quite a few scholars would quietly dedicate their lives to some important work, with no intention or possibility of publishing it. And more than in any other country, there were men who, despite wide knowledge and insight, could not be prevailed upon to enter into written, let alone printed, communication. But Winckelmann quickly found access to such people. Among them, he names Giacomelli[27] and Baldani[28] in particular, and refers with pleasure to his growing circle of acquaintances and to his increasing influence.

Cardinal Albani

What helped him most of all was his good fortune in becoming a member of Cardinal Albani's household.[29] The latter, who enjoyed considerable means and a highly influential position, had shown since his youth a marked predilection for art. He had had every opportunity to indulge his tastes, and his luck as a collector had been little short of miraculous. In later years, his chief pleasure consisted in arranging his collection in a fitting manner, and thereby competing with those Roman families who had discovered the worth of such treasures before him; indeed, his taste resembled that of the ancients, in that he delighted in filling the available space to the limit. Buildings crowded upon each other, room upon room and hall upon hall; fountains and obelisks, caryatids and bas-reliefs, statues and urns filled courtyards and gardens alike, while larger and smaller rooms, galleries and cabinets contained the most remarkable monuments of all ages.

We noted in passing that the ancients filled the space at their disposal in precisely the same way. Thus the Romans crowded so much on to their Capitol that it seems inconceivable that there was enough space to accommodate it all. Similarly, the Via Sacra, the Forum, and the Palatine were so overcrowded with buildings and monuments that we could scarcely imagine a mass of people in these areas as well, were it not for the real evidence of excavated cities, from which we can see for ourselves how small and confined the plan of their buildings was: they seem, as it were, no larger than models. This is true even of the Villa of Hadrian, although sufficient land and resources were available for a far larger edifice at the time when it was constructed.

It was in an overcrowded state such as this that Winckelmann left the villa of his master and friend, the place where he had completed the most advanced and enjoyable phase of his education. It remained in this condition long after the cardinal's death, to the delight and admiration of the world at large, until it was stripped of all its ornaments by the ever-moving, all-dissolving current of time.[30] The statues were lifted from their niches and pedestals, the bas-reliefs were torn from the walls, and the huge collection was packed in crates in readiness for transport. But through an extraordinary turn of events, these treasures got no further than the Tiber. In a short time, they were returned to their owner, and the majority of pieces – with the exception of a few choice items – are now back in their original positions. Winckelmann might well have lived to experience that first blow of fate which struck this artistic Elysium, and to see it restored again by a curious twist of circumstances. But it was as well for him that he had already outgrown earthly sufferings, as well as that pleasure which is not always sufficient to outweigh them.

Propitious events

But external good fortune also came his way at various times: for not only was the excavation of antiquities proceeding vigorously and successfully in Rome, but the discoveries in Herculaneum and Pompeii were in part new, and in part still unknown as a result of jealousy, secrecy, and dilatoriness.[31] He thus entered into a harvest which was more than enough to occupy his mind and energies.

It is sad when we have to regard our present collections as closed and complete. Armouries, galleries, and museums which acquire nothing new have a funereal and spectral atmosphere. So restricted a range of art has a restricting effect on the mind, for we tend to regard such collections as complete wholes, whereas we ought instead to be reminded by constant acquisitions that, in art as in life, nothing closed and complete can endure, and that all is an endless process.

Winckelmann was fortunate in this respect. The earth gave up its treasures, and the ever-changing art-market brought to light many older items from private collections which passed before his eyes, stimulated his interest, invited his judgement, and increased his knowledge.

His relationship with the heir to the vast Stosch[32] collection was of no small advantage to him. It was only after the death of the collector himself that Winckelmann came to know this little universe of art, and ruled over it according to his own insights and convictions. It is true that not every part of this extremely valuable collection was treated with equal respect, despite the fact that all of it deserved to be catalogued for the pleasure and profit of later generations of art-lovers and collectors. Some items were simply discarded; but in order to make the splendid collection of gems better known and more attractive to purchasers, Winckelmann, in collaboration with Stosch's heir, undertook the compilation of a catalogue. The surviving correspondence provides a remarkable record of this enterprise, and of the hurried but always imaginative manner in which it was carried out.

This disintegrating corpus of art, along with the ever-growing and increasingly unified collection of Cardinal Albani, kept our friend constantly busy; and everything which passed through his hands for sale or purchase increased the store of knowledge he had begun to build up in his mind.

Projected writings

Already in Dresden, when Winckelmann first took an interest in art and artists and made his debut in this field, his success as a writer was assured. He was well versed both in history and in contemporary knowledge. Even in his profoundly oppressed circumstances, he had a true perception of antiquity, and of genuine worth in the present, both in life and in character. He had already developed a style of his own. In the new school which he now entered, he listened to his masters as a pupil who was not only anxious to learn, but was himself already learned; he easily assimilated such specific knowledge as they had to offer, and at once began to apply and utilise it.

Translated to a higher sphere than that of Dresden, and inspired by a higher sense of purpose, he still remained true to type. He did not, for example, jealously retain what he had learned from Mengs or what his new surroundings had taught him; he did not wait until the process of fermentation was complete, but, just as we are said to learn through teaching, so did Winckelmann learn by means of drafts and written compositions. How many titles of projected works he has left us, how many subjects he planned to write books on! And these beginnings foreshadow his whole antiquarian career. We find him in constant activity, preoccupied with the present moment, seizing and holding fast to it as if the moment could itself be complete and satisfying; and then he would learn from the following moment in turn. This perspective is useful when it comes to appreciating his works.

That the latter took the form they did when they were first committed to paper and subsequently fixed for posterity on the printed page, was the result of an infinitely varied combination of minor circumstances. Had each been written only a month later, we should have had another work, more accurate in content and more definite in form, and perhaps something altogether different. And for this reason we must deeply regret his premature death, because he would have revised his works continually, always incorporating his earlier and most recent experiences in what he wrote.

And thus everything he has left us was written as a living thing for living people, not as a dead letter for pedantic scholars. His works, along with his correspondence, are a biography, a life in themselves. Like most people's lives, they look more like a preparation than a finished œuvre. They fill us with hopes, desires, and intuitions; if we try to improve on them, we see that we ought to improve ourselves; if we try to find fault with them, we see that we may ourselves be guilty of the same faults, perhaps on a higher level of cognition: for limitation is our universal lot.

Philosophy

In the progress of culture, not all areas of human activity and behaviour in which our individual development is expressed flourish with equal strength. On the contrary, more or less favourable circumstances and personal attributes mean that one individual will outstrip the other and attract more widespread interest. This gives rise to a certain jealous displeasure among members of the vast and immensely ramified human family, whose incompatibility often increases with the closeness of their relationship.

It is admittedly usually a hollow complaint when those engaged in a particular art or science protest that their own subject is neglected by their contemporaries: for as soon as an able master emerges, he will become a focus of attention. If Raphael were to appear again today, he would be assured of honours and riches in plenty. An able master attracts worthy pupils, and their activity in turn forms endless new branches. It is true, however, that philosophers especially have always attracted the hatred not only of their fellow thinkers, but also of practical men of affairs, and perhaps rather because of the position they occupy than through any fault of their own. For since philosophy, by its very nature, claims universal and ultimate validity, it is bound to regard practical concerns as entailed in and subordinate to itself, and to treat them accordingly.

Furthermore, no one expressly repudiates these presumptuous claims; on the contrary, everyone thinks he has a right to share in the discoveries of philosophy, to avail himself of its maxims, and to make use of whatever else it may provide. But since, in the interests of universality, it has to employ specialised terms, unusual combinations of words, and unfamiliar premises which do not exactly coincide with the particular circumstances of practical people and their immediate needs, it is vilified by those who cannot find a ready means of access to it.

If, however, we were to accuse the philosophers themselves of being unable to make a satisfactory transition to life, and if we were to argue that it is precisely in their attempts to put their convictions actively into effect that they make most of their mistakes, thereby reducing their own credit in the eyes of the world, it would not be difficult to cite appropriate examples.

Winckelmann complains bitterly about the philosophers of his time and their widespread influence;[33] but it seems to me that one can escape from any external influence simply by withdrawing into one's own subject. It is strange that Winckelmann did not enrol at Leipzig University, where he could more conveniently have pursued his main field of interest under the guidance of Johann Friedrich Christ,[34] and ignored the philosophers completely.

But in the light of more recent events, we may perhaps mention one particular experience which many of us may encounter in our lives: no scholar has been able to dismiss, oppose, or despise with impunity that great philosophical movement which began with Kant[35] – except perhaps for genuine classical scholars, who seem to have a unique advantage over all other men because of the peculiar nature of their research.

For since they are exclusively concerned with the best things the world has ever produced, and need take account of the trivial or indeed the mediocre only in relation to the excellent, their knowledge becomes so extensive, their judgements so reliable, and their taste so consistent that their education, within their own sphere, seems remarkably, indeed astonishingly, complete.

Winckelmann also enjoyed this good fortune, which was of course enhanced by the powerful influences of visual art and of life itself.

Poetry

However carefully Winckelman read the poets in his studies of ancient literature, we nevertheless find, if we look more closely at his career and scholarship, that he had no real liking for poetry; in fact, it could sooner be said that he at times seems actually to dislike it. In the same way, his love of the familiar old Lutheran hymns and his desire, even in Rome, to possess an authentic Lutheran hymnal merely confirm that he was a good and honest German, but not exactly a friend of poetry.

The poets of antiquity appear to have interested him at first as documents of the ancient languages and literatures, and later as a commentary on the visual arts. It is therefore all the more remarkable and gratifying when he himself emerges as a competent and undisputed poet, not only in his descriptions of the ancient statues,[36] but also virtually throughout his later writings. His eyes can see and his mind can comprehend ineffable works of art, but he still feels an irresistible impulse to come to terms with them by means of words and letters. The consummate splendour of the work, the idea which gave birth to it, and the feeling it aroused in him when he contemplated it must be communicated to the reader or listener; and as he reviews all the resources at his disposal, he feels compelled to deploy the most powerful and exalted medium he can find. He must be a poet, whether or not he realises it or intends to be one.

New insights

However much Winckelmann valued a measure of public esteem, however much he coveted literary renown, however concerned he was with the outward appearance of his books and with raising their tone by means of a certain solemnity of style, he was nevertheless by no means blind to their deficiencies; on the contrary, he was very quick to note them, as inevitably happened in consequence of his ever-developing nature, which constantly grasped at new objects to work upon. The more dogmatically and didactically he had gone to work in a given essay, insisting upon and firmly upholding this or that interpretation and application of a particular passage, the more clearly he could see his mistake as soon as new data had convinced him of it, and the more readily he was inclined to correct it by one means or another.

If the manuscript was still in his hands, he revised it; if it had already gone to the printer, he sent corrections and addenda after it. And he made no secret to this friends of all these acts of penitence: for his whole character was based on truthfulness, integrity, directness, and honesty.

Later works

But one happy idea did become fully clear in his mind – not all at once, it is true, but in the course of implementing it: namely his plan for the *Monumenti inediti*.[37]

It is obvious enough that he was first attracted to this project by his delight in making known new discoveries, in offering convincing interpretations of them, and in thereby significantly enlarging the bounds of classical scholarship. To this was added his interest in testing once more the method he had already introduced to art history, this time on objects he would represent in visual form for the reader's benefit.[38] And finally, he formed the happy intention of using his introductory essay to the new work as a means of tacitly correcting his earlier work on the history of art, which he had by now completed – as a means of refining it, condensing it, and perhaps even to some extent superseding it.[39]

Since he was aware that he had earlier laboured under certain misconceptions which people outside Rome would scarcely be in a position to correct, he wrote this work in Italian, hoping that it would gain recognition in Rome as well as elsewhere. Not only did he give it his fullest attention; he also sought expert advice among his friends, asking them to go carefully through it with him, and making the wisest possible use of their judgement. As a result, he managed to complete a work which will live on as a legacy to all future ages. And he did not merely write it himself: he undertook and supervised the whole project, and accomplished as a private individual of limited means a task which would do credit to a well-established publisher or to an academic enterprise.

The pope

With so many references to Rome, we must not forget the pope, who, at least indirectly, was of considerable service to Winckelmann.

Winckelmann's sojourn in Rome fell largely within the pontificate of Benedict XIV (Lambertini), who, as a cheerful and easy man, preferred to let others govern for him instead of governing himself; and accordingly, the various positions which Winckelmann held may well have come his way rather through the goodwill of friends in high places than through the pope's own awareness of his merits.

Nevertheless, we find him on one significant occasion in the presence of the head of the Church; he was granted the special privilege of being permitted to read some extracts from the *Monumenti inediti* aloud to the pope, thereby gaining in this further respect the highest honour a writer can attain.[40]

Character

The most important quality about many people, and about scholars in particular, is their actual achievement, whereas their character remains little in evidence. But the opposite is true of Winckelmann: everything he produced is remarkable and valuable chiefly because his character is invariably manifest in it. We have already discussed his character in general terms at the beginning of this essay (under the headings of 'Antiquity', 'Paganism', 'Friendship', and 'Beauty'), but some more specific remarks may not be out of place here towards the end.

Winckelmann's whole nature was to be honest with himself and with others; his innate love of truth became ever more apparent the more independent and autonomous he felt himself to be, so that he finally came to regard it as a crime to treat one's own past mistakes with polite indulgence, however common this practice may be in life and in literature.

With such a nature as this, he could comfortably have withdrawn into himself; but here again we notice in him that antique characteristic of always being preoccupied with himself without actually observing himself. He thinks only *of* himself, not *about* himself; his mind is full of his present intentions, he is interested in his whole being in all its aspects, and is confident that his friends will be interested in it too. We accordingly find that, in his letters, he mentions everything from the highest moral necessity to the most ordinary physical need; indeed, he says explicitly that he would rather discuss minor personal affairs than matters of importance. At the same time, he remains a complete enigma to himself, and he is sometimes amazed at his own personality, particularly in the light of what he formerly was and what he has now become. But in fact, every individual may be likened to a many-syllabled charade, of which the individual in question can piece together only a few syllables, while others can easily decipher the entire word.

Nor does Winckelmann appear to have any expressly formulated principles; his sure instinct and cultivated mind are his guide in both moral and aesthetic matters. He has notions of some kind of natural religion, but God figures in it rather as the primary source of beauty than as a being with any personal relationship to man. We must, however, admire the way in which Winckelmann recognises the obligations of duty and gratitude.

He makes only modest provision for his own needs, and not always consistently. But he does work hard to secure his future in old age. His methods are morally admirable; in his pursuit of each objective he is honest, direct, and even defiant, and at the same time shrewd and pertinacious. He never works systematically, but always by instinct and with passion. His joy in each new discovery is intense, so that errors are inevitable; but he sets them right as soon as he detects them, and presses on as vigorously as before. Here again, his antique disposition is fully in evidence: his point of departure is certain, the goal he pursues is uncertain, and his practical approach is defective and incomplete as soon as he extends it to too wide an area.

Society

Although he did not at first feel wholly at ease in society – ill-prepared as he was by his earlier way of life – a feeling of his own worth soon made up for lack of training and practice, and he very quickly learned to behave as circumstances required. His pleasure in associating with distinguished, rich, and famous people, and his delight at enjoying their esteem are always conspicuous; and as regards ease of social relations, he could not have found a more favourable environment than that of Rome.

He himself observes that prominent people there, particularly in clerical circles, live on a relaxed and familiar footing with members of their households, however ceremonious they may outwardly appear; but he failed to observe that this familiarity is in fact a disguise for the oriental relationship between master and servant. All the southern nations would find it infinitely tedious if they had to sustain that constant reciprocal tension to which the northerners are accustomed in their domestic relations. Travellers have remarked that Turkish slaves behave with much greater informality towards their masters than do northern courtiers towards their superiors; but on closer scrutiny, we can see that such displays of deference have actually been introduced for the benefit of the subordinates, as constant reminders to those in authority of what they owe to them.

But the southerner likes to have periods of relaxation, and those around him benefit accordingly. Winckelmann describes such scenes with great satisfaction; they make his otherwise dependent position more tolerable and sustain his sense of freedom, which dreads any threat of servitude.

Foreigners

While Winckelmann found much happiness in associating with native Italians, his relations with foreigners were a constant source of tribulation. It is a fact that there is nothing more dreadful than the typical foreigner in Rome. In every other place, the traveller can look to his own interests and find something to suit him; but for the truly Roman mentality, those who do not adapt to Rome are simply abhorrent.

The English are criticised for carrying a teapot wherever they go, even dragging it with them up Mount Etna; but does not every nation have its own kind of teapot in which, even abroad, it brews up its bundle of dried herbs from home?

More than once, Winckelmann curses such narrow-minded and presumptuous foreigners, blind to their surroundings and with no time to spare; he vows
never to act as guide to them again, but is eventually talked round once more.
He jokes about his schoolmasterly tendencies, his love of teaching and
persuading others; yet he does in fact reap various benefits from his encounters
with men of distinguished rank and achievements. We need mention only the
Prince of Dessau, the Crown Princes of Mecklenburg-Strelitz and Brunswick,
and Baron von Riedesel,[41] a man who proved entirely worthy of our friend
in his attitude towards art and antiquity.

World reputation

We see how Winckelmann strives unremittingly for esteem and consideration;
but he wants to win these by real achievements. He is always concerned with
the real qualities of objects, and of the means and methods of approaching them;
this is why he is so hostile towards French superficiality.

Having had the opportunity in Rome to mix with foreigners from all
countries, he continued to foster such connections in a skilful and active
manner. Distinctions conferred on him by academies and learned societies gave
him much pleasure – indeed, he went out of his way to obtain them.

But what enhanced his status more than anything else was that splendid
product of quiet and painstaking research, namely the *History of the Art of
Antiquity*.[42] It was immediately translated into French, and Winckelmann
became famous far and wide.

What such a work has achieved can perhaps most readily be recognised at
the moment of its publication: its repercussions are felt immediately, its novelty
is readily acknowledged, and men are amazed at the sudden advancement they
receive from it. A colder posterity, on the other hand, has a jaded palate; it
tastes bits and pieces from the works of its masters and teachers, and makes
demands of them such as it would never have dreamed of making if their
original achievement had not been as great as it was.

Winckelmann thus became known to the educated nations of Europe at a
time when he already commanded sufficient respect in Rome to be honoured
with the important office of Prefect of Antiquities.[43]

Restlessness

In spite of that acknowledged happiness of which he himself often boasted, he
was still the constant victim of an inner unrest which, being deeply rooted in
his character, assumed many different forms.

He had eked out a meagre existence in his early days, and had subsequently
lived on court patronage and the favours of various well-disposed individuals;
in so doing, he had confined himself to the most basic necessities, in order not
to lose his independence, or to become even more dependent than he already

was. But meanwhile, he was valiantly striving to provide for the present and future from his own resources, an aim which the successful publication of his illustrated work at last gave him fair hopes of realising.

But his uncertain circumstances had made him accustomed to look in ever new directions for his subsistence, now finding a place with modest advantages in the house of a cardinal, in the Vatican, or elsewhere, now magnanimously renouncing his position when a new prospect emerged, and then looking round yet again for other employment and lending an ear to various proposals.

Living in Rome also means that one is exposed to all kinds of temptations to travel abroad. One is at the centre of the ancient world, and all the countries of most interest to the antiquarian are in close proximity. Magna Graecia and Sicily, Dalmatia, the Peloponnese, Ionia, and Egypt – all of them beckon, as it were, to the inhabitants of Rome; and in someone who, like Winckelmann, has an innate desire to use his eyes, they arouse from time to time an inexpressible longing, which is intensified by the presence of so many foreigners passing through, now with purposeful (or aimless) plans to visit those countries, now returning from them with endless stories and reports of the marvels of distant lands.

And so our friend Winckelmann also had ambitions to travel, sometimes independently, sometimes in the company of wealthy travellers who were in varying degrees able to appreciate the value of an informed and talented travelling companion.

A further cause of his inner restlessness and uneasiness does credit to his sentiments, namely his irresistible longing for his absent friends. On this point especially the nostalgia of a man who otherwise lived so very much in the present seems to have concentrated itself. He sees his friends before him, he converses with them in letters, he longs to embrace them, and wants to relive the days he has shared with them in the past.

The restoration of peace[44] had rekindled these desires, which were focussed on the north in particular. It was his proud intention to seek an audience with that great king who had already honoured him with an invitation to serve him;[45] to see again the Prince of Dessau, whose serene and exalted nature Winckelmann regarded as divinely bestowed; to pay his respects to the Duke of Brunswick, whose outstanding qualities he had recognised; to offer his personal homage to the Hanoverian Minister von Münchhausen, who had done so much for learning, and to admire his immortal foundation in Göttingen;[46] to delight once more in lively intimacy with his friends in Switzerland[47] – such were the temptations which re-echoed in his heart and imagination. He turned them over in his mind and toyed with them for a considerable time, until, unhappily, he at last surrendered to his impulse and so went to his death.

He was by now dedicated body and soul to his Italian existence, and every alternative seemed insupportable to him. And whereas his earlier journey to Italy through the rocks and mountains of the Tyrol had filled him with interest, indeed with rapture, he now felt, on his way back to his native land, as if he were being dragged through a Cimmerian gate, plunged into anxiety, and tormented by the notion that it was impossible to go any further.[48]

Demise

Thus, in possession of the greatest happiness he could have wished for, Winckelmann departed from this world. His fatherland awaited him, his friends reached out to welcome him, and all the expressions of love he so much craved for, all the testimonies of public esteem he valued so highly were about to be lavished on him as soon as he arrived. And in this respect we may well call him fortunate, for he ascended to the realm of the blessed from the summit of human existence, and was removed from the world of the living by a passing shock and a short-lived pain.[49] He did not experience the infirmities of age or the waning of his mental powers; and when, as he had foretold, the artistic treasures were dispersed (although not quite in the way he had predicted), he did not have to witness the spectacle.[50] He lived as a man, and as a complete man he went from hence. He now enjoys in the remembrance of posterity the distinction of appearing eternally able and eternally strong: for it is in the form in which a man leaves the earth that he walks among the shades, and so Achilles remains ever-present to us as an eternally aspiring youth. That Winckelmann departed early is also a gain for us. A breath of his strength invigorates us from his grave, and arouses in us the keenest impulse to continue and perpetuate, with love and enthusiasm, the work which he began.[51]

Notes

Introduction

1. P. 42 below. Subsequent page references in the Introduction are to the present volume.
2. See Horst Rüdiger, 'Winckelmanns Persönlichkeit', in *Johann Joachim Winckelmann 1768–1968*, a commemorative volume of essays published by Inter Nationes (Bad Godesberg, 1968), pp. 20–40 (pp. 28–32), first published in *Der Deutschunterricht*, 8 (1956).
3. See Hugh Honour, *Neo-classicism* (Harmondsworth, 1968; reprinted 1981), p. 60.
4. Compare Honour, *Neo-classicism*, p. 46, on puritanical reactions to the more scurrilous aspects of art which came to light in Herculaneum and Pompeii in the 1750s.
5. Goethe in conversation with Eckermann, 16 February 1827, in *Goethes Gespräche mit Eckermann*, edited by Franz Deibel (Leipzig, 1921), p. 280.
6. For a full account of its reception in Germany, see H. B. Nisbet, 'Laocoon in Germany: The Reception of the Group since Winckelmann', *Oxford German Studies*, 10 (1979), 22–63.
7. See, for example, Hugo Blümner's introduction to his edition of *Lessings Laokoon*, second edition (Berlin, 1880), pp. 1–79; William Guild Howard, *Laokoon: Lessing, Herder, Goethe. Selections* (New York, 1910), pp. lxxi ff.; and C. R. Bingham, 'Lessing's *Laokoon* and its English Predecessors', unpublished M.A. dissertation (University of London, 1937). Various of Lessing's ideas were anticipated by Shaftesbury, Dubos, James Harris, Diderot, and Moses Mendelssohn, among others.
8. These aspects of Lessing's aesthetics are admirably analysed in David E. Wellbery's *Lessing's 'Laocoon': Semiotics and Aesthetics in the Age of Reason* (Cambridge, 1984). As Wellbery points out, Lessing's treatise, despite its fragmentary nature, is the Enlightenment's most complete and impressive statement on the semiotics of poetry and art. See also *Das Laokoon-Projekt: Pläne einer semiotischen Ästhetik*, edited by Gunter Gebauer (Stuttgart, 1984) and Victor Anthony Rudowski, *Lessing's 'Aesthetica in nuce': An Analysis of the May 26, 1769, Letter to Nicolai* (Chapel Hill, North Carolina, 1971).
9. E. H. Gombrich, 'Lessing: Lecture on a Master Mind', *Proceedings of the British Academy*, 43 (1957), 133–56 (p. 140).
10. See Hamann to J. C. Häfeli, 2 July 1780, in J. G. Hamann, *Briefwechsel*, edited by Walther Ziesemer and Arthur Henkel, 7 vols. (Wiesbaden, 1955–79), IV, 202.
11. See especially Hans-Martin Lumpp, *Philologia crucis: Zu Johann Georg Hamanns Auffassung von der Dichtkunst. Mit einem Kommentar zur 'Aesthetica in nuce'* (1762) (Tübingen, 1970); Johann Georg Hamann, *Sokratische Denkwürdigkeiten. Aesthetica*

in nuce, edited with a commentary by Sven-Aage Jørgensen (Reclams Universal-Bibliothek, 926) (Stuttgart, 1968).

12. See Sven-Aage Jørgensen, 'Hamanns hermeneutische Grundsätze', in *Aufklärung und Humanismus*, edited by Richard Toellner (Wolfenbütteler Studien zur Aufklärung, 6) (Heidelberg, 1980), pp. 219–31.

13. See H. B. Nisbet, *Herder and the Philosophy and History of Science* (Cambridge, 1970), pp. 272 f., and Robert T. Clark, *Herder. His Life and Thought* (Berkeley and Los Angeles, 1955), pp. 204 and 315.

14. See Nisbet, *Herder*, pp. 1–5.

15. See Kenneth Dewhurst and Nigel Reeves, *Friedrich Schiller. Medicine, Psychology and Literature* (Oxford, 1978).

16. See the excellent bilingual edition of Schiller's *On the Aesthetic Education of Man, in a Series of Letters*, edited, translated and introduced by Elizabeth M. Wilkinson and L. A. Willoughby (Oxford, 1967).

17. See T. J. Reed, *The Classical Centre: Goethe and Weimar 1775–1832* (London, 1980), pp. 163 f.

18. See Schiller's letter to Wilhelm von Humboldt of 26 October 1795, in which he declares that the aim of his essay is to answer the question: 'How far, given this distance which separates me from the spirit of Greek poetry, can I still be a poet, and indeed a better poet than the magnitude of this distance would seem to allow?' He goes on to suggest that his own, idealising approach is less limiting than that of the more 'natural' Goethe (*Schillers Werke. Nationalausgabe*, edited by Julius Petersen and others (Weimar, 1943–), XXVIII, 83–6).

19. The affinities between Schiller's and Hegel's presentation of the dynamic of history are obvious and have often been remarked upon. Hegel was influenced by Schiller's *Aesthetic Letters* in particular: see Walter Kaufmann, *Hegel. Reinterpretation, Texts, and Commentary* (London, 1966), pp. 50–7.

20. See Schiller's letter to Wilhelm von Humboldt of 29 November 1795: 'The marriage of Hercules and Hebe would be the content of my idyll...The chief characters would indeed be gods, but through Hercules I may still link them with humanity and bring movement into the portrait. If this plan succeeded, I would hope thereby to have triumphed by means of sentimental poetry over naive poetry itself' (*Schillers Werke. Nationalausgabe*, XXVIII, 119).

21. For a detailed analysis of this passage see Emil Staiger, 'Ein Satz aus Goethes Winckelmannschrift', *Schweizer Monatshefte*, 37 (1957), 196–207.

22. The parallel between this idea and T. S. Eliot's notion of a 'dissociation of sensibility', a dislocation of thought and feeling in the modern era, has often been noticed: see, for example, George Watson, *The Literary Critics* (Harmondsworth, 1962), p. 189; also René Wellek, *A History of Modern Criticism* (new edition, Cambridge, 1981), I, 236.

23. See Ludwig Uhlig, 'Klassik und Geschichtsbewußtsein in Goethes Winckelmannschrift', *Germanisch-Romanische Monatsschrift*, N.F. 31 (1981), 143–55 (p. 146).

24. See *Goethes Werke*, Hamburger Ausgabe (Hamburg, 1948–64), XII, 597 f.; 'monasticising' is an allusion to the *Herzensergießungen eines kunstliebenden Klosterbruders* (*Outpourings from the Heart of an Art-loving Friar*) of 1796 by the Romantics W. H. Wackenroder and Ludwig Tieck, a work full of ecstasies on Christian art, and 'Sternbaldising' is a reference to a related work, Tieck's novel *Franz Sternbalds Wanderungen* (*Franz Sternbald's Wanderings*) of 1798.

25. Compare Uhlig, 'Goethes Winckelmannschrift', p. 153.

26. Walter Pater, *The Renaissance. Studies in Art and Poetry*, sixth edition (London, 1902), p. 226.

Winckelmann: Thoughts on the Imitation of the Painting and Sculpture of the Greeks

1. This essay was first published in 1755 in Dresden, before Winckelmann's departure for Rome. The 176 paragraphs of the work are numbered (inaccurately) in Eiselein's edition, but these numbers are omitted here as unnecessary. The seven section-headings, added by later editors, have been included here, since they accurately identify the main topics dealt with.
2. Plato, *Timaeus*, 24 c.
3. Friedrich August I, Elector of Saxony, and (as Augustus II) King of Poland (Augustus the Strong).
4. Friedrich August II, Elector of Saxony and (as Augustus III) King of Poland, likened by Winckelmann to the benevolent Roman Emperor Titus.
5. Polycleitus of Argos, Greek sculptor of the fifth century B.C. who wrote a work on the theory of proportion.
6. Proclus, commentary on Plato's *Timaeus*.
7. Euphranor, Greek artist of the fourth century B.C.
8. Pindar, seventh Olympic ode.
9. Spartan magistrates.
10. Claude Quillet, *Callipaedia* (Paris, 1655), on the procreation of beautiful children.
11. Aristotle, *Politics*, Book 5.
12. An eighteenth-century term, much used on the continent, for states of depression, often associated with suicidal tendencies.
13. Winckelmann's note refers to the French translation (1724) of Philipp von Stosch, *Gemmae antiquae caelatae*, Plate 33.
14. Winckelmann's note refers to Baldinucci's biography of Bernini, published in 1682.
15. Along with the Laocoon group and the so-called Belvedere Apollo, one of the most famous statues in the Vatican museum, supposedly after Praxiteles.
16. The so-called Belvedere Apollo, also in the Vatican.
17. 'whose hearts the Titan [i.e. Prometheus] formed with auspicious art and better material' (Juvenal, *Satires*, 14) (Winckelmann's own note).
18. Roger de Piles (1635–1709), French theorist of art; source of quotation not specified.
19. Jacob Jordaens (1593–1678), Flemish painter of Antwerp.
20. Jacques Stella (1596–1657), friend and imitator of Poussin.
21. Winckelmann's note refers to Plates 29 and 30 of Stosch's work (cf. note 13 above).
22. Winckelmann's note refers to Plate 5 in Volume II of Antonio Francesco Gori's *Museum Florentinum* (Florence, 1731–42).
23. Winckelmann's note refers to Antonio Maria Zanetti, *Antiche Statue nell'Antisala della Libreria di S. Marco* (Venice, 1740–3).
24. By the Emperor Tiberius in 29 A.D., for alleging that he had connived at the murder of her husband Germanicus.
25. basement room (Italian) (Winckelmann's own note).
26. Lorenzo Mattielli, died 1748, who executed fifty-nine statues for the outside of the Hofkirche in Dresden.
27. Francesco Algarotti (1712–64), a leading Italian critic. According to David Irwin,

in his edition of Winckelmann's *Writings on Art* (London, 1972), p. 153, the poem quoted here appears in Algarotti's *Opere Varie* (Venice, 1757), II, 428.

28. Carlo Maratta (1625–1713), along with Poussin a pupil of Andrea Sacchi.

29. Francesco Solimena (1657–1747), like Maratta, a baroque painter influenced by classical models, who painted frescoes for many major churches.

30. This famous paragraph provides Lessing with the starting-point of his treatise *Laokoon* of 1766 (see p. 60 below).

31. Jacopo Sadoleto (1477–1547), Italian cardinal and author of a Latin poem on the Laocoon group.

32. Metrodorus of Athens, a philosopher and painter of the second century B.C. On his dual accomplishment cf. Pliny's *Natural History*, xxv, 135.

33. Excessive or immoderate expression in art (Winckelmann's own note).

34. frankness, openness (Italian) (Winckelmann' own note).

35. Heracleitus (c. 540–475 B.C.), Greek thinker known as the 'dark philosopher' for the obscurity of his sayings.

36. 'so that each may hope to achieve the same himself, may sweat much and toil in vain when attempting the same' (Horace, *Ars poetica*, 240 f.) (Winckelmann's own note).

37. Raymond Lafage (1656–90), best known as an engraver.

38. 'When they should see a man dignified by goodness and meritorious deeds, they fall silent and stand around with pricked-up ears' (Virgil, *Aeneid*, I, 151 f.) (Winckelmann's own note).

39. Alessandro Algardi (1602–54), Italian sculptor, one of whose principal works is the enormous relief *La Fuega d'Attila*, the two main figures of which are around ten feet high.

40. Sebastiano Conca (1680–1764), a pupil of Solimena and pioneer of the Roman Rococo style.

41. The reference is to Joseph Addison's poem 'The Campaign', on Marlborough's victory at Blenheim.

42. Raphael's famous Sistine Madonna, still in the Zwinger Gallery in Dresden.

43. Caspar Netscher (1639–84), Dutch genre painter and pupil of Terborch.

44. Gerrit Dou (1613–75), genre painter and pupil of Rembrandt.

45. Adriaen Van der Werff (1659–1722), exponent of the precise and careful finish of the Leiden school of painters.

46. Mentioned by Pliny in *Natural History*, xxv, 151 f.

47. Sculptor active in Rome in the first century B.C.

48. George Turnbull, *Treatise of Ancient Painting* (London, 1740).

49. Parrhasius, a celebrated Greek painter who flourished in Athens around 400 B.C.

50. Aristides of Thebes, a Greek military painter who flourished around 360–330 B.C.

51. Cesare Ripa, *Iconologia deorum* (1593).

52. Romein de Hooghe, Dutch painter and engraver, *Hieroglyphica of Merkbeelden der oude Volkeren* (Amsterdam, 1735).

53. François Lemoyne (1688–1737), teacher of Boucher and official painter to Louis XV.

54. Vitruvius Pollio, *De Architectura*, VII, Chapter 5.

55. Morto da Feltro, painter of c. 1467–1512.

56. '[it] knows how to give each individual his fitting part' (Horace, *Ars poetica*, 316) (Winckelmann's own note).

57. 'vain fancies shall be formed like the dreams of a sick man' (Horace, *Ars poetica*, 7 f.) (Winckelmann's own note).

58. 'rich in lands and in monies lent for interest' (Horace, *Ars poetica*, 421) (Winckelmann's own note).
59. The bronze doors of St Peter's, completed in 1445 by Filarete (c. 1400 – c. 1469), are decorated with a mixture of religious and historical subjects and complex classical allegories.
60. Quotation from Horace, *Ars poetica*, 333.

Lessing: Laocoon

1. There is a useful commentary on the *Laocoon* in Lessing's *Werke*, edited by Herbert G. Göpfert, 8 vols. (Munich, 1970–9), VI, 861–917. The fullest collection of drafts, variants, and background materials is still that in Hugo Blümner's edition of Lessing's *Laokoon*, second edition (Berlin, 1880). In the present translation, those of Lessing's long and learned footnotes which are now of only antiquarian interest are omitted. Where his footnotes contain material essential to his argument or to an understanding of the text, their substance is incorporated in the notes which follow here.
2. Greek painters of the fourth century B.C.
3. The Greek lyric poet Simonides of Ceos, 556–467 B.C.
4. 'They differ in their objects and mode of imitation.' The quotation, used by Lessing as a motto on the title page of his work, is from Plutarch, 'Whether the Athenians were more Famous for their Martial Accomplishments or for their Knowledge', Chapter 3.
5. This claim is not strictly true. See Introduction, pp. 8 f.
6. Alexander Gottlieb Baumgarten (1714–62), the founder of aesthetics as a philosophical discipline (*Aesthetica*, 1750).
7. Johann Matthias Gesner (1691–1761), humanist and antiquary; the work referred to is his *Novus linguae et eruditionis romanae Thesaurus*.
8. See note 31 to p. 42 above; the translation here of the extract from Winckelmann differs in minor particulars from my own translation on p. 42 above.
9. See note 32 to p. 42 above.
10. Exclamations of pain.
11. See note 10.
12. Danish hero and legendary founder of the town of Jomsburg.
13. 'shedding hot tears.'
14. 'but the great Priam forbade them to weep.'
15. Anne Lefèvre Dacier (1654–1720), philologist and translator of classical texts, including the *Iliad* (Paris, 1711).
16. 'I in no way condemn weeping.'
17. In the *Trachiniae* of Sophocles.
18. The French.
19. Jean Baptiste Vivien de Chateaubrun (1686–1775), author of the drama *Philoctète* (1775).
20. This legend is reported by Pliny, *Natural History*, XXXV, 151.
21. Greek genre painters of the fifth century B.C. and the Hellenistic period respectively.
22. Franciscus Junius (1589–1677), French antiquarian and author of *De pictura veterum* (1637).
23. Pier Leone Ghezzi (1674–1755), historical painter and caricaturist.
24. Judges at the ancient Olympic games.

25. That is, a portrait likeness.

26. An allusion to the popular superstition that pregnant mothers exposed to frightening impressions produced malformed offspring.

27. An error of Lessing's; intended is perhaps Aratus of Sicyon, 271– 213 B.C., whose mother's name was Aristodama, or Aristodemus, a hero of the first Messenian War (c. 735–715 B.C.).

28. Lessing adds a learned footnote, in which he tries to prove that supposed representations of the Furies in ancient art are in fact of other mythological figures.

29. Greek painter (c. 420–380 B.C.).

30. Bernard de Montfaucon (1655–1741), *L'antiquité expliquée et représentée en figures*, 5 vols. (Paris, 1719–24), I, 50.

31. Valerius Maximus, Roman historian of the first century A.D., and author of *De factis dictisque memorabilibus libri IX*.

32. Greek sculptor of Rhegium, fifth century B.C.

33. Julien Offray de La Mettrie (1709–51), materialistic philosopher and author of *L'homme machine* (1748); Democritus of Abdera (c. 460–370 B.C.), 'the laughing philosopher', traditionally opposed in iconography to the mournful Heracleitus.

34. Greek painter of the Hellenistic period.

35. Flavius Philostratus, second to third century A.D., author of the *Life of Apollonius of Tyana*; Lessing's reference is to Book II, Chapter 22 of this work.

36. 'He raises terrible shouts to the stars above' (*Aeneid*, II, 222).

37. Figure of Greek mythology, whose life depended on a piece of wood rescued from the fire by his mother. His mother, when Meleager slew her brothers, cast the wood upon the fire and Meleager was himself consumed.

38. See note 19 above.

39. Lessing's footnote refers to the *Mercure de France*, April 1755, p. 177.

40. Or rather, a Scotsman: Adam Smith (1723–90), *The Theory of Moral Sentiments* (London, 1761).

41. In Lessing's day, Seneca's authorship of the tragedies traditionally attributed to him was doubted.

42. Lessing's error; intended is probably Cresilas, an artist of the first century A.D. to whom Pliny (XXXVI, 77) attributes a statue of a dying gladiator.

43. Chateaubrun; see note 19 above.

44. The actor David Garrick (1717–79) was revered in Germany, where he had appeared on tour in 1763, no less than in England.

45. This and the following chapter deal with the dating of the Laocoon group, a question which archaeologists still debate. For recent arguments, see Margarete Bieber, *Laocoon: The Influence of the Group since its Rediscovery*, revised edition (Detroit, 1967), pp. 37–41; Gisela M. A. Richter, *The Sculpture and Sculptors of the Greeks*, fourth edition (New Haven and London, 1970), pp. 237 ff.; and A. F. Stewart, 'To Entertain an Emperor: Sperlonga, Laokoon and Tiberius at the Dinner Table', *Journal of Roman Studies*, 67 (1977), 76–94. According to Stewart, the latest evidence suggests that the group was executed in the reign of Augustus or even Tiberius, not up to a century earlier, as was until recently believed. If this is indeed the case, Lessing's conjecture that the group post-dates Virgil's *Aeneid* (c. 26–19 B.C.) could well be correct.

46. Bartolomeo Marliani (died c. 1560), author of *Topographia urbis Romae* (1544); Lessing's reference is to Book IV, Chapter 14 of this work.

47. See note 30 above; Lessing's reference is to the supplement to *L'antiquité expliquée*, Part I, p. 242.

48. Aurelius Ambrosius Theodosius Macrobius (c. 400 A.D.), author of *Saturnalia sive conviviorum libri VII*; Lessing's reference is to Book V, Chapter 2.

49. Pisander, Greek epic poet of the seventh century B.C., of whose work only fragments survive.

50. 'Recited by schoolchildren' (the phrase is quoted from Macrobius).

51. Quintus Calaber or Smyrnaeus (third to fourth century A.D.), author of *Posthomerica*, a continuation of Homer's *Iliad*.

52. Lycophron, grammarian and poet (third century B.C.), author of the monodrama *Cassandra*.

53. Virgil's account of Laocoon's death is in Book II of the *Aeneid*, lines 199–224.

54. *Aeneid*, II, 212–17: 'they forged on, straight at Laocoon. First each snake took one of his little sons, twined round him, tightening, and bit, and devoured the tiny limbs. Next they seized Laocoon, who had armed himself and was hastening to the rescue; they bound him in the giant spirals of their scaly length' (*The Aeneid*, translated by W. F. Jackson Knight (Harmondsworth, 1956)).

55. Tiberius Claudius Donatus (fourth century A.D.), author of *Interpretationes Vergilianae*, a commentary on Virgil. Lessing's footnote quotes Donatus's comment on *Aeneid*, II, 227, which confirms his own reconstruction of the serpents' attack on Laocoon as described by Virgil.

56. *Aeneid*, II, 220: 'His hands strove frantically to wrench the knots apart.'

57. *Aeneid*, II, 218–19: 'twice round his middle, twice round his throat; and still their heads and necks towered above him'.

58. Franz Cleyn (1590–1658), Dutch painter and engraver who died in London.

59. (London, 1697).

60. *Aeneid*, II, 221: 'Filth and black venom drenched his priestly bands.'

61. On 'arbitrary' and 'natural' signs, see Lessing's explanations in Chapter 17 below (p. 103).

62. Jonathan Richardson (1665–1745), author of *The Theory of Painting* (1715), which Lessing's footnote cites in a French translation of 1728.

63. 'The one snake darts upwards and seizes Laocoon, winds round him from top to bottom and wounds him in the side with a furious bite...But the slippery serpent turns downward in repeated circles and binds his knees in a tight knot.'

64. Jacopo Sadoleto (1477–1547), cardinal and poet, author of the poem *De Laocoontis statua* from which the quotation here is taken.

65. See note 57 above.

66. Joseph Spence (1699–1768), historian and antiquary, author of *Polymetis: or, An Enquiry concerning the Agreement between the Works of the Roman Poets and the Remains of the Antient Artists* (London, 1747). Characteristically, Lessing develops his own views by attacking those of another, just as he subsequently does with Caylus in Chapter 11. That he is far from fair to Spence, misrepresenting his arguments when it suits him, has been shown by Donald T. Siebert, 'Laokoon and *Polymetis*: Lessing's Treatment of Joseph Spence', *Lessing Yearbook*, 3 (1971), 71–83.

67. 'And you were not the first, Roman warrior, to bear the rays of gleaming lightning nor the reddish wings on your shield'; from Valerius Flaccus (died c. 90 A.D.), author of the *Argonautica*, an unfinished poem in eight books; Lessing's reference is to Book VI, 55–6.

68. Joseph Addison (1672–1719), *Dialogues upon the Usefulness of Ancient Medals* (1702); Lessing's lengthy footnote discusses Spence's and Addisons's comments on Juvenal, *Satires*, XI, 100–7 and related images on antique coins.

69. Ovid, *Metamorphoses*, VII, 813 f.: 'Come, Zephyr, to my breast, a most welcome visitor, and soothe me.'

70. Juvenal, *Satires*, VIII, 52–5.

71. Albius Tibullus (c. 54–18 B.C.), author of *Elegiae*; Lessing's reference is to the fourth elegy of Book III, and to Spence's comments in *Polymetis*, Dialogue VIII, p. 84.

72. Aetion (fourth century B.C.), famed for his pictures of the marriage of Alexander the Great.

73. 'newly wed bride distinguished by her bashfulness'.

74. P. Papinius Statius (c. 61–96 A.D.), author of five books of *Silvae* and other poems; Lessing's reference is to *Silvae*, I, 5, line 8, and to Spence's comments in *Polymetis*, Dialogue VIII, p. 81.

75. Titus Lucretius Carus (95 – c. 52 B.C.), *De rerum natura*, V, 736–47. Lessing's footnote contains another polemic against Spence.

76. *Aeneid*, VIII, 725, 'Araxes enraged at the bridge'; Lessing's reference to Spence is to *Polymetis*, Dialogue XIV, p. 230.

77. See note 68 above.

78. Ovid, *Metamorphoses*, IV, 19 f.: 'When you stand there without horns, your head is like that of a maiden.'

79. 'of two shapes'.

80. Lessing's reference is to *Polymetis*, Dialogue VI, p. 63.

81. See note 74 above.

82. See note 67 above.

83. Lessing's footnote cites *Polymetis*, Dialogue XX, p. 311: 'Scarce any thing can be good in a poetical description, which would appear absurd, if represented in a statue or picture.'

84. Lessing's reference is to *Polymetis*, Dialogue VII, p. 74.

85. *Argonautica* (cf. note 67), II, 102–6: 'Now she no longer wishes to appear as a lovely goddess, and her hair, no longer fastened with gold, falls down on her divine breast. Wild and terrible, her cheeks stained, bearing a blazing torch, and dressed in black, she resembles the Stygian maidens [i.e. the Eumenides].'

86. Statius (cf. note 74), *Thebaïs* (a heroic poem in twelve books), V, 61–9: 'She [Venus] left ancient Paphos and its hundred altars, her face and hair transformed; she unloosed her girdle and sent the Idalian doves far from her. Some even say that, in the darkness of midnight, bearing other flames and larger arrows than usual, she appeared in the nuptial chambers amidst the Stygian sisters [the Eumenides], and filled the innermost parts of the houses with writhing serpents and all their thresholds with holy terror.'

87. Lessing's footnote cites Valerius Flaccus, *Argonautica*, II, 263–73.

88. Lessing adds a long footnote in which he argues that the Furies, as ugly objects, were never represented as such in ancient works of art, other than perhaps in miniature form on gems etc.

89. Lessing's reference is to *Polymetis*, Dialogue VII, p. 81.

90. Ovid, *Fasti*, VI, 295–8.

91. Legendary second king of Rome.

92. Ovid, *Fasti*, III, 45 f.

93. 'Priest of Vesta'.

94. Pliny, *Natural History*, XXXVI, Section 4, p. 727 (Lessing's reference).

95. Sacred image of Pallas (Athene).

96. Cultic drum.

97. Georgius Codinus (fifteenth century), Byzantine historian, supposed author of *De originibus Constantinopolitanis*, included in *Corpus Byzantinae historiae* (Venice, 1729); Lessing's reference is to p. 12 of this edition, and his footnote discusses the significance of the tympanum.

98. Lessing's reference is to *Polymetis*, Dialogue VIII, p. 91.

99. Statius, *Thebaïs*, (cf. note 86), VIII, 551: 'Urania had long since foretold his death from the position of the stars.' Lessing adds a reference to *Polymetis*, Dialogue X, p. 137.

100. Lessing's reference is to *Polymetis*, Dialogue X, pp. 137–9.

101. Lessing adds a long footnote in which he criticises Spence on further points of detail.

102. Anne Claude Philippe de Tubières, Comte de Caylus (1692–1765), antiquarian and author of *Tableaux tirés de l'Iliade* (Paris, 1757), the work with which Lessing here takes issue. His greatest work, however, was the monumental *Recueil d'antiquités*, 7 vols. (Paris, 1752–67). Lessing adds a footnote in which he takes issue with Caylus on the manner in which ancient artists depicted death. He later devoted a separate treatise to this problem, entitled *How the Ancients portrayed Death* (1769).

103. James Thomson (1700–48), author of *The Seasons*, a poem which was greatly admired and imitated in eighteenth-century Germany.

104. Horace, *Ars Poetica*, lines 128–30: 'it is better for you to put the song of Troy [the *Iliad*] into dramatic form than to be the first to treat unknown and unsung subjects.'

105. See note 2 above.

106. 'an inner compulsion and a desire for artistic production'; Lessing's reference is to Pliny, *Natural History*, XXXV, Section 36, p. 700.

107. Ialysus, a hero of Rhodes; Cydippe, mother of Ialysus.

108. Homer, *Iliad*, XXI, 403–5: 'But she gave ground, and seized with her stout hand a stone that lay upon the plain, black and jagged and great, that men of former days had set to be the boundary mark of a field' (*The Iliad*, translated by A. T. Murray, Loeb Classical Library (London, 1925)).

109. Cassius Longinus (c. 213–73 A.D.), to whom the aesthetic treatise *On the Sublime* was traditionally attributed. Lessing's reference is to Chapter 9 of that work.

110. *Iliad*, XX, 446: 'And thrice he stabbed the dense mist.'

111. *Iliad*, I, 44–53: Lessing adds a reference to Caylus, *Tableaux*, p. 7.

112. *Iliad*, I, 44–52: 'Down from the peaks of Olympus he strode, wroth at heart, bearing on his shoulders his bow and covered quiver. The arrows rattled on the shoulders of the angry god, as he moved; and his coming was like the night. Then he sate him down apart from the ships and let fly a shaft: terrible was the twang of the silver bow. The mules he assailed first and the swift dogs, but thereafter on the men themselves he let fly his stinging arrows, and smote; and ever did the pyres of the dead burn thick.'

113. *Iliad*, IV, 1–4: 'Now the gods, seated by the side of Zeus, were holding assembly on the golden floor, and in their midst the queenly Hebe poured them nectar, and they with golden goblets pledged one another as they looked forth upon the city of the Trojans'; Lessing adds a reference to Caylus, *Tableaux*, p. 30.

114. Apollonius of Rhodes (third century B.C.), epic poet, author of the *Argonautica*.

115. Lessing's footnote quotes Caylus, *Tableaux*, Avertissement, p. v, as follows: 'On est toujours convenu, que plus un Poëme fournissoit d'images et d'actions, plus il avoit de supériorité en Poësie. Cette réflexion m'avoit conduit à penser que le

calcul des differens Tableaux, qu'offrent les Poëmes, pouvoit servir à comparer le merite respectif des Poëmes et des Poëtes. Le nombre et le genre des Tableaux que presentent ces grands ouvrages, auroient été une espèce de pierre de touche, ou plutôt une balance certaine du mérite de ces Poëmes et du Genie de leurs Auteurs.'

116. *Iliad*, IV, 105–26.

117. The following deductive argument had in fact formed the basis of Lessing's plan for the whole work: see Introduction, pp. 8 f.

118. *Iliad*, V, 722–31: 'Hebe quickly put to the car on either side the curved wheels of bronze, eight-spoked, about the iron axle-tree. Of these the felloe verily is of gold imperishable, and thereover are tyres of bronze fitted, a marvel to behold; and the naves are of silver, revolving on this side and on that; and the body is plaited tight with gold and silver thongs, and two rims there are that run about it. From the body stood forth the pole of silver, and on the end thereof she bound the fair golden yoke, and cast thereon the fair golden breast-straps.'

119. *Iliad*, II, 42–6: 'He put on his soft tunic, fair and glistening, and about him cast his great cloak, and beneath his shining feet he bound his fair sandals, and about his shoulders flung his silver-studded sword; and he grasped the sceptre of his fathers, imperishable ever.'

120. *Iliad*, II, 101–8: '...bearing in his hands the sceptre which Hephaestus had wrought with toil. Hephaestus gave it to king Zeus, son of Cronos, and Zeus gave it to the messenger Argeiphontes; and Hermes, the lord, gave it to Pelops, driver of horses, and Pelops in turn gave it to Atreus, shepherd of the host; and Atreus at his death left it to Thyestes, rich in flocks, and Thyestes again left it to Agamemnon to bear, so that he might be lord of many isles and of all Argos.'

121. 'Zeus, son of Cronos'; Lessing here accepts the false equation of the latter name with 'Chronos' (time).

122. 'the messenger Argeiphontes'.

123. 'Pelops, driver of horses'.

124. 'shepherd of the host' (Atreus).

125. 'Thyestes, rich in flocks'.

126. *Iliad*, I, 234–9: 'Verily by this staff, that shall no more put forth leaves or shoots since at the first it left its stump among the mountains, neither shall it again grow green, for the bronze hath stripped it of leaves and bark, and now the sons of the Achaeans that give judgement bear it in their hands, even they that guard the dooms by ordinance of Zeus.'

127. *Iliad*, IV, 105–11: '...his polished bow of the horn of a wild ibex, that he had himself smitten beneath the breast as it came forth from a rock, he lying in wait the while in a place of ambush, and had struck it in the chest, so that it fell backward in a cleft of the rock. From its head the horns grew to a length of sixteen palms; these the worker in horn had wrought and fitted together, and smoothed all with care, and set thereon a tip of gold.'

128. On 'natural' and 'arbitrary' signs, see Introduction pp. 9 f.

129. The following quotation consists of stanzas 39 and 40 of the didactic poem *The Alps* (*Die Alpen*, 1729) by the Swiss poet and scientist Albrecht von Haller (1708–77): 'There the high head of the noble gentian towers far above the lowly chorus of the vulgar herbs. A whole nation of flowers serves under his banner, and even his blue brother [a lesser species of gentian] bows low and honours him. The bright gold of the flowers, radiating outwards [centaury], ascends the stalk and crowns its grey garment; the smooth white of the leaves, streaked with dark

green, shines with the coloured sparkle of the dewy diamond. Most equitable law! That strength should join with ornament; in a beautiful body there dwells a more beautiful soul.

Here creeps a lowly herb [antirrhinum], like a grey mist, whose leaf nature has formed in a cross; the lovely flower displays the two gilded beaks of a bird made of amethyst. There a gleaming leaf, its edges divided into fingers, casts its green reflection on a bright rivulet; the delicate snow of the flowers, dyed with crimson, surrounds a striped star with its white rays [Astrantia major, masterwort]. Emerald and roses bloom even on the trodden heath [wild rosemary], and rocks are clothed in a dress of purple [campion].' (Haller himself, in footnotes to the poem, elucidates the botanical references.)

130. The praise of Haller quoted here is by his fellow Swiss, Johann Jakob Breitinger (1701–76), in his *Kritische Dichtkunst* (*Critical Poetics* (Zurich, 1740)), Part II, p. 407 (Lessing's reference).

131. Jan van Huysum (1682–1749), one of the most famous Dutch flower-painters of his day.

132. Virgil, *Georgics*, III, 51–9:

In a cow the following
Points should be looked for – a rough appearance, a coarse head,
Generous neck, and dewlaps hanging from jaw to leg;
Flanks as roomy as you like; everything built on a large scale,
Even the hoof; and shaggy ears under the crooked horns.
I have nothing against an animal of prominent white markings,
Or one that rejects the yoke and is hasty at times with her horn –
More like a bull to look at,
Tall all over, dusting the ground with her tail as she goes.

(Virgil, The *Eclogues, Georgics and Aeneid*, translated by C. Day Lewis (London, 1966))

133. Virgil, *Georgics*, III, 79–81:

He shows a proud neck,
A finely tapering head, short barrel and fleshy back,
And his spirited chest ripples with muscle.
(Translated by C. Day Lewis)

134. Horace, *Ars Poetica*, lines 16–18: 'they describe Diana's grove and altar, the meanderings of a stream through a pleasant landscape, or the River Rhine, or a rainbow'.

135. Alexander Pope (1688–1744); Lessing's reference is to his *Epistle to Arbuthnot* (*Prologue to the Satires*), lines 148 f. and 340 f. Lessing's footnote shows that he is aware that Warburton, in his commentary on the poem, is the author of the culinary reference he cites, but he (Lessing) maintains that Warburton is merely echoing Pope's own sentiments.

136. Christian Ewald von Kleist (1715–59), poet and officer in Frederick the Great's army, who died of wounds received in the Seven Years' War. His descriptive poem *Der Frühling* (*The Spring*) was greatly admired in Lessing's day. Kleist had been a close friend of Lessing's.

137. Jean François de Marmontel (1723–99), French critic, author of a *Poétique française* (1763); Lessing's reference is to Part II, p. 501, of this work.

138. The reference is to Kleist's (not Marmontel's) Eclogues or pastoral poems.

139. Francesco Mazzola Parmigianino (1503–40), Italian painter.

140. Anton Raphael Mengs (1728–79), painter and friend of Winckelmann in Rome, author of *Gedanken über die Schönheit und über den Geschmack in der Malerei* (Zurich, 1762); Lessing's reference is to p. 69 of that work.

141. *Iliad*, v, 722 f.

142. *Iliad*, xii, 296.

143. See note 15 above.

144. 'the round, brazen, eight-spoked'.

145. 'wheels'.

146. Virgil, *Aeneid*, viii, 447–53: 'They shape an enormous shield...Others, with bellows full of wind, draw in and discharge the air. Others again temper the hissing bronze in a vessel of water. The cave resounds with the blows on the anvils. They powerfully raise their arms together in rhythm and turn the mass of metal with the grip of their tongs.'

147. *Aeneid*, viii, 730: 'he delights in the image, though ignorant of the things represented'.

148. That is, Vulcan.

149. A reference to the famous *Querelle des anciens et des modernes* of the late seventeenth and early eighteenth centuries. Perrault and Terrasson were among those who, from the perspective of modern rationalism, criticised the supposed backwardness of the classical writers; the last three, as critics or translators, adopted a more sympathetic attitude. Julius Caesar Scaliger (1484–1558), classical philologist; Charles Perrault (1628–1703), author of *Le parallèle des anciens et des modernes* (1688–98); Jean Terrasson (1670–1750), author of *Dissertations critiques sur L'Iliade de Homère* (1715); André Dacier (1651–1722), editor of *La poétique d'Aristote* (1692); Jean Boivin de Villeneuve (1649–1722), author of the *Apologie d'Homère et du bouclier d'Achille* (1715); Alexander Pope (1688–1744), whose translation of Homer included 'Observations on the Shield of Achilles'.

150. Lessing's reference is to Pliny, *Natural History*, xxxvi, Section 4, p. 726.

151. *Iliad*, xviii, 497–507: 'But the folk were gathered in the place of assembly; for there a strife had arisen, and two men were striving about the blood-price of a man slain; the one avowed that he had paid all, declaring his cause to the people, but the other denied that he had received anything; and each was anxious to win the issue in the word of an arbitrator. Moreover, the people were cheering both, showing favour to this side and to that. And heralds held back the people, and the elders were sitting upon polished stones in the sacred circle, holding in their hands the staves of the loud-voiced heralds. Therewith then they would spring up and give judgement, each in turn. And in the midst lay two talents of gold.'

152. *actu...virtute*: in fact...in essence.

153. *Iliad*, xviii, 509–40 (Lessing's reference).

154. 'there he created', 'there he made', 'there he placed', 'there the lame one [Vulcan] fashioned'.

155. Polygnotus (fifth century B.C.), whose compositions at Delphi of the Sack of Troy and of the descent of Odysseus into Hades are described by the traveller and geographer Pausanias (second century A.D.) in his *Itinerary of Greece*; Lessing's reference is to Pausanias's description of Phocis in that work, Chapters 25–31.

156. See *The Iliad of Homer*, translated by Alexander Pope, edited by Gilbert Wakefield, new edition, 3 vols. (London, 1817), iii, 93.

157. Lessing bases this conclusion on Vitruvius (first century B.C.), *De architectura*, preface to Book vii.

158. Lessing's footnote to this sentence reads 'Written in the year 1763'. His *Laocoon*

was not published until 1766, by which time Winckelmann's *History of the Art of Antiquity* (1764) had already appeared.

159. Constantinus Manasses (twelfth century), Byzantine monk, author of a verse chronicle of the world up to 1080 A.D.; Lessing quotes it from the collection *Corpus Byzantinae historiae* (Venice, 1729), p. 20.

160. 'She was a beautiful woman, with a fair brow, fine complexion and cheeks, a lovely face, large eyes, pale skin, curling eyelashes, her breast a seat of the graces, with white arms, in the full radiance of beauty, her countenance very pale, her cheeks rosy, her expression delightful, her eyes bright, with youthful charm; without artifice, in the adornment of her natural beauty, white and delicate but tinged with a rosy glow, like ivory dyed in radiant purple; with a long, white, shining neck, recalling the legend that the lovely Helen was born of the race of swans.'

161. *Stichos politikos*, an epic verse-form used in medieval Greek.

162. Ludovico Ariosto (1474–1533), *Orlando furioso*, Canto VII, verses 11–15: 'She was so beautifully modelled, no painter, however much he applied himself, could have achieved anything more perfect. Her long blonde tresses were gathered in a knot: pure gold itself could have no finer lustre. Roses and white privet blooms lent their colours to suffuse her delicate cheeks. Her serene brow was like polished ivory, and in perfect proportion. Beneath two of the thinnest black arches, two dark eyes – or rather, two bright suns; soft was their look, gentle their movement. Love seemed to flit, frolicsome, about them; indeed, Love from this vantage point would let fly his full quiver and openly steal away all hearts. Down the midst of the face, the nose – Envy herself could find no way of bettering it. Below this, the mouth, set between two dimples; it was imbued with native cinnabar. Here a beautiful soft pair of lips opened to disclose a double row of choicest pearls. Here was the course of those winning words which could not but soften every heart, however rugged and uncouth. Here was formed the melodious laughter which made a paradise on earth. Snow-white was her neck, milky her breast; the neck was round, the breast broad and full. A pair of apples, not yet ripe, fashioned in ivory, rose and fell like the sea-swell at times when a gentle breeze stirs the ocean. Argus himself could not see them entire, but you could easily judge that what lay hidden did not fall short of what was exposed to view. Her arms were justly proportioned, and her lily-white hands were often to be glimpsed: they were slender and tapering, and quite without a knot or swelling vein. A pair of small, neat, rounded feet completes the picture of this august person. Her looks were angelic, heaven-sent – no veil could have concealed them' (*Orlando furioso*, translated by Guido Waldman (Oxford, 1974), pp. 61–2).

163. Milton, *Paradise Lost*, I, 731 f.

164. Lodovico Dolce (1508–66), *Dialogo della Pittura, intitolato L'Aretino* (Florence, 1735), p. 178.

165. 'She was so beautifully modelled, no painter, however much he applied himself, could have achieved anything more perfect.'

166. 'Roses and white privet blooms lent their colours to suffuse her delicate cheeks.'

167. 'Down the midst of the face, the nose –'.

168. 'Her brow was in perfect proportion.'

169. 'Envy herself could find no way of bettering it.'

170. 'They were slender and tapering.'

171. 'most beautiful Dido'.

172. *Aeneid*, IV, 136–9: 'At last she steps forth...dressed in a Sidonian mantle with

embroidered hem. Her quiver is of gold, her hair is held in a gold clasp, and a golden brooch fastens her purple tunic.'

173. Anacreon (fifth and sixth centuries B.C.), Greek lyric poet; Lessing refers to his *Odes*, 15 [28] and 16 [29].

174. Anacreon, *Odes*, 15 [28], lines 33–4: 'Enough! I see her as real. Her image is about to address me.'

175. Anacreon, *Odes*, 16 [29], lines 27–33 and 43–4: 'Paint beneath his face an ivory neck surpassing that of Adonis. Model his breast and hands on those of Mercury, his hips on Pollux, his abdomen on Bacchus...Transform Apollo to create Bathyllus!'

176. Lucian (second century A.D.) wrote the dialogue Εἰκόνες in praise of Panthea, mistress of the Emperor Lucius Aurelius Verus; Lessing's reference is to Section 3, Part II, of this dialogue.

177. *Iliad*, III, 156–8: 'Small blame that Trojans and well-greaved Achaeans should for such a woman suffer woes for so long; for she is indeed like an immortal goddess to look upon.'

178. Sappho (c. 600 B.C.), poetess of Lesbos.

179. Ovid, *Amores*, I, 5, lines 19–22:

> What arms and shoulders did I touch and see,
> How apt her breasts were to be press'd by me!
> How smooth a belly under her waist saw I!
> How large a leg, and what a lusty thigh!

(Translation by Christopher Marlowe). The name of Ovid's mistress was in fact Corinna; Lesbia was the mistress of Catullus.

180. Ariosto, *Orlando furioso* (see note 162 above): 'A pair of apples, not yet ripe, fashioned in ivory, rose and fell like the sea-swell at times when a gentle breeze stirs the ocean.'

181. 'In the dimple of her soft chin and round her marble neck let all the Graces play.'

182. 'impressed by Amor's finger'.

183. Zeuxis (fifth century B.C.), Greek painter of Heraclea.

184. Town in southern Italy; the painting was for the temple of Hera there.

185. 'Base is the lust of old men' (Ovid, *Amores*, I, 9, line 4).

186. *Iliad*, III, 159 f.: 'But even so, despite her attractiveness, let her depart upon the ships, and not be left here to be a bane to us and to our children after us.'

187. *Iliad*, III, 141 f.: 'and straightway she veiled herself with shining linen, and went forth from her chamber'.

188. 'Helen, covered in a white veil'.

189. Lessing's reference is to Pliny, *Natural History*, XXXV, Section 36, p. 698, and he quotes the passage: 'Fecit et Dianam sacrificantium virginum choro mixtam: quibus vicisse Homeri versus videtur id ipsum describentis.' ('He also painted a Diana in a group of sacrificing virgins; he seems thereby to have surpassed the verses in which Homer describes the same scene.') Lessing finds the reading *sacrificantium* ('sacrificing') implausible, and suggests *venantium* ('hunting') or *sylvis vagantium* ('wandering in the woods') instead. He goes on to criticise Spence (see note 66 above) for accepting the reading *sacrificantium* at face value.

190. Phidias (fifth century B.C.), the greatest of the Greek sculptors.

191. *Iliad*, I, 528–30: 'The son of Cronos spake, and bowed his dark brow in assent, and the ambrosial locks waved from the king's immortal head; and he made great Olympus to quake.'

192. 'almost as if fetched from heaven itself'.
193. 'how large a part of the *soul*'; Lessing's reference is to Pliny, x, Section 51, p. 616.
194. Lessing's reference is to Pliny, xxxiv, Section 19, p. 651; Myron (fifth century B.C.), Greek sculptor, who worked mainly in bronze; Pythagoras Leontinus (fifth century B.C.), Greek sculptor of Rhegium.
195. William Hogarth (1697–1764), painter and engraver, author of the *Analysis of Beauty* (1753, German translation, Berlin, 1754); Lessing's reference is to p. 47 of the German translation. The statue of 'Antinous' in the Vatican is now reckoned to be of Hermes.
196. *Iliad*, iii, 210 f.
197. *Iliad*, ii, 216–19.
198. Moses Mendelssohn (1729–86), Jewish philosopher and close friend of Lessing.
199. Aesop (sixth century B.C.), author of fables, who was reputedly extremely ugly; 'monastic whim' is an allusion to the commentaries of medieval scholastics.
200. 'ridiculousness'.
201. Alexander Pope; William Wycherley (c. 1640–1716), English Restoration dramatist.
202. 'harmlessness'; Aristotle, *Poetics*, Chapter 5.
203. See note 51 above.
204. 'which makes even the wisest man foolish' (*Posthomerica*, i, 737).
205. *King Lear*, i, 2.
206. *Richard III*, i, 1.
207. Lessing again quotes his friend Moses Mendelssohn (see note 198); the source is Letter 82 in the series *Letters concerning Recent Literature* (*Briefe, die neueste Literatur betreffend*, 1759–65), a collaborative and anonymous publication to which Lessing himself contributed.
208. Aristotle, *Poetics*, Chapter 4.
209. Christian Adolf Klotz (1738–71), philologist and Professor of Rhetoric at Halle, with whom Lessing, a few years later, had an acrimonious controversy which destroyed Klotz's reputation as a scholar. Lessing refers to Klotz's *Epistolae Homericae* (1764), pp. 33 ff.
210. That is, Moses Mendelssohn (see note 207 above).
211. In fact, a lizard.
212. Aristophanes (c. 444–380 B.C.), comic dramatist; the quotation is from his *Clouds*, lines 169–74:

> *Student*   And yet last night a mighty thought we lost
> Through a green lizard.
> *Strepsiades*   Tell me, how was that?
> *Student*   Why, as Himself, with eyes and mouth wide open,
> Mused on the moon, her paths and revolutions,
> A lizard from the roof squirted full on him.
> *Strepsiades* He, he, he, he. I like the lizard's spattering Socrates.'

213. Lessing's reference is to *The Connoisseur*, vol. i, no. 21. His footnote quotes the original at length.
214. Longinus: see note 109 above.
215. Hesiod (c. 700 B.C.), among the earliest of the Greek poets; Lessing's reference is to *The Shield of Hercules* (a poem often ascribed to Hesiod), line 266: 'slime streamed from her nostrils'.
216. 'blood flowed down her cheeks to the ground'.

217. Sophocles, *Philoctetes*, lines 31–9:

Neoptolemus The chamber's empty; no man is within.
Odysseus And no provision for a man's abode?
Neoptolemus Litter of trodden leaves as for a couch.
Odysseus And that is all – no other sign of life?
Neoptolemus A cup of uncouth handiwork, rough hewn
From out a log; some tinder, too, I see.
Odysseus These are his household treasures.
Neoptolemus Faugh! and here
Spread in the sun to dry, are filthy rags
Dank with the ooze of some malignant sore.

(translated by F. Storr, Loeb Classical Library (London, 1913))
218. *Aeneid*, II, 277: 'his beard was ragged, his hair clotted with blood'.
219. Ovid, *Metamorphoses*, VI, 387–91: 'Despite his cries, the skin was ripped from his whole body: it was all a single wound. Blood flowed everywhere, his nerves were exposed, his veins pulsed with no skin to cover them. One could count his throbbing entrails and the fibres shining through his breast.'
220. Ovid, *Metamorphoses*, VIII, 809–12: 'When she saw her [Hunger]...she told her the instructions of the goddess, and after a short time, although she stood at a distance and had only just arrived, she seemed to feel hunger herself.'
221. Callimachus (third century B.C.), Alexandrian poet and scholar; Lessing's reference is to his *Hymn to Ceres*, lines 111–16.
222. *Hymn to Ceres*, lines 109–12 and 115 f.: 'And he devoured the cow which his mother had raised for Hestia [Vesta], as well as the racehorse and the martial steed; and then the cat, at which small animals had trembled. Then this son of a royal house sat down at the wayside and begged for crusts and the refuse of meals.'
223. Ovid, *Metamorphoses*, VIII, 875–8: 'However, after the violence of his malady had consumed everything available,...he began to tear pieces off his own limbs with his teeth, and fed his body by eating it away.'
224. The Harpies, ravenous monsters with the bodies of birds and the heads of maidens, sent by the gods to torment the blind Phineas by stealing or defiling his food.
225. *Argonautica* (see note 114 above), II, 228–33: 'And if they leave me any food at all it stinks of putrefaction, the smell is intolerable, and no one could bear to come near it, even for a moment, even if he had an adamantine will. Yet bitter necessity that cannot be gainsaid, not only keeps me there, but forces me to pamper my accursed belly' (translation by E. V. Rieu).
226. *Aeneid*, III, 211 ff.
227. Dante, *Divine Comedy*, XXXII, 124–39.
228. Francis Beaumont (1584–1616) and John Fletcher (1576–1625), English dramatists; Lessing's reference is to the starvation of the shipwrecked pirates in Act III, Scene 1 of *The Sea-Voyage*, which he quotes at length in his footnote.
229. Giovanni Antonio de Sacchis Pordenone (1483–1539), Italian Mannerist painter.
230. Lessing's reference is to the French translation of Richardson's *Theory of Painting* (see note 62 above), p. 74.
231. The argument of Lessing's *Laocoon* ends at this point. The remaining four chapters, which are omitted here, are simply an appendix in which Lessing gives his initial reactions on the publication of Winckelmann's *History of the Art of Antiquity*: he defends his own dating of the Laocoon group against Winckelmann's contention that it dates from the age of Alexander the Great; he tries to prove (unsuccessfully, as it later emerged) that the statue of the so-called 'Borghese Gladiator' is in

fact a representation of the Athenian general Chabrias; and he corrects various minor errors in Winckelmann's references to ancient literary sources.

Lessing: Letter to Nicolai

1. The first paragraph, in which Lessing briefly discusses his current publications and a projected journey to Austria, is omitted in this translation.
2. The review was by Christian Garve (1742–98), and it appeared in 1769 in the *Allgemeine Deutsche Bibliothek*, a journal edited by Lessing's friend Christoph Friedrich Nicolai (1733–1811), to whom the present letter is addressed. The review is reprinted in *Lessings Laokoon*, edited by Hugo Blümner, second edition (Berlin, 1880), pp. 683–703.
3. Lessing refers to the planned continuation of the *Laocoon*, in which he intended to deal, among other things, with music, dance, and mime, and to elaborate at greater length his theory of 'natural' and 'arbitrary' signs in the arts. The continuation, which was never written, would have consisted of two further parts.
4. On Lessing's theory of signs, see Introduction, pp. 9 f.
5. The philosopher Moses Mendelssohn (1729–86), a close friend of Lessing and Nicolai.
6. The concluding paragraph, in which Lessing criticises a review of an unrelated work, is omitted in this translation.

Hamann: Aesthetica in nuce

Hamann's own notes

a. Judges, v, 10.
b. See Plato's *Cratylus*: '*Hermogenes* Indeed, Socrates, you do seem to me to be uttering oracles, exactly like an inspired prophet.

   Socrates Yes, Hermogenes, and I am convinced that the inspiration came to me from Euthyphro the Prospaltian [Hamann's text: the son of Pantios]. For I was with him and listening to him for a long time early this morning. So he must have been inspired, and he not only filled my ears but took possession of my soul with his superhuman wisdom. So I think this is our duty: we ought today to make use of this wisdom...but tomorrow, if the rest of you agree, we will conjure it away and purify ourselves, when we have found someone, whether priest or sophist, who is skilled in that kind of purifying...But ask me about any others [i.e. other names] you please, "that you may see what" Euthyphro's "horses are".' [Plato, *Cratylus*, translated by H. N. Fowler, Loeb Classical Library (London, 1926), 396d–397a and 407d; the quotation at the end is from Homer, *Iliad*, v, 221 f.].
c. '...as hieroglyphs are older than letters, so are parables older than arguments', says Bacon, my Euthyphro.
d. Ephesians, v, 13: 'for whatsoever doth make manifest is light'.
e. Manilius Astron. Lib. iv. [Marcus Manilius, *Astronomica*, iv, 895].
f. 'for being as a plant which comes from the lust of the earth without a formal seed, poetry has sprung up and spread abroad more than any other kind of learning' (Bacon, *de Augm. Scient.* Lib. ii Cap. 13). See Councillor Johann David Michaelis's observations on Robert Lowth, *de sacra poesi Praelectionibus Academicis Oxonii habitis*, p. 100 (18).

g. Judges, IX; II Chronicles, XXV, 18.

h. You learn to compose verses with a divided name;
   Thus you will become an imitator of the singer Lucilius.
            Ausonius *Epist.* v. [Ausonius, *Epistolae*, XVI, 37–8]

i. For an explanation, consult Wachter's *Naturae et Scripturae Concordia. Commentatio de literis ac numeris primaevis aliisque rebus memorabilibus cum ortu literarum coniunctis.* Lips. et Hafn. 1752, in the first section.[11]

j. The following passage in Petronius is to be understood as being of this kind of sign. I am obliged to quote it in its context, even if it has to be read as a satire on the philologist himself and his contemporaries:[12] 'Your flatulent and formless flow of words is a modern immigrant from Asia to Athens. Its breath fell upon the mind of ambitious youth like the influence of a baleful planet, and when the old tradition was once broken, eloquence halted and grew dumb. In a word, who after this came to equal the splendour of Thucydides? (He is called the Pindar of historians.) [Hamann's parenthesis] Or of Hyperides? (who bared Phryne's bosom to convince the judges of his good cause) [Hamann's parenthesis] Even poetry did not glow with the colour of health, but the whole of art, nourished on one universal diet, lacked the vigour to reach the grey hairs of old age. The decadence in painting was the same, as soon as Egyptian charlatans had found a short cut to this high calling.' [Petronius, *Satyricon*, 2; translated by Michael Heseltine, Loeb Classical Library (London, 1913)]. Compare this with the profound prophecy which Socrates put into the mouth of the Egyptian King Thamus about the inventions of Thoth, such that Phaedrus was moved to cry: 'Socrates, you easily make up stories of Egypt or any country you please.' [Plato, *Phaedrus*, 275 b].

k. The one metaphor comes from the Earl of Roscommon's *Essay on Translated Verse* and Howel's *Letters*.[14] Both, if I am not mistaken, borrowed the comparison from Saavedra.[15] The other is borrowed from one of the most excellent weekly journals, *The Adventurer*.[16] But there they are used *ad illustrationem* (to adorn the garment), here they are used *ad involucrum* (as a covering for the naked body), as Euthyphro's muse would distinguish.

l. Psalms, XXXIII, 9.

m. John, XX, 15–17.

n. Romans, IX, 21.

o. See Dr Young's *Letter to the Author of Grandison on Original Composition*.[23]

p. Acts, X, 11.

q. Lib. I, Od. 22. [Horace, *Odes*, I, 22; ode on Lalage to Aristius Fuscus]

r. 'Orgia nec Pentheum nec Orpheum tolerant.' Bacon, *de Augm. Scient.* Lib. II, Cap. XIII.[33]

s. Tibullus Libr. II, Eleg. I. [Tibullus, *Elegies*, II, 1]

t. 'L'art de personifier ouvre un champ bien moins borné et plus fertile que l'ancienne Mythologie.' Fontenelle sur la poésie en général. Tom. VIII.

u. John, III, 11. The following passage from Bacon, *de Augm.* Lib. IX may help to guard against the crude and ignorant idea of pronouncing the present imitation of cabbalistic style to be good or bad: 'in the free way of interpreting Scripture, there occur two excesses. The one presupposes such perfection in Scripture, that all philosophy likewise should be derived from its sources; as if all other philosophy were something profane and heathen. This distemper has principally grown up in the school of Paracelsus and some others; but the beginnings thereof came from the Rabbis and Cabalists. But these men do not gain their object; and instead of giving honour to the Scriptures as they suppose, they rather embase and pollute them...and as to seek divinity in philosophy is to seek the living among the dead, so to seek philosophy in divinity is to seek the dead among the living. The other method of interpretation which I set down as an excess, appears at the first glance sober and modest, yet in reality it both dishonours the Scriptures themselves, and is very injurious to the Church. This is, (in a word), when the divinely-inspired Scriptures are explained in the same way as human writings. But we ought to remember that there are two things which are known to God the author of the Scriptures, but unknown to man; namely, the secrets of the heart, and the successions of time. And therefore as the dictates of Scripture are written to the hearts of men, and comprehend the vicissitudes of all ages; with an eternal and certain foreknowledge of all heresies, contradictions, and differing and changing estates of the Church, as well in general as of the individual elect, they are not to be interpreted only according to the latitude and obvious sense of the place; or with respect to the occasion whereon the words were uttered; or in precise context with the words before or after; or in contemplation of the principal scope of the passage; but we must consider them to have in themselves, not only totally or collectively, but distributively also in clauses and words, infinite springs and streams of doctrines, to water every part of the Church and the souls of the faithful. For it has been well observed that the answers of our Saviour to many of the questions which were propounded to Him do not appear to the point, but as it were impertinent thereto. The reason whereof is twofold; the one, that knowing the thoughts of his questioners not as we men do by their words, but immediately and of himself, he answered their thoughts and not their words; the other, that He did not speak only to the persons then present, but to us also now living, and to men of every age and nation to whom the Gospel was to be preached. And this also holds good in other passages of Scripture.' [Bacon, *Works*, IV, 116–18].

v. See Kortholt's collection of letters by Leibniz, Vol. 3, Ep. 29.
w. See the poetic edict of the Emperor Octavius Augustus, according to which Virgil's last will *de abolenda Aeneide* [i.e. that the *Aeneid* should be destroyed] is said to have been nullified. One can concede whole-heartedly what Dr George Benson[45] has to say about the unity of sense, though he has scarcely developed his ideas, rather pulled them together with little thought, selection or smoothness. If he had tried to convey some earthly propositions about the unity of reading, his thoroughness would strike us more strongly. One cannot leaf through the four volumes of this paraphrastic explanation without a sly smile, nor miss the frequent passages where Dr Benson, the beam of popery in his own eye, inveighs against the mote in the Roman Church's, passages where he imitates our own official theologians when they applaud any blind and over-hasty bright idea honouring the creature more than the creator. First I would want to ask Dr Benson whether unity cannot exist without multiplicity? A lover of Homer is exposed to the same danger of losing his unity of sense by French paraphrasts like de la Motte or thoughtful dogmatists like Samuel Clarke. The literal or grammatical sense, the corporeal or dialectical sense, the Capernaitic[46] or historical sense are all profoundly mystical, and they are determined by minor circumstances of such a fleeting, arbitrary, spiritual nature that without ascending to heaven we cannot find the key to their understanding. We must not shrink from any journey across the seas or to the regions of such shadows as have believed, spoken, suffered for a day, for two, for a hundred or a thousand years – oh mysteries! –. The general history of the world can tell us hardly as much about them as can be writ on the

narrowest tombstone, or as can be retained by Echo, that nymph of the laconic memory. The thinker who wants to intimate to us the schemes which thoughtful writers in a critical place devise in order to convert their unbelieving brethren must have the keys to heaven and hell. Because Moses placed life in the blood,[47] all the baptised rabbis are afraid of the spirit and life of the prophets, which make a sacrifice of the literal understanding, the child of their heart (ἐν παραβολῇ)[48] and turn the streams of Eastern wisdom to blood. A dainty stomach will have no use for these stifled thoughts. – *Abstracta initiis occultis; Concreta maturitati conveniunt*, according to Bengel's *Sonnenweiser*.[49] (*plane pollex, non index.*[50])

x. Acts, II, 19.

y. Psalms, LXXIII, 21, 22.

z. 'La seule politique dans un Poème doit être de faire de bons vers', says M. Voltaire in his credo on the epic [Voltaire's *Idée de la Henriade*].

aa. Whatever M. Voltaire understands by religion, *Grammatici certant et adhuc sub Judice lis est*;[51] the philologist has as little to worry about here as his readers. We may look for it in the liberties of the Gallican Church, or in the flowers of sulphur of refined Naturalism, but neither explanation will do any harm to the unity of the sense.

bb. 'I take mythological fables to be a kind of breath from the traditions of more ancient nations, which fell into the pipes of the Greeks.' *De augm. scient.* Lib. II, Cap. XIII [Bacon, *Works*, IV, 317].

cc. 'Qu'un homme ait du jugement ou non, il profite également de vos ouvrages: il ne lui faut que de la MEMOIRE', is what a writer who utters prophecy has said to M. Voltaire's face. 'The rhapsodist should not forget this': Socrates in Plato's *Ion* [*Ion*, 539 e].

dd. Photius (in his *Amphilochiis Quaest.* CXX, which Johann Christoph Wolf has added to his cornucopia of critical and philological whimsies)[52] looks for a prophecy in the words of Herod to the Wise Men of the East – 'that I may come and worship him also' – and compares them with Caiaphas's statement in John XI, 49–52. He observes: 'There are perhaps other remarks of this kind, spoken by one of evil intention and murderous heart, which are ultimately prophetic.' Photius conceives Herod as a Janus bifrons,[53] who represented the Gentiles by his race and the Jews by his office. Many malicious and empty utterances (on which both master and servant pride themselves) might appear in a wholly different light if we were to ask ourselves from time to time whether they are speaking of their own accord or whether they should be understood as prophetic.

ee. Fontenelle sur la Poésie en général. 'Quand on saura employer d'une manière nouvelle les images fabuleuses, il est sûr qu'elles feront un grand effet.'

ff. '...et notho... – ...lumine...' Catull. *Carm Sec. ad Dian.* ['and with borrowed light', Catullus, *Hymn to Diana*, ll. 15 f.]

gg. '...And yet more bright
Shines out the Julian star, as moon outglows
        Each lesser light'

[Horace, *Odes*, I, 12, lines 46–8;
translation by John Marshall]

hh. II Corinthians, IV, 6.

ii. Revelation, XVI, 15.

jj. 'the image of the invisible God', Colossians, I, 15.

kk. 'partakers of the divine nature', II Peter, I, 4; 'to be conformed to the image of his Son', Romans, VIII, 29.

ll. Acts, xvii, 27, etc.

mm. Malachi, iii, 2.

nn. Bacon, *de interpretatione Naturae et regno Hominis*, Aphorism. cxxiv: 'But I say that those foolish and apish images of worlds which the fancies of men have created in philosophical systems must be utterly scattered to the winds. Be it known then how vast a difference there is between the Idols of the human mind and the Ideas of the divine. The former are nothing more than arbitrary abstractions; the latter are the creator's own stamp upon creation, impressed and defined in matter by true and exquisite lines. Truth therefore and utility are here the very same things: and the works of nature themselves are of greater value as pledges of truth than as contributing to the comforts of life' [Bacon, *Novum organum*, i, Aphorism 124, in *Works*, iv, 110]. Elsewhere Bacon repeats this reminder that we should use the works of nature not only as amenities of living but also as pledges of truth.

oo. 'for the gods also have a sense of humour'. Socrates in *Cratylus* [Plato, *Cratylus*, 406c.]

pp. Socrates to Phaedrus: 'They used to say, my friend, that the words of the oak in the holy place of Zeus at Dodona were the first prophetic utterances. The people of that time, not being so wise as you young folks, were content in their simplicity to hear an oak or a rock, provided only it spoke the truth; but to you, perhaps, it makes a difference who the speaker is and where he comes from, for you do not consider only whether his words are true or not.' [Plato, *Phaedrus*, 275 b–c; translated by H. N. Fowler, Loeb Classical Library (London, 1914)]

qq. I Samuel, xiv, 24.

rr. 'Brief as the lightning in the collied night,
That (in a spleen) unfolds heav'n and earth
And ere man has power to say: Behold!
The jaws of darkness do devour it up.'
                                    Shakespeare, *A Midsummer Night's Dream*

ss. 'C'est l'effet ordinaire de notre ignorance de nous peindre tout semblable à nous et de repandre nos portraits dans toute la nature', says Fontenelle in his *Histoire du Théâtre Franç.* 'Une grande passion est une espèce d'Ame, immortelle à sa manière et presque indépendante des Organes', Fontenelle in *Eloge de M. du Verney.*

tt. 'for Plato alone is worth all of them to me'. Cicero, *Brutus.*[62]

uu. Psalms, lix, 12.

vv. See Part 11 of the *Letters concerning Recent Literature* (*Briefe, die neueste Literatur betreffend*) passim, a little here, a little there, but mainly p. 131.[65]

ww. Ovid, *Metamorph.*, Lib. iii. [Hamann, in this footnote, goes on to quote Ovid's version of the myth of Narcissus at length, from *Metamorphoses*, iii, 415–510.]

xx. James, ii, 7.

yy. 'But indeed the chief business of magic was to note the correspondences between the architectures and fabrics of things natural and things civil. Neither are these only similitudes (as men of narrow observation may perhaps conceive them to be), but plainly the same footsteps of nature treading or printing upon different subjects and matters.' So Bacon in the third book of *De augmentis scientiarum*, in which he claims to explain the magic art also by means of a 'science of the universal consents of things', and in the light of this, the appearance of the Wise Men at Bethlehem. [Bacon, *Works*, iv, 339 and 366.]

zz. I Corinthians, xii, 31: 'and yet I show unto you a more excellent way'.

aaa. Revelation, xix, 10.

bbb. See pp. 66 and 67 of the *Answer to the Question as to the Influence of Opinions on Language*

and of Language on Opinions which received the prize awarded by the Royal
Academy of Sciences in 1759.[75] Also to be consulted in this connection: *Ars Punica
sive Flos Linguarum: The Art of Punning, or the Flower of Languages in seventy-nine Rules
for the farther Improvement of Conversation and Help of Memory.* By the Labour and
Industry of TUM PUN-SIBI.[76]

'Bons-mots prompted by an equivocation are deemed the very wittiest, though
not always concerned with jesting, but often even with what is important...for
the power to divert the force of a word into a sense quite different from that in
which other folk understand it seems to indicate a man of talent' (Cicero, *De Orat.*,
lib. 2) [Cicero, *De Oratore*, II, 250 and 254].

See the second edition [of *Ars Punica*], 1719, octavo. The author of this learned
work (of which I have, unfortunately, only a defective copy) is Swift, the glory
of the priesthood ('The glory of the Priesthood and the shame!', *Essay on
Criticism*).[77] It begins with definitions: logical, physical, and moral. In the logical
sense, 'Punning is essentially something of which it is said that it applies to
something else or is in any manner applied to something else.' According to the
natural science of the extravagant and whimsical Cardanus, 'Punning is an Art
of Harmonious Jingling upon Words, which passing in at the Ears and falling
upon the Diaphragma, excites a titillary Motion in those Parts, and this being
convey'd by the Animal Spirits into the Muscles of the Face raises the Cockles
of the Heart.' But according to Casuistry, it is 'a Virtue, that most effectually
promotes the End of good Fellowship'. An example of this artful virtue can be
found among others of the same ilk in the answer quoted above to the Punic
comparison between Mahomet the Prophet and Augustine the Church Father,
which resembles a hybrid lover of poetry, with an imagination half inspirational,
half scholastic, who is not nearly learned enough to appreciate the use of figurative
language properly, let alone be able to scrutinise religious experience.[78] The good
Bishop spoke Hebrew without knowing it, just as M. Jourdain spoke prose without
knowing it, and just as even today this raising and answering of learned questions
without knowing it, can reveal the barbarism of the age and the treachery of the
heart, at the cost of this profound truth: that we are all sinners, and devoid of
the glory that is ascribed to us, the lying prophet of Arabia as much as the good
African shepherd, as well as that clever wit (whom I should have named first of
all) who thought up that far-fetched comparison between the two believers in
providence by putting together such ridiculous parallel passages according to the
Punic theory of reason of our modern cabbalists, for whom every fig-leaf yields
a sufficient reason, and every insinuation a fulfilment.[79]

ccc. Our Luther's words (reading Augustine, it is said, spoiled his taste somewhat),
taken from his famous Preface to the Epistle to the Romans,[81] which I never weary
of reading, just as I never tire of his Preface to the Psalms. I have introduced this
passage by means of an accommodation, as they say, because in it Luther speaks
of the abyss of Divine Providence, and, after his admirable custom, rests upon
his dictum: 'that one cannot without suffering the cross and the pains of death
trade Providence against God without harm and secret rage'.

ddd. The devout reader will be able to complete the hymnic cadence of this section
for himself. My memory abandons me out of sheer wilfulness; 'Ever hastening
to the end...and what he cannot hope to accomplish...he omits'.[83]

eee. II Peter, II, 8.

fff. See note 76 of the editor, Lowth's *Praelect.*, xv; Algarotti, Vol. III.[88]

ggg. Gently rhyme creepeth into the heart, if 'tis not under compulsion; Harmony's staff and adornment, speech in our mem'ry it fixes. *Elegien und Briefe*, Strasburg, 1760.[89]

hhh. See the editor's fourth note to Lowth's third lecture, p. 149, and the fifty-first letter in the third part of the *Letters concerning Recent Literature*.

iii. Wouldn't it be funny if Herr Klopstock were to specify to his printer or to some Margot la Ravaudeuse,[93] as the philologist's muse, the reasons why he had his poetic feelings printed in separate lines, when the vulgar think they are concerned with *qualitatibus occultis* and the language of dalliance calls them feelings par excellence. Despite the gibberish of my dialect, I would willingly acknowledge Herr Klopstock's prosaic manner to be a model of classical perfection. From having read a few small specimens, I would credit this writer with a profound knowledge of his mother tongue, particularly of its prosody. Indeed, his musical metre would seem highly appropriate as a lyrical garb for a poet who seeks to shun the commonplace. I distinguish the original compositions of our Asaph[94] from his transformations of old church hymns, indeed even from his epic,[95] whose story is well-known, and resembles Milton's in profile at least, if not entirely.

jjj. 'the rhapsodists – interpreters of the interpreters' (Socrates in Plato's *Ion*).[99]

kkk. Procopius, *De bello persico*, I, 18.

lll. 'An asterisk [= little star] makes a light shine out, an obelisk [= little dagger] stabs and pierces' (Jerome's preface to the Pentateuch, cf. Diogenes Laertius on Plato). In skilful hands, these masoretic signs could equally well be used to rejuvenate the writings of Solomon, as one of the most recent commentators has interpreted two Epistles of St Paul by the method of paragraphs and tables.

Editor's notes

1. 'Aesthetics in a Nutshell'; the title is probably modelled on that of Christoph Otto von Schönaich's (1725–1809) *Complete Aesthetics in a Nutshell* (*Die ganze Ästhetik in einer Nuß*, 1754), a satirical work against Klopstock.

2. This, and the previous quotation from Judges, are given by Hamann in the original Hebrew.

3. Hamann quotes Horace in the original Latin (as he does with subsequent Latin authors). The translation is by John Marshall (1908).

4. The 'Archangel' (Michael) is an allusion to Johann David Michaelis (1717–91), theologian and philologist, whose rationalistic approach to the poetic language of the Old Testament aroused Hamann's strong opposition.

5. The 'wise idiot' is Socrates – and Hamann himself.

6. The allusion is again to Michaelis. The latter's work on Lowth, referred to in Hamann's footnote (f), is his annotated edition of Robert Lowth's (1710–87) lectures on Hebrew poetry, *Praelectiones de Sacra Poesi Hebraeorum* (originally published in England in 1753). The quotation from Bacon in the same footnote is from *De augmentis scientiarum*, Book II, Chapter 13. Translations of this and subsequent Latin quotations from Bacon's works are from the English versions in vols. IV and V of Francis Bacon, *Works*, edited by James Spedding, Robert Leslie Ellis, and Douglas Denon Heath, 14 vols. (London, 1857–74); the present quotation is from IV, 318.

7. The reference is to Antoine Yves Goguet (1716–58), *De l'origine des loix, des arts et des sciences et leur progrès chez les anciens peuples* (1758), I, 114 f. Goguet maintained

that the original purpose of clothing cannot have been to protect man from the elements, since it was worn in countries whose climate made such protection unnecessary.

8. A satirical reference to Lessing, whose essay *On the Use of Animals in Fables* (1759) argues that the writers of fables employed animals rather than men because of the 'universally known constancy of animal characters'; see G. E. Lessing, *Werke*, edited by Herbert G. Göpfert, 8 vols. (Munich, 1970–9), v, 398. Hamann, of course, finds Lessing's rationalistic explanation unacceptable.

9. Abaddon...Apollyon: see Revelation, IX, 11.

10. 'the limbs of the dismembered poet' (Horace, *Satires*, I, 4, line 62).

11. The philologist Johann Georg Wachter (1673–1757), in the work referred to, distinguished three phases in the development of writing (cyriological, symbolic or hieroglyphic, and characteristic) from pictorial representation to abstract signs. Hamann adds the terms 'poetic', 'historic', and 'philosophical' to indicate parallel phases in the development of human thought.

12. Hamann's satirical reference and quotation are aimed at the rationalistic philology of Michaelis (and its prolix expression).

13. See the Earl of Roscommon, *Poems*, (London, 1717), p. 9 (on a prose translation of Horace).

14. James Howell (c. 1594–1666), *Familiar Letters* (1645–55).

15. That is, Cervantes (Miguel Cervantes de Saavedra).

16. *The Adventurer*, No. 49, 24 April 1753.

17. The reference is to Bacon's distinction between two types of knowledge: divine revelation, and the empirical data of the senses (Bacon, *Works*, I, 520).

18. See Revelation, IV, 6.

19. See I Kings, XVIII, 44.

20. The reference is to St Paul, as Apostle to the Gentiles and a scholar learned in the Scriptures.

21. A combined reference to the creation of woman from Adam's rib (Genesis, II, 21–3) and to Endymion, the beautiful youth whom the moon-goddess Selene visited while he slept.

22. A reference to Edward Young's (1683–1765) poem *Night Thoughts* (1742–4).

23. A reference to Edward Young's *Conjectures on Original Composition, in a Letter to the Author of Sir Charles Grandison* (1759).

24. A reference to the Jewish philosopher and critic Moses Mendelssohn (1729–86), friend of Lessing and contributor, with Lessing and Nicolai, to the *Letters concerning Recent Literature* (1759–65); the 'passing Levite' alludes to Luke, x, 32 (the parable of the Good Samaritan).

25. See Mark, VII, 4 and 8.

26. Horace, *Ars poetica*, 127 (*Difficile est proprie communia dicere*): 'It is difficult to deal adequately with familiar subjects'; or, in Hamann's context, 'It is utterly impossible to call vulgar things by their proper name.'

27. See Genesis, XVII, 12.

28. According to Adelung's dictionary 'white gentian' was a vulgar expression in German for the white excrement of dogs.

29. A reference to the proverbial ugliness of Aesop.

30. A reference to Lessing, whose *Fables* were published in 1759.

31. The geographical names are taken from Horace's ode (I, 22) to Aristius; the target of satire is again Lessing, who wrote frivolous Anacreontic poetry in his early years.

32. A reference to Lessing's contention, in the *Letters concerning Recent Literature*, that

the private life of an author is irrelevant to his writing (see Lessing, *Werke*, ed. Göpfert, v, 43).

33. 'Orgies cannot endure either Pentheus or Orpheus' (that is, both were torn to pieces by frenzied Maenads); see Bacon, *Works*, iv, 335.

34. Another reference to Michaelis; also to John, iii, 10.

35. Personification (prosopopoeia) was employed in ancient rhetoric not only as an everyday figure of speech, but also as a means of introducing deceased personages as spokesmen in dialogues. (Hamann himself is about to address an ironic dialogue to the 'Rabbi' Michaelis.)

36. 'if as a NUT I count as one of them' (Ovid, *Nux*, 19); an allusion to the title of Hamann's essay.

37. A reference to the weekly newspaper *Ordentliche Wöchentliche Kayserliche Reichs-Postzeitung*, published in the Imperial city of Frankfurt; its motto was *Relata refero* ('I report reports').

38. Hamann refers to the newspaper announcement of the publication of the second part of Michaelis's edition of Lowth's work on Hebrew poetry (see note 6 above), which appeared in 1761.

39. See Judges, v, 28.

40. *sermones fideles*: true expressions (as distinct from the 'cabbalistic' style of the present work).

41. *Orbis pictus sensualium* (1657) by the Czech scholar and educationalist Johann Amos Comenius (1592–1671), an illustrated textbook designed to teach children by concrete, visual methods.

42. Friedrich Muzelius (1684–1753), philologist and author of school textbooks.

43. A reference to Michaelis's emphasis on geographical and climatic factors in his rationalistic exegesis of the Scriptures.

44. Quoted by Hamann in Latin from *Anthologia Latina*, 672, lines 4, 20, and 8. The quotation expresses Hamann's unease at the violence done to Scripture by such interpreters as Michaelis.

45. George Benson (1699–1762), liberal theologian and author of various paraphrases, with commentaries, of books of the New Testament. (Michaelis had translated some of Benson's work.) Benson rejected the notion of the multiple sense of Scriptural passages, arguing for the unity of sense (that is, every passage has only a single meaning). Antoine Houdart de la Motte (1672–1731) and Samuel Clarke (1675–1729) applied the same thesis to Homer; for further details, see Sven-Aage Jørgensen's notes to his edition of Hamann's *Sokratische Denkwürdigkeiten* and *Aesthetica in nuce* (Stuttgart, 1968), pp. 102–4.

46. Capernaitic: pertaining to the doctrine of transubstantiation.

47. See Leviticus, xvii, 11.

48. 'as an example'.

49. 'The abstract is appropriate to dark beginnings, the concrete to maturity': inaccurate quotation from Johann Albrecht Bengel's (1687–1752) *Gnomon* [= German *Sonnenweiser*] *Novi Testamenti* (1742). Hamann wishes to suggest by this quotation that the true prophetic sense of the Scriptures, denied by the literalist Benson, will come to light in the fullness of time.

50. 'Plainly a thumb, not an index finger': pun from Cicero, *Epistles to Atticus*, xiii, 46, as a humorous indication (*index*) of the importance of the preceding quotation.

51. Horace, *Ars poetica*, line 78: 'scholars argue, and the case is so far undecided'. Hamann now transfers his satire to Voltaire as a leader of the rationalistic Enlightenment.

52. Johann Christoph Wolf (1683–1739) quotes the passage from Photius (820–91) in his *Curae philologicae et criticae*, IV (Hamburg, 1735).

53. Janus bifrons: the Roman god of doorways, with two faces looking in opposite directions.

54. A reference to the *querelle des anciens et des modernes*.

55. Typically oblique reference to the academic degrees of Master (M) and Doctor (D, the Roman numeral for 500, and half of M or 1,000).

56. Bernhard Nieuwentyt (1654–1720), Dutch scientist and physico-theologian; he, Newton, and Buffon are named simply as representatives of modern science, the Enlightenment's faith in which Hamann did not share.

57. Homer, *Iliad*, I, 1; Hamann omits the alphas and omegas in quoting the Greek, producing an effect similar to that of deleting the 'a's and 'o's from the English translation 'Sing, O Goddess, the wrath of Peleus's son Achilles'.

58. A reference to such secular philosophers and freethinkers of the Enlightenment as Gassendi, La Mettrie, and Frederick the Great (who much admired the Epicurean philosophy of Lucretius).

59. A reference to modern scientific determinism, as a counterpart to the determinism of the ancient Stoics.

60. An allusion to Matthew, XIX, 12 and to the Church Father Origen (c. 185 – c. 254), who castrated himself for the sake of religion.

61. The 'prince of this aeon' is Frederick the Great; the 'court fools', 'Gauls', and *esprits forts* are the French freethinkers (La Mettrie, Voltaire, etc.) with whom Frederick associated.

62. Antimachus, in the anecdote alluded to, was reading a long poem, and all of his audience except Plato left the lecture room. He then made the remark quoted by Hamann (Cicero, *Brutus*, LI, 191).

63. Horace, *Ars poetica*, line 476 (the final line of the poem).

64. An allusion to Winckelmann, and an example of Hamann's hostility towards neo-classicism.

65. The reference is to an (anonymous) attack by Nicolai, in the *Letters* referred to, on a volume of poems which had impressed Hamann favourably. Hamann throws back at the anonymous critic some of the abuse the latter had directed at the poems. For further details, see Hans-Martin Lumpp, *Philologia crucis. Zu Johann Georg Hamanns Auffassung von der Dichtkunst* (Tübingen, 1970), pp. 87–9.

66. See John, IV, 22.

67. See Bacon, *Works*, IV, 319–20: Pan (Nature) is the son of Penelope (formless matter) and her suitors (the Platonic Ideas or Forms), according to one myth discussed by Bacon, who himself suggests that Nature is rather the son of matter and Mercury (the Logos or Word of God). Hamann's following sentence presents Odysseus, the true master, as a typological forerunner of Christ, appearing in lowly form (as a beggar).

68. Allusion to a Danish scientific expedition (1761–7) to 'Arabia felix' (Southern Arabia) under Carstens Niebuhr (1733–1815), which was mounted at the suggestion of Michaelis, who remains the chief target of Hamann's satire.

69. Another allusion to Frederick the Great and his circle of *philosophes*.

70. See II Kings, IV, 38–42.

71. See Isaiah, LXIII, 10.

72. Psalms, L, 13.

73. See John, I, 18 and XIII, 23–5.

74. See John, II, 8–10.

75. The prize essay referred to is by Michaelis, and the reference is to remarks by him on Augustine's Punic (Carthaginian) origin and native language. Hamann goes on to pun on the word 'Punic' in his footnote, and makes fun, at considerable length, of Michaelis's learned deliberations.

76. Hamann, as his subsequent comments make clear, shares the belief of his contemporaries that the work was by Jonathan Swift. It is now ascribed to Thomas Sheridan (see Jørgensen, p. 132).

77. Pope, *Essay on Criticism*, line 694 (on Erasmus).

78. All of this is oblique criticism of Michaelis and his attempts to rationalise Biblical references to miracles etc. as merely figurative expressions.

79. Satirical references to the philosophical doctrines of the Enlightenment such as the Leibnizian principle of sufficient reason.

80. The quotation is from St Augustine's commentary (IX, 3) on St John: see J. P. Migne, *Patrologia Latina*, XXXV, 1379 f.

81. See Martin Luther, *Vorreden zur Heiligen Schrift* (Munich, 1934), pp. 78–93. Luther warns, in the passage referred to, against philosophical speculation on the mysteries of predestination and divine grace.

82. The quotation is from Luther's translation of the *Te Deum*.

83. Fragmentary quotation from Horace, *Ars poetica*, lines 148 ff.

84. See II Kings, VI, 25.

85. The reference is to Cleopatra, who dissolved a pearl to drink Antony's health.

86. That is, in the Catholic mass (Rome) or the austere Calvinist church (Geneva).

87. Persius, *Satires*, I, 113; snakes, sacred to the house, were used as a sign to warn against desecration. Here, the satirist responds ironically to protests by influential persons against his attacks.

88. Michaelis, in his edition of Lowth, discusses wordplay at length, and considers it of little aesthetic merit; the second reference is to Francesco Algarotti's (1712–64) *Oeuvres*, III, 76 (*Essai sur la rime*).

89. The collection of poems quoted is by Ludwig Heinrich von Nicolay (1737–1820).

90. Plato, *Symposium*, 185c–e; Paul Scarron (1610–60), French poet.

91. Friedrich Gottlieb Klopstock (1724–1803), the most acclaimed lyric poet in Germany in the 1760s and 1770s, established the use of free rhythms and rhymeless verse in German.

92. The 'thorough critics' are Michaelis (as editor of Lowth's lecture) and Lessing, whose comments (in the *Letters concerning Recent Literature*) Hamann here quotes. The praise of the 'thorough critics' is, of course, ironic. Hamann valued Klopstock for his piety and Biblical language as well as for his verse.

93. According to Jørgensen, p. 142, the title of a novel by Fougeret de Monbron.

94. Asaph: psalmist (see Psalms, L and LXXIII–LXXXIII); circumlocution for Klopstock as a singer of sacred songs.

95. References to Klopstock's *Geistliche Lieder* (1758) and his epic poem *The Messiah*, of which only part had been published when Hamann wrote.

96. Note Hamann's interest in folk poetry, which Herder was soon to echo more fully in his essay on Ossian (see pp. 154–61).

97. Cicero, *Brutus*, LXXV, 262; that is, 'who will merely use my writings as wastepaper'.

98. Horace, *Odes*, I, 2, lines 1–8 (translation by John Marshall); the reference in the poem to Deucalion's flood and the return of ancient chaos is for Hamann a figure for the coming Day of Judgement.

99. Plato, *Ion*, 535a; compare p. 144 above: 'The opinions of the philosophers are

variant readings of Nature, and the precepts of the theologians variants of the Scriptures. The author is the best interpreter of his own words.'

100. Revelation, xiv, 7.

Herder: Extract from a Correspondence on Ossian and the Songs of Ancient Peoples

1. This work was first published in an anonymous collection of five essays, edited by Johann Gottfried Herder, entitled *Von deutscher Art und Kunst. Einige fliegende Blätter (On German Character and Art. A Collection of Broadsheets)* (Hamburg, 1773). Herder's epistolary essay on Ossian was the first item in the collection. His essay on Shakespeare, also included here (pp. 161–76), was the second. The remaining contributions were Johann Wolfgang Goethe's *Von deutscher Baukunst (On German Architecture)*, a eulogy of Gothic architecture, and of Strasbourg Cathedral in particular; Paolo Frisi's *Versuch über die Gothische Baukunst (Essay on Gothic Architecture)*, translated from the Italian original of 1766; and Justus Möser's *Deutsche Geschichte (German History)*, an extract from the preface to Möser's *History of Osnabrück* (1768). The present translation of Herder's essay on Ossian omits the numerous folksongs and ballads from various countries which Herder cites as examples of folk poetry, as well as sections in which he discusses Klopstock and various lesser poets of the time.
2. The correspondent is fictitious. His supposed contempt for folk poetry is a rhetorical device which enables Herder to defend such literature in a direct and vigorous manner.
3. James Macpherson's *The Works of Ossian, the Son of Fingal*, 2 vols. (London, 1765) appeared in the German translation of Michael Denis as *Die Gedichte Ossians, eines alten celtischen Dichters*, 3 vols. (Vienna, 1768–9).
4. 'among the dregs of Rome' (Cicero, *Letters to Atticus*, ii, 1).
5. Herder dismissed all (justified) suggestions that the poems were largely the work of Macpherson himself, and accepted the latter's claim that he had merely translated authentic poems by the ancient Celtic bard.
6. The break in the text is Herder's. It is designed to preserve the fiction that this is a series of extracts from an actual correspondence.
7. Denis's translation is in German hexameters, a form popularised in Germany by the poets Friedrich Gottlieb Klopstock (1724–1803) and Christian Ewald von Kleist (1715–59).
8. 'hence the tears' (Terence, *Andria*, i, 126).
9. Herder here ironically alludes to his own earlier review of Denis's translation in the periodical *Allgemeine deutsche Bibliothek* (1768).
10. The following passage, in which Herder cites other popular poems which would resist translation into the formal hexameter, is omitted.
11. The references are to Olaus Wormius (1588–1654), author of *Danica litteratura antiquissima vulga gothica dicta* (Copenhagen, 1636) and other works on ancient Norse poetry; Thomas Bartholinus (died 1690), author of *Antiquitatum de causis contemptae a Danis adhuc gentilibus mortis libri tres* (Copenhagen, 1689); Johann Peringer de Peringskiöld (1654–1720), author of *Monumenta Sueo-Gothica* (Stockholm, 1710–19); and Olaus Verelius (1618–82), editor of the *Hervarar-Saga* (Upsala, 1672) and other Norse sagas.
12. The following short discussion of alliterative verse-forms in Old Norse poetry is omitted here.

13. Pierre François Xavier de Charlevoix (1682–1761), *Histoire et description générale de la Nouvelle-France* (Paris, 1744); Joseph François Lafiteau, *Moeurs des Sauvages Amériquains, comparées aus moeurs des premiers temps* (Paris, 1723); Woodes Rogers (died 1732), *A Cruising Voyage Round the World* (London, 1712); Cadwallader Colden (1688–1776), *The History of the Five Indian Nations* (New York, 1727).

14. Henry Timberlake, *Memoirs of Lt Henry Timberlake...* (London, 1765).

15. In his letter to Rousseau of 30 August 1755, Voltaire ironically distanced himself in such terms from Rousseau's praise of primitive society in his *Discours sur les origines et les fondements de l'inégalité parmi les hommes.*

16. A long section follows, in which Herder describes how his appreciation for primitive poetry was first awakened by reading it in an appropriately 'natural' environment (on board ship, in stormy weather, on his voyage from the Baltic to France in 1769). He then describes hearing Latvian folksongs at first hand, and, after further criticisms of Denis's hexameter translation of Ossian, quotes a selection of folk poems from various countries, including the ballad 'Edward' from Thomas Percy's *Reliques of Ancient Poetry.*

17. 'poets' or 'singers'.

18. Greek painter of the fourth century B.C., renowned for the likelike quality of his work.

19. There follows a discussion (omitted here) of various contemporary German poets, who are classified under the two headings which Herder has just specified. More examples of genuine folksong, including 'Sweet William's Ghost' from Percy's *Reliques*, are then quoted.

20. 'Sweet William's Ghost', which Herder has just quoted in full in his own German translation.

21. Lessing edited and published a collection of epigrams by the German baroque poet Friedrich von Logau (1604–55) in 1759, and a collection of poems by Andreas Scultetus (c. 1622–47) in 1771.

22. Justus Friedrich Wilhelm Zachariae (1726–77), a friend of Lessing's and himself a poet, published a two-volume anthology (Brunswick, 1766–71) of German poetry which included works by the baroque poets Martin Opitz (1597–1639), Paul Fleming (1609–40), and Andreas Gryphius (1616–64).

23. Herder proceeds, in the following (omitted) passage, to quote German poems, including Goethe's famous 'Heidenröslein', which is presented as an anonymous folksong like the rest. He praises its popular language and elisions as the antithesis of over-polished modern verse.

24. Herder goes on to quote further examples of the free use of language in popular poetry, and praises Luther's hymns in particular. He again attacks slavish adherents of (neo-classical) poetic rules, and defends Klopstock's odes for their bold inversions and innovative language.

25. Thomas Gray (1716–71), *Odes* ('The Progress of Poesy', 'The Bard') (Strawberry Hill, 1757); Mark Akenside (1721–70), author of *The Pleasures of the Imagination* (1744) and of various odes which appeared in his collected poems in 1772; William Mason (1725–97), a friend of Gray and author of *Poems* (London, 1764).

26. The essay concludes with a 'Postscript', in which Herder ecstatically praises Klopstock's newly published *Odes* (1771), and laments the inadequacy of recent musical settings of German poetry.

Herder: Shakespeare

1. On the original edition of this essay, see note 1 to the preceding essay by Herder (p. 286 above).

2. The image is taken from Mark Akenside's didactic poem *The Pleasures of the Imagination* (1744), III, 550–9, which Herder paraphrases; cf. also note 25 to Herder's essay on Ossian (p. 287 above).

3. The editors whom Herder has in mind probably include Alexander Pope, Samuel Johnson, and Christoph Martin Wieland (1733–1813), whose eight-volume translation of *Shakespears theatralische Werke* was published at Zurich in 1762–6.

4. Herder, without naming him, is here contradicting Lessing who, in Section 46 of his *Hamburg Dramaturgy*, had declared that the Greek tragedies simplified originally complex plots in the interests of those unities of place and time which were necessitated by the constant presence of one and the same chorus on stage: see Lessing, *Werke*, edited by Herbert G. Göpfert, 8 vols. (Munich, 1970–9), IV, 443.

5. Herder's account of Greek tragedy in this paragraph closely follows that of Aristotle in Chapters 4 and 6 of his *Poetics*.

6. Herder's criticism is directed at the poetics of Corneille and French classical tragedy, and at its German imitators such as Johann Christoph Gottsched (1700–66), whose *Critical Poetics* (*Kritische Dichtkunst*) of 1740 had attempted to legislate for the German stage.

7. Aristotle's *Poetics*, Chapter 7.

8. That is, the French. Herder's contemptuous remarks on French neo-classicism echo Lessing's strictures on it in his *Hamburg Dramaturgy* of 1767–9.

9. The reference is again to Lessing's *Hamburg Dramaturgy*, particularly Sections 46–8: see Lessing's *Werke*, ed. Göpfert, IV, 443–56.

10. Prosper Jolyot de Crébillon (1674–1762), French tragedian whose dramas include *Idoménée* (1705), *Rhadamiste et Zénobie* (1711), and *Catilina* (1748).

11. *Astrée*, a pastoral romance in five volumes (Paris, 1607–28) by Honoré d'Urfé (1567–1625).

12. *Clélie*, a romance in ten volumes (Paris, 1654–60) by Madeleine de Scudéry (1607–1701).

13. *Aspasia*: the name of more than one French novel of the eighteenth century. It is uncertain whether Herder is referring to one of them in particular, or to them all as a class. Aspasia is also, however, a character in Madeleine de Scudéry's romance of chivalry *Artamène ou le Grand Cyrus* (1648).

14. 'The Britons, divided from the rest of the world'; after Virgil, *Eclogues*, I, 66.

15. 'pupil [literally 'chicken'] of Aristotle'.

16. Henry Home (Lord Kames) (1696–1782); author of *Elements of Criticism* (Edinburgh, 1762).

17. Richard Hurd (1720–1808), editor of *Q. Horatii Flacci Ars Poetica. Epistola ad Pisones* (London, 1749), the commentary to which contained an analysis of the different kinds of drama.

18. Aristotle, *Poetics*, Chapter 7: 'a whole is that which has a beginning, a middle, and an end... well-constructed plots must neither begin nor end in a haphazard way, but must conform to the pattern I have been describing'.

19. Aristotle, *Poetics*, Chapter 7: 'in just the same way as living creatures and organisms compounded of many parts must be of a reasonable size, so that they can be easily taken in by the eye, so too plots must be of a reasonable length, so that they may be easily held in the memory'.

20. In his comparison, in the *Hamburg Dramaturgy* (Sections 11–12), of the unconvincing ghost in Voltaire's *Semiramis* with the far more effective ghost in Shakespeare's *Hamlet* (Lessing's *Werke*, ed. Göpfert, IV, 281–6).

21. The young Herder was already studying the much decried heretic Spinoza. Along with Lessing and Goethe, he was shortly to initiate a wave of enthusiasm in Germany for Spinoza's nature pantheism, an enthusiasm which was shared by Schelling, Novalis, and other German Romantics: see David Bell, *Spinoza in Germany from 1670 to the Age of Goethe* (London, 1984), especially pp. 38–70 and 97–146.

22. Herder's criticisms here are directed in particular at Pierre Corneille's *Discours des trois unités* (*Théâtre de Pierre Corneille*, vol. III (Amsterdam, 1664)).

23. Mohammed's dream of his assumption into heaven.

24. Order of succession and simultaneity (order in time and space); cf. Lessing's use of these categories in Chapter 16 of his *Laocoon* (pp. 98–103 above).

25. The reference is to William Warburton's (1698–1779) eight-volume edition of Shakespeare (London, 1747).

26. Elizabeth Montagu (1720–1800), *An Essay on the Writings and Genius of Shakespeare, compared with the Greek and French dramatic Poets, with some Remarks upon the Misrepresentations of Mons. de Voltaire* (London, 1769); Herder reviewed the German translation (by J. J. Eschenburg) of the work in 1771 (*Sämtliche Werke*, v, 312–17).

27. See note 16 above.

28. Heinrich Wilhelm von Gerstenberg (1737–1823), 'Versuch über Shakespears Werke und Genie', in Gerstenbergs periodical *Briefe über Merkwürdigkeiten der Literatur*, 2, Letters 14–18 (1766); the classification after Polonius occurs in Letter 17 (reprinted in *Sturm und Drang. Kritische Schriften*, edited by Erich Loewenthal, third edition (Heidelberg, 1972), pp. 27–30).

29. Johannes Stobaeus, Greek anthologist of the sixth century A.D., whose *Florilegium* contained numerous extracts from a wide range of Greek authors. The English anthology of Shakespeare to which Herder refers is William Dodd's *The Beauties of Shakespeare*, 2 vols. (London, 1752). J. J. Eschenburg (1743–1820), German translator of Shakespeare, planned a similar anthology in German.

30. Richard II and Falstaff.

31. *Hamlet*, II, 2, 88.

32. The actor David Garrick (1717–79).

33. These words are addressed to the young Goethe, who had already been infected by Herder's enthusiasm for Shakespeare, and whose essay *Von deutscher Baukunst* (*On German Architecture*), in praise of Gothic architecture, was printed immediately after Herder's essay on Shakespeare in the collection *On German Character and Art* (1773) in which these works first appeared.

34. The reference is to the original version (1771) of Goethe's drama of chivalry, *Götz von Berlichingen*, which was entitled *History of Gottfried von Berlichingen with the Iron Hand*. Although Herder was privately much impressed by the drama, the sharp criticisms he sent in a (now lost) letter to Goethe led Goethe to revise the play before it was published in 1773.

35. 'He has striven! now he rests!'

Schiller: On Naive and Sentimental Poetry

Schiller's own notes

a. Kant, who was the first, as far as I know, who began to reflect purposefully upon this phenomenon, remarks that if we were to hear the song of the nightingale imitated with the utmost deception by a human voice and had abandoned ourselves to the impression with all our feelings, our entire delight would disappear with the destruction of the illusion. See the chapter on the intellectual interest in the beautiful in the *Critique of Aesthetic Judgment*.[2] Anyone who has learned to admire the author only as a great thinker will be pleased here to come upon a trace of his heart and be convinced by this discovery of the man's high philosophical calling (which absolutely requires the combination of both characteristics).

b. In a note appended to the 'Analytic of the Sublime' (*Critique of Aesthetic Judgment*, p. 225, 1st edition) Kant likewise distinguishes these threefold ingredients in the feeling of the naive, but he supplies another explanation. 'Something compounded of both (the animal feeling of pleasure and the spiritual feeling of respect) is found in naivety, which is the bursting forth of that sincerity originally natural to mankind in opposition to the art of dissimulation that has become second nature. We laugh at a simplicity that does not yet understand how to conceal itself, yet we are delighted at the simplicity of nature which here thwarts that art. We expected some routine mode of utterance, artificial and carefully contrived to make a fine impression, and yet we see unspoiled innocent nature which we no more expected to see than he who displayed it intended it to be exposed. That the fair but false impression which ordinarily weighs so much in our judgement is now suddenly transformed into nothing – that the scoundrel in us, as it were, is revealed – sets the mind in motion in two opposed directions one after the other, giving the body a salutary shock. A mixture of solemnity and high esteem appears in this play of the faculty of judgement, because something infinitely superior to all conventional manners, namely, purity of thought (or ar least an inclination thereto) is, after all, not wholly extinguished in human nature. But since it appears only fleetingly and the art of dissimulation swiftly draws a veil before it, there is at the same time an admixture of regret, which is an emotion of tenderness; an emotion which, taken as a joke, is very easily combined with good-humoured laughter (and in fact is usually so combined), and which simultaneously compensates for the embarrassment of whoever gave rise to the occasion for not yet being experienced in the ways of men.'[8] – I confess that this mode of explanation does not entirely satisfy me, and this principally because it asserts of the naive as a whole what is at most true only of a species of it, the naive of surprise, of which I shall speak later. It certainly arouses laughter if somebody exposes himself by naivety, and in some cases this laughter may derive from a preceding expectation that fails to materialise. But even naivety of the noblest sort, the naive of temperament, arouses a smile always, which however is scarcely due to any expectation that comes to nothing, but that can only be explained by the contrast between certain behaviour and the conventionally accepted and expected forms. I doubt also whether the regret which is mingled in our feeling about the latter kind of naivety refers to the naive person and not rather to ourselves or to humanity at large, whose decay we are reminded of in such cases. It is too clearly a moral regret which must have some nobler object than the physical ills by which sincerity is threatened in the ordinary course of things, and this object can hardly be any other than the loss of truth and simplicity in mankind.

c. Perhaps I should say quite briefly: *truth victorious over deceit*; but the concept of the naive seems to me still more inclusive, since any form of simplicity that triumphs over artifice, and natural freedom over stiffness and constraint, excites a similar emotion in us.

d. A child is badly behaved if, out of greediness, foolhardiness, or impetuosity, it acts in opposition to the prescripts of a good education, but it is naive if its free and healthy nature rids it of the mannerisms of an irrational education, such as the awkward posturings of the dancing master. The same occurs with the naive in its wholly figurative meaning, when it is transferred from the human to the inanimate. Nobody would find naive the spectacle of a badly tended garden in which the weeds have the upper hand, but there is certainly something naive when the free growth of spreading branches undoes the painstaking work of the topiarist in a French garden. Likewise, it is in no way naive if a trained horse performs its lessons badly out of natural stupidity, but something of the naive is present if it forgets them out of natural freedom.

e. Since the naive depends solely on the manner in which something is said or done, this characteristic disappears from view as soon as the matter itself assumes a predominant or even contradictory impression either by its causes or its effects. Naivety of this kind can even disclose a crime, but then we have neither the calm nor the time to direct our attention to the form of the disclosure, and revulsion at the personal character swallows up our pleasure in the natural character. Just as our outraged feelings deprive us of moral delight in the sincerity of nature when we discover a crime as a result of naivety, so also the compassion excited destroys our malicious joy when we witness someone endangered by his naivety.
[Translator's note: the references to disclosure of a crime appear to anticipate Schiller's poem of 1797, *Die Kraniche des Ibykus*, in which a pair of murderers betray themselves because they see in the cranes flying overhead an omen of the pursuing Furies.]

f. But also only with the Greeks; since just such an active motion and such a rich fullness of human life as surrounded the Greeks was required to breathe life even into the lifeless and to pursue the image of humanity with this avidity. For example, the world peopled by Ossian was shabby and uniform;[13] the inanimate world that surrounded it, however, was broad, colossal and powerful, so it imposed itself and asserted its rights even over the people. In the songs of this poet, therefore, inanimate nature (in contrast with the people) figures much more as an object of sentiment. Yet even Ossian complains of a decline of humanity and, as small among his people as the extent of civilisation and its perversions was, yet the awareness of it was still lively and penetrating enough to drive the emotion-laden moral poet back to the inanimate and to pour out in his songs that elegiac tone that makes them so moving and attractive to us.

g. It is perhaps not superfluous to remark that if here the modern poets are set over against the ancients, the difference of manner rather than of time is to be understood. We possess in modern times, even most recently, naive works of poetry in all classes, even if no longer of the purest kind and, among the old Latin, even among the Greek poets, there is no lack of sentimental ones. Not only in the same poet, even in the same work one often encounters both species combined, as, for example, in *The Sorrows of Werther*, and such creations will always produce the greater effects.

h. Molière, as a naive poet, is said to have left it in every case to the opinion of his chambermaid what should stand or fall in his comedies; it might also be wished that the masters of the French buskin had occasionally tried the same experiment with their tragedies. But I would not advise that a similar experiment be undertaken with Klopstock's *Odes*, with the finest passages in the *Messiah*, in Paradise Lost, in *Nathan the Wise*, or in many other pieces.[20] Yet what am I saying? – the test has really been undertaken, and Molière's chambermaid chops logic back and forth in our critical literature, philosophical and belletristic journals and travel accounts, on poetry, art and the like, except that, as is proper, she does so less tastefully on German soil than on French, as only becomes the servants' hall of German literature.

i. Anyone who observes the impression that naive poetry makes on him and is able to separate from it that part which is due to the content will find this impression always joyous, always pure, always serene, even in the case of very pathetic objects; with sentimental poetry it will always be somewhat solemn and intense. This is because with naive accounts, regardless of their subject matter, we always rejoice in the truth, in the living presence of the object in our imagination, and seek nothing further beyond these; whereas with the sentimental we have to reconcile the representation of imagination with an idea of reason and hence always fluctuate between two different conditions.

j. In *Nathan the Wise* this is not the case; here the frosty nature of the theme has cooled the whole art work. But Lessing himself knew that he was not writing a tragedy and simply forgot in his own case, humanly enough, his own doctrine propounded in the *Hamburg Dramaturgy*[26] that the poet is not permitted to employ the tragic form for other than a tragic purpose. Without very substantial changes it would hardly be possible to transform this dramatic poem into a good tragedy; but with merely incidental changes it might have yielded a good comedy. For the latter purpose the pathetic would have to be sacrificed, for the former its reasoning, and there can be no question upon which of the two the beauty of the poem most depends.

k. That I employ the terms satire, elegy, and idyll in a wider sense than is customary, I will hardly have to explain to readers who penetrate deeper into the matter. My intention in doing so is by no means to disrupt the boundaries which have been set for good reasons by usage hitherto for satire and elegy as well as idyll; I look merely at the *mode of perception* predominant in these poetic categories, and it is sufficiently well known that this cannot be accommodated at all within those narrow limits. We are not moved elegiacally solely by the elegy which is exclusively so called: the dramatic and epic poets can also move us in the elegiac manner. In the *Messiah*,[31] in Thomson's *Seasons*, in *Paradise Lost*, in *Jerusalem Delivered*, we find numerous depictions which are otherwise proper only to the .idyll, the elegy, and to satire. Likewise, to a greater or lesser degree, in almost every pathetic poem. But that I account the idyll as an elegiac category does seem to require justification. It should be recalled, though, that here I speak only of that kind of idyll that is a species of sentimental poetry, to the essence of which belongs the notion that nature is *opposed* to art, and the ideal to actuality. Even if this is not rendered explicit by the artist and he offers to our view a pure and spontaneous portrait of unspoiled nature or of the ideal fulfilled, yet that opposition is still within his heart and will betray itself in every stroke of the brush, even against his will. For even if this were not so, then the very language which he must employ, because it bears the spirit of the age and has undergone the influence of art, would serve to remind us of actuality and its limitations, of civilisation with its mannerism; indeed, our own heart would oppose to that picture of pure nature its experience of corruption and thus render the mode of perception elegiac in us even though this had not been sought by the poet. This last is so unavoidable that even the highest delight which the finest works of the naive genus of ancient and modern times assure to the cultivated individual does not for long remain pure, but sooner or later will be accompanied by an elegiac mood. Finally, I would still observe that the division attempted here, for the very reason that it is simply based on the distinction of mode of perception, should by no means whatever determine the division of poetry itself nor the derivation of poetic genres; since the poet is in no way bound, even in a single work, to the same mode of perception, that division therefore cannot be based upon it, but must be taken from the form of the presentation.

l. See, for example, the superb poem entitled *Carthon*.

m. I say *musical* to recall here the dual relationship of poetry with music and plastic art. According as poetry either imitates a given *object* as the plastic arts do, or whether, like music, simply produces a given *state of mind*, without requiring a given object for the purpose, it can be called plastic or musical. The latter expression, therefore, does not refer exclusively to whatever is music in poetry actually and in relation to its material, but rather in general to all those effects which it is able to produce without subordinating the imagination to a given object; and in this sense I call Klopstock a musical poet above all.

n. 'The tendency', as Herr Adelung[49] defines it, 'to sensitive, tender feelings without a rational intention and beyond due measure.' – Herr Adelung is very fortunate that he feels only by intention, and even only by rational intention.

o. The wretched pleasures of certain readers should not, indeed, be marred, and in the final analysis, what concern is it of criticism if there are people who can regale and edify themselves with the sordid wit of Herr Blumauer.[51] But the critics should at least refrain from speaking with a certain respect of works the existence of which might decently remain a secret from good taste. One cannot, indeed, mistake either the talent or the caprice they contain, but it is all the more to be regretted that both qualities are not more purified. I say nothing of our German comedies; the poets depict the age in which they live.

p. And *heart*: for the merely sensuous ardour of the portrayal and the luxuriant richness of imagination do not by far make it so. Thus *Ardinghello*[55] remains, despite all its sensuous energy and all the fire of its coloration, only a sensuous caricature without truth and without aesthetic dignity. Still, this unusual production will always remain remarkable as an example of the almost poetic impetus which *mere appetite* was capable of supplying.

q. If I mention the immortal author of *Agathon, Oberon*, etc., in this company I must declare expressly that I do not mean to confuse him with them. His portrayals, even those most objectionable from this point of view, have no material tendency (as a recent, somewhat thoughtless, critic permitted himself to suggest not long ago); the author of *Love for Love* and of so many other naive and gifted works, in all of which the features of a beautiful and noble soul are unmistakable, could not possess such a tendency at all. But he seems to me to be pursued by the quite exceptional misfortune that portrayals of this kind are made necessary by the plan of his works. The cold understanding that designed that plan demanded them of him and his feeling seems to me so far removed from favouring them by preference that I believe I can still recognise that cold understanding in their execution. And this very coldness in depiction is damaging to them in judgement since only naive feeling can justify such portrayals aesthetically as well as morally. Whether the poet, however, is permitted in the designing of his plan to expose himself to such a danger in its execution, and whether a plan can be called poetic at all which, allowing the foregoing for the moment, cannot be executed without outraging the chaste feeling of the poet as well as of the reader, and without forcing both to dwell on subjects from which refined feeling gladly retreats – this is what I doubt, and on which I would be glad to hear a reasonable opinion.

r. I must repeat once again that satire, elegy, and idyll, as they are here laid down as the only three possible species of sentimental poetry, have nothing in common with the three particular genres of poem which are known by these names, other than the *modes of perception* which are proper to the former as well as to the latter. But that, beyond the limits of naive poetry, only this tripartite mode of perception and poetic composition is possible, consequently that the area of sentimental poetry is completely exhausted by this division, can be easily deduced from the concept of the latter.

Sentimental is distinguished from naive poetry, namely, in that it refers actual conditions, at which the latter halts, to ideas, and applies ideas to actuality. Hence it has always, as has already been observed above, to contend simultaneously with two conflicting objects, i.e., with the ideal and with experience, between which neither more nor less than just these three following relationships can be conceived of. Either it is the *contradiction* with actual conditions, or it is its *correspondence* with the ideal, which is the preferred attitude of mind, or it is divided between the two. In the first case it is satisfied by the force of the inner conflict, by *energetic movement*; in the second, it is satisfied by the *harmony* of the inner life, by *dynamic calm*; in the third, conflict *alternates* with harmony, calm alternates with motion. This triadic state of feeling gives rise to three different modes of poetry to which the customary names, *satire, idyll, elegy*, correspond exactly, provided only that one recalls the mood into which the poetic species known by these names place the mind, and abstracts from the means by which they achieve it.

Anyone who could now still ask me to which of the three species I assign the epic, the novel, the tragedy, etc., would not have understood me at all. For the concept of these last, as individual *genres of composition*, is either not at all or at least not solely determined by the mode of perception; it is clear, rather, that they can be executed in more than one mode of perception, consequently in more than one of the species of poetry I have established.

Finally, I have still to remark that if one is inclined to take sentimental poetry, as is reasonable, as a genuine order (and not simply as a degenerate species) and as an extension of true poetic art, then some attention must be paid to it in the determination of poetic types as well as generally in the whole of poetic legislation, which is still onesidedly based on the observances of the ancient and naive poets. The sentimental poet deviates too radically from the naive for those forms which the latter introduced to accommodate him at all times without strain. In such cases it is indeed difficult to distinguish correctly always the exceptions which the differentiation between the species demands, from the subterfuges to which incompetence resorts: but this much we learn from experience, that in the hands of sentimental poets (even the most outstanding) no single type of composition has ever remained entirely what it was among the ancients, and that often very new types have been executed under the old names.

s. Herr Voss has recently not only enriched our German literature with such a work, his *Luise*, but has also truly extended it.[66] This idyll, if not completely free of sentimental influences, does belong wholly to the naive mode, and vies with rare success by its individual truth and unalloyed nature with the best Greek models. It cannot therefore (and this accrues much to its credit) be compared with any modern poem, but must be compared with Greek models, with which it also shares the exceedingly rare advantage of according us a pure, certain, and always unmixed pleasure.

t. For the reader whose scrutiny is critical I add that both modes of perception considered in their ultimate concepts are related to one another like the first and third categories, in that the last always arises by the combination of the first with its exact opposite.[68] The opposite of naive perception is, namely, reflective understanding, and the sentimental mood is the result of the effort, *even under the conditions of reflection*, to restore naive feeling according to its content. This would occur through the fulfilled ideal in which art again encounters nature. If one considers those three concepts in relation to the categories one will always find *nature* and the naive mood corresponding to her in the first; *art*, as the overcoming of nature by the freely functioning understanding, always in the second; the *ideal*, in which consummated art returns to nature, in the third category.

u. How very much the naive poet is dependent upon his subject and how much, even everything, depends upon his feelings, is best exemplified by ancient poetry. To the extent that nature within and without them is beautiful, the poetry of the ancients is likewise so; but if, on the contrary, nature is vulgar, then the spirit has fled from their poetry. Every reader of finer feeling must sense, for example, in their depictions of feminine nature, of the relation between the two sexes and of love in particular, a certain emptiness and satiety that all the truth and naivety of the representation cannot overcome. Without advocating fanatical enthusiasm which, of course, does not ennoble nature but detracts from it, one may, it is to be hoped, assume that in reference to that relationship of the sexes and the passion of love nature is capable of a nobler character than the ancients gave it; we know too of the *incidental* circumstances which for them stood as an obstacle to the refinement of those feelings. That it was narrowness, not inner necessity, that kept the ancients at a lower level is shown by the example of the modern poets who have gone so much further than their predecessors, still without exceeding the bounds of nature. Here we are not speaking of that which sentimental poets have made of this subject, for they do go beyond nature into the ideal, and, therefore, their example cannot be applied against the ancients; but we are speaking of the manner in which this subject has been treated by truly naive poets as, for example, in the *Sakuntala*,[69] by the minnesingers, in many a courtly tale and knightly epic, or by Shakespeare, Fielding, and many others, even by German poets. This would then have provided the occasion for the ancients to spiritualise from within themselves a theme which externally was too crude, to supply the poetic meaning, which was lacking in external perception, by means of reflection, to supplement nature by the idea; in a word, to make a limited object into an infinite one by a sentimental operation. But these were naive, not sentimental, poetic geniuses; their work was, therefore, terminated with external perception.

v. These gentle friends[77] have received very unkindly what a reviewer in the *Allgemeine Literatur-Zeitung* criticised a few years ago in Bürger's poems, and the spite with which they lick at this thorn seems to be an acknowledgement that with the cause of this poet they believe that they are contesting their own. But in this they are much in error. That censure could only apply to a true poetic genius, richly endowed by nature, but who had failed by his own education to cultivate that rare gift. Such an individual ought to and must be subjected to the highest criteria of art, because he possessed the ability, if only he seriously intended to be equal to it; but it would be at once ridiculous and cruel to proceed in like manner with people whom nature has not favoured, and who in every work they place upon the market display a completely convincing certificate of indigence.

w. I note, in order to forestall any misunderstanding, that this division is by no means undertaken in order to promote a choice between them or therewith the preference of one to the exclusion of the other. It is just this *exclusion* which is found in experience that I am combatting; and the result of the present observations will be the proof that only by completely equal *inclusion* of both can justice be done to the rational concept of mankind. Moreover, I take both in their most dignified sense and in the whole wealth of their connotations which can only subsist together with their purity and the retention of their specific differences. It will also be apparent that a high degree of human truth is compatible with each and that their diversion from one another may indeed make a difference in detail but not in the whole; in the form perhaps, but not in the content.

Editor's notes

1. Commentaries to the work can be found in *Schillers Werke. Nationalausgabe*, edited by Petersen and others (1943–), xxi, 278–314 and in Schiller, *Über naive und sentimentalische Dichtung*, edited by William F. Mainland (Oxford, 1957).

2. Kant, *The Critique of Judgement (Kritik der Urteilskraft)*, Part i, *Critique of Aesthetic Judgement*, Section 42. Kant says of such artificial nightingales, employed to entertain guests at country houses: 'But as soon as the deception is discovered, no one will for long be able to endure listening to this song which had previously seemed so enrapturing; and the same applies to all other songbirds. It has to be nature, or to be taken for nature by us, for us to be able to take an immediate interest in the beautiful as such' (Immanuel Kant, *Gesammelte Schriften*, edited by the Königliche Preußische Akademie der Wissenschaften (Berlin, 1902–), v, 302.

3. Schiller alludes to the vogue for *sensibilité* in European literature of the later eighteenth century, as in Rousseau's novel *La nouvelle Héloïse* (1761), Goethe's *The Sorrows of Werther* (1774), Laurence Sterne's *A Sentimental Journey through France and Italy* (1768), etc.

4. 'Determination' and 'determinability' (*Bestimmung und Bestimmbarkeit*): one of Schiller's key conceptual antitheses, between the extent to which an individual's potential is already determined or realised, and the extent to which it exists as infinite and unfulfilled possibility. Schiller develops this antithesis at greater length in his *Aesthetic Letters* (see Introduction, pp. 22 f.), letters 19–21.

5. 'Determination' (*Bestimmung*) is used here in a rather different sense from above, closer to its common eighteenth-century meaning of 'destiny'. In the child, its (future) destiny is as yet unrealised; in the adult, it is fulfilled. This is a characteristic instance of Schiller's use of the same term in shifting senses (see Introduction, p. 23).

6. 'Understanding' and 'reason' (*Verstand* and *Vernunft*) are used by Schiller in the Kantian sense of the faculties of (conceptual) explanation and judgement on the one hand and of (*a priori* or moral) reason on the other. Reason is the higher of the two, in that it brings general principles to bear upon the operations of the understanding. The understanding relates to the empirical world, reason to the world of ideas and principles.

7. '*theoretical*'...'*practical*': Schiller adopts Kant's antithesis, in which the terms refer to the spheres of cognition and morality respectively.

8. The passage occurs at the end of Part I of the *Critique of Judgement*, Section 54 (Kant, *Gesammelte Schriften*, v, 335).

9. 'Affect' (*Affekt*): spontaneous feeling or reaction.

10. Johann Matthias Schröckh (1733–1808), whose life of Pope Adrian VI (1522–3) Schiller had read in Schröckh's *Allgemeine Biographie* (1767–78).

11. Schiller's Protestant bias is evident in this passage.

12. That is, freedom of the will.

13. It is noteworthy that Schiller, who was unaware that the poems of Ossian were largely a modern forgery (by James Macpherson), has recognised their essentially modern and 'sentimental' character. Compare Herder's assessment of them, in his essay on Ossian (pp. 154–61 above), as primitive and 'natural' poetry.

14. Homer, *Odyssey*, xiv, 72 ff. and Goethe, *The Sorrows of Werther*, Book ii, letter of 15 March.

15. The modern Tivoli, where Horace had his rural retreat.

16. Schiller is probably referring to Johann Christoph Gottsched (1700–66), who had on various occasions roundly condemned Shakespeare for failing to observe the rules of French neo-classical poetics: for examples of his censures, see *Shakespeare-Rezeption. Die Diskussion um Shakespeare in Deutschland*, edited by Hansjürgen Blinn, vol. I (Berlin, 1982), pp. 40 f. and 62 f.

17. *Orlando Furioso*, Canto I, verse 22.

18. *Iliad*, vi, 224–33 (translation by E. V. Rieu).

19. Schiller's 'wit' (*Witz*) translates the French *esprit*; note the continuity with Lessing and Herder in Schiller's anti-French sentiments.

20. '*Messiade*...*Nathan the Wise*': Friedrich Gottlieb Klopstock's (1724–1803) religious epic *Der Messias* and Lessing's drama on religious tolerance *Nathan der Weise*.

21. Schiller builds here on Lessing's antithesis, in his *Laocoon*, between the circumscribed sphere of visual art and the unlimited sphere of poetry, and links it to his own antithesis between 'naive' (finite) and 'sentimental' (infinite) modes of perception.

22. Of these often satirical writers, Albrecht von Haller (1708–77) will be the least familiar to English readers. He is the Swiss poet and scientist whose descriptive poem *The Alps* Lessing criticised so vigorously in the *Laocoon* (see pp. 104–5 above), but also a writer of satirical verse, akin to that of Pope, as in the poems 'The Falseness of Human Virtues' (1730) and 'On the Origin of Evil' (1734).

23. Schiller was not the first to associate the sublime with tragedy and the beautiful with comedy. Kant had already done so in his essay 'Observations on the Feelings of the Sublime and the Beautiful' in 1764 (Kant, *Gesammelte Schriften*, ii, 205–56). Schiller's own theory of tragedy, as expressed in his *On Pathos* (*Über das Pathetische*) of 1793, is based on the principle of sublimity. The tragic hero attains sublimity by asserting his moral freedom, in situations of suffering, over the weakness of the senses.

24. 'theoretically' and 'practically': cf. note 7 above.

25. *Nathan*: cf. note 20 above.
26. *Hamburg Dramaturgy*: see Introduction, p. 9. The reference here is to Section 80 of the work.
27. Lucian (second century A.D.), Sophist and rhetorician, author of the satirical *Dialogues*, some of which Schiller goes on to mention.
28. Tom Jones and Sophia Western, characters in Henry Fielding's (1707–54) novel *The History of Tom Jones* (1749).
29. The hero of Laurence Sterne's (1713–68) *A Sentimental Journey through France and Italy* (1768).
30. Christoph Martin Wieland (1733–1813), German poet, and translator of Shakespeare and other classics of world literature (Schiller has just quoted a passage from Wieland's translation of Lucian's *Dialogues*).
31. See note 20 above.
32. Rousseau's novel *Julie, ou La nouvelle Héloïse* (1761).
33. On Haller, see note 22 above; Christian Ewald von Kleist (1715–59), writer of pastoral poems, and friend of Lessing; on Klopstock, see note 20 above.
34. From Haller's 'Ode of Mourning' ('Trauer-Ode') of 1736.
35. See note 6 above.
36. From Kleist's poem 'Longing for Calm' ('Sehnsucht nach Ruhe'), lines 115–20.
37. An allusion to Kleist's long descriptive poem *Spring* (*Der Frühling*) of 1749, which was influenced by James Thomson's (1700–48) poem *The Seasons* (1758). Lessing, in his *Laocoon*, had criticised Kleist's *Spring* as an example of descriptive poetry (see p. 106 above).
38. The references are to Kleist's epic *Cissides and Paches* (1759) and his tragedy *Seneca* (1758).
39. Thomson: see note 37 above.
40. Characters in Klopstock's religious epic *The Messiah*.
41. Klopstock's tragedy *Solomon* (*Salomo*) appeared in 1764.
42. Edward Young (1683–1765), author of the long verse meditation *Night Thoughts* (1742–4), which enjoyed immense popularity in Germany as well as in England.
43. Harp, lyre, lute: symbols of epic, lyric, and elegiac poetry.
44. Johann Peter Uz (1720–96), lyric poet in the Anacreontic style; Michael Denis (1729–1800), translator of Ossian into German (see Herder's criticism of his translation on pp. 154 f. above) and writer of 'bardic' poems; Salomon Geßner (1730–88), Swiss painter and poet, whose prose *Idylls* and religious epic *The Death of Abel* were enormously successful in their day; Johann Georg Jacobi (1740–1814), minor poet and brother of the philosopher Friedrich Heinrich Jacobi; Heinrich Wilhelm von Gerstenberg (1737–1823), dramatist (*Ugolino*, 1768) and writer of 'bardic' poetry; Ludwig Heinrich Christoph Hölty (1748–76), lyric poet of the *Sturm und Drang* generation; Leopold Friedrich von Göckingk (1748–1828), literary editor and minor poet.
45. The allusion is to Goethe, and his treatment of the theme of suicide in *The Sorrows of Werther* (1774).
46. Goethe's drama *Torquato Tasso* (1790).
47. *Wilhelm Meister's Apprenticeship* (1795–6).
48. Schiller refers to *Faust. A Fragment* (1790), the only portion of Goethe's *Faust* to have been published by the time at which Schiller was writing.
49. The definition is from the *Dictionary of the High-German Dialect* (*Wörterbuch der hochdeutschen Mundart*) of 1774–86 by Johann Christoph Adelung (1732–1806).

50. That is, in 1777, the date of publication of Johann Martin Miller's (1750–1814) sentimental novel *Siegwart*, referred to by Schiller in the next paragraph.

51. Alois Blumauer (1755–98), Austrian poet and author of the mock-heroic epic *Adventures of the Pious Hero Aeneas* (1783).

52. See note 50 above.

53. Moritz August von Thümmel's (1738–1817) novel *Journey to the Southern Provinces of France in 1785–86*, 10 vols. (1791–1805).

54. Schiller is thinking above all of Goethe's *Roman Elegies* (published 1795), whose uninhibited sensuality had been found morally offensive by many.

55. Wilhelm Heinse's (1746–1803) novel *Ardinghello* (1787) glorifies Renaissance amoralism and sensuality.

56. Christoph Martin Wieland (see note 30 above).

57. The 'German Ovid' is Johann Kaspar Friedrich Manso (1759–1826), author of the didactic poem *The Art of Loving* (1794).

58. Claude Prosper Jolyot de Crébillon (1707–77), author of various licentious novels.

59. Jean François Marmontel (1723–99), author of *Contes moraux* (1766) and *Bélisaire* (1767).

60. Pierre-Ambroise-François Choderlos de Laclos (1741–1803), author of *Les Liaisons dangereuses* (1782).

61. That is, Goethe (as author of the *Roman Elegies*).

62. Denis Diderot's (1713–84) novels *Les Bijoux indiscrets* (1747) and *La Religieuse* (published 1790).

63. This plan was never carried out.

64. The reference is, of course, to Rousseau.

65. The titles of idylls by Salomon Geßner (see note 44 above).

66. Johann Heinrich Voss's (1751–1826) verse-idyll *Luise* (1795).

67. On Schiller's own plan for a sentimental idyll of the kind specified, see Introduction, pp. 23 f.

68. Schiller is referring to the doctrine of categories formulated by Kant in Section 11 of the *Critique of Pure Reason*. In his later years, Schiller frequently structures his arguments on the triadic model outlined here.

69. *Sakuntala*, an ancient Sanskrit play by Kalidasa, first became known in Germany through Johann Georg Forster's (1754–94) translation of 1791.

70. Johann Jakob Bodmer (1698–1783), Swiss poet and critic, author of several lengthy religious epics on Old Testament themes.

71. Jean François Regnard (1655–1709), French comic dramatist.

72. Ludwig Holberg (1684–1754), Danish comic dramatist whose work much influenced German comedy in the mid-eighteenth century.

73. Johann Elias Schlegel (1719–49), critic and dramatist, uncle of the brothers August Wilhelm and Friedrich Schlegel.

74. Christian Fürchtegott Gellert (1715–69), poet, moralist, and writer of sentimental dramas.

75. Gottlieb Wilhelm Rabener (1714–71), journalist and writer of prose satires.

76. Camenae: fountain nymphs, sometimes identified with the Muses.

77. The identity of the poets Schiller is attacking is hinted at by the names of the rivers he associates them with: the Pleiße (Leipzig), Leine (Göttingen), and Elbe (Hamburg). He has in mind contributors to the *Leipziger Musenalmanach*, the Göttingen poets (and in particular Gottfried August Bürger (1747–94), whose poems Schiller had reviewed adversely in 1791), and contributors to the *Voßsche*

Musenalmanach in Hamburg respectively. The reference to the review of Bürger's poems is in fact to Schiller's own review.

78. Christian Gotthilf Salzmann's (1744–1811) novel *Karl von Karlsberg, or On Human Misery* (1783–8).

79. The novel *History of a Fat Man* (1784) by Lessing's friend Friedrich Nicolai (1733–1811), in which he pours scorn on the philosophy of Kant.

80. St Preux, Julie: the lovers in Rousseau's novel *Julie, ou La nouvelle Héloïse*.

81. Agathon, Phanias, Peregrinus Proteus: the main figures in Wieland's (see note 30 above) *The History of Agathon* (1766–7), *Musarion* (1768), and *Peregrinus Proteus* (1791). All of them are inclined to excessive enthusiasm for their ideals.

82. Thalia and Melpomene: the Muses of comedy and tragedy respectively.

Goethe: Winckelmann

1. Twenty-seven letters from Winckelmann to his friend Hieronymus Dietrich Berends, which formed the first part of the anthology *Winckelmann und sein Jahrhundert* (*Winckelmann and his Century*), edited by Goethe (Tübingen, 1805), in which Goethe's own essay also appeared.

2. Compare Schiller's parallel distinction between ancients and moderns in his essay *On Naive and Sentimental Poetry*: see above, p. 190.

3. Winckelmann's role here as an antique spirit in the modern age recalls, and is doubtless to some extent modelled on, that of Goethe himself as portrayed in Schiller's essay: see p. 206 and note 45 (p. 298) above.

4. The dire consequences of over-specialisation and the division of labour are a frequent theme in the late eighteenth century in Germany. This problem is discussed at length, with suggested remedies, by Schiller in his *On the Aesthetic Education of Man: In a Series of Letters* (1795): see the bilingual edition of this work, with an excellent introduction and commentary, by Elizabeth M. Wilkinson and L. A. Willoughby (Oxford, 1967).

5. The following glorification of pagan attitudes is doubtless intended by Goethe in part as a counterblast to the Catholicising tendencies of the German Romantics, which he deplores on various occasions around this time.

6. Mythological figures: Chloris, the only surviving daughter of Niobe, and Thyia, who became by Apollo the mother of Delphus.

7. Friedrich Wilhelm Lamprecht, a pupil of Winckelmann in his school-teaching days, with whom he subsequently lived for a time.

8. *der sich immer steigernden Natur*: on Goethe's concept of *Steigerung* see above, Introduction, p. 25.

9. *steigert*: see previous note.

10. Lost work by Phidias in gold and ivory, among the most celebrated sculptures of antiquity.

11. Heinrich, Graf von Bünau (1697–1762), diplomat and Imperial Minister, whose service Winckelmann entered as librarian at Nötnitz near Dresden in 1748.

12. As the letters to Berends, published in the same anthology as Goethe's essay, reveal particularly clearly.

13. See above, pp. 32–54.

14. In the first of these supplements, Winckelmann assumed the guise of a hostile critic of his own essay; in the second, written soon after his arrival in Rome (1756), he refuted this supposed critic's objections.

15. Goethe somewhat exaggerates the difficulties of Winckelmann's first major work:

its central theses, at least, are perfectly intelligible without detailed knowledge of Winckelmann's associates in Dresden. This background information is, however, fully presented in Carl Justi's *Winckelmann: Sein Leben, seine Werke und seine Zeitgenossen*, 3 vols. (third edition, Leipzig, 1923), which remains the standard biography.

16. Philipp Daniel Lippert (1702–85), teacher of drawing in Dresden, from 1764 Professor of Classical Studies at the Dresden Academy; Christian Ludwig von Hagedorn (1713–80), from 1763 Director of the Dresden Academy; Adam Friedrich Oeser (1713–99), from 1764 Director of the Leipzig Academy, with whom Goethe studied drawing during his time at Leipzig University (1765–8); Christian Wilhelm Ernst Dietrich (1712–74), court painter in Dresden from 1741; Karl Heinrich von Heinecken (1707–91), from 1746 curator of the art gallery in Dresden; Matthias Oesterreich (1716–78), Director of the Dresden gallery, and subsequently (from 1757) of the gallery in Potsdam.

17. This friend is Wilhelm von Humboldt, Prussian representative in Rome from 1802 to 1808; Goethe quotes from Humboldt's letter to him of 24 August 1804.

18. Compare Schiller's essay above, p. 196; Humboldt was not only a friend of Goethe and Schiller, but also shared their classical ideals.

19. Ancient name for the modern Tivoli.

20. Horace, *Epodes*, 2, line 1: 'Happy the man who, far from town affairs...'.

21. Anton Raphael Mengs (1728–79), a leading exponent of neo-classicism in painting. Winckelmann dedicated his *History of the Art of Antiquity* to him.

22. One of Winckelmann's many planned but unwritten works.

23. Likewise never completed.

24. Velleius Paterculus, author of a compendium of Roman history, born around 19 B.C., died after A.D. 30; Goethe's quotation is from the *Historiae Romanae*, Book I, 17, 4–7.

25. Marcus Fabius Quintilianus, c. A.D. 35–95, Roman rhetorician and author of the *Institutio Oratoria*; Goethe's quotation is from Book XII, Chapter 10 of this work.

26. Domenico Passionei (1682–1761), Director of the Vatican Library in Rome and owner of a major private library to which Winckelmann had access.

27. Michelangelo Giacomelli (1695–1774), clergyman and scholar, much respected by Winckelmann.

28. Antonio Baldani (1691–1765), clergyman and scholar, an employee of Winckelmann's patron Cardinal Albani.

29. Alessandro Albani (1692–1779), diplomat and cardinal, Librarian to the Vatican from 1761; Winckelmann resided in his palace from 1759, and worked as Librarian and adviser to the Cardinal on his collection of antiquities.

30. Goethe refers to the plundering of the Villa Albani by French forces in January 1796.

31. Excavations began at Herculaneum in 1738 and at Pompeii in 1748. Winckelmann made several visits to Naples to follow the progress of the discoveries, and published reports on the subject in 1762 and 1764.

32. Baron Philipp von Stosch (1691–1757) amassed the greatest collection of ancient engraved gems in his times. Winckelmann's catalogue, the *Description des pierres gravées du feu Baron de Stosch*, appeared in 1760.

33. In 1738, Winckelmann matriculated at the University of Halle to study theology and philosophy, and attended the lectures of Christian Wolff (1679–1754), whose extensive writings popularised and systematised the philosophy of Leibniz, and Alexander Gottlieb Baumgarten (1714–62), who founded the science of aesthetics.

For Winckelmann, with his growing interest in history and in art, the systems of these philosophers were excessively abstract and remote from experience.

34. Johann Friedrich Christ (1700–56), Professor of Poetry at the University of Leipzig, was a pioneer of art history and an inspiring teacher. It was he who first introduced Lessing to antiquarian studies.

35. Goethe had encountered the philosophy of Kant through his friendship with Schiller during the preceding decade. Though Kant's uncompromising dualism was foreign to his nature – Goethe is a monist, for whom man and nature form a single unity – he realised that the Kantian system was an intellectual force of the first magnitude.

36. Winckelmann's descriptions of the ancient statutes – for example, the Belvedere Apollo – are indeed highly poetic, and were deservedly famous in the later eighteenth century. This poetic quality is already evident, though to a lesser degree, in his description of Laocoon in the essay of 1755 on the imitation of the Greeks (see above, p. 42). On Winckelmann's alleged indifference to poetry, Herbert von Einem, in his commentary on Goethe's essay in *Goethes Werke*, Hamburg edition, 14 vols. (Hamburg, 1948–64), XII, 604, rightly takes issue with Goethe, and stresses Winckelmann's profound love of Homer and other ancient poets from early in his career.

37. The *Monumenti antichi inediti spiegati ed illustrati da Winckelmann* were published in two volumes in 1767.

38. The *Monumenti inediti* contained 216 engraved plates.

39. The first volume of the *Monumenti inediti* contains a general introduction, in which Winckelmann revises the scheme of art history he had advanced in 1764 in his *Geschichte der Kunst des Altertums* (*History of the Art of Antiquity*).

40. The papal patronage to which Goethe refers was chiefly that of Benedict XIV's successor, Clement XIII. (Benedict died in 1758, only three years after Winckelmann's arrival in Rome.)

41. Leopold Friedrich Franz von Dessau (1740–1817), visited Rome in 1765; Georg August von Mecklenburg-Strelitz (1748–85), visited Rome in the same year; Karl Wilhelm Ferdinand von Braunschweig (1735–1806), visited Rome in 1766; Johann Hermann von Riedesel (1740–85), Prussian Ambassador in Vienna, visited Rome in 1762–3.

42. The *Geschichte der Kunst des Altertums* was published in Dresden in 1764.

43. This appointment was made in 1763, a year before the *History* appeared.

44. The Peace of Hubertusberg, which terminated the Seven Years War.

45. Frederick the Great; Winckelmann was approached in 1765 concerning the post of Royal Librarian in Berlin.

46. Gerlach Adolf von Münchhausen (1688–1770), who was instrumental in founding the University of Göttingen in 1737.

47. These included the painter Heinrich Füßli (Henry Fuseli, 1741–1825), and the poet and painter Salomon Geßner (1730–88); for his relations with them see Hugo Blümner (ed.), *Winckelmanns Briefe an seine Züricher Freunde* (Freiburg, 1882).

48. His journey north into Germany in 1768 got no further than Regensburg, where he turned back. He did, however, visit Vienna, where he was received by the Empress Maria Theresia; the gold coins which she presented to him furnished the motive for his subsequent murder.

49. Winckelmann was stabbed to death on 8 June 1768 in Trieste, on his way back to Rome, by one Francesco Arcangeli, to whom he had rashly shown the presents from Maria Theresia. The principal documents surrounding this affair are

printed in Horst Rüdiger (ed.), *Winckelmanns Tod. Die Originalberichte* (Wiesbaden, 1959).

50. See note 30 above.

51. The final sentence reveals the underlying aim of Goethe's essay: to keep alive, in face of the rising tide of Romanticism, the neo-classical ideals he shared with Winckelmann.

Bibliography

Alexander, W. M., *Johann Georg Hamann: Philosophy and Faith* (The Hague, 1966).
Allison, Henry E., *Lessing and the Enlightenment* (Ann Arbor, Michigan, 1966).
Barnard, F. M., *Herder's Social and Political Thought. From Enlightenment to Nationalism* (Oxford, 1965).
Berger, Arnold E., *Der junge Herder und Winckelmann* (Halle, 1903).
Berlin, Isaiah, *Vico and Herder. Two Studies in the History of Ideas* (New York, 1976).
Bieber, Margarete, *Laocoon: The Influence of the Group since its Rediscovery*, revised edition (Detroit, 1967).
Bingham, C. R., 'Lessing's "Laokoon" and its English Predecessors', unpublished M.A. dissertation (University of London, 1937).
Blackall, Eric A., *The Emergence of German as a Literary Language 1700–1775*, second edition (Ithaca and London, 1978).
Blanning, T. C. W., 'The Enlightenment in Catholic Germany', in *The Enlightenment in National Context*, edited by Roy Porter and Mikuláš Teich (Cambridge, 1981), pp. 118–26.
Boyd, James, *Goethe's Knowledge of English Literature* (Oxford, 1932).
Brown, F. Andrew, *Gotthold Ephraim Lessing* (New York, 1971).
Bruford, W. H., *Culture and Society in Classical Weimar 1775–1806* (Cambridge, 1962; reprinted 1975).
  Germany in the Eighteenth Century: The Social Background of the Literary Revival (Cambridge, 1935; reprinted 1965).
  'Goethe's Reputation in England since 1832', in *Essays on Goethe*, edited by William Rose (London, 1949), pp. 187–206.
Butler, Elsie M., *Byron and Goethe. Analysis of a Passion* (London, 1956).
  The Tyranny of Greece over Germany (Cambridge, 1935).
Carlyle, Thomas, *The Life of Friedrich Schiller*, second edition (London, 1845).
Carré, Jean-Marie, *Goethe en Angleterre* (Paris, 1920).
  Bibliographie de Goethe en Angleterre (Paris, 1920).
Cassirer, Ernst, *The Philosophy of the Enlightenment* (Princeton, 1951).
Clark, R. T., *Herder. His Life and Thought* (Berkeley and Los Angeles, 1955).
Conrady, Karl Otto, *Goethe: Leben und Werk*, 2 vols. (Königstein/Taunus, 1982–3).
Constantine, David, *Early Greek Travellers and the Hellenic Ideal* (Cambridge, 1984).
Dewhurst, Kenneth and Nigel Reeves, *Friedrich Schiller: Medicine, Psychology and Literature* (Oxford, 1978).
Ellis, J. M., *Schiller's 'Kalliasbriefe' and the Study of his Aesthetic Theory*, Anglica Germanica, 12 (The Hague and Paris, 1969).
Fairley, Barker, *A Study of Goethe* (Oxford, 1947).
Flavell, M. Kay, 'Winckelmann and the German Enlightenment', *Modern Language Review*, 74 (1979), 79–96.

Friedenthal, Richard, *Goethe. His Life and Times* (London, 1965).

Fugate, Joe K., *The Psychological Basis of Herder's Aesthetics*, Studies in Philosophy, 10 (The Hague and Paris, 1966).

Garland, H. B., *Lessing: The Founder of Modern German Literature*, second edition (London, 1962).

Schiller (London, 1949).

Gay, Peter, *The Enlightenment: An Interpretation*, 2 vols. (London, 1967–70).

Gebauer, Gunter (ed.), *Das Laokoon-Projekt: Pläne einer semiotischen Ästhetik* (Stuttgart, 1984).

Gillies, Alexander, *Herder* (Oxford, 1945).

'Herder and Goethe', in *German Studies presented to Leonard A. Willoughby* (Oxford, 1952), pp. 82–97.

Goethe, Johann Wolfgang von, *Werke*, Weimar edition, 133 vols. (Weimar, 1887–1919).

Goethes Werke, Briefe und Gespräche, Gedenkausgabe, edited by Ernst Beutler, 24 vols. (Zurich, 1948–60).

Goethes Werke, Hamburg edition, edited by Erich Trunz, 14 vols. (Hamburg, 1948–64).

The Autobiography of Johann Wolfgang von Goethe, translated by John Oxenford, 2 vols. (Chicago and London, 1974).

Conversations and Encounters, translated by David Luke and Robert Pick (Chicago and London, 1966).

Eckermann's Conversations with Goethe, translated by John Oxenford, edited by J. K. Moorhead (London and New York, 1971).

Goethe on Art, edited by John Gage (Berkeley and Los Angeles, 1980).

The Italian Journey, 1786–88, translated by W. H. Auden and Elizabeth Mayer (New York and London, 1962).

Literary Essays, edited by J. E. Spingarn (New York, 1964).

Winckelmann und sein Jahrhundert. In Briefen und Aufsätzen herausgegeben von Goethe (Tübingen, 1805); new edition, edited by E. Howald (Zurich, 1943).

Gombrich, E. H., 'Lessing. Lecture on a Master Mind', *Proceedings of the British Academy*, 43 (1957), 133–56.

Hamann, Johann Georg, *Sämtliche Werke*, edited by Josef Nadler, 6 vols. (Vienna, 1949–57).

Briefwechsel, edited by Walther Ziesemer and Arthur Henkel, 7 vols. (Wiesbaden, 1955–79).

Hamann's 'Socratic Memorabilia'. A Translation and Commentary, by James C. O'Flaherty (Baltimore, 1967).

Sokratische Denkwürdigkeiten. Aesthetica in nuce, edited with a commentary by Sven-Aage Jørgensen (Stuttgart, 1968).

Harrold, Charles Frederick, *Carlyle and German Thought. 1818–1834*, Yale Studies in English, 82 (New Haven, Connecticut, 1934).

Hatfield, Henry, *Aesthetic Paganism in German Literature from Winckelmann to the Death of Goethe* (Cambridge, Mass., 1964).

Winckelmann and his German Critics 1755–1781 (New York, 1943).

Haym, Rudolf, *Herder*, 2 vols. (Berlin, 1880–5); new edition, with an introduction by Wolfgang Harich (Berlin, 1954).

Herder, Johann Gottfried, *Sämtliche Werke*, edited by Bernhard Suphan, 33 vols. (Berlin, 1877–1913).

Briefe. Gesamtausgabe 1763–1803, edited by Karl-Heinz Hahn, 8 vols. (Weimar, 1977–85).

J. G. Herder on Social and Political Culture, translated and edited by F. M. Barnard (Cambridge, 1969).

Essay on the Origin of Language [together with J.-J. Rousseau, *Essay on the Origin of Languages*], translated by John H. Moran and Alexander Gode (New York, 1967).

God. Some Conversations, translated by Frederick H. Burkhardt, third edition (Indianapolis and New York, 1962).

Outlines of a Philosophy of the History of Man, translated by T. O. Churchill, new edition (New York, 1966; first published 1800).

(Herder, Goethe, Frisi, Möser) *Von deutscher Art und Kunst. Einige fliegende Blätter*, edited by Hans Dietrich Irmscher (Stuttgart, 1968).

(Herder, Goethe, Frisi, Möser) *Von deutscher Art und Kunst. Einige fliegende Blätter*, edited by Edna Purdie (Oxford, 1924).

Hettner, Hermann, *Geschichte der deutschen Literatur im achtzehnten Jahrhundert*, 4 vols. (Leipzig, 1928); new edition, 2 vols. (Berlin, 1961).

Honour, Hugh, *Neo-classicism* (Harmondsworth, 1968).

Howard, William Guild, *Laokoon: Lessing, Herder, Goethe. Selections* (New York, 1910).

Justi, Carl, *Winckelmann und seine Zeitgenossen*, fifth edition, 3 vols. (Cologne, 1956).

Kerry, S. S., *Schiller's Writings on Aesthetics* (Manchester, 1961).

Kohlschmidt, Werner, *A History of German Literature 1760–1805*, translated by Ian Hilton (London, 1975).

Lamport, F. J., *Lessing and the Drama* (Oxford, 1981).

Lange, Victor, *The Classical Age of German Literature 1740–1815* (London, 1982).

Leppmann, Wolfgang, *Winckelmann* (New York, 1970).

Lessing, Gotthold Ephraim, *Sämtliche Schriften*, edited by Karl Lachmann and Franz Muncker, 23 vols. (Stuttgart and Leipzig, 1886–1924).

Gesammelte Werke, edited by Paul Rilla, 10 vols., second edition (Berlin and Weimar, 1968).

Werke, edited by Herbert G. Göpfert, 8 vols. (Munich, 1970–9).

Lessing im Gespräch. Berichte und Urteile von Freunden und Zeitgenossen, edited by Richard Daunicht (Munich, 1971).

Hamburg Dramaturgy, translated by Helen Zimmern (New York, 1962).

Laocoon. Nathan the Wise. Minna von Barnhelm, edited by William A. Steel (London and New York, 1930, reprinted 1967).

Lessings 'Laokoon', edited by Hugo Blümner, second edition (Berlin, 1880).

Theological Writings, translated and introduced by Henry Chadwick (London, 1956).

Loewenthal, Erich (ed.), *Sturm und Drang. Kritische Schriften*, third edition (Heidelberg, 1972).

Lowrie, Walter, *Johann Georg Hamann: An Existentialist* (Princeton, 1950).

Lumpp, Hans-Martin, *Philologia crucis. Zu Johann Georg Hamanns Auffassung von der Dichtkunst. Mit einem Kommentar zur 'Aesthetica in nuce'* (Tübingen, 1970).

May, Kurt, *Lessings und Herders kunsttheoretische Gedanken in ihrem Zusammenhang*, Germanische Studien, 25 (Berlin, 1923).

Minor, Jacob, *Schiller, Sein Leben und seine Werke*, 2 vols. (Berlin, 1890).

Nadler, Josef, *Johann Georg Hamann. Der Zeuge des Corpus Mysticum* (Salzburg, 1949).

Nisbet, H. B., *Herder and the Philosophy and History of Science* (Cambridge, 1970).

'Laocoon in Germany: The Reception of the Group since Winckelmann', *Oxford German Studies*, 10 (1979), 22–63.

Nivelle, Armand, *Les théories esthétiques en Allemagne de Baumgarten à Kant* (Paris, 1955).

O'Flaherty, James C., *Johann Georg Hamann*, Twayne's World Authors Series, 527 (Boston, 1979).

Unity and Language: A Study in the Philosophy of Hamann, second edition (New York, 1966).

O'Neill, Patrick, *German Literature in English Translation. A Select Bibliography* (Toronto, 1981).

Pascal, Roy, *The German Sturm und Drang* (Manchester, 1953).

Shakespeare in Germany 1740–1815 (Cambridge, 1937).

Pater, Walter, 'Winckelmann', in Pater, *The Renaissance: Studies in Art and Poetry*, sixth edition (London, 1902).

Pick, Robert, 'Schiller in England, 1787–1960. A Bibliography', *Publications of the English Goethe Society*, 30 (1961), 1–123.

Price, Lawrence Marsden, *The Reception of English Literature in Germany* (Berkeley, 1932).

Price, Mary Bell and Lawrence Marsden Price, *The Publication of English Literature in Germany in the Eighteenth Century* (Berkeley, 1934).

The Publication of English Humaniora in Germany in the Eighteenth Century (Berkeley and Los Angeles, 1955).

Prudhoe, John, *The Theatre of Goethe and Schiller* (Oxford, 1973).

Reed, T. J., *The Classical Centre: Goethe and Weimar 1775–1832* (London, 1980).

Rehm, Walther, 'Winckelmann und Lessing', in Rehm, *Götterstille und Göttertrauer. Aufsätze zur deutsch-antiken Bewegung* (Salzburg, 1951), pp. 183–201.

Robertson, John G., *Lessing's Dramatic Theory* (Cambridge, 1939; second edition 1965).

Robson-Scott, W. D., *The Literary Background of the Gothic Revival in Germany* (Oxford, 1965).

The Younger Goethe and the Visual Arts (Cambridge, 1981).

Rudowski, Victor Anthony, *Lessing's 'Aesthetica in nuce': An Analysis of the May 26, 1769, Letter to Nicolai* (Chapel Hill, 1971).

Schiller, Friedrich, *Schillers Werke. Nationalausgabe*, edited by Julius Petersen and others (Weimar, 1943–).

Sämtliche Werke, edited by Gerhard Fricke and Herbert G. Göpfert, 5 vols. (Munich, 1958–9).

Schillers Briefe, edited by Fritz Jonas, 7 vols. (Stuttgart, 1892–6).

On the Aesthetic Education of Man, in a Series of Letters, edited, translated and introduced by Elizabeth M. Wilkinson and L. A. Willoughby (Oxford, 1967).

Mary Stuart, translated by F. J. Lamport, in Lamport (ed.), *Five German Tragedies* (Harmondsworth, 1969); also contains translations of Lessing's *Emilia Galotti* and Goethe's *Egmont*.

The Robbers. Wallenstein, translated by F. J. Lamport (Harmondsworth, 1979).

Über naive und sentimentalische Dichtung, edited with an introduction and annotations by William F. Mainland (Oxford, 1957).

Schmidt, Erich, *Lessing. Geschichte seines Lebens und seiner Schriften*, 2 vols., fourth edition (Berlin, 1923).

Schmitt, Albert R., *Herder und Amerika*, Studies in German Literature, 10 (The Hague and Paris, 1967).

Simpson, David (ed.), *German Aesthetic and Literary Criticism: Kant, Fichte, Schelling, Schopenhauer, Hegel* (Cambridge, 1984).

Simpson, James, *Matthew Arnold and Goethe*, MHRA Texts and Dissertations, 11 (London, 1979).

Smith, Ronald Gregor, *J. G. Hamann: A Study in Christian Existence* (New York, 1960).

Staiger, Emil, 'Ein Satz aus Goethes Winckelmannschrift', *Schweizer Monatshefte*, 37 (1957), 196–207.

Goethe, 3 vols. (Zurich and Freiburg, 1952–9).

308 Bibliography

Stockley, V., *German Literature as Known in England 1750–1830* (London, 1929).
Stokoe, F. N., *German Influence in the English Romantic Period, 1788–1818* (Cambridge, 1926).
Strich, Fritz, *Goethe and World Literature* (London, 1949).
Todt, W., *Lessing in England* (Heidelberg, 1912).
Trevelyan, Humphry, *Goethe and the Greeks*, new edition with a foreword by Hugh Lloyd-Jones (Cambridge, 1981; first published 1941).
Uhlig, Ludwig, 'Klassik und Geschichtsbewußtsein in Goethes Winckelmannschrift', *Germanisch-Romanische Monatsschrift*, N.F. 31 (1981), 143–55.
Unger, Rudolf, *Hamann und die Aufklärung*, 2 vols. (Jena, 1911).
Vail, Curtis C. D., *Lessing's Relation to the English Language and Literature* (New York, 1936).
Ward, Albert, *Book Production, Fiction and the German Reading Public 1740–1800* (Oxford, 1974).
Wellbery, David E., *Lessing's 'Laocoon': Semiotics and Aesthetics in the Age of Reason* (Cambridge, 1984).
Wellek, René, *A History of Modern Criticism 1750–1950*, Vol. 1, *The Later Eighteenth Century*, new edition (Cambridge, 1981).
Wells, George A., *Herder and After. A Study in the Development of Sociology*, Anglica Germanica, 1 (The Hague, 1959).
Whaley, Joachim, 'The Protestant Enlightenment in Germany', in *The Enlightenment in National Context*, edited by Roy Porter and Mikuláš Teich (Cambridge, 1981), pp. 106–17.
Wheeler, Kathleen M., *German Aesthetic and Literary Criticism: The Romantic Ironists and Goethe* (Cambridge, 1984).
Wiese, Benno von, *Friedrich Schiller*, fourth edition (Stuttgart, 1978).
Wilkinson, Elizabeth M. (ed.), *Goethe Revisited. A Collection of Essays* (London and New York, 1984); pp. 185–8 contain a bibliography of works in English on Goethe.
and L. A. Willoughby, *Goethe. Poet and Thinker*, second edition (London, 1970).
Winckelmann, Johann Joachim, *Sämtliche Werke*, edited by Joseph Eiselein, 12 vols. (Donaueschingen, 1825–9).
Winckelmanns Briefe, edited by Walther Rehm, 3 vols. (Berlin, 1952–7).
Writings on Art, edited by David Irwin (London, 1972).
Witte, William, *Schiller* (Oxford, 1949).
Zeydel, Edwin H., 'Goethe's Reputation in America', in *Essays on Goethe*, edited by William Rose (London, 1949), pp. 207–32.
Zimmermann, R., *Kant, Schiller and Hegel: A Study in Metaphysical Aesthetics* (New York, 1962).

Index